BLOODY MONDAY

VOLUME 7

Story by Ryou Ryumon
Art by Kouji Megumi

Translated by Sebastian Girner

Lettered by Christy Sawyer

KC
KODANSHA
COMICS

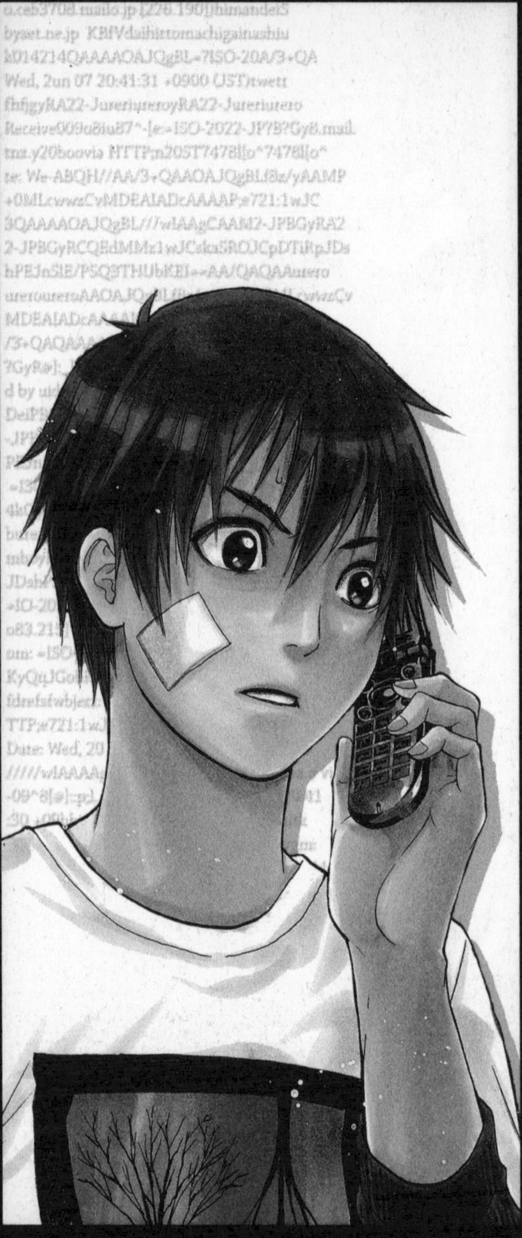

AUTHOR'S NOTES:

Have you ever heard about conspiracies? It's the theory that there are secret historic events, unbeknownst to regular folks like you and me, that allow the authorities to stay in power. I heard this story from an old friend of mine, though I don't know if he was pulling my chain. During his University days he worked next to a research laboratory that was apparently developing a high-powered laser designed to be used as a weapon. Before too long government agents shut down the laboratory and stopped the development of the laser. Not long after that it was rumored that the professor who was working on the project was reported dead. It seems like beneath the surface of what we know lies another world.

-RYUMON

I really have no affinity for touch pads. I'll probably give up on it completely. I'm too stubborn to change my ways now. I'm content to miss out on all the wonders of the future.

-MEGUMI

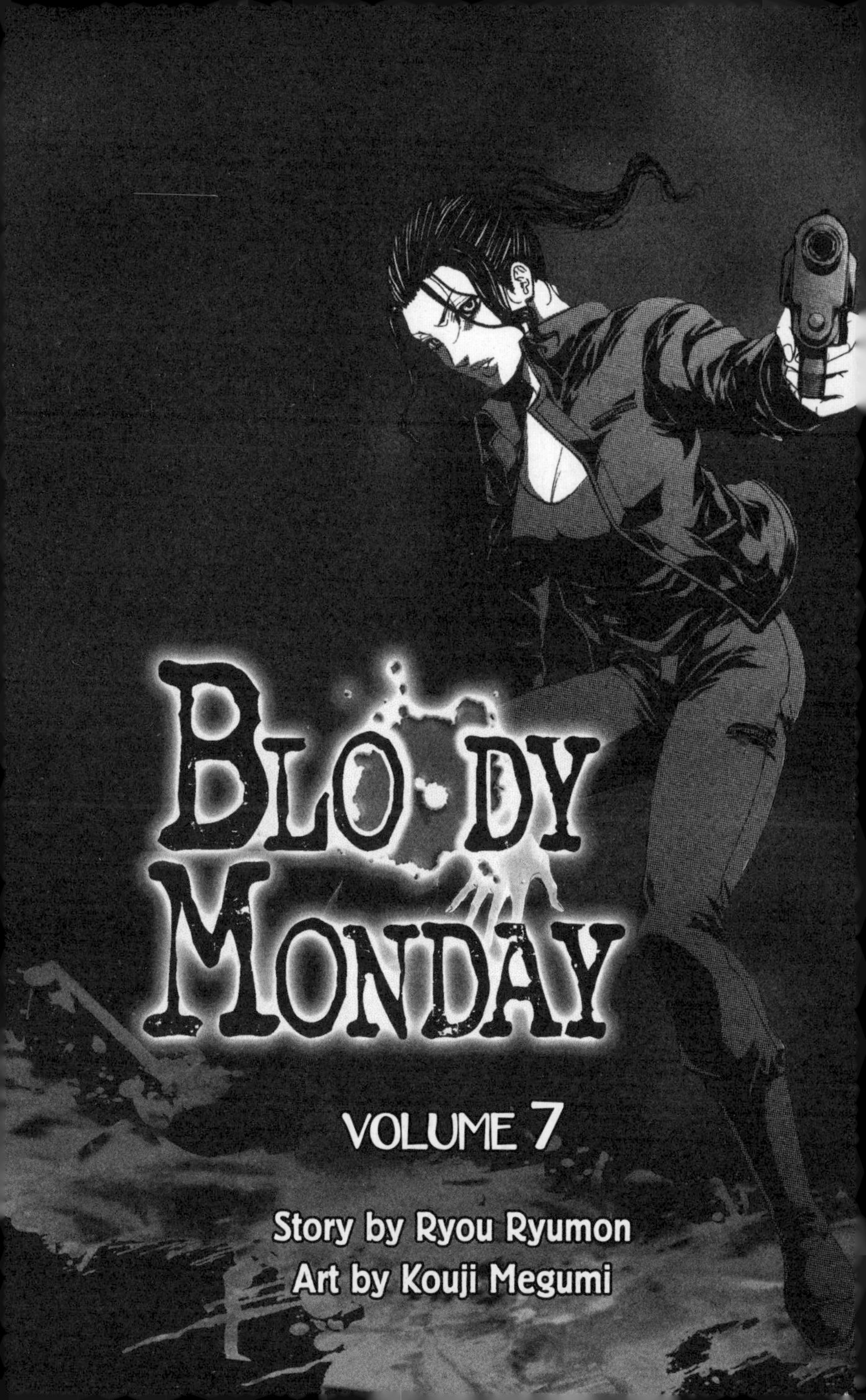
BLOODY MONDAY
VOLUME 7
Story by Ryou Ryumon
Art by Kouji Megumi

BLOODY MONDAY
Character Introductions

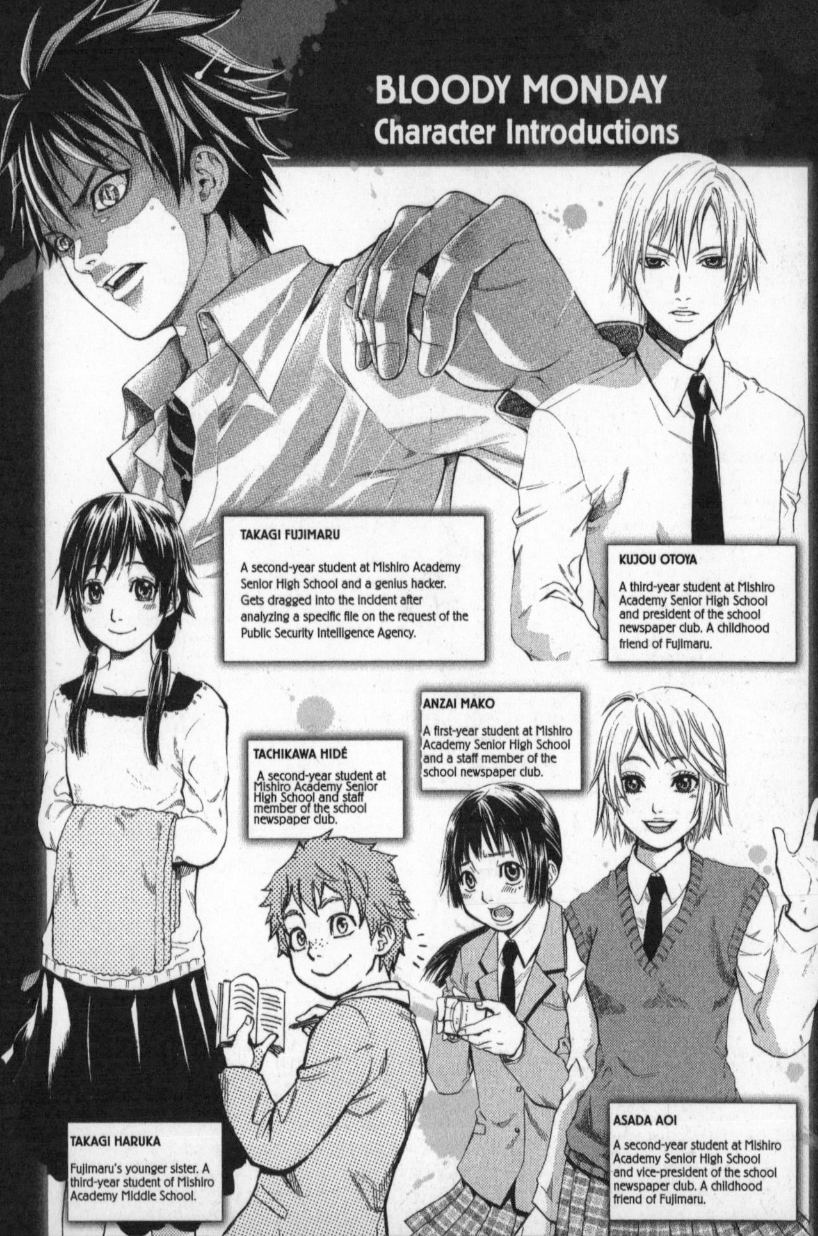
TAKAGI FUJIMARU
A second-year student at Mishiro Academy Senior High School and a genius hacker. Gets dragged into the incident after analyzing a specific file on the request of the Public Security Intelligence Agency.
KUJOU OTOYA
A third-year student at Mishiro Academy Senior High School and president of the school newspaper club. A childhood friend of Fujimaru.
ANZAI MAKO
A first-year student at Mishiro Academy Senior High School and a staff member of the school newspaper club.
TACHIKAWA HIDÉ
A second-year student at Mishiro Academy Senior High School and staff member of the school newspaper club.
TAKAGI HARUKA
Fujimaru's younger sister. A third-year student of Mishiro Academy Middle School.
ASADA AOI
A second-year student at Mishiro Academy Senior High School and vice-president of the school newspaper club. A childhood friend of Fujimaru.

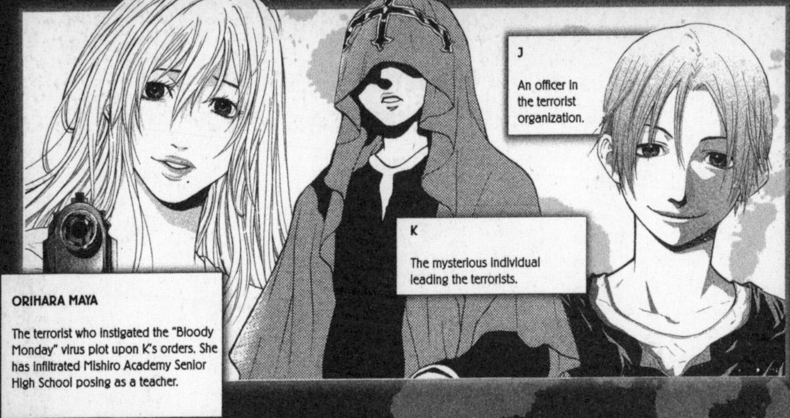
J
An officer in the terrorist organization.
K
The mysterious individual leading the terrorists.
ORIHARA MAYA
The terrorist who instigated the "Bloody Monday" virus plot upon K's orders. She has infiltrated Mishiro Academy Senior High School posing as a teacher.

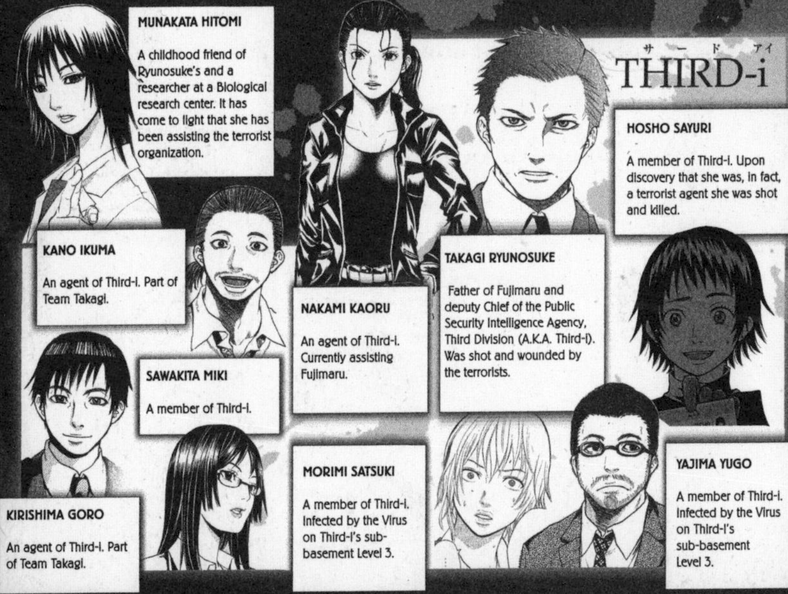
THIRD-i
サードアイ
MUNAKATA HITOMI
A childhood friend of Ryunosuke's and a researcher at a Biological research center. It has come to light that she has been assisting the terrorist organization.
HOSHO SAYURI
A member of Third-i. Upon discovery that she was, in fact, a terrorist agent she was shot and killed.
KANO IKUMA
An agent of Third-i. Part of Team Takagi.
TAKAGI RYUNOSUKE
Father of Fujimaru and deputy Chief of the Public Security Intelligence Agency, Third Division (A.K.A. Third-i). Was shot and wounded by the terrorists.
NAKAMI KAORU
An agent of Third-i. Currently assisting Fujimaru.
SAWAKITA MIKI
A member of Third-i.
MORIMI SATSUKI
A member of Third-i. Infected by the Virus on Third-i's sub-basement Level 3.
YAJIMA YUGO
A member of Third-i. Infected by the Virus on Third-i's sub-basement Level 3.
KIRISHIMA GORO
An agent of Third-i. Part of Team Takagi.

The Story So Far

To regain the original chip containing the data of the "Christmas Massacre", J and his terrorist group have released the "Bloody-X" virus in basement Level 3 of the Third-i headquarters. Fujimaru is on the hunt for the antivirus in order to save the lives of Yajima and Morimi who are still trapped on Level 3. He seeks out the aid of his father's childhood friend, Minakata but he discovers that Minakata has been conspiring with the terrorists. Risking it all, Fujimaru manages to capture Minakata and learns that the antivirus is already at Third-I Headquarters.

Contents

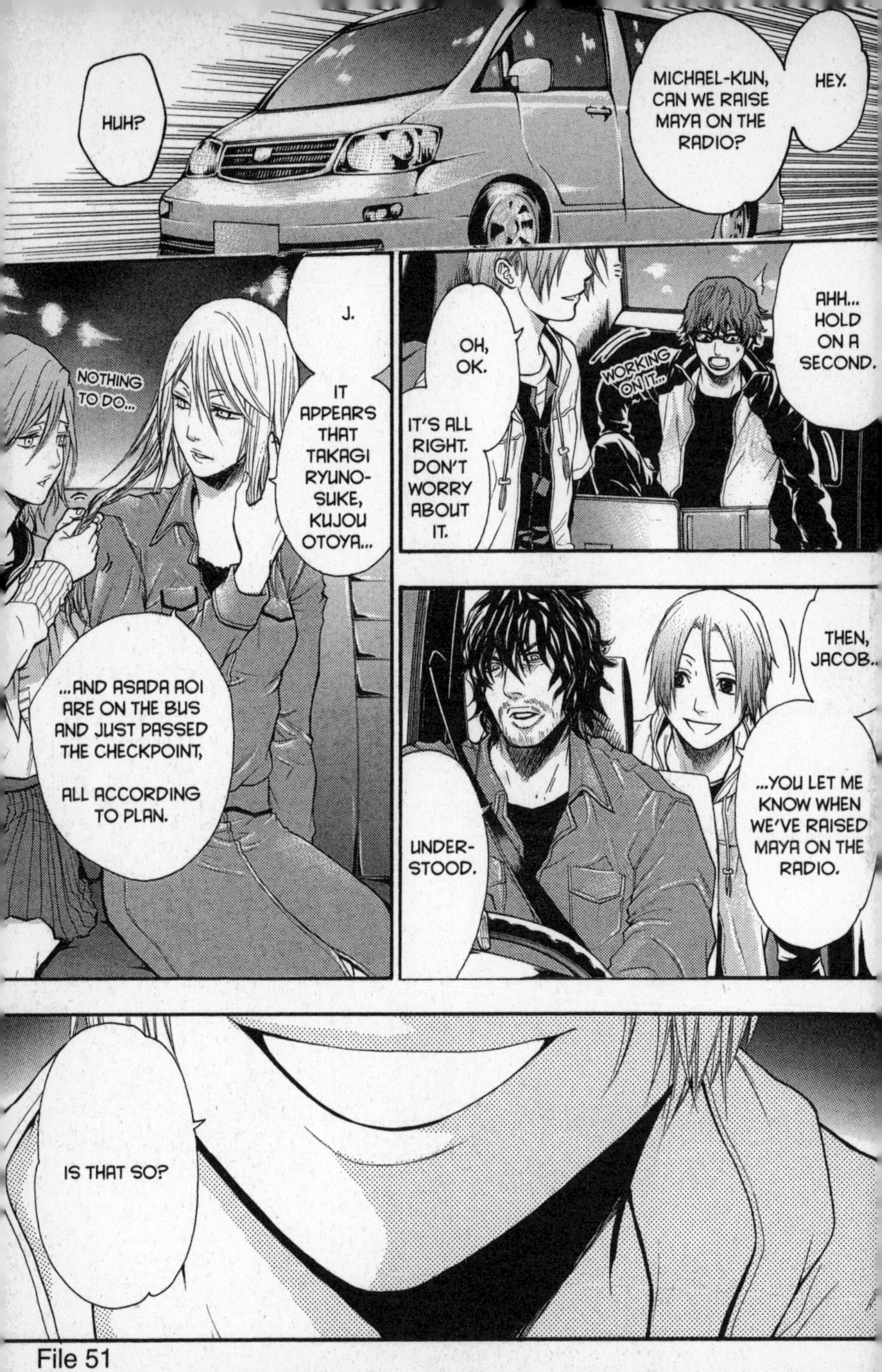
HEY.
MICHAEL-KUN, CAN WE RAISE MAYA ON THE RADIO?
HUH?
AHH... HOLD ON A SECOND.
WORKING ON IT...
OH, OK.
IT'S ALL RIGHT. DON'T WORRY ABOUT IT.
THEN, JACOB...
...YOU LET ME KNOW WHEN WE'VE RAISED MAYA ON THE RADIO.
UNDER-STOOD.
J.
IT APPEARS THAT TAKAGI RYUNO-SUKE, KUJOU OTOYA...
NOTHING TO DO...
...AND ASADA AOI ARE ON THE BUS AND JUST PASSED THE CHECKPOINT,
ALL ACCORDING TO PLAN.
IS THAT SO?

File 51
What we've been fighting to get.

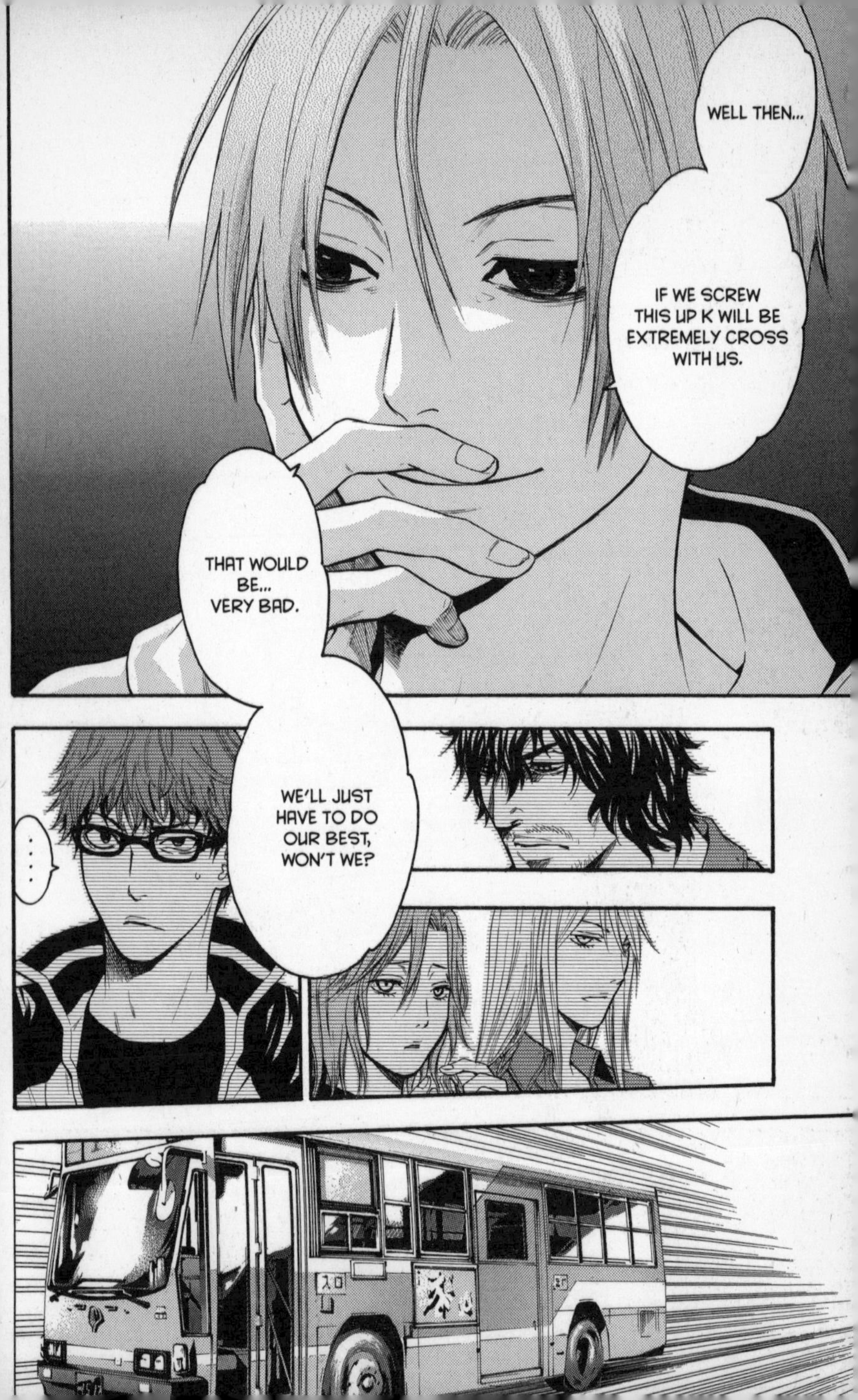
WELL THEN...
IF WE SCREW THIS UP K WILL BE EXTREMELY CROSS WITH US.
THAT WOULD BE... VERY BAD.
WE'LL JUST HAVE TO DO OUR BEST, WON'T WE?
.....

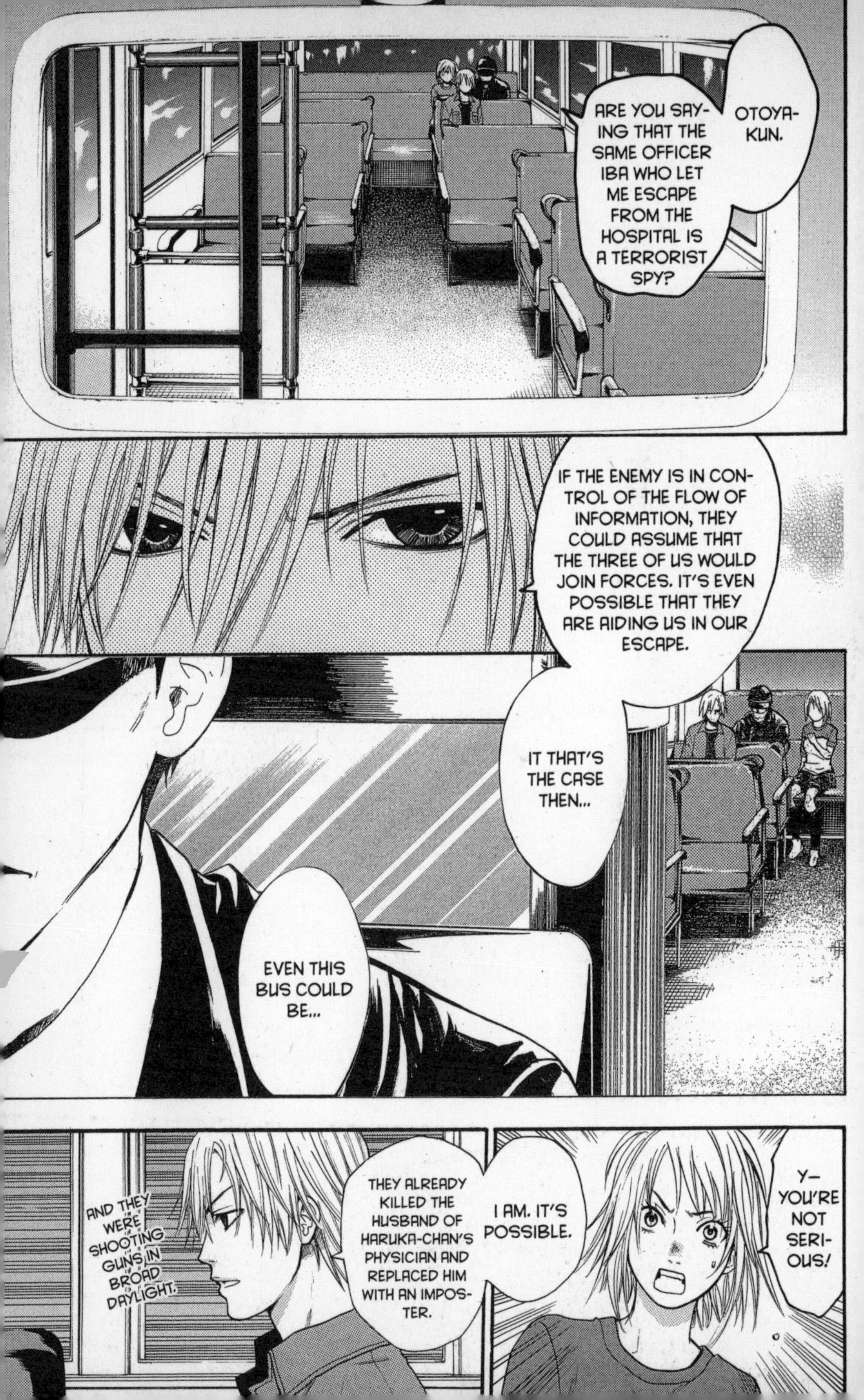
OTOYA-KUN.
ARE YOU SAYING THAT THE SAME OFFICER IBA WHO LET ME ESCAPE FROM THE HOSPITAL IS A TERRORIST SPY?
IF THE ENEMY IS IN CONTROL OF THE FLOW OF INFORMATION, THEY COULD ASSUME THAT THE THREE OF US WOULD JOIN FORCES. IT'S EVEN POSSIBLE THAT THEY ARE AIDING US IN OUR ESCAPE.
IT THAT'S THE CASE THEN...
EVEN THIS BUS COULD BE...
Y— YOU'RE NOT SERIOUS!
I AM. IT'S POSSIBLE.
THEY ALREADY KILLED THE HUSBAND OF HARUKA-CHAN'S PHYSICIAN AND REPLACED HIM WITH AN IMPOSTER.
AND THEY WERE SHOOTING GUNS IN BROAD DAYLIGHT.

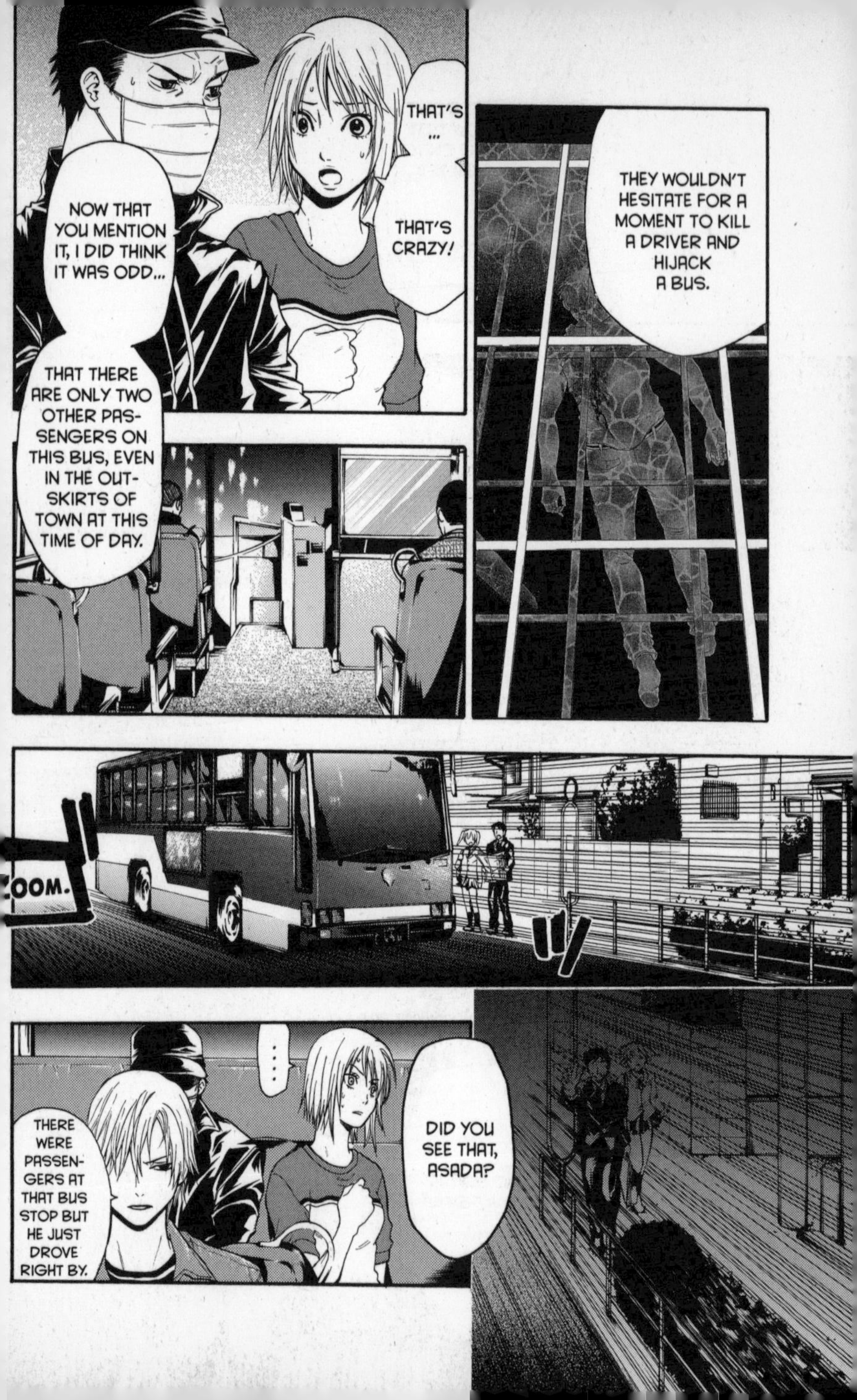
THEY WOULDN'T HESITATE FOR A MOMENT TO KILL A DRIVER AND HIJACK A BUS.
THAT'S ...
THAT'S CRAZY!
NOW THAT YOU MENTION IT, I DID THINK IT WAS ODD...
THAT THERE ARE ONLY TWO OTHER PAS-SENGERS ON THIS BUS, EVEN IN THE OUT-SKIRTS OF TOWN AT THIS TIME OF DAY.
OOM.
DID YOU SEE THAT, ASADA?
....
THERE WERE PASSEN-GERS AT THAT BUS STOP BUT HE JUST DROVE RIGHT BY.

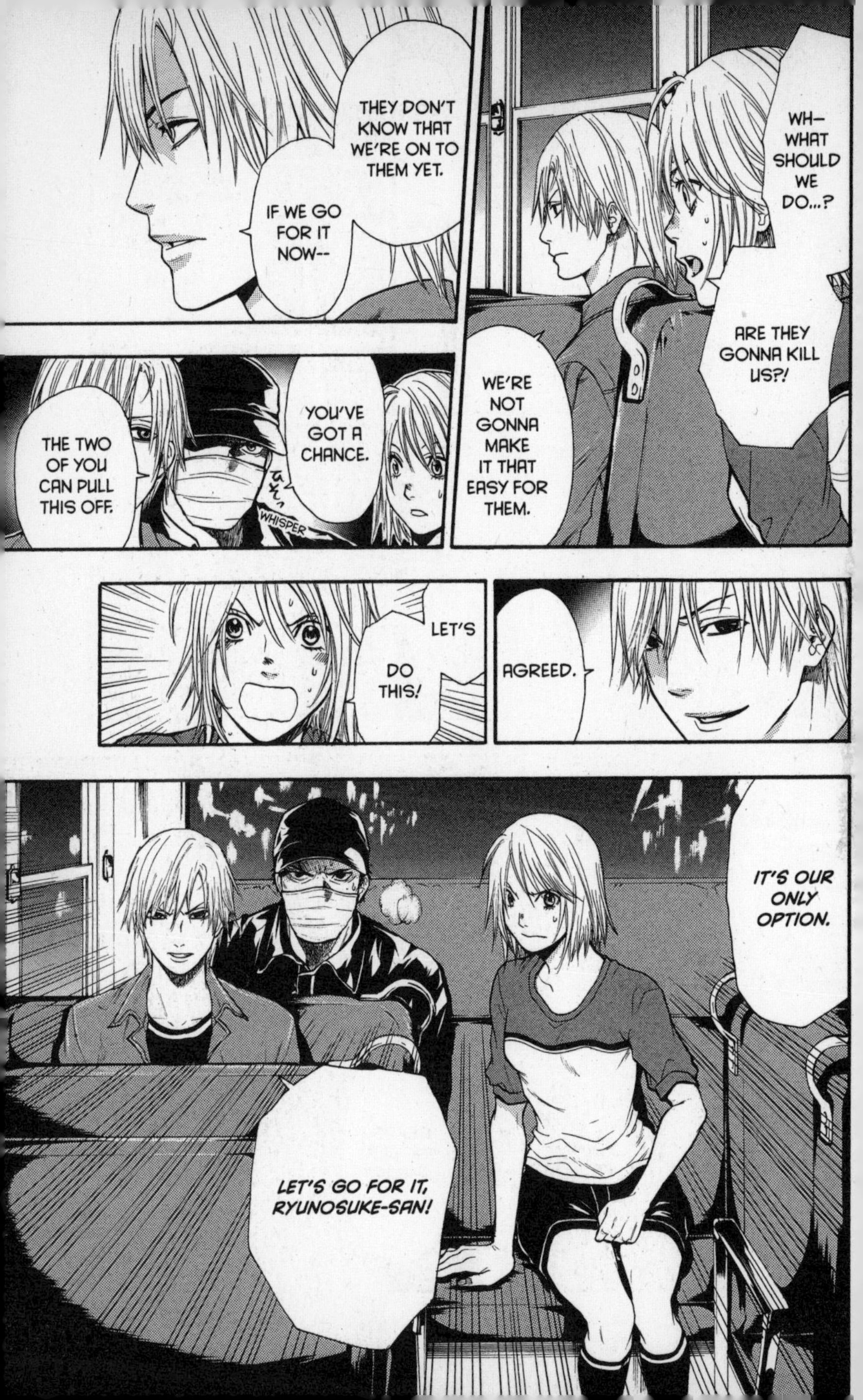
WH—WHAT SHOULD WE DO...?
ARE THEY GONNA KILL US?!
WE'RE NOT GONNA MAKE IT THAT EASY FOR THEM.
THEY DON'T KNOW THAT WE'RE ON TO THEM YET.
IF WE GO FOR IT NOW--
YOU'VE GOT A CHANCE.
WHISPER
THE TWO OF YOU CAN PULL THIS OFF.
AGREED.
LET'S DO THIS!
IT'S OUR ONLY OPTION.
LET'S GO FOR IT, RYUNOSUKE-SAN!

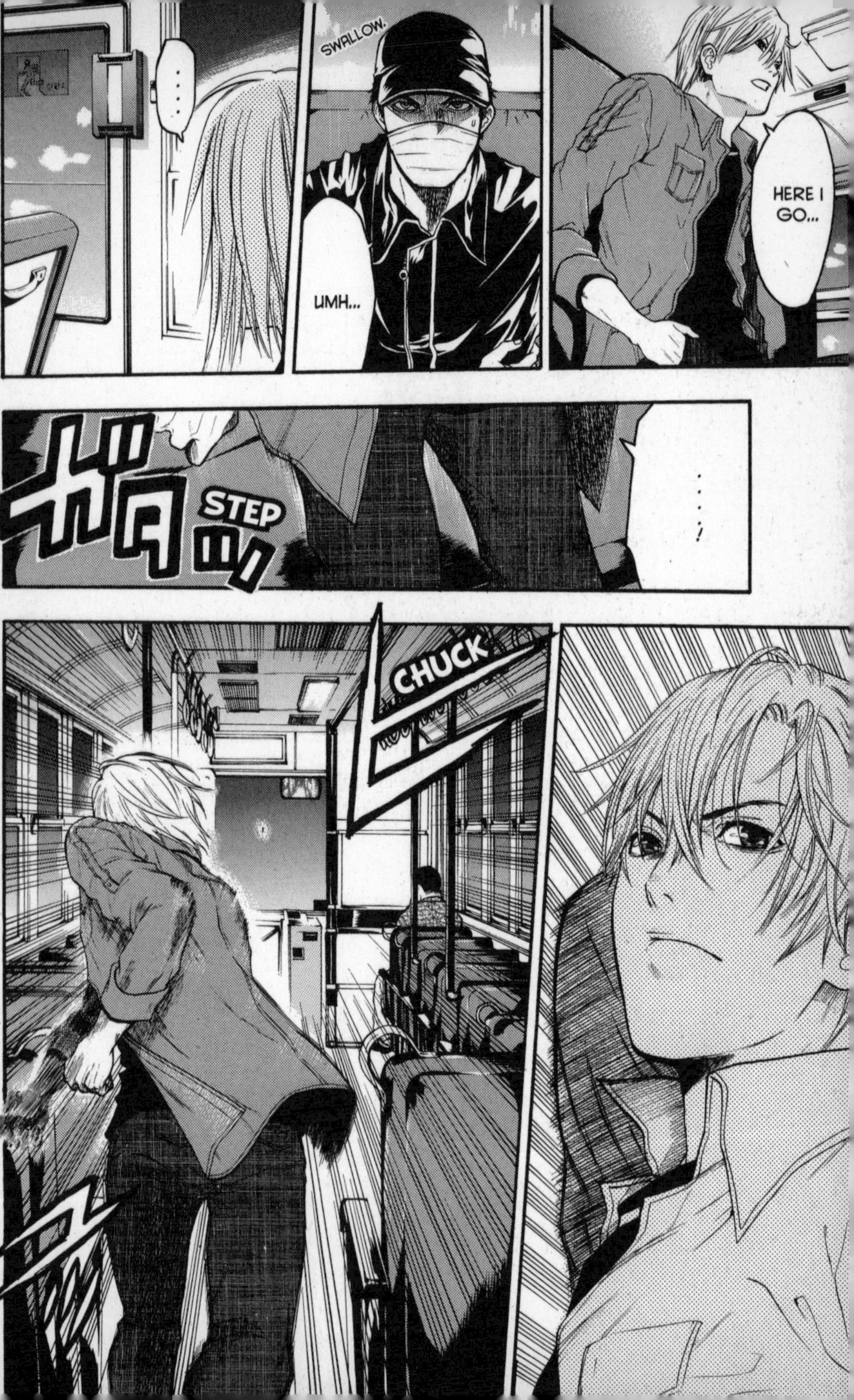
HERE I GO...
SWALLOW.
UMH...
...
...!
STEP
CHUCK

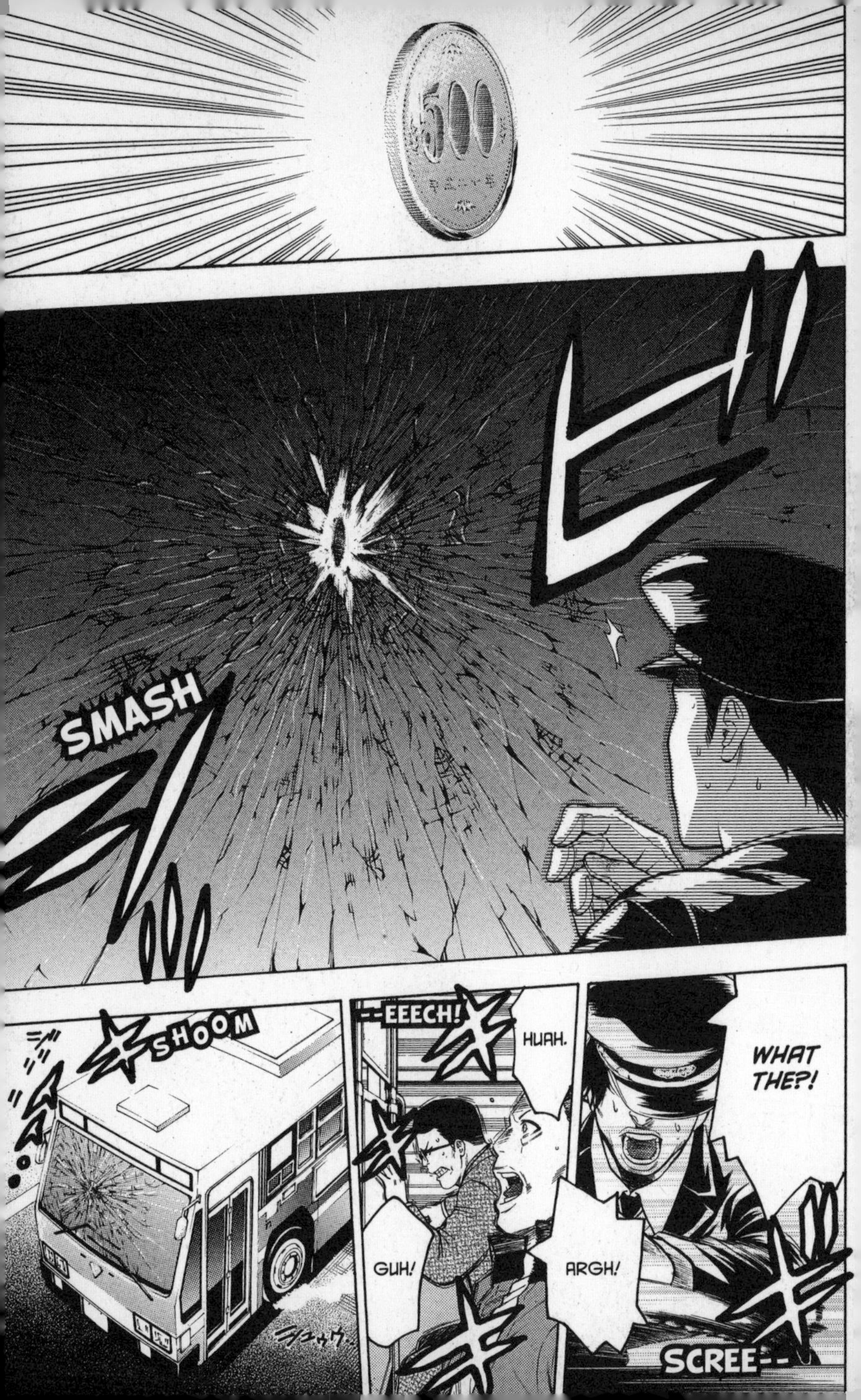
500
SMASH
WHAT THE?!
SCREE--
--EEECH!
HUAH.
ARGH!
GUH!
SHOOM

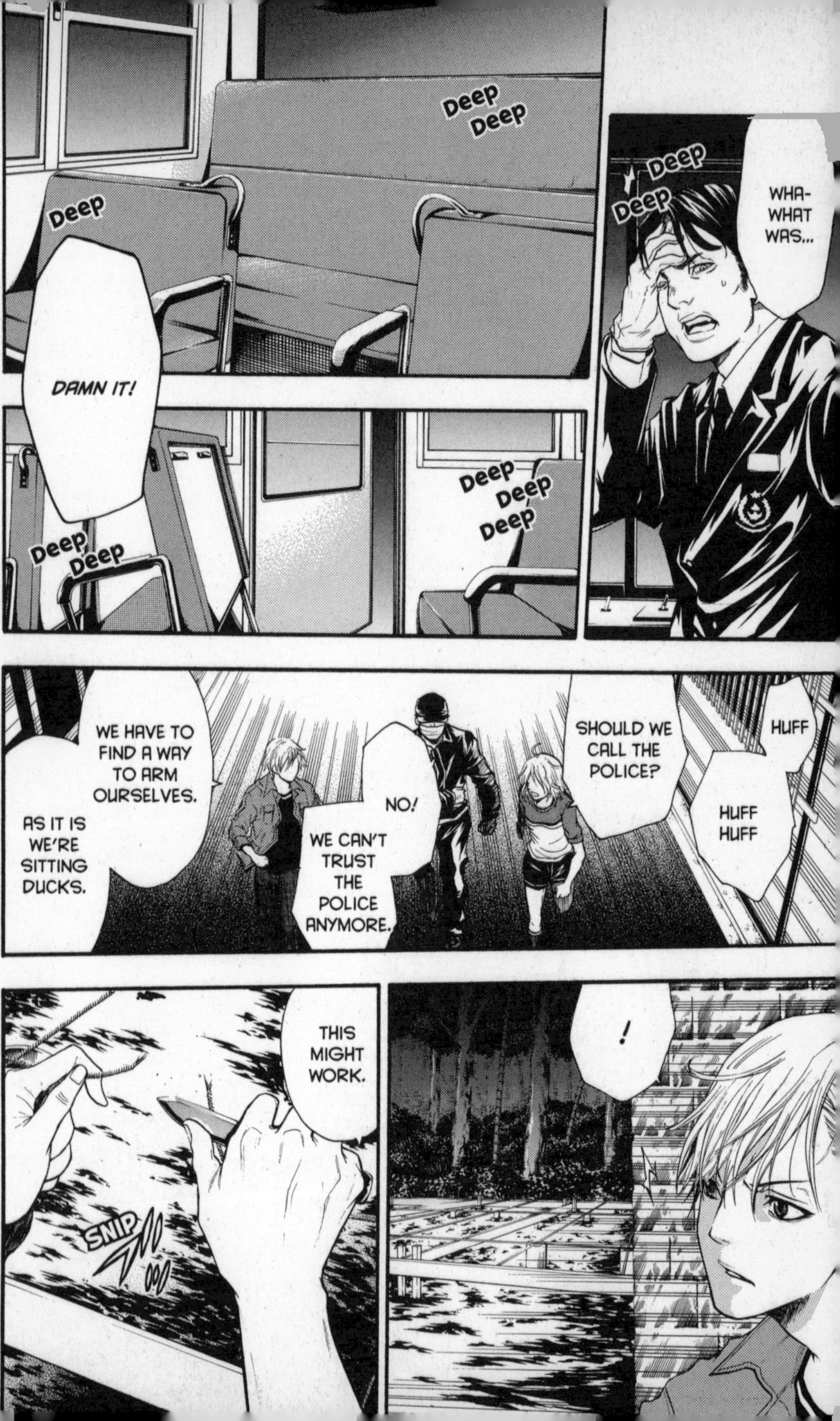
WHA- WHAT WAS...
Deep Deep
Deep Deep
Deep
DAMN IT!
Deep Deep Deep
Deep Deep
HUFF
HUFF HUFF
SHOULD WE CALL THE POLICE?
NO!
WE CAN'T TRUST THE POLICE ANYMORE.
WE HAVE TO FIND A WAY TO ARM OURSELVES.
AS IT IS WE'RE SITTING DUCKS.
!
THIS MIGHT WORK.
SNIP

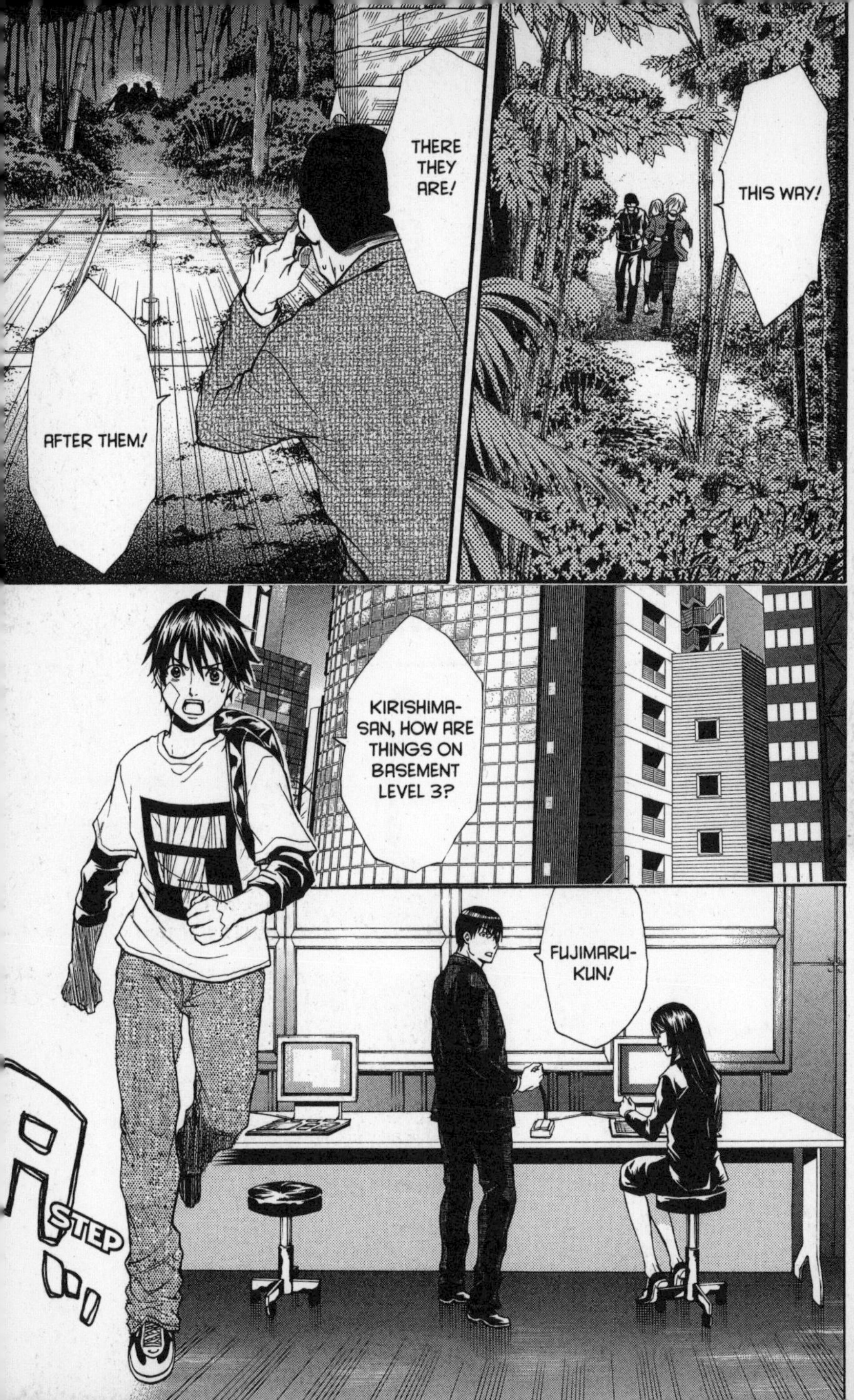
THIS WAY!
THERE THEY ARE!
AFTER THEM!
KIRISHIMA-SAN, HOW ARE THINGS ON BASEMENT LEVEL 3?
FUJIMARU-KUN!
STEP

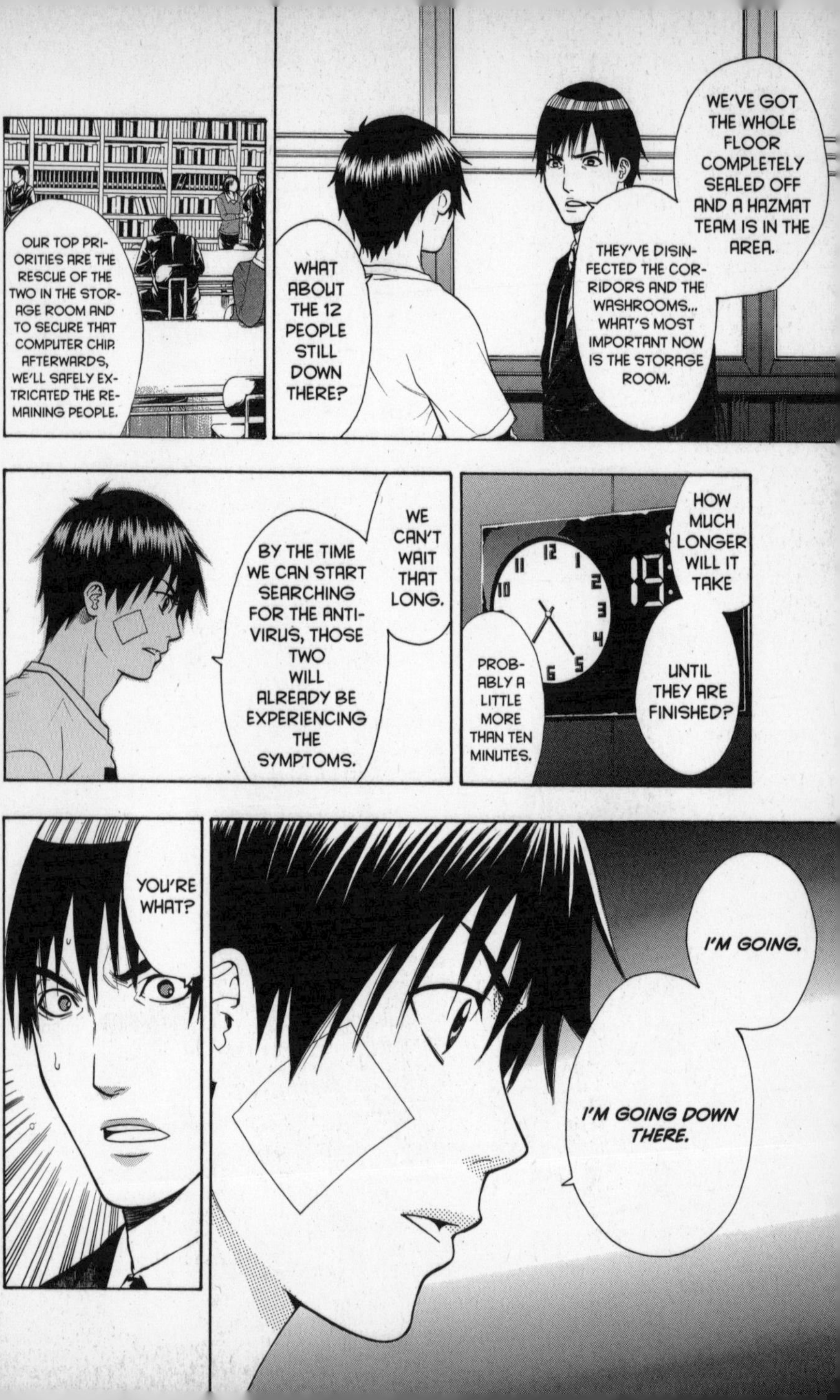
WE'VE GOT THE WHOLE FLOOR COMPLETELY SEALED OFF AND A HAZMAT TEAM IS IN THE AREA.
THEY'VE DISINFECTED THE CORRIDORS AND THE WASHROOMS... WHAT'S MOST IMPORTANT NOW IS THE STORAGE ROOM.
WHAT ABOUT THE 12 PEOPLE STILL DOWN THERE?
OUR TOP PRIORITIES ARE THE RESCUE OF THE TWO IN THE STORAGE ROOM AND TO SECURE THAT COMPUTER CHIP. AFTERWARDS, WE'LL SAFELY EXTRICATED THE REMAINING PEOPLE.
HOW MUCH LONGER WILL IT TAKE
UNTIL THEY ARE FINISHED?
PROBABLY A LITTLE MORE THAN TEN MINUTES.
WE CAN'T WAIT THAT LONG.
BY THE TIME WE CAN START SEARCHING FOR THE ANTI-VIRUS, THOSE TWO WILL ALREADY BE EXPERIENCING THE SYMPTOMS.
I'M GOING.
I'M GOING DOWN THERE.
YOU'RE WHAT?

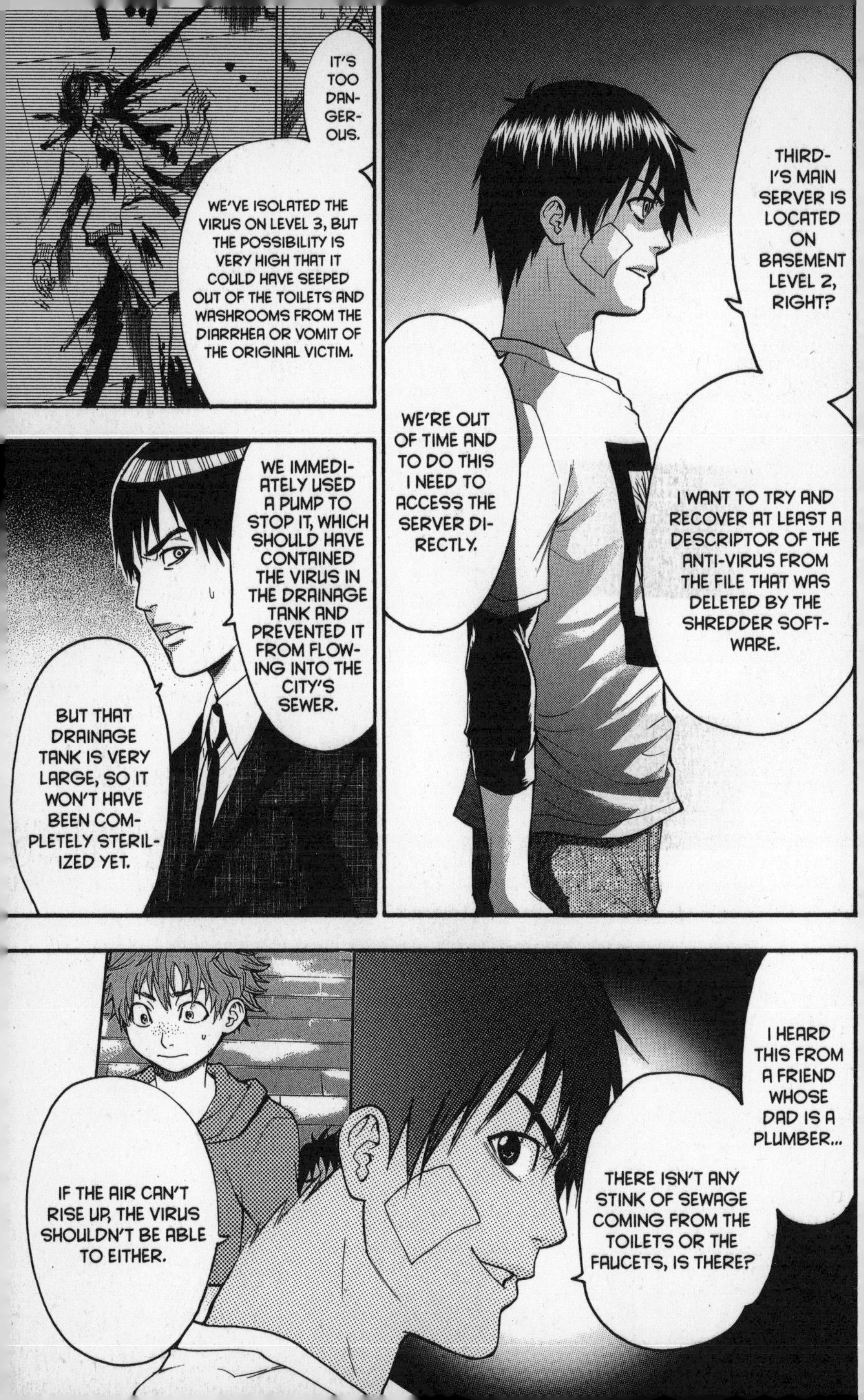
THIRD-I'S MAIN SERVER IS LOCATED ON BASEMENT LEVEL 2, RIGHT?
I WANT TO TRY AND RECOVER AT LEAST A DESCRIPTOR OF THE ANTI-VIRUS FROM THE FILE THAT WAS DELETED BY THE SHREDDER SOFTWARE.
WE'RE OUT OF TIME AND TO DO THIS I NEED TO ACCESS THE SERVER DIRECTLY.
IT'S TOO DANGEROUS.
WE'VE ISOLATED THE VIRUS ON LEVEL 3, BUT THE POSSIBILITY IS VERY HIGH THAT IT COULD HAVE SEEPED OUT OF THE TOILETS AND WASHROOMS FROM THE DIARRHEA OR VOMIT OF THE ORIGINAL VICTIM.
WE IMMEDIATELY USED A PUMP TO STOP IT, WHICH SHOULD HAVE CONTAINED THE VIRUS IN THE DRAINAGE TANK AND PREVENTED IT FROM FLOWING INTO THE CITY'S SEWER.
BUT THAT DRAINAGE TANK IS VERY LARGE, SO IT WON'T HAVE BEEN COMPLETELY STERILIZED YET.
I HEARD THIS FROM A FRIEND WHOSE DAD IS A PLUMBER...
THERE ISN'T ANY STINK OF SEWAGE COMING FROM THE TOILETS OR THE FAUCETS, IS THERE?
IF THE AIR CAN'T RISE UP, THE VIRUS SHOULDN'T BE ABLE TO EITHER.

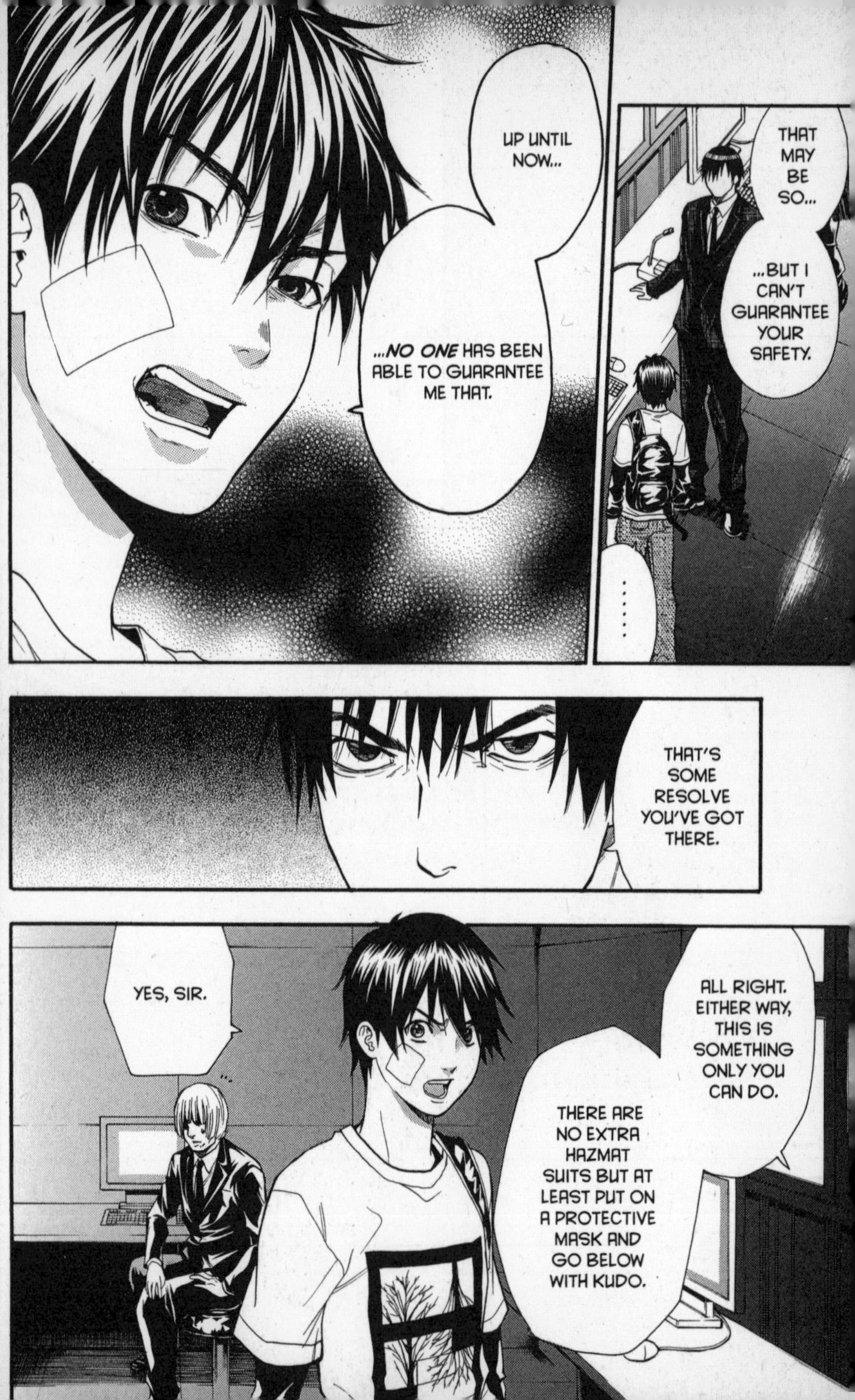
THAT MAY BE SO...
...BUT I CAN'T GUARANTEE YOUR SAFETY.
......
UP UNTIL NOW...
...NO ONE HAS BEEN ABLE TO GUARANTEE ME THAT.
THAT'S SOME RESOLVE YOU'VE GOT THERE.
ALL RIGHT. EITHER WAY, THIS IS SOMETHING ONLY YOU CAN DO.
THERE ARE NO EXTRA HAZMAT SUITS BUT AT LEAST PUT ON A PROTECTIVE MASK AND GO BELOW WITH KUDO.
YES, SIR.

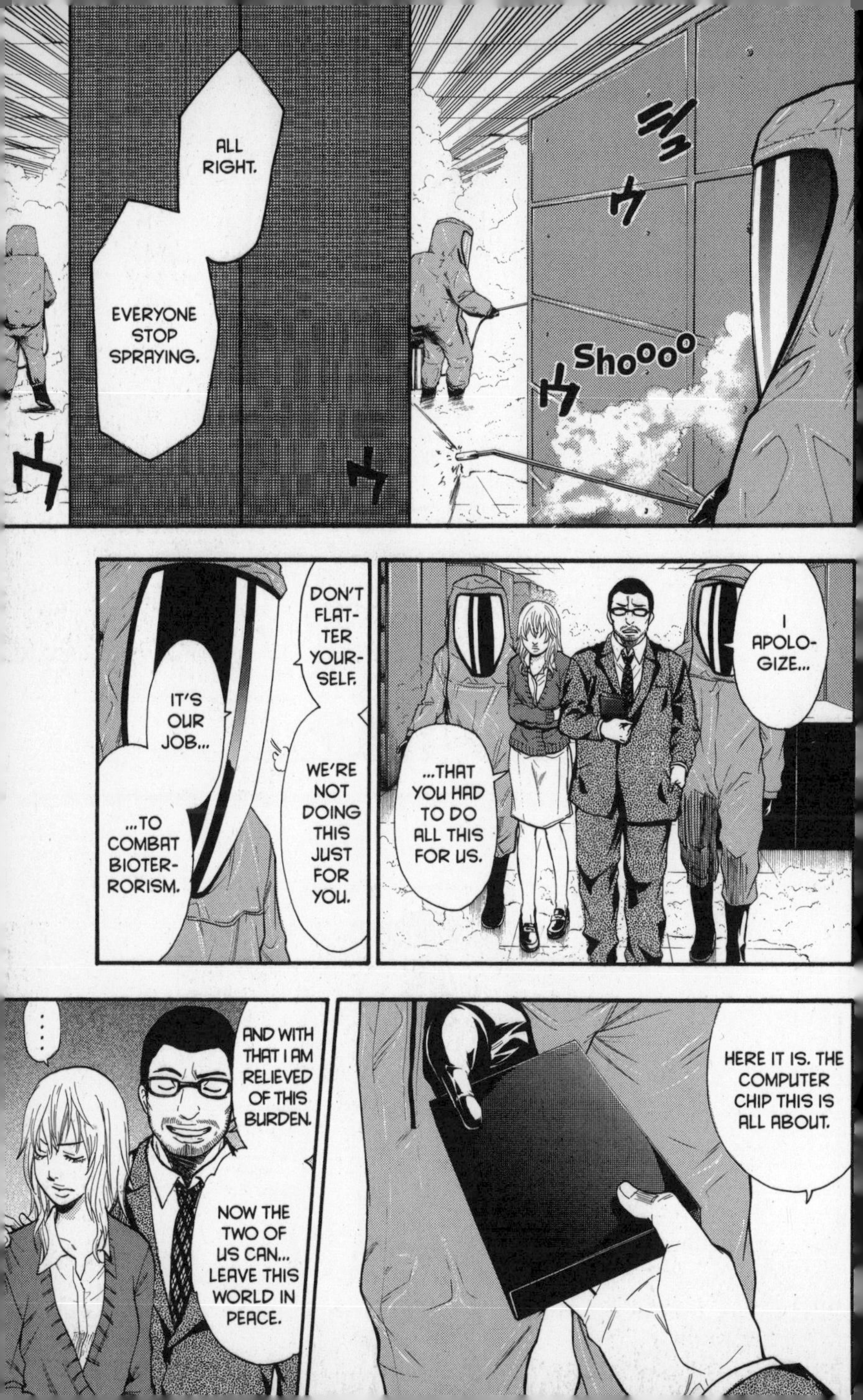
Shoooo
ALL RIGHT.
EVERYONE STOP SPRAYING.
I APOLOGIZE...
...THAT YOU HAD TO DO ALL THIS FOR US.
DON'T FLATTER YOURSELF.
WE'RE NOT DOING THIS JUST FOR YOU.
IT'S OUR JOB...
...TO COMBAT BIOTERRORISM.
HERE IT IS. THE COMPUTER CHIP THIS IS ALL ABOUT.
AND WITH THAT I AM RELIEVED OF THIS BURDEN.
NOW THE TWO OF US CAN... LEAVE THIS WORLD IN PEACE.
.....

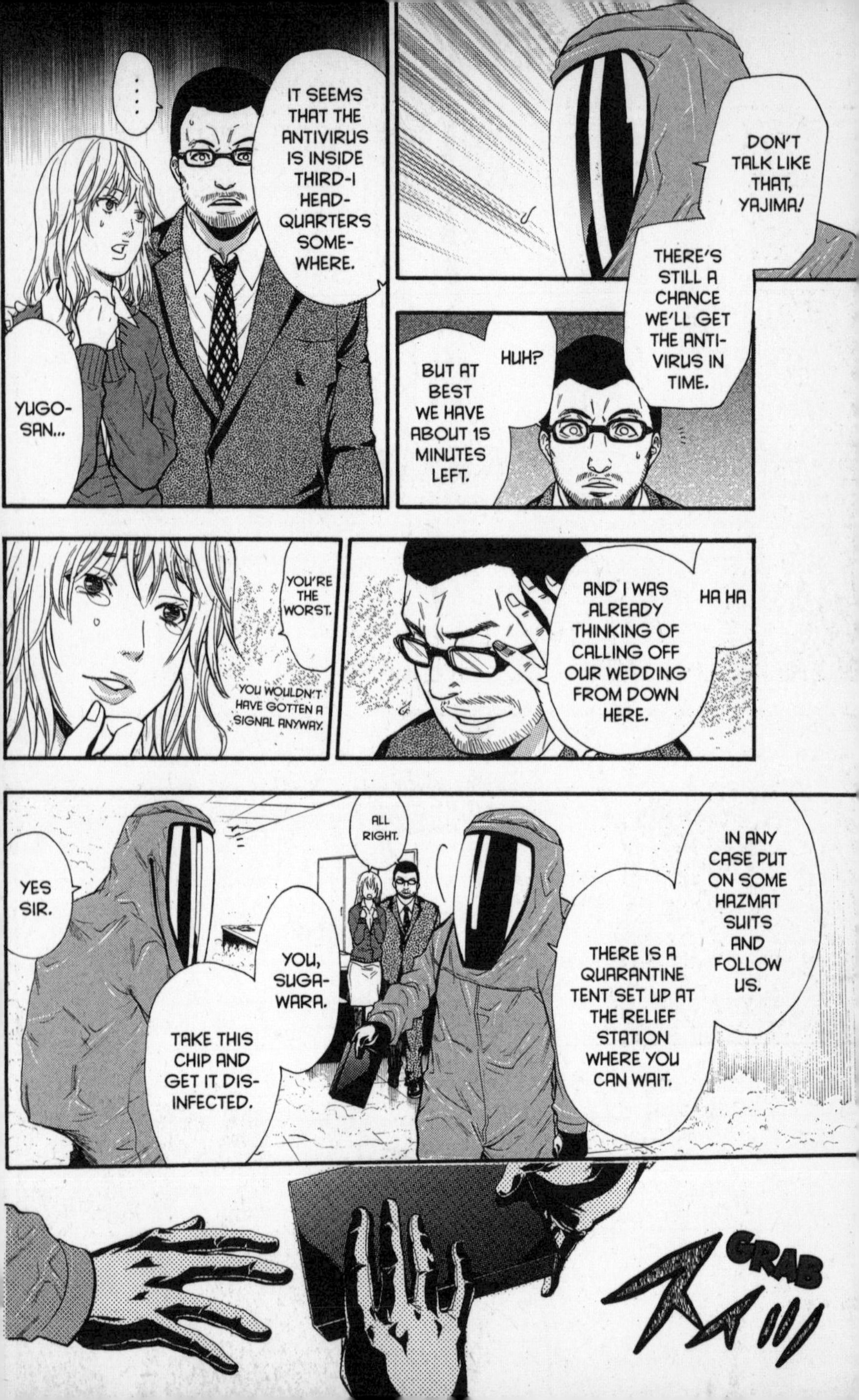
DON'T TALK LIKE THAT, YAJIMA!
THERE'S STILL A CHANCE WE'LL GET THE ANTI-VIRUS IN TIME.
HUH?
BUT AT BEST WE HAVE ABOUT 15 MINUTES LEFT.
IT SEEMS THAT THE ANTIVIRUS IS INSIDE THIRD-I HEAD-QUARTERS SOME-WHERE.
. . . .
YUGO-SAN...
AND I WAS ALREADY THINKING OF CALLING OFF OUR WEDDING FROM DOWN HERE.
HA HA
YOU'RE THE WORST.
YOU WOULDN'T HAVE GOTTEN A SIGNAL ANYWAY.
IN ANY CASE PUT ON SOME HAZMAT SUITS AND FOLLOW US.
THERE IS A QUARANTINE TENT SET UP AT THE RELIEF STATION WHERE YOU CAN WAIT.
ALL RIGHT.
YOU, SUGA-WARA.
TAKE THIS CHIP AND GET IT DIS-INFECTED.
YES SIR.
GRAB

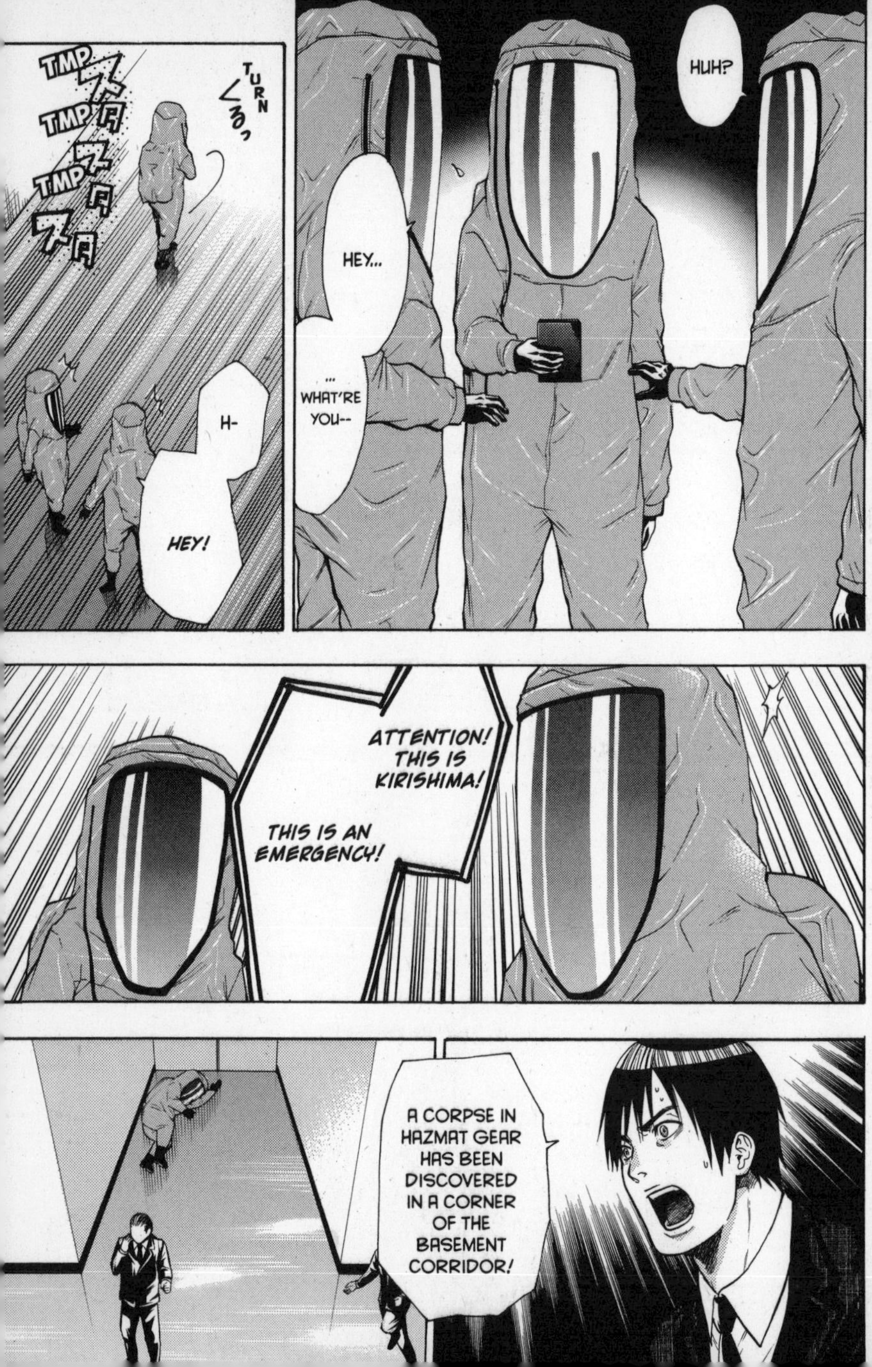
HUH?
HEY...
... WHAT'RE YOU--
TURN くるっ
TMP TMP TMP
H-
HEY!
ATTENTION! THIS IS KIRISHIMA!
THIS IS AN EMERGENCY!
A CORPSE IN HAZMAT GEAR HAS BEEN DISCOVERED IN A CORNER OF THE BASEMENT CORRIDOR!

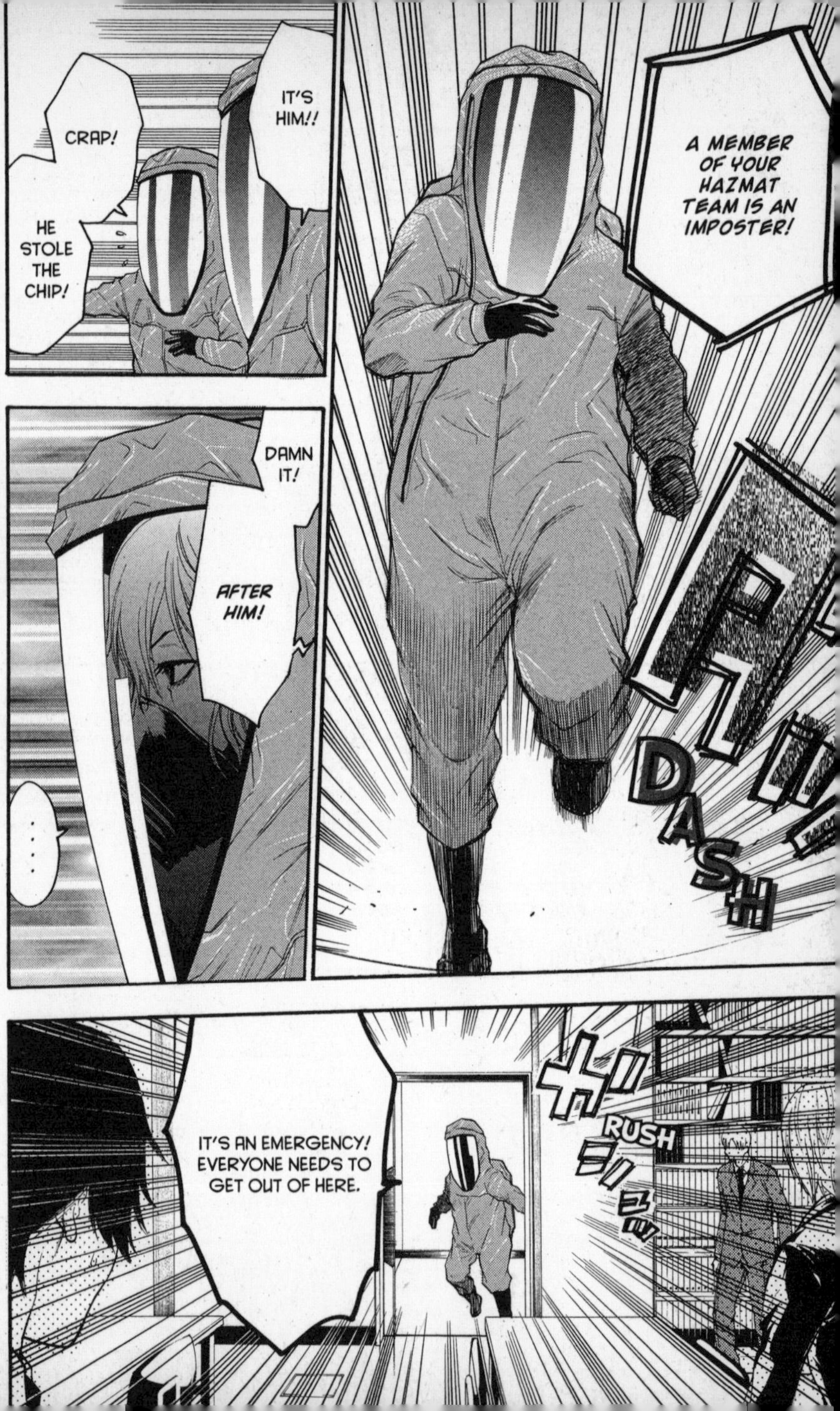
A MEMBER OF YOUR HAZMAT TEAM IS AN IMPOSTER!
DASH
IT'S HIM!!
CRAP!
HE STOLE THE CHIP!
DAMN IT!
AFTER HIM!
...
RUSH
IT'S AN EMERGENCY! EVERYONE NEEDS TO GET OUT OF HERE.

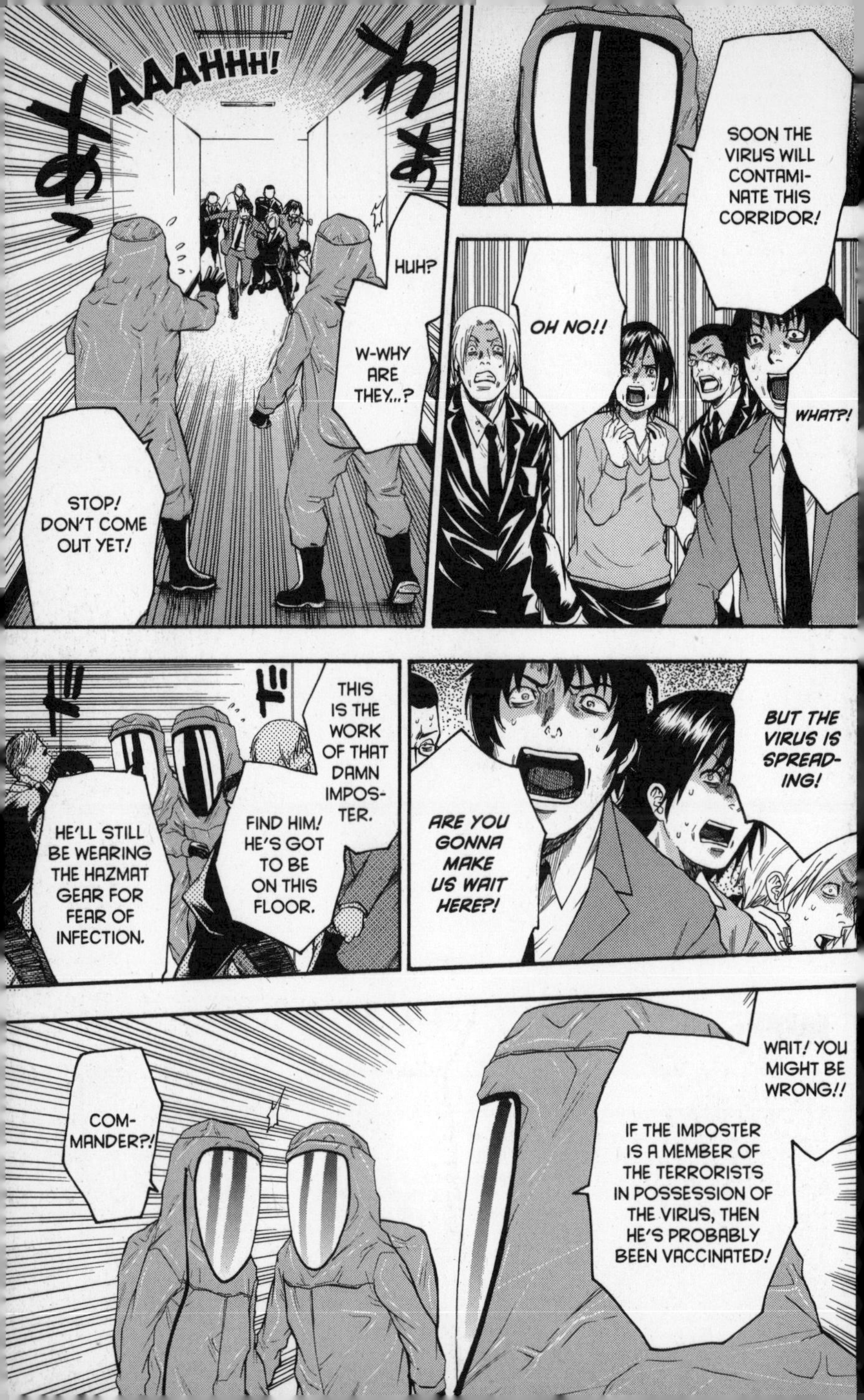
SOON THE VIRUS WILL CONTAMINATE THIS CORRIDOR!
WHAT?!
OH NO!!
わぁ
AAAHHH!
あぁっ
HUH?
W-WHY ARE THEY...?
STOP! DON'T COME OUT YET!
BUT THE VIRUS IS SPREADING!
ARE YOU GONNA MAKE US WAIT HERE?!
ド
THIS IS THE WORK OF THAT DAMN IMPOSTER.
FIND HIM! HE'S GOT TO BE ON THIS FLOOR.
ド
HE'LL STILL BE WEARING THE HAZMAT GEAR FOR FEAR OF INFECTION.
WAIT! YOU MIGHT BE WRONG!!
IF THE IMPOSTER IS A MEMBER OF THE TERRORISTS IN POSSESSION OF THE VIRUS, THEN HE'S PROBABLY BEEN VACCINATED!
COMMANDER?!

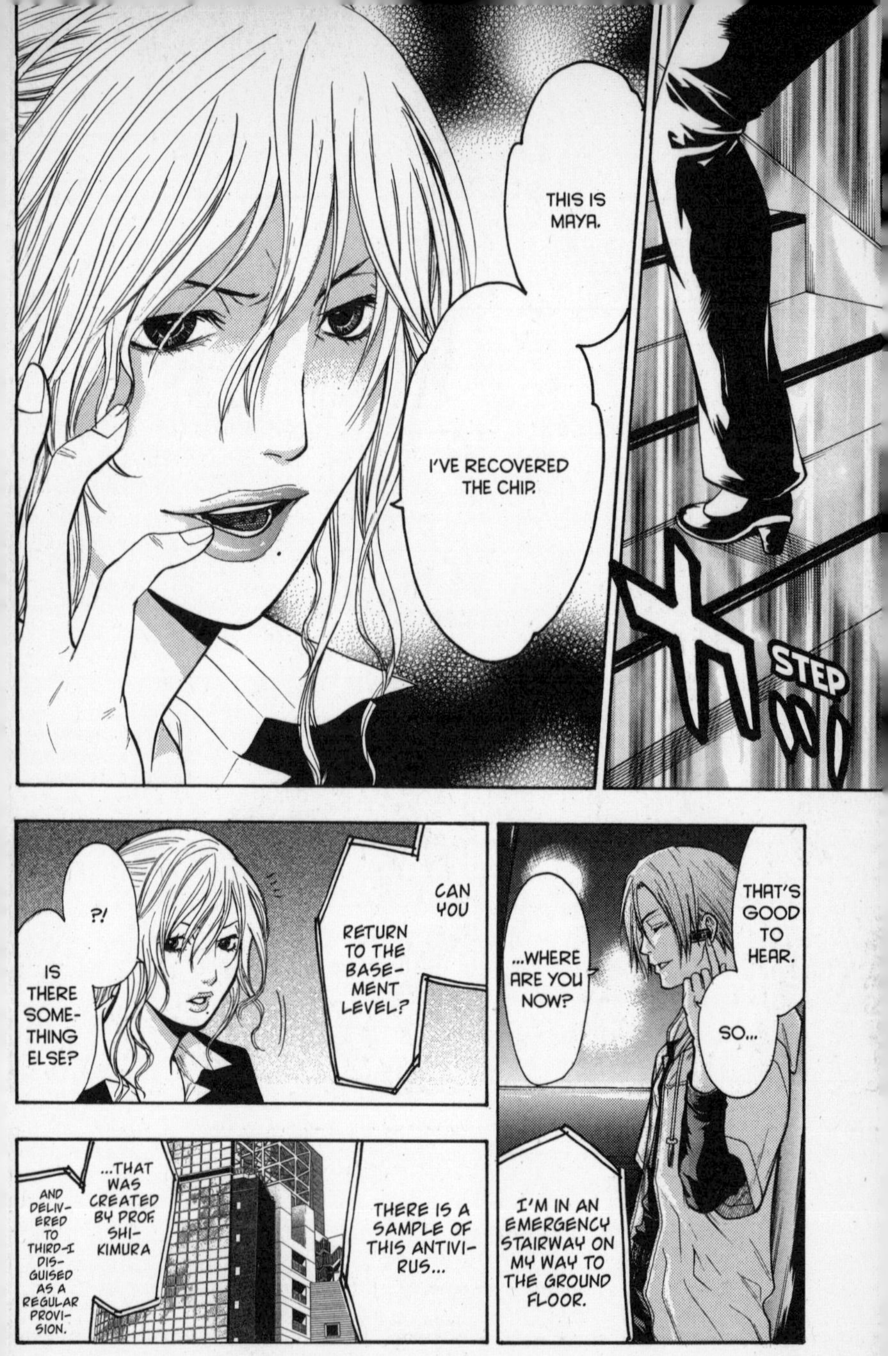
STEP
THIS IS MAYA.
I'VE RECOVERED THE CHIP.
THAT'S GOOD TO HEAR.
SO...
...WHERE ARE YOU NOW?
I'M IN AN EMERGENCY STAIRWAY ON MY WAY TO THE GROUND FLOOR.
CAN YOU RETURN TO THE BASEMENT LEVEL?
?!
IS THERE SOMETHING ELSE?
THERE IS A SAMPLE OF THIS ANTIVIRUS...
...THAT WAS CREATED BY PROF. SHIKIMURA
AND DELIVERED TO THIRD-I DISGUISED AS A REGULAR PROVISION.

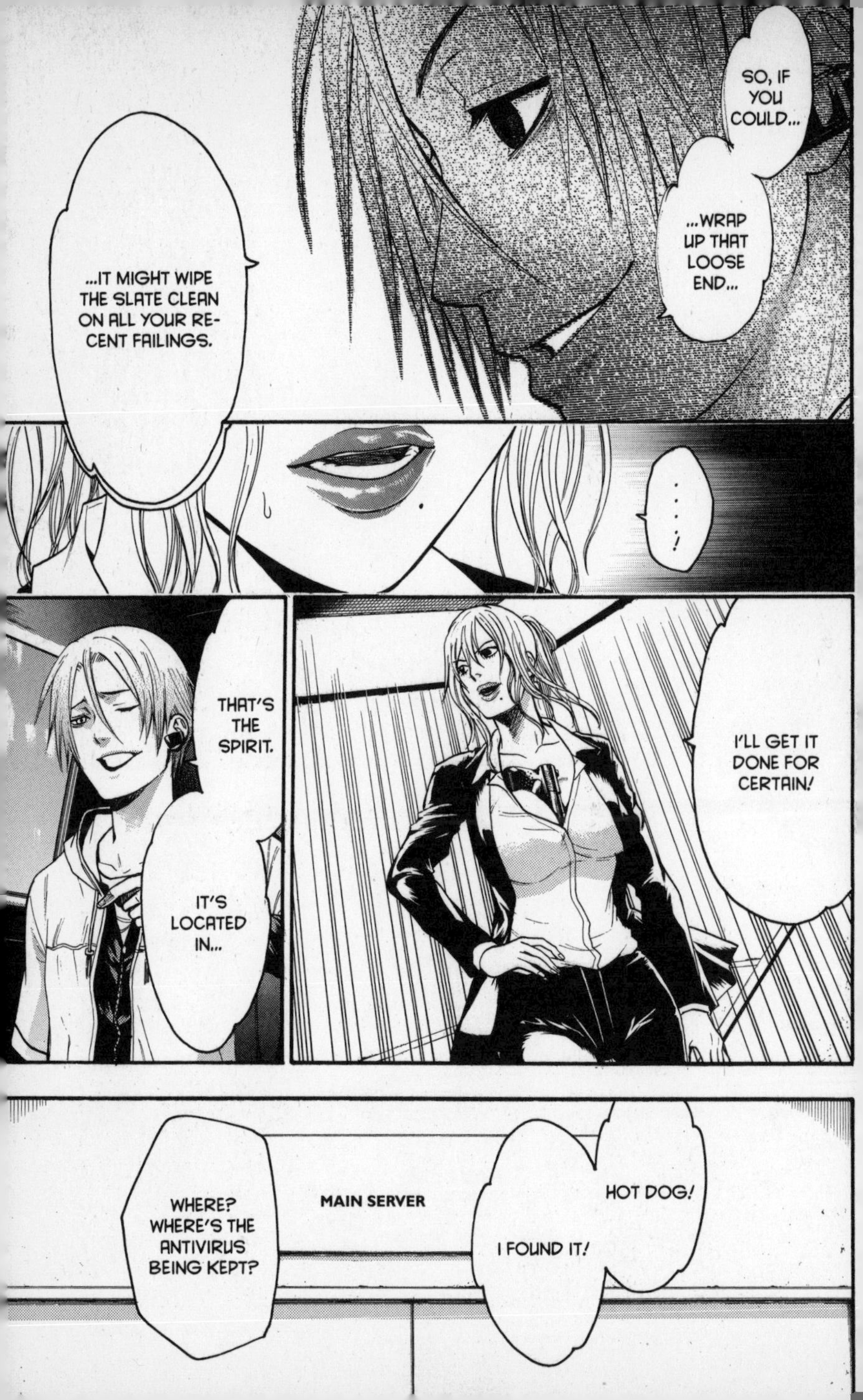
SO, IF YOU COULD...
...WRAP UP THAT LOOSE END...
...IT MIGHT WIPE THE SLATE CLEAN ON ALL YOUR RE-CENT FAILINGS.
...!
I'LL GET IT DONE FOR CERTAIN!
THAT'S THE SPIRIT.
IT'S LOCATED IN...
HOT DOG!
I FOUND IT!
MAIN SERVER
WHERE? WHERE'S THE ANTIVIRUS BEING KEPT?

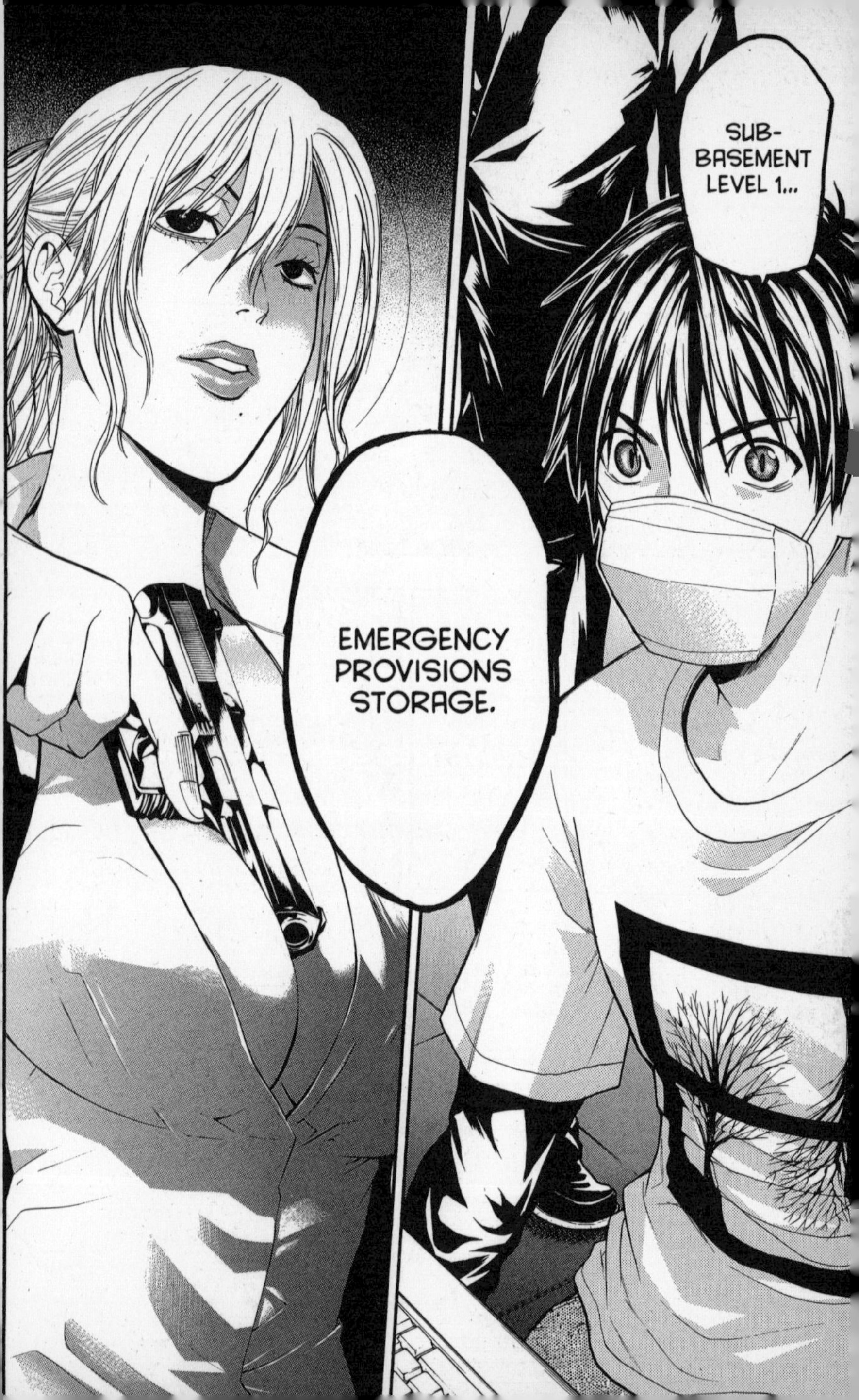
SUB-BASEMENT LEVEL 1...
EMERGENCY PROVISIONS STORAGE.

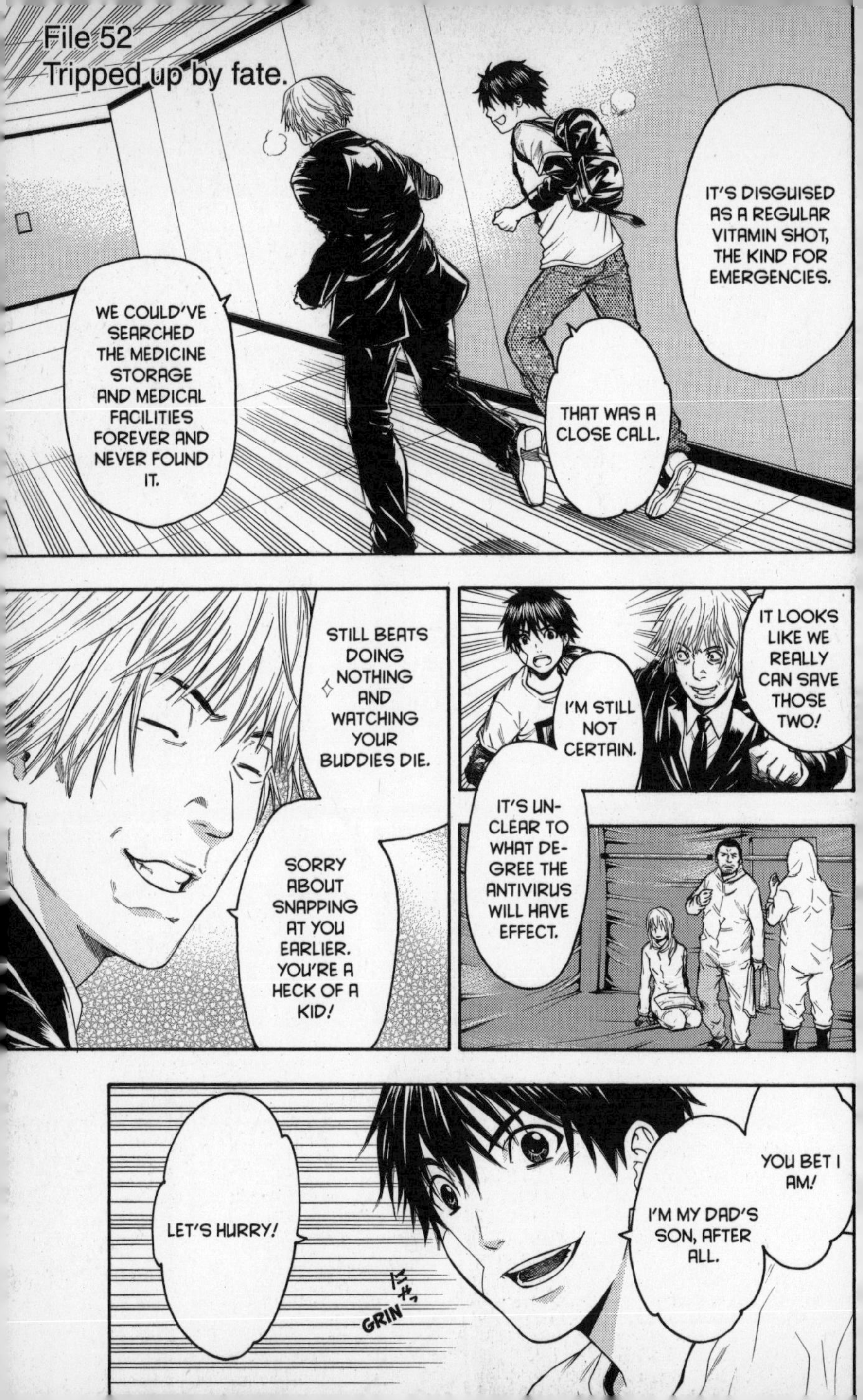
File 52
Tripped up by fate.
IT'S DISGUISED AS A REGULAR VITAMIN SHOT, THE KIND FOR EMERGENCIES.
THAT WAS A CLOSE CALL.
WE COULD'VE SEARCHED THE MEDICINE STORAGE AND MEDICAL FACILITIES FOREVER AND NEVER FOUND IT.
IT LOOKS LIKE WE REALLY CAN SAVE THOSE TWO!
I'M STILL NOT CERTAIN.
IT'S UN-CLEAR TO WHAT DE-GREE THE ANTIVIRUS WILL HAVE EFFECT.
STILL BEATS DOING NOTHING AND WATCHING YOUR BUDDIES DIE.
SORRY ABOUT SNAPPING AT YOU EARLIER. YOU'RE A HECK OF A KID!
YOU BET I AM!
I'M MY DAD'S SON, AFTER ALL.
GRIN
LET'S HURRY!

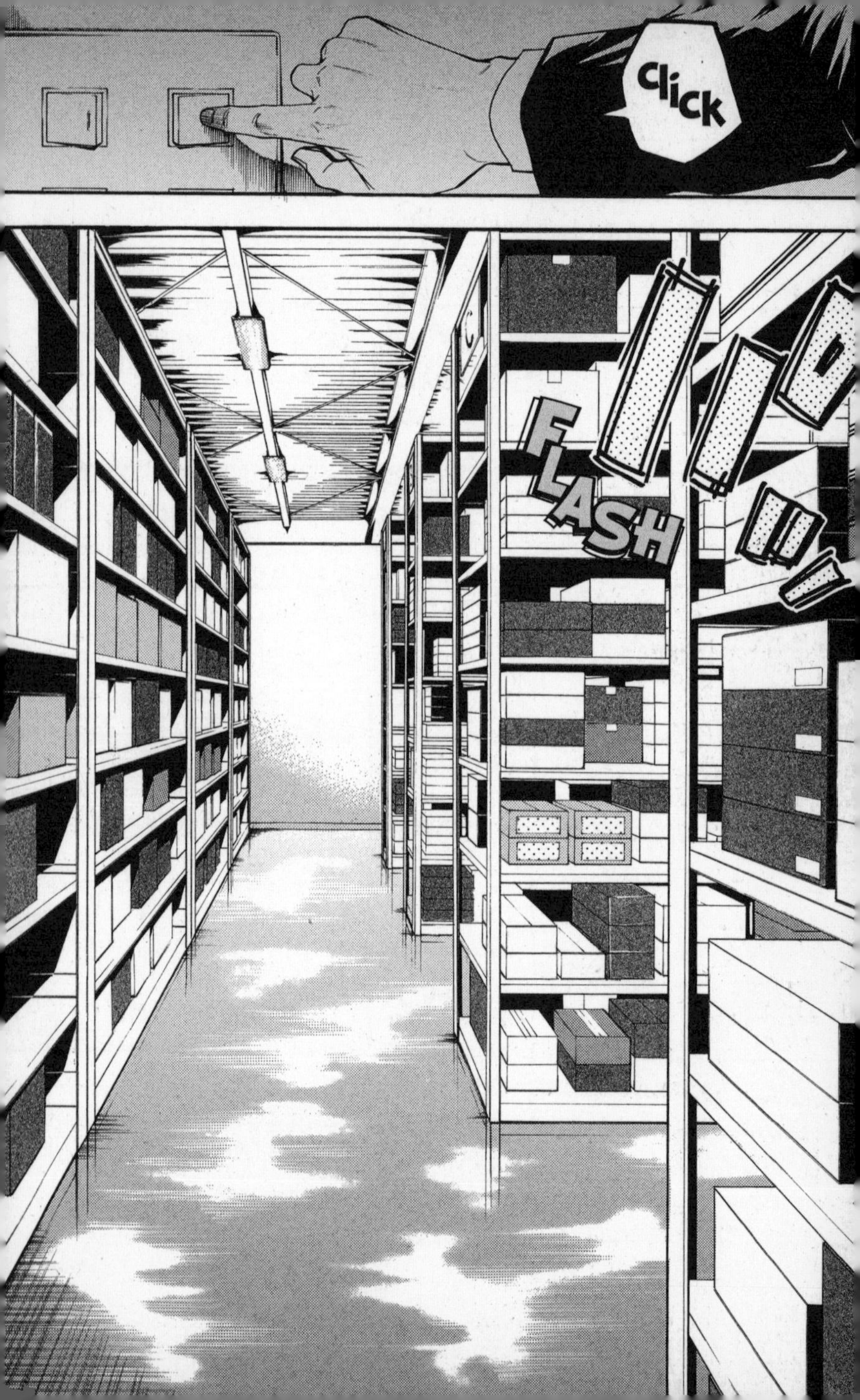
Click
FLASH

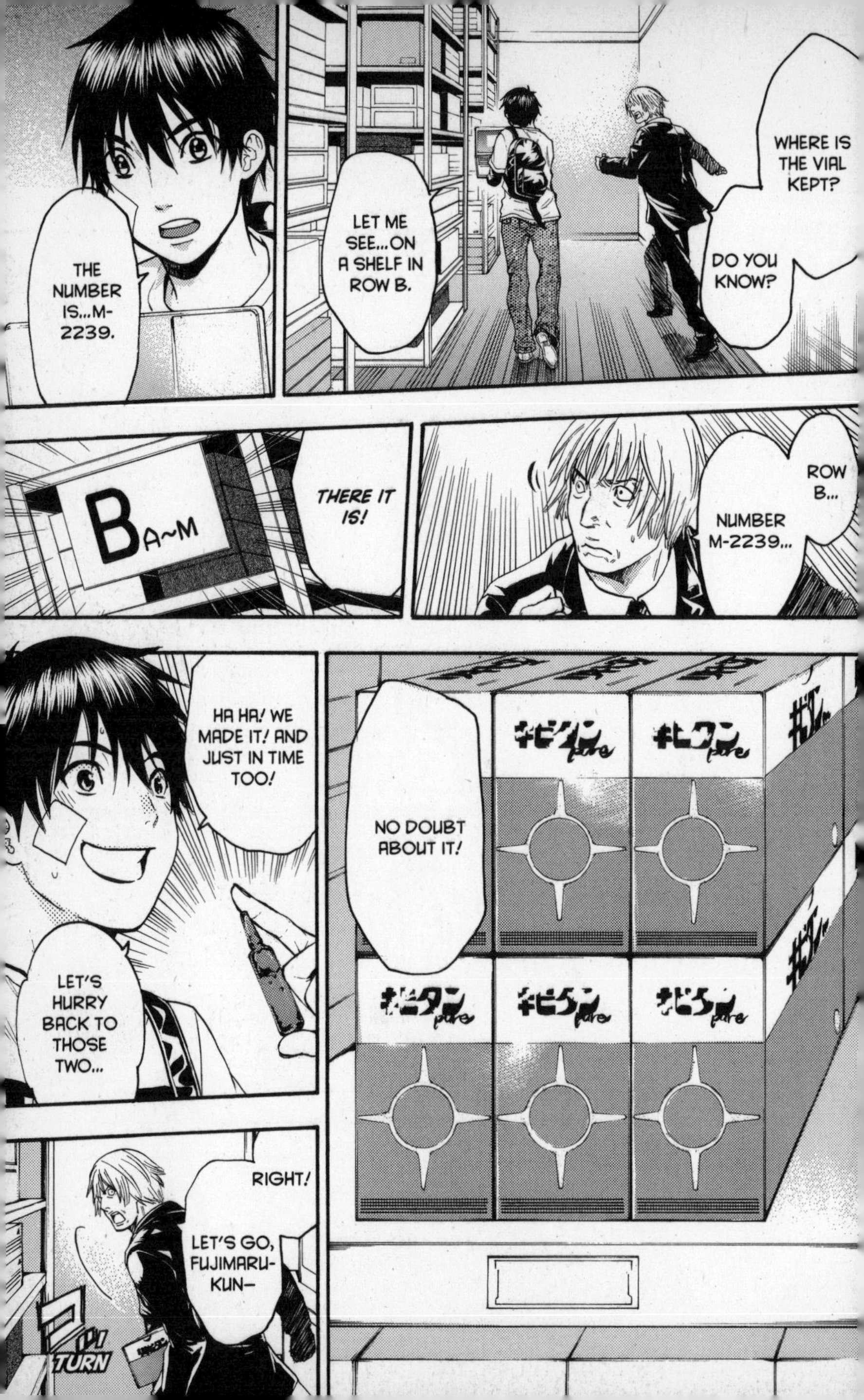
WHERE IS THE VIAL KEPT?
DO YOU KNOW?
LET ME SEE...ON A SHELF IN ROW B.
THE NUMBER IS...M-2239.
ROW B...
NUMBER M-2239...
THERE IT IS!
B A~M
NO DOUBT ABOUT IT!
HA HA! WE MADE IT! AND JUST IN TIME TOO!
LET'S HURRY BACK TO THOSE TWO...
RIGHT!
LET'S GO, FUJIMARU-KUN—
TURN

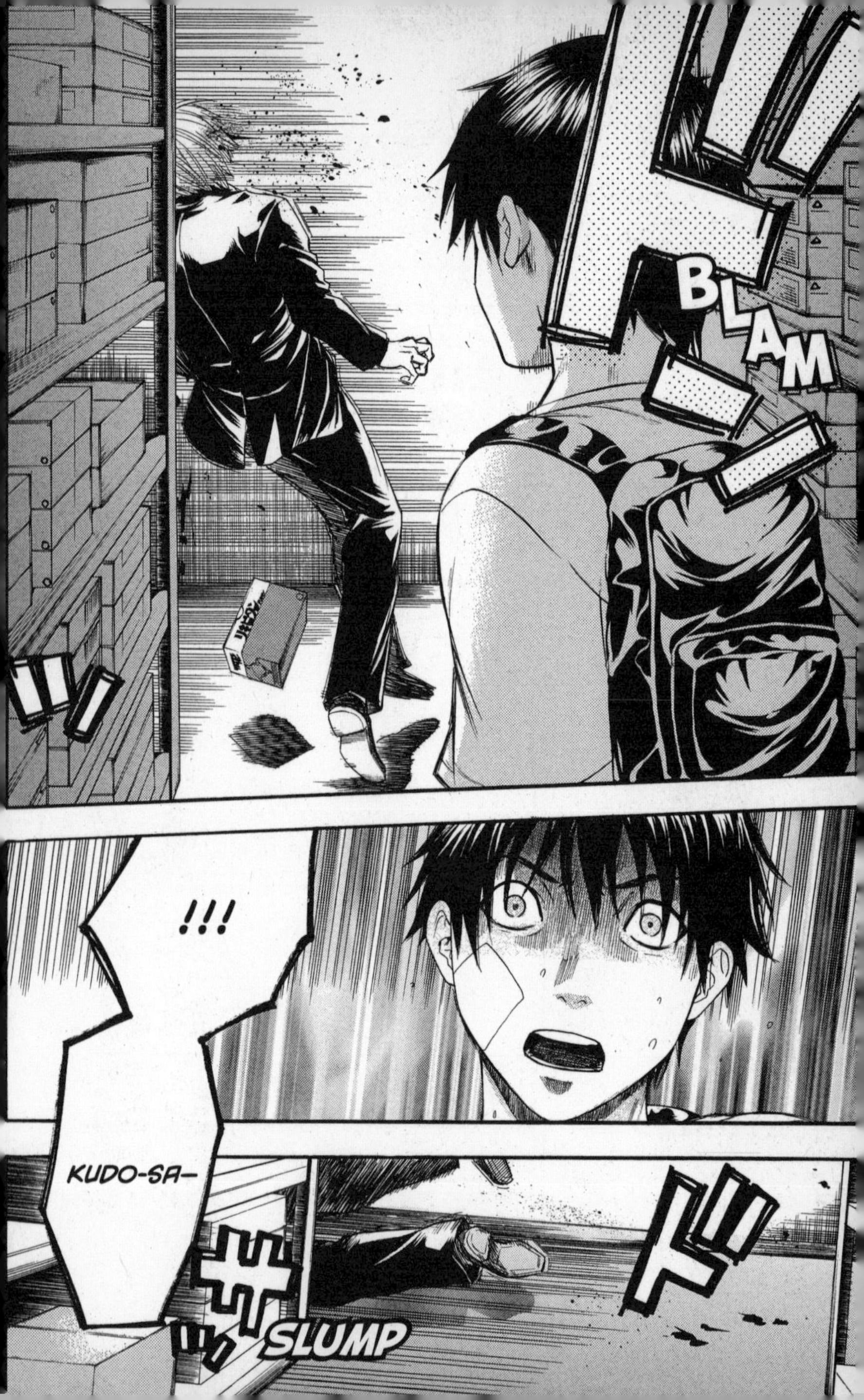
BLAM
!!!
KUDO-SA—
SLUMP

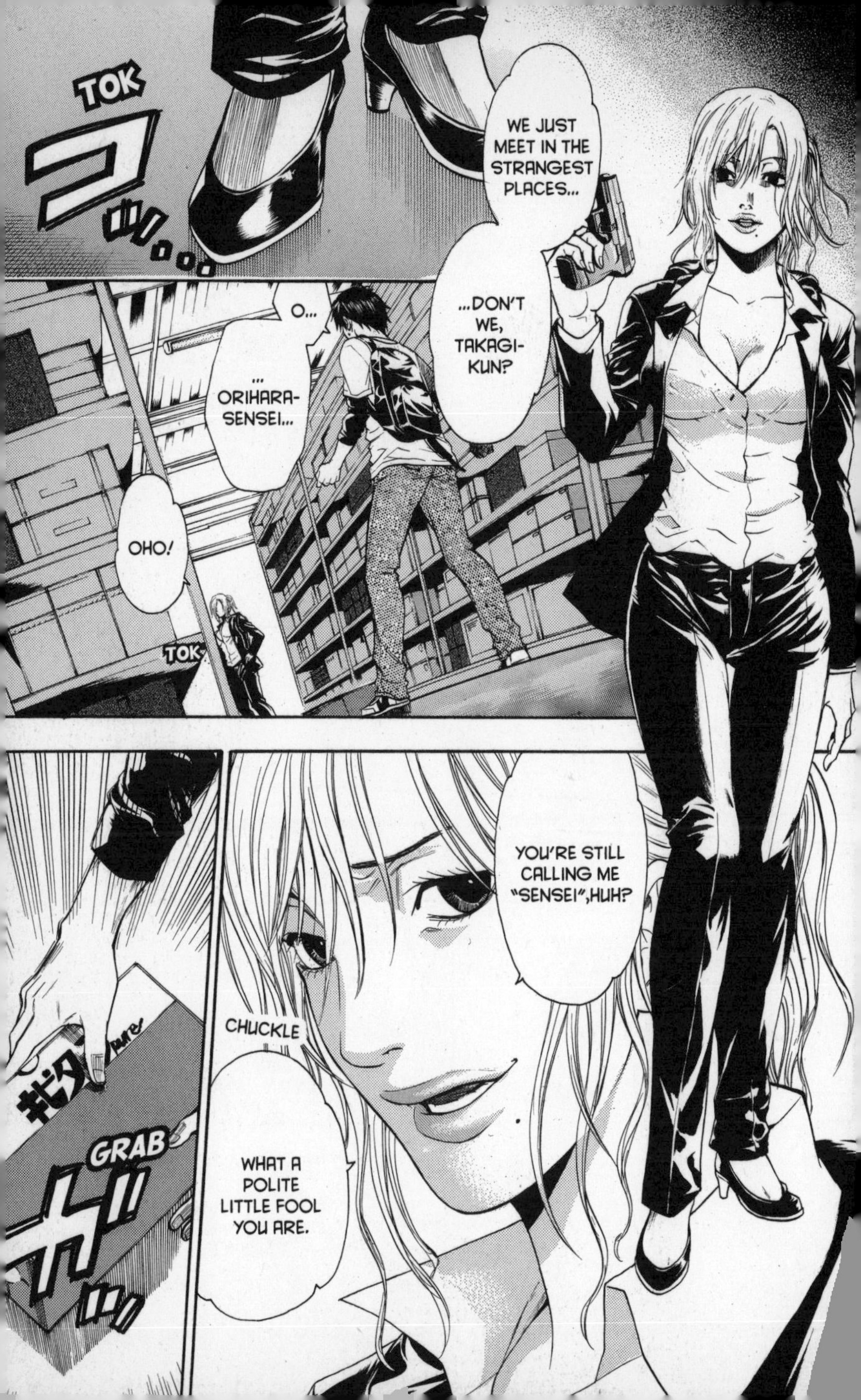
WE JUST MEET IN THE STRANGEST PLACES...
...DON'T WE, TAKAGI-KUN?
TOK
O...
...ORIHARA-SENSEI...
OHO!
TOK
YOU'RE STILL CALLING ME "SENSEI",HUH?
CHUCKLE
WHAT A POLITE LITTLE FOOL YOU ARE.
GRAB

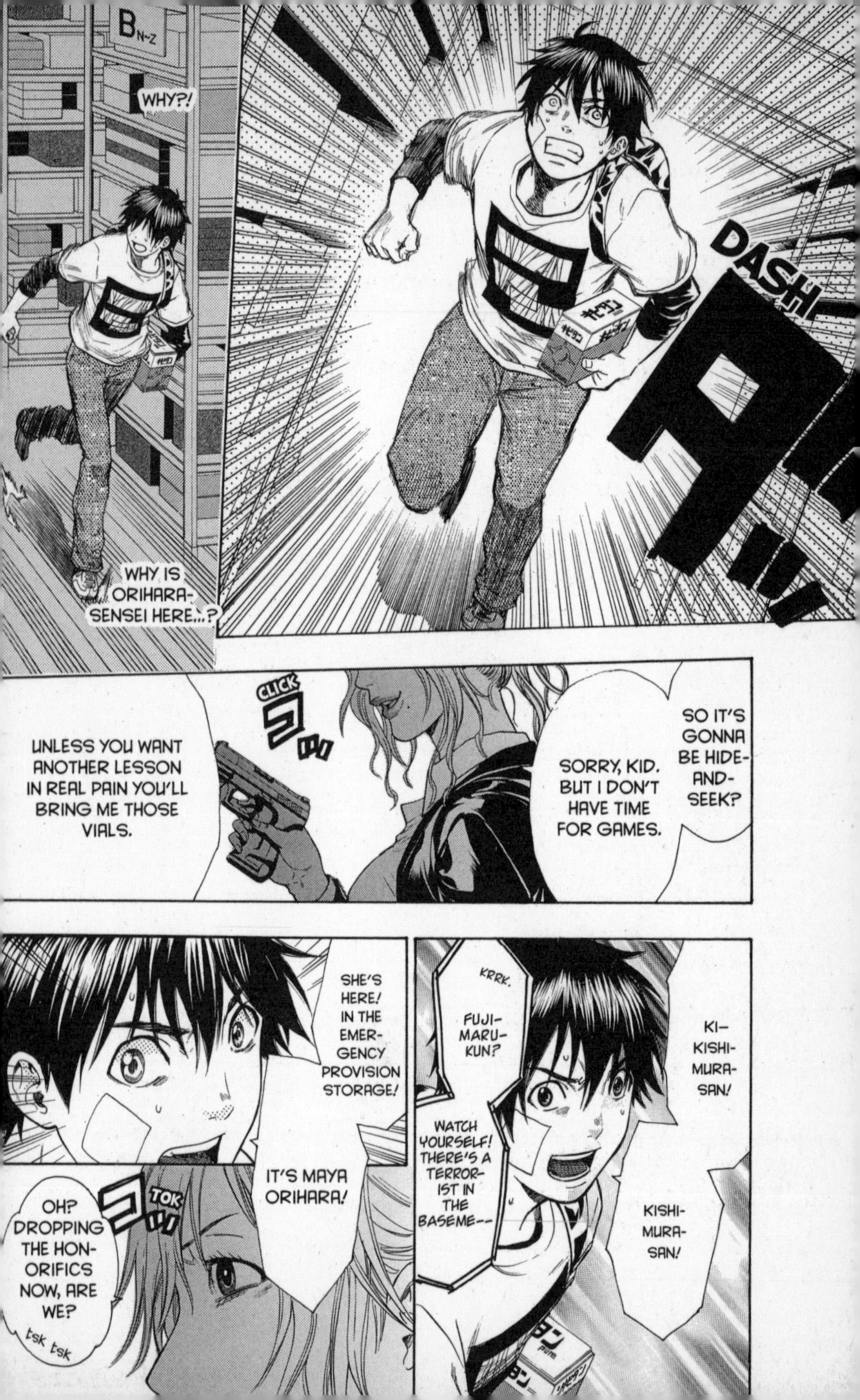
DASH
WHY?!
WHY IS ORIHARA-SENSEI HERE...?
SO IT'S GONNA BE HIDE-AND-SEEK?
SORRY, KID. BUT I DON'T HAVE TIME FOR GAMES.
CLICK
UNLESS YOU WANT ANOTHER LESSON IN REAL PAIN YOU'LL BRING ME THOSE VIALS.
KI-KISHI-MURA-SAN!
KRRK.
FUJI-MARU-KUN?
KISHI-MURA-SAN!
WATCH YOURSELF! THERE'S A TERROR-IST IN THE BASEME--
SHE'S HERE! IN THE EMER-GENCY PROVISION STORAGE!
IT'S MAYA ORIHARA!
TOK
OH? DROPPING THE HON-ORIFICS NOW, ARE WE?
tsk tsk

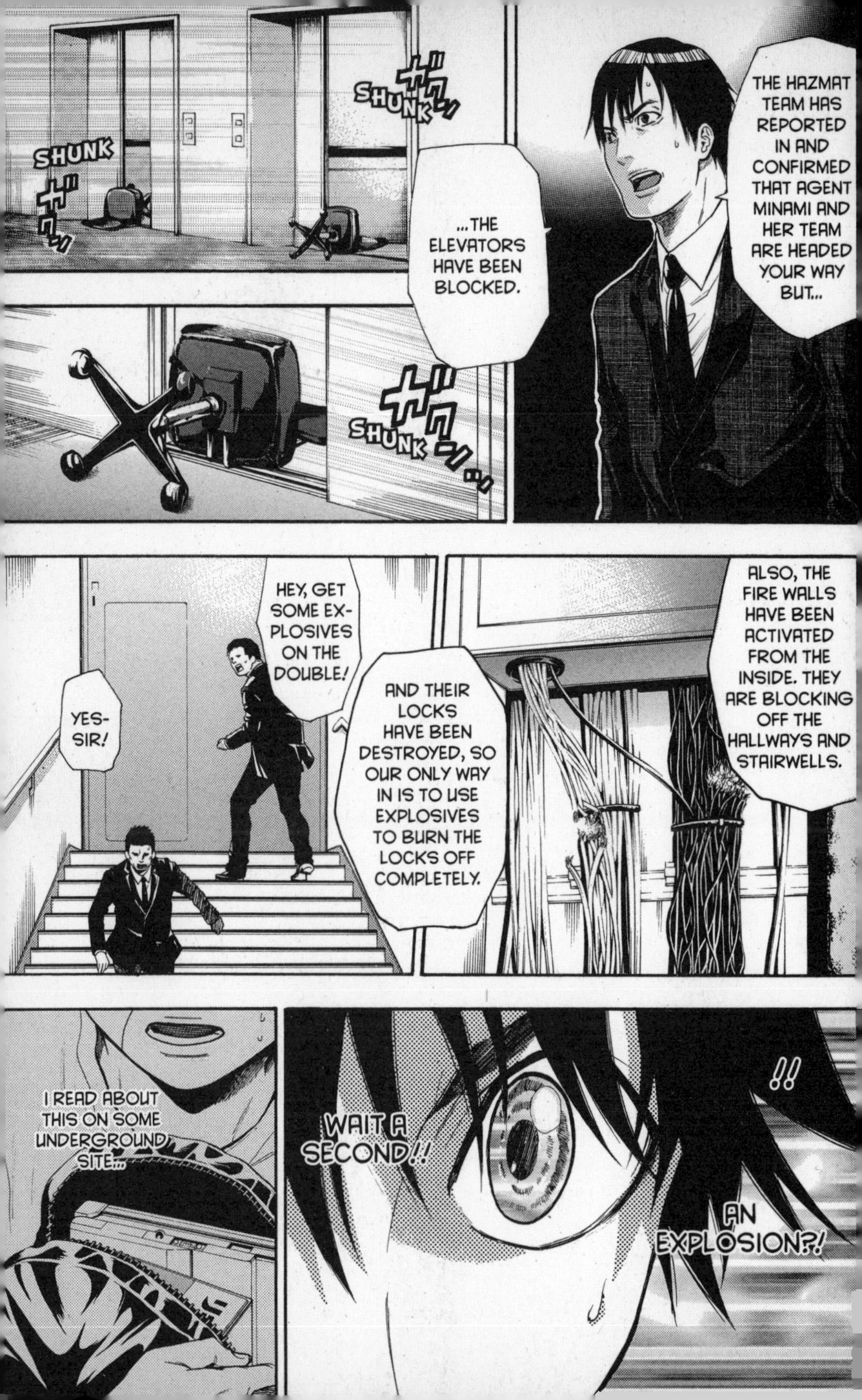
THE HAZMAT TEAM HAS REPORTED IN AND CONFIRMED THAT AGENT MINAMI AND HER TEAM ARE HEADED YOUR WAY BUT...
...THE ELEVATORS HAVE BEEN BLOCKED.
SHUNK
SHUNK
SHUNK
ALSO, THE FIRE WALLS HAVE BEEN ACTIVATED FROM THE INSIDE. THEY ARE BLOCKING OFF THE HALLWAYS AND STAIRWELLS.
AND THEIR LOCKS HAVE BEEN DESTROYED, SO OUR ONLY WAY IN IS TO USE EXPLOSIVES TO BURN THE LOCKS OFF COMPLETELY.
HEY, GET SOME EXPLOSIVES ON THE DOUBLE!
YES-SIR!
!!
WAIT A SECOND!!
AN EXPLOSION?!
I READ ABOUT THIS ON SOME UNDERGROUND SITE...

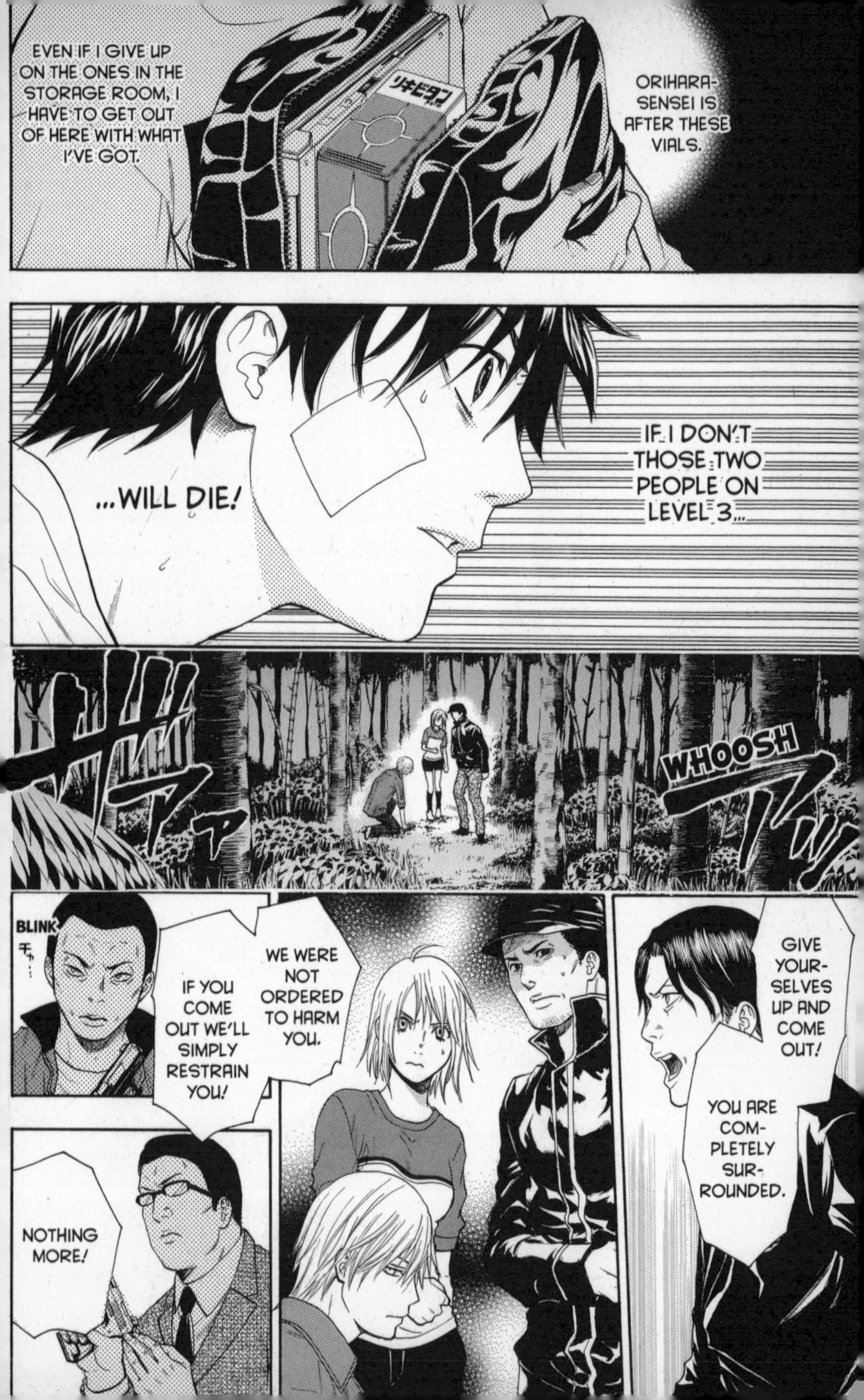

ORIHARA-SENSEI IS AFTER THESE VIALS.
EVEN IF I GIVE UP ON THE ONES IN THE STORAGE ROOM, I HAVE TO GET OUT OF HERE WITH WHAT I'VE GOT.
IF I DON'T THOSE TWO PEOPLE ON LEVEL 3...
...WILL DIE!
WHOOSH
GIVE YOUR-SELVES UP AND COME OUT!
YOU ARE COM-PLETELY SUR-ROUNDED.
WE WERE NOT ORDERED TO HARM YOU.
IF YOU COME OUT WE'LL SIMPLY RESTRAIN YOU!
BLINK
NOTHING MORE!

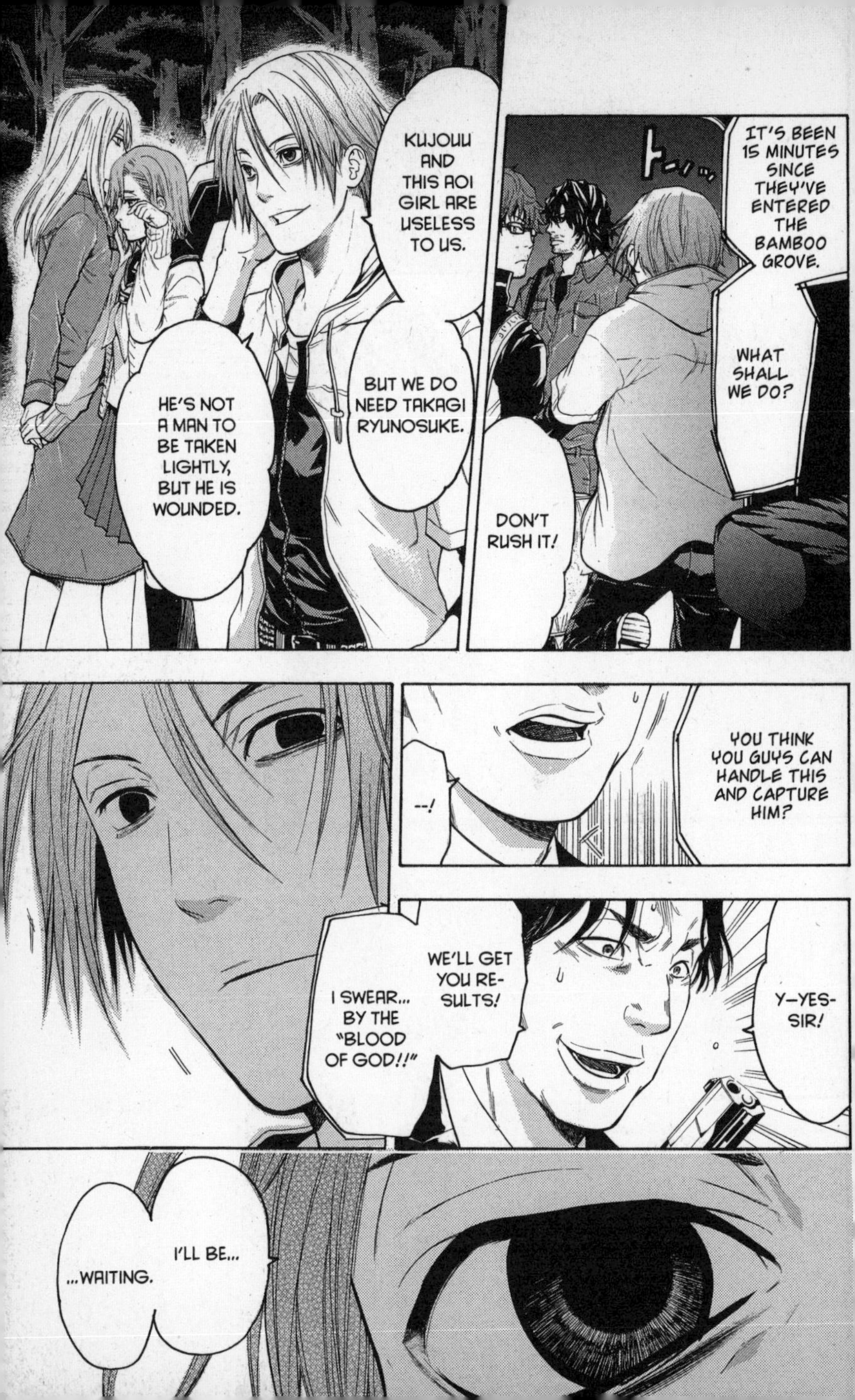
IT'S BEEN 15 MINUTES SINCE THEY'VE ENTERED THE BAMBOO GROVE.
WHAT SHALL WE DO?
DON'T RUSH IT!
KUJOUU AND THIS AOI GIRL ARE USELESS TO US.
BUT WE DO NEED TAKAGI RYUNOSUKE.
HE'S NOT A MAN TO BE TAKEN LIGHTLY, BUT HE IS WOUNDED.
YOU THINK YOU GUYS CAN HANDLE THIS AND CAPTURE HIM?
--!
Y—YES-SIR!
WE'LL GET YOU RE-SULTS!
I SWEAR... BY THE "BLOOD OF GOD!!"
I'LL BE...
...WAITING.

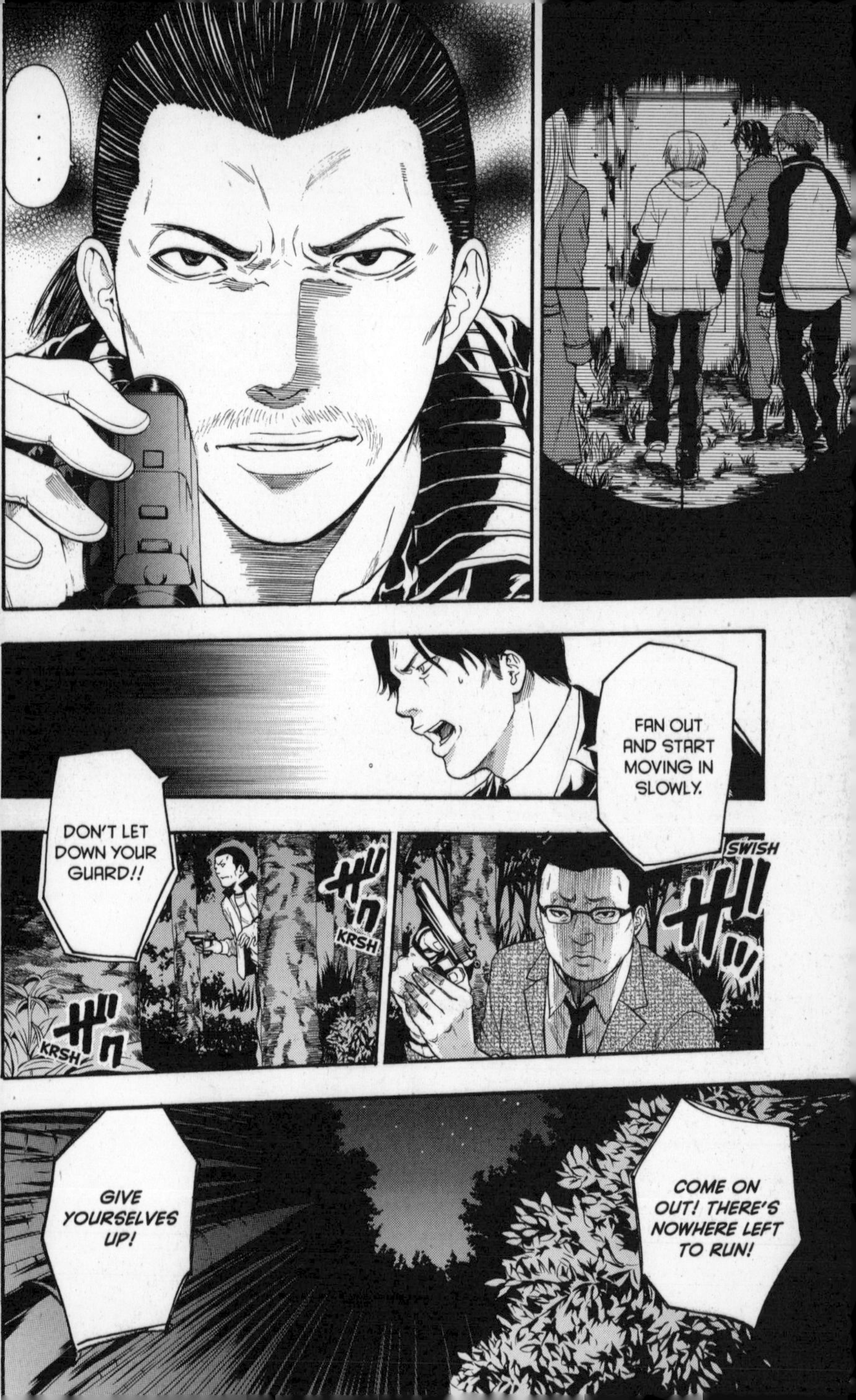
. . . .
FAN OUT AND START MOVING IN SLOWLY.
SWISH
DON'T LET DOWN YOUR GUARD!!
KRSH
KRSH
COME ON OUT! THERE'S NOWHERE LEFT TO RUN!
GIVE YOURSELVES UP!

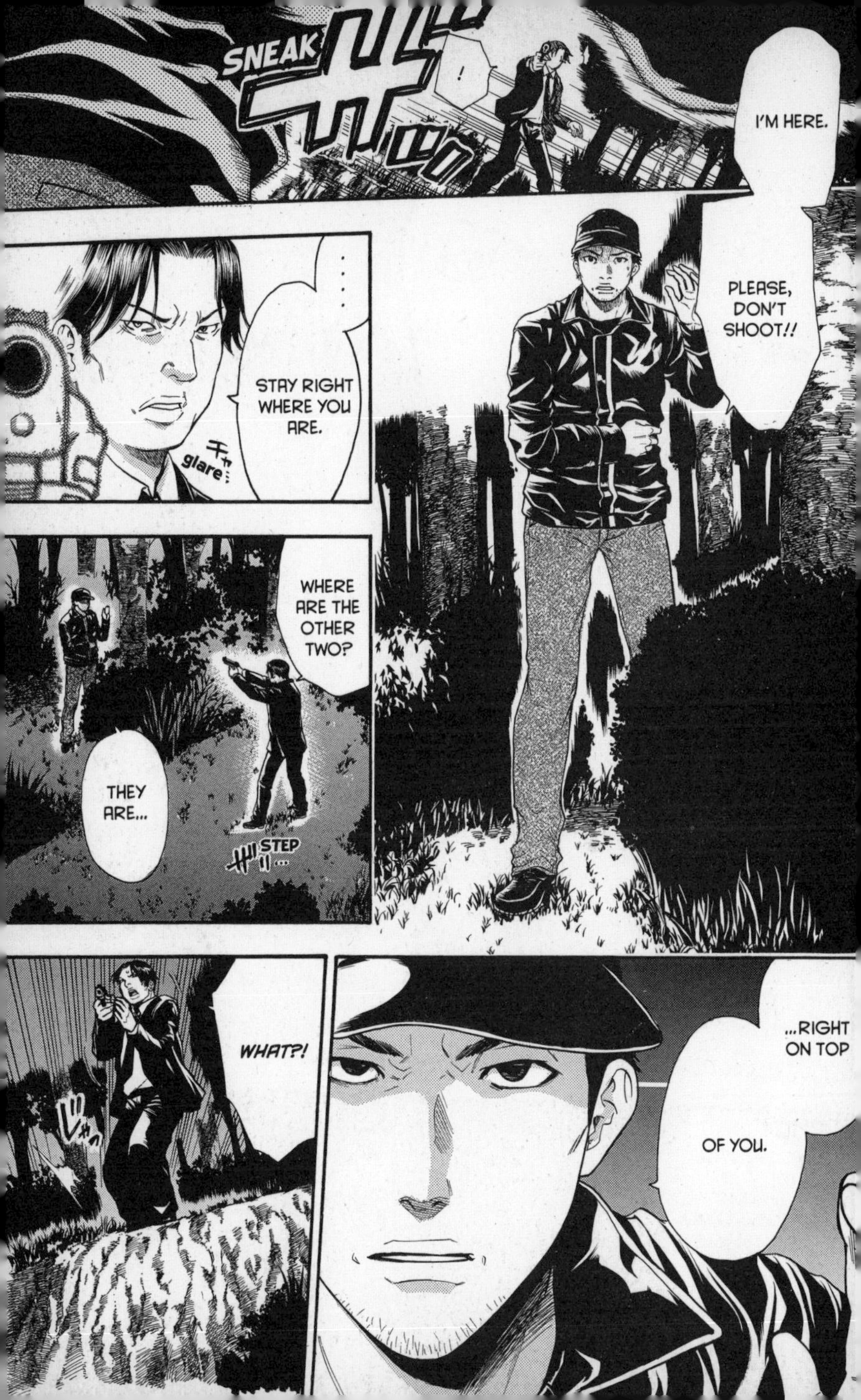
SNEAK
!
I'M HERE.
PLEASE, DON'T SHOOT!!
...
STAY RIGHT WHERE YOU ARE.
glare
WHERE ARE THE OTHER TWO?
THEY ARE...
STEP
...RIGHT ON TOP OF YOU.
WHAT?!

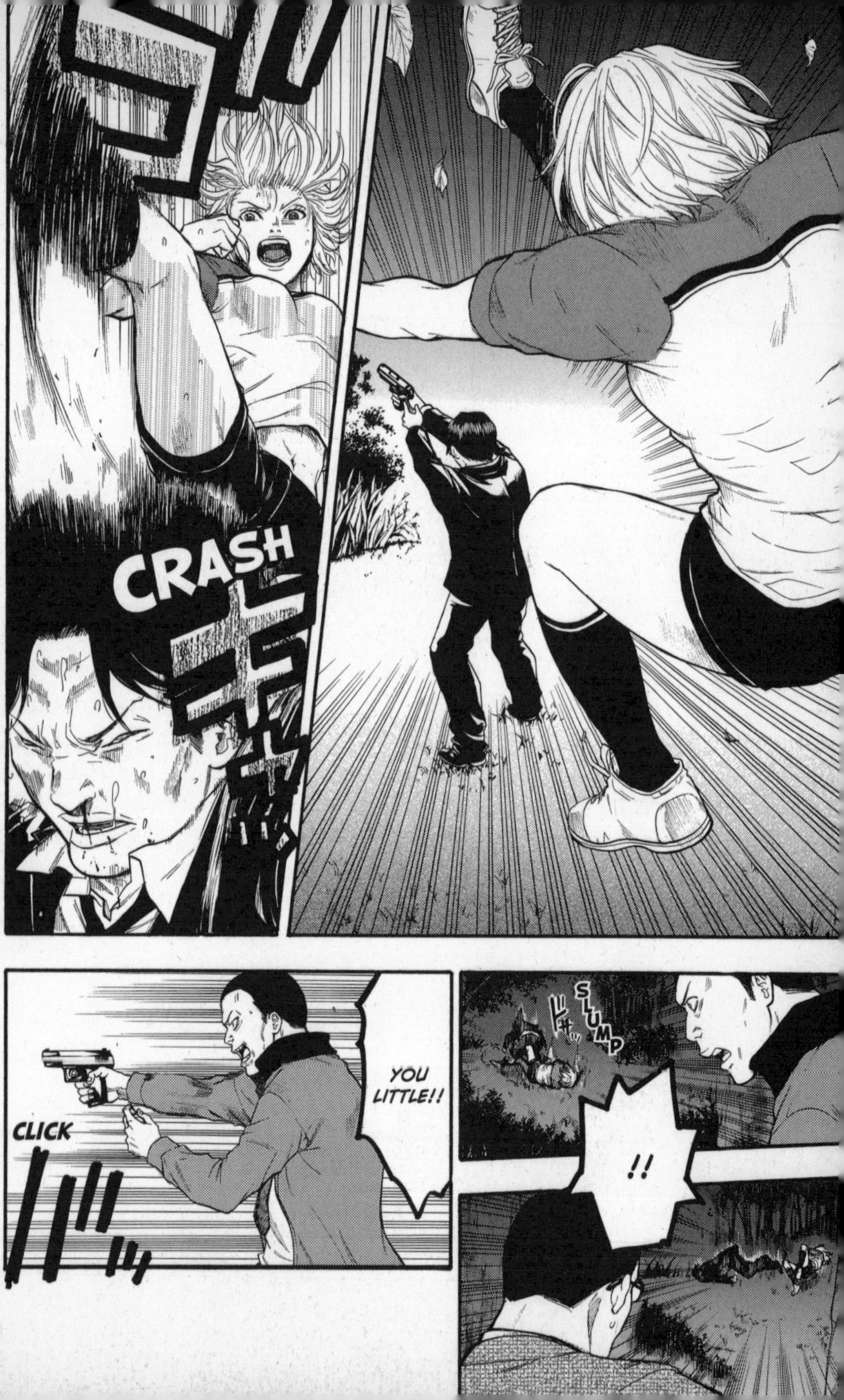
CRASH
SLUMP
!!
YOU LITTLE!!
CLICK

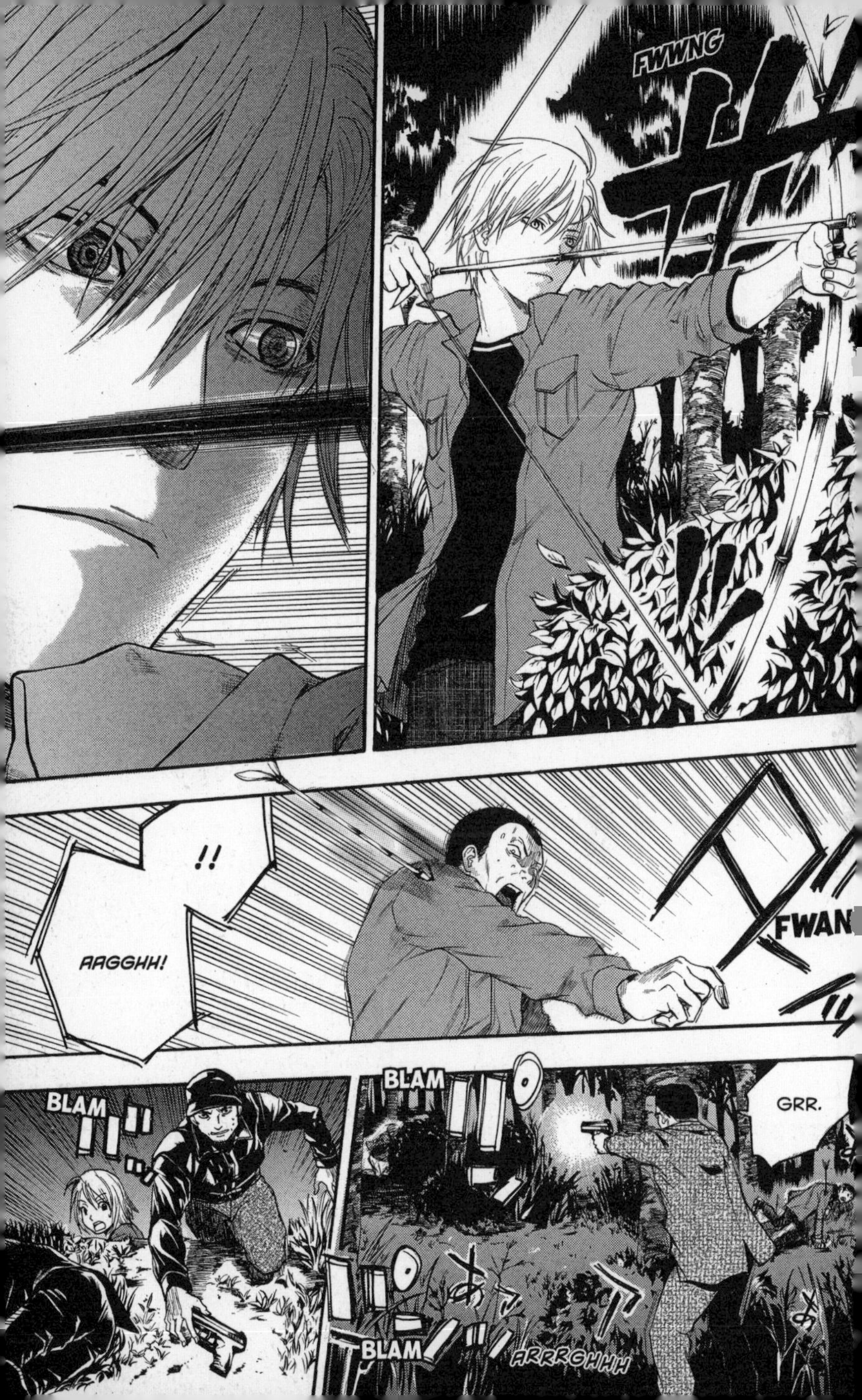

FWWNG
FWAN
!!
AAGGHH!
GRR.
BLAM
BLAM
ARRRGHHH
BLAM

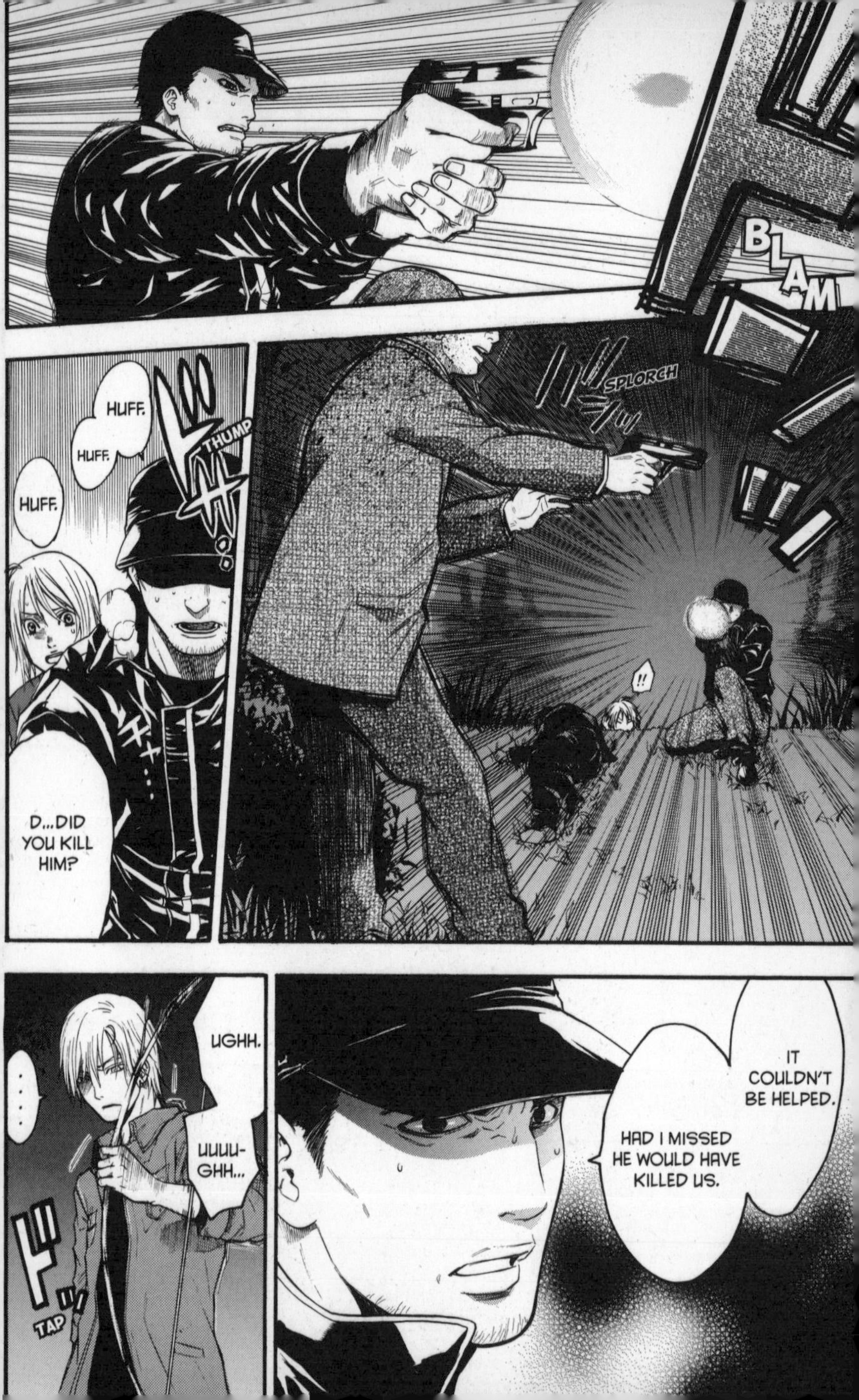
BLAM
SPLORCH
!!
THUMP
HUFF.
HUFF.
HUFF.
D...DID YOU KILL HIM?
IT COULDN'T BE HELPED.
HAD I MISSED HE WOULD HAVE KILLED US.
UGHH.
UUUU-GHH...
....
TAP

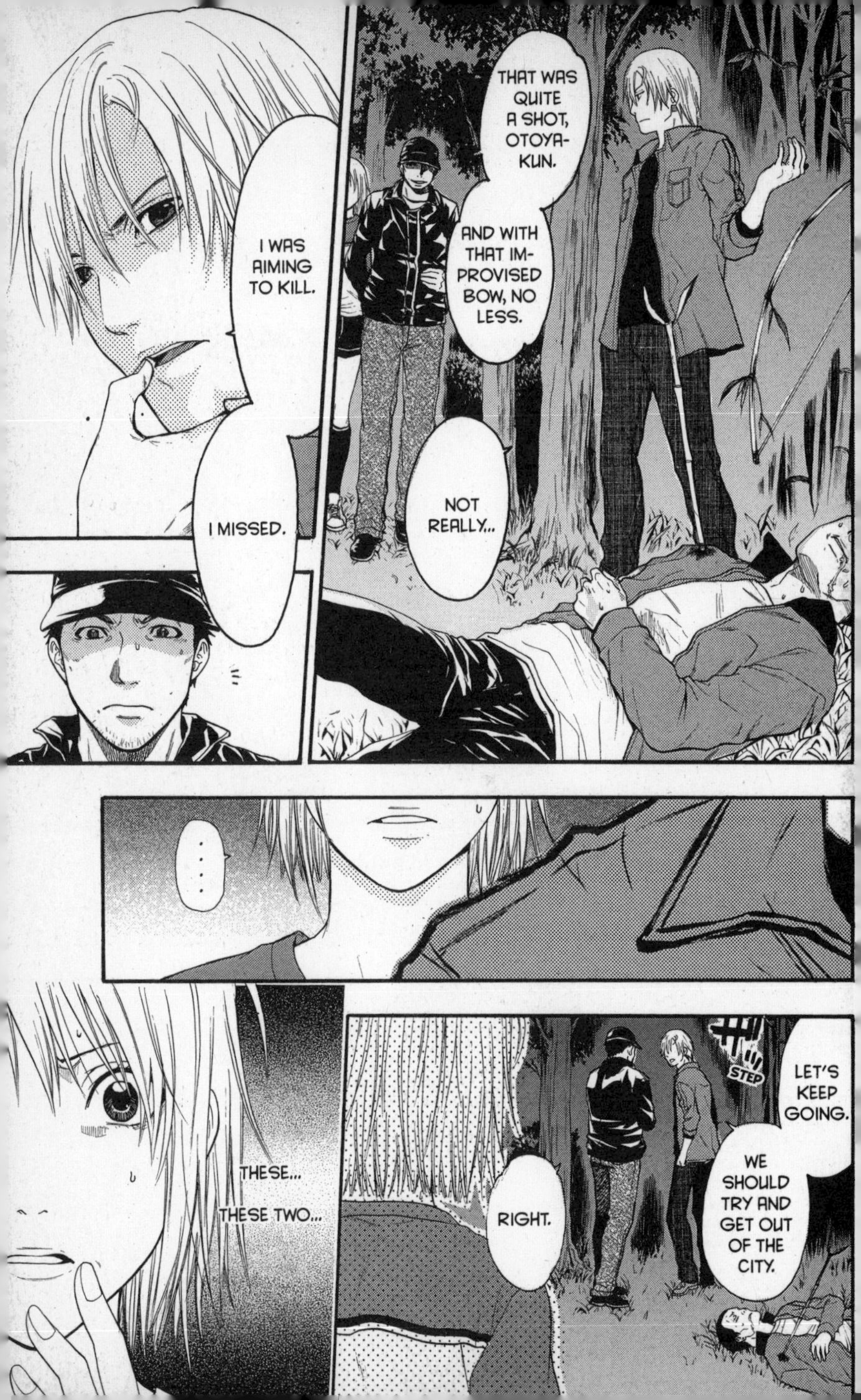
THAT WAS QUITE A SHOT, OTOYA-KUN.
AND WITH THAT IMPROVISED BOW, NO LESS.
NOT REALLY...
I WAS AIMING TO KILL.
I MISSED.
....
STEP
LET'S KEEP GOING.
WE SHOULD TRY AND GET OUT OF THE CITY.
RIGHT.
THESE...
THESE TWO...

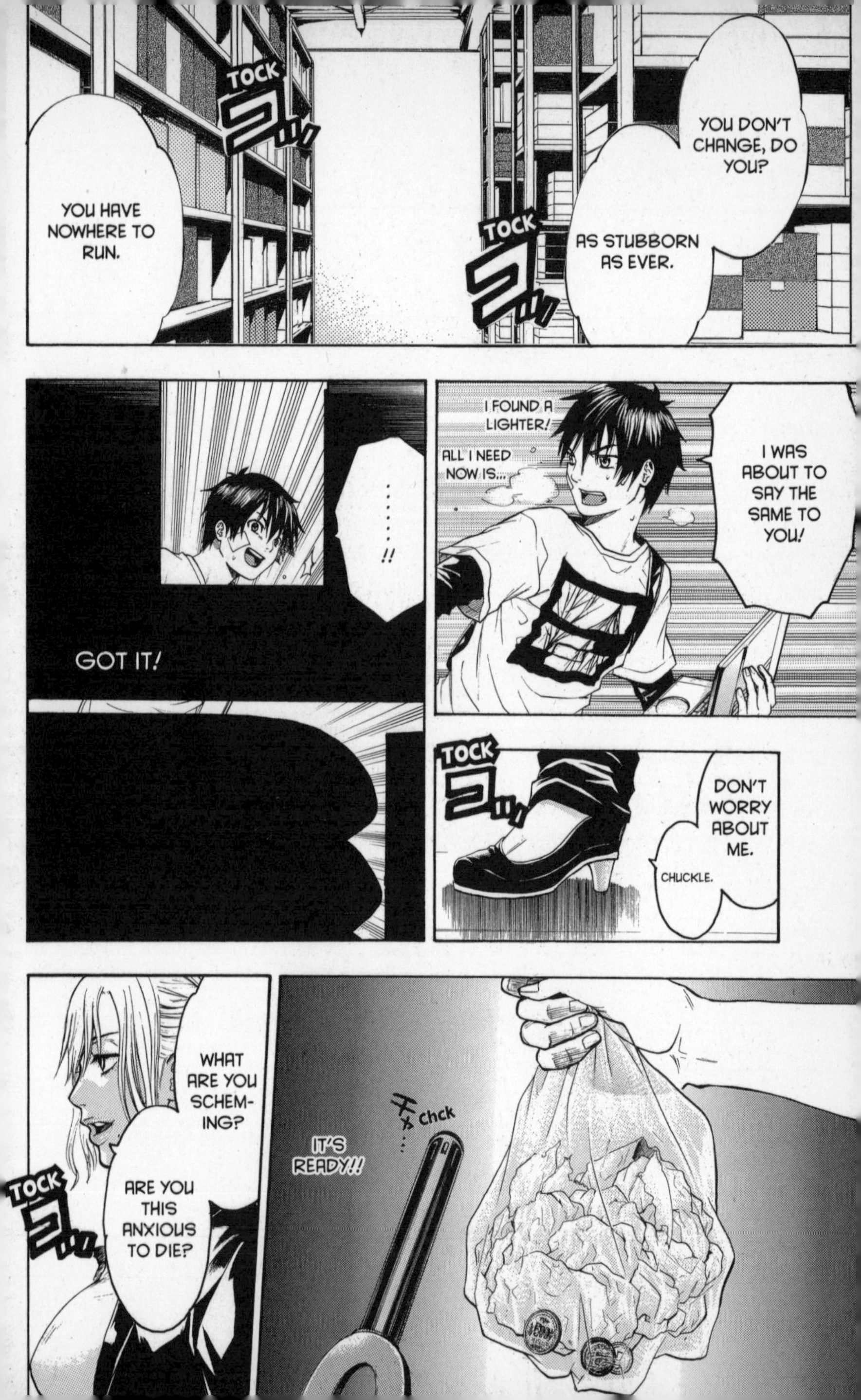
YOU DON'T CHANGE, DO YOU?
AS STUBBORN AS EVER.
TOCK
TOCK
YOU HAVE NOWHERE TO RUN.
I WAS ABOUT TO SAY THE SAME TO YOU!
I FOUND A LIGHTER!
ALL I NEED NOW IS...
TOCK
DON'T WORRY ABOUT ME.
CHUCKLE.
......!!
GOT IT!
chck
IT'S READY!!
WHAT ARE YOU SCHEM-ING?
ARE YOU THIS ANXIOUS TO DIE?
TOCK

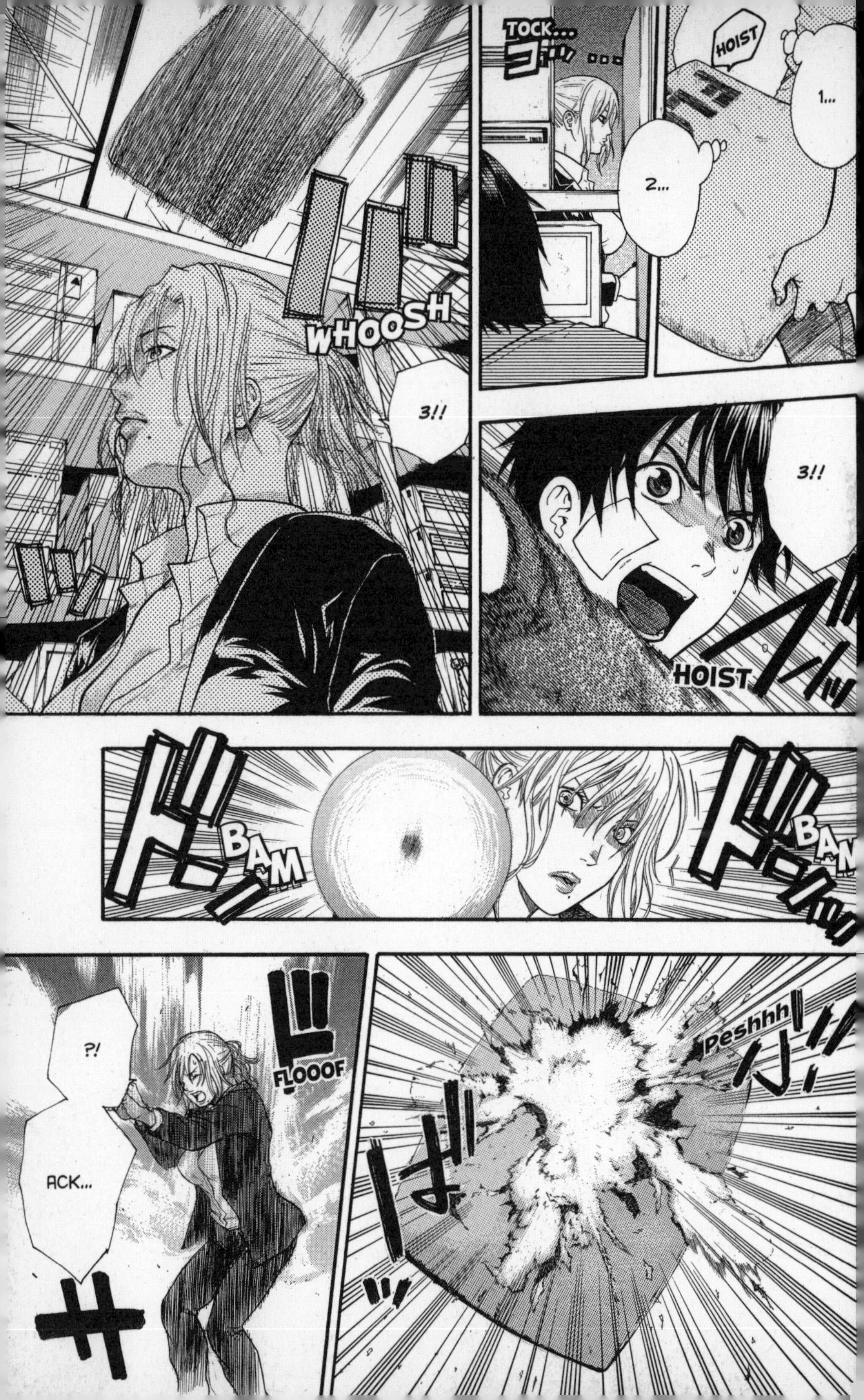
HOIST
1...
2...
TOCK...
3!!
HOIST
3!!
WHOOSH
BAM
BAM
Peshhh
FLOOOF
?!
ACK...

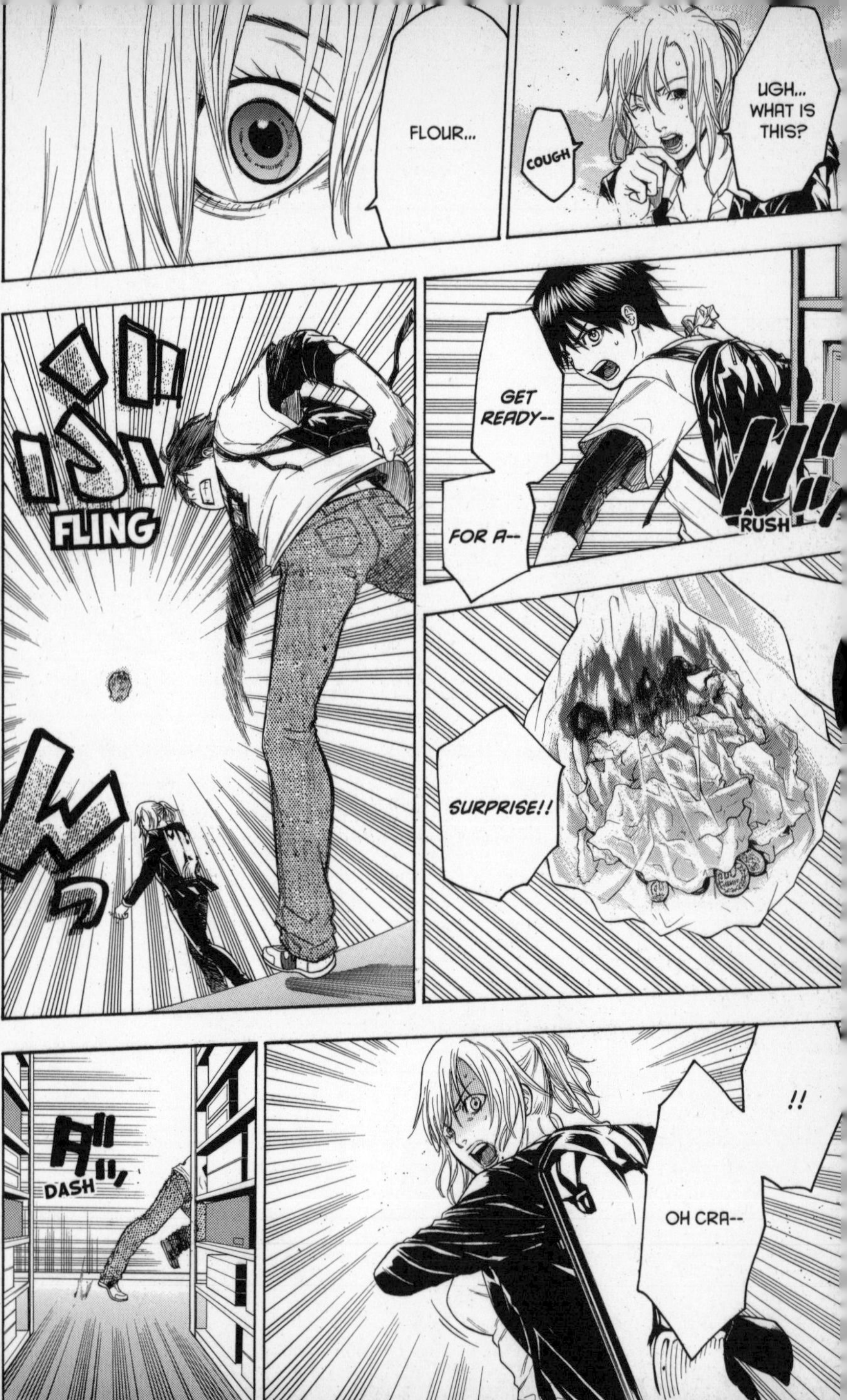
UGH... WHAT IS THIS?
COUGH
FLOUR...
GET READY--
FOR A--
RUSH
SURPRISE!!
FLING
!!
OH CRA--
DASH

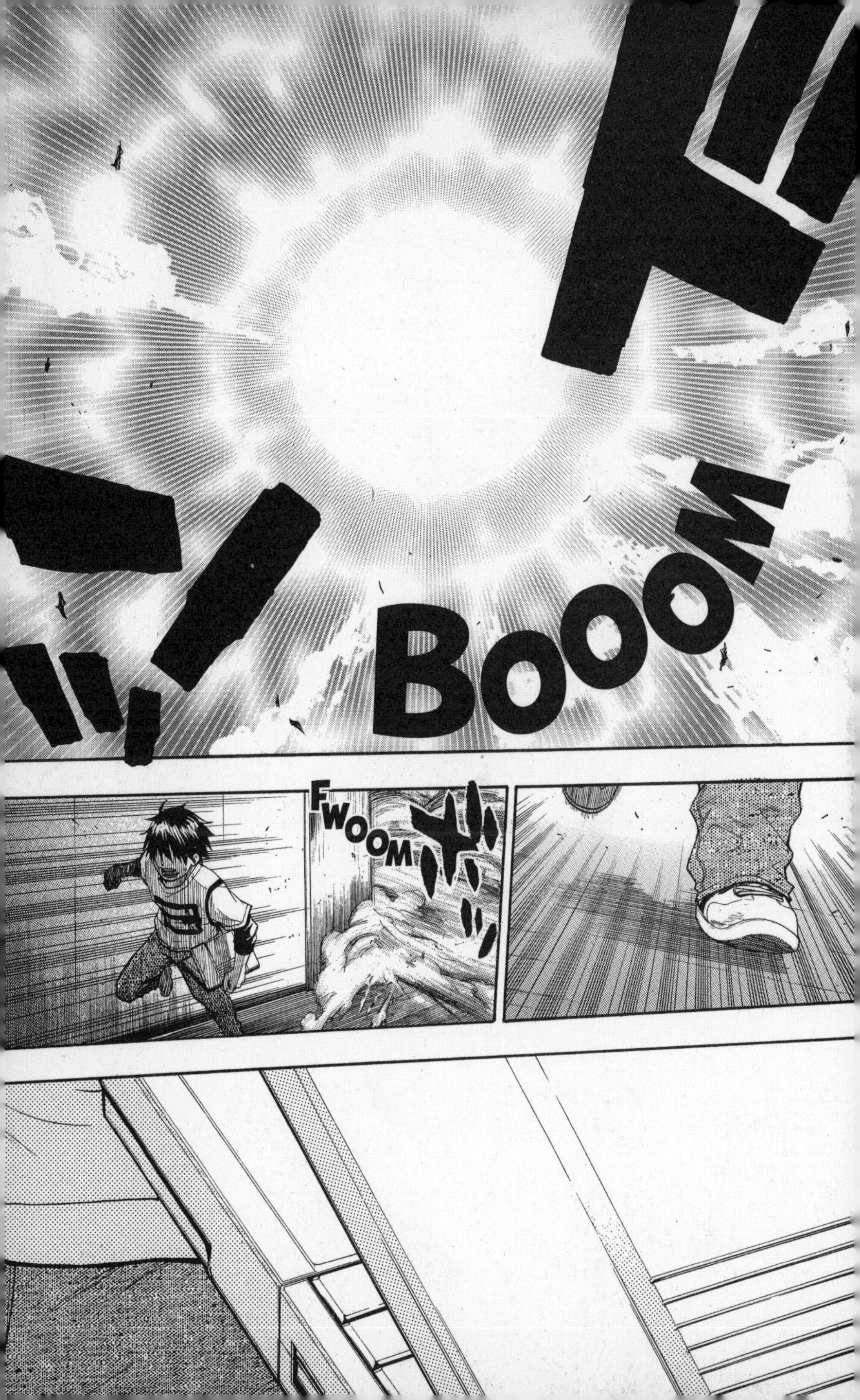
BOOOM
FWOOM

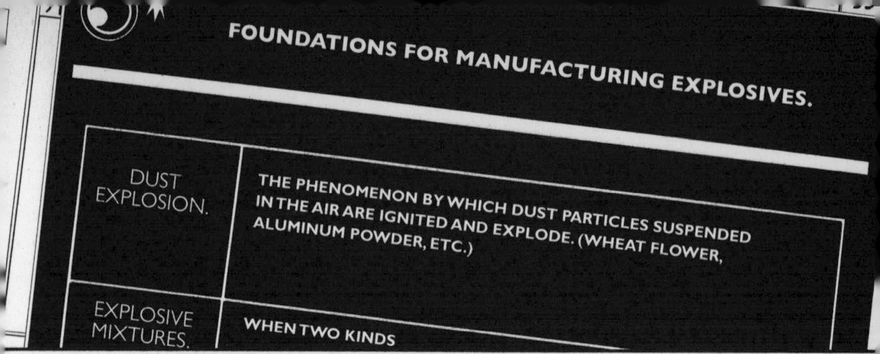
FOUNDATIONS FOR MANUFACTURING EXPLOSIVES.
DUST EXPLOSION.
THE PHENOMENON BY WHICH DUST PARTICLES SUSPENDED IN THE AIR ARE IGNITED AND EXPLODE. (WHEAT FLOWER, ALUMINUM POWDER, ETC.)
EXPLOSIVE MIXTURES.
WHEN TWO KINDS

This is extremely dangerous. Do not try this at home.

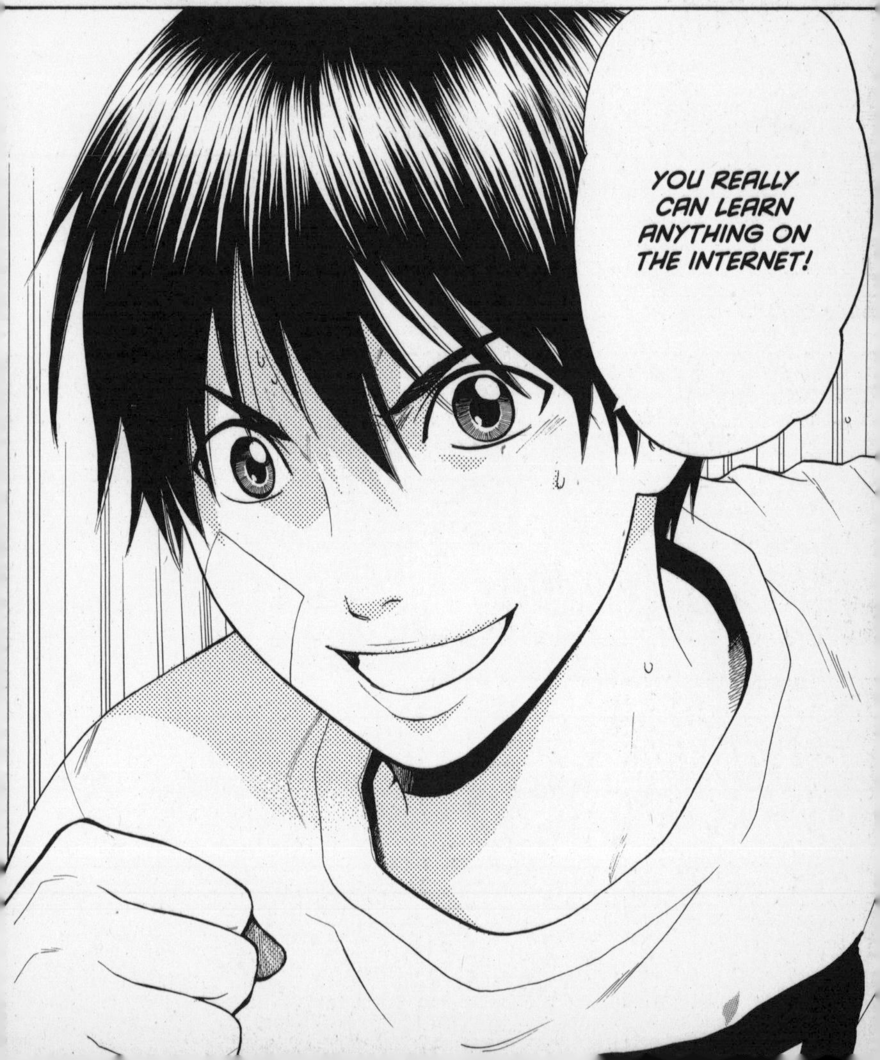
YOU REALLY CAN LEARN ANYTHING ON THE INTERNET!

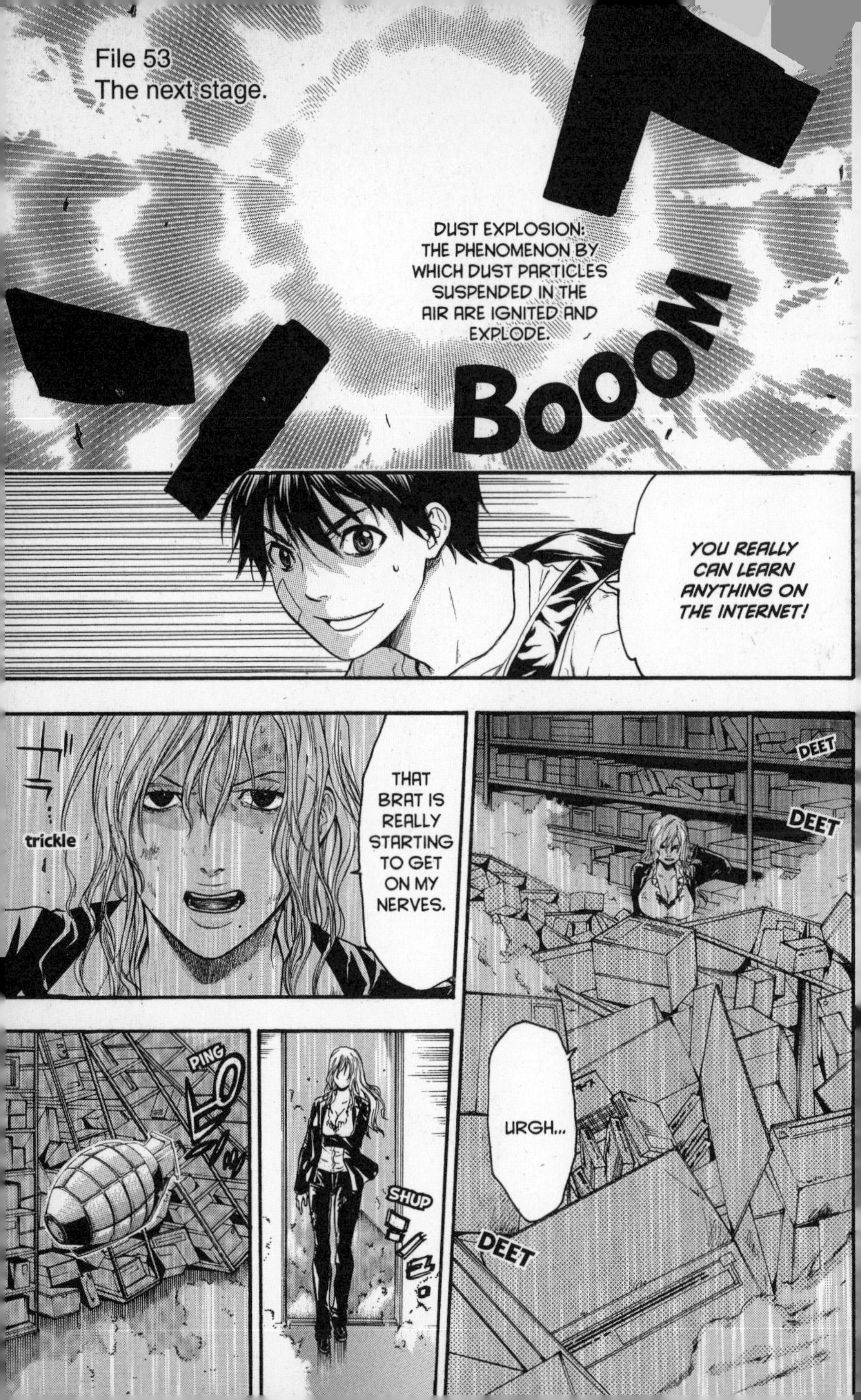
File 53
The next stage.
DUST EXPLOSION: THE PHENOMENON BY WHICH DUST PARTICLES SUSPENDED IN THE AIR ARE IGNITED AND EXPLODE.
BOOOOM
YOU REALLY CAN LEARN ANYTHING ON THE INTERNET!
DEET
DEET
URGH...
DEET
THAT BRAT IS REALLY STARTING TO GET ON MY NERVES.
trickle
SHUP
PING

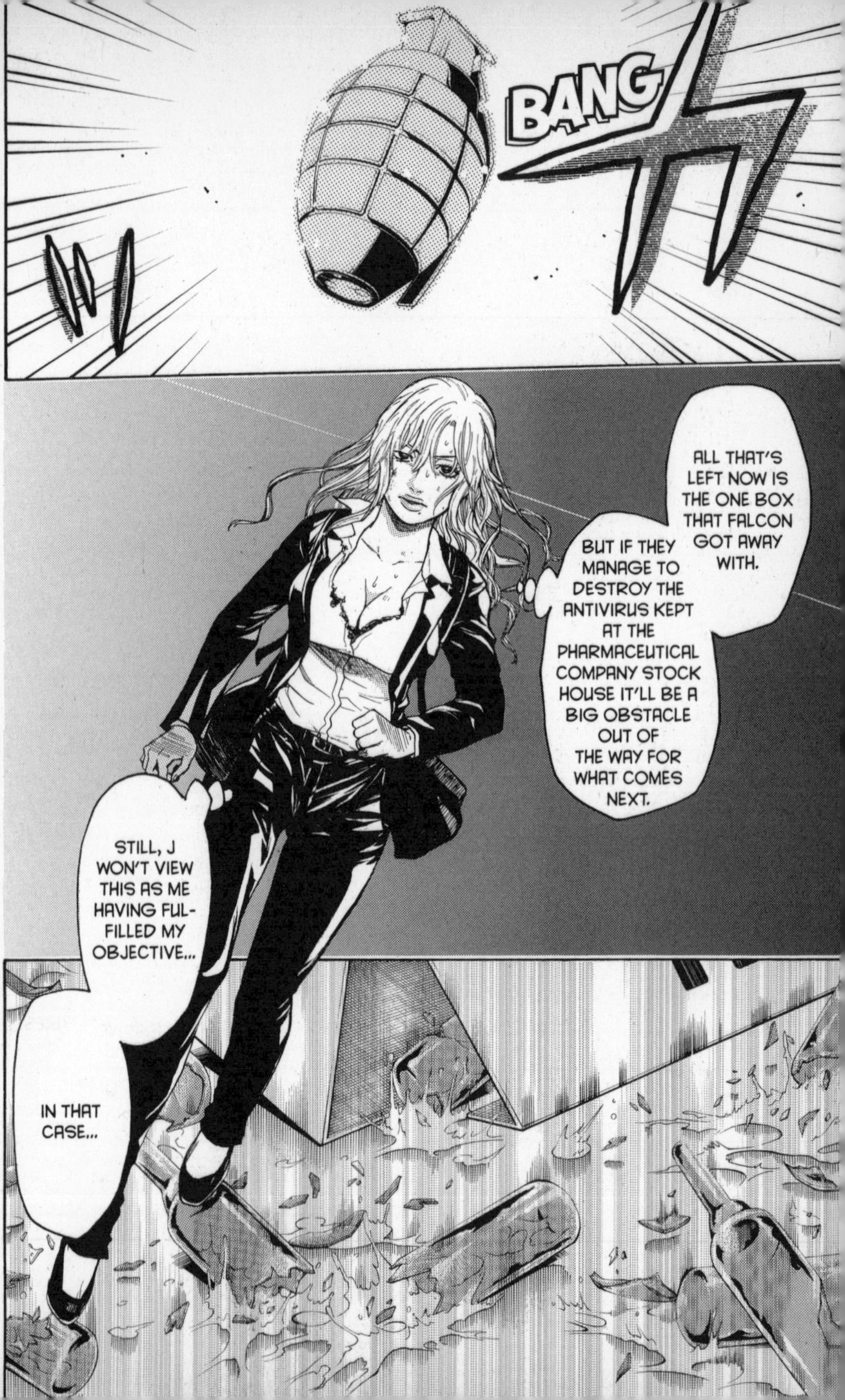
BANG
ALL THAT'S LEFT NOW IS THE ONE BOX THAT FALCON GOT AWAY WITH.
BUT IF THEY MANAGE TO DESTROY THE ANTIVIRUS KEPT AT THE PHARMACEUTICAL COMPANY STOCK HOUSE IT'LL BE A BIG OBSTACLE OUT OF THE WAY FOR WHAT COMES NEXT.
STILL, J WON'T VIEW THIS AS ME HAVING FUL-FILLED MY OBJECTIVE...
IN THAT CASE...

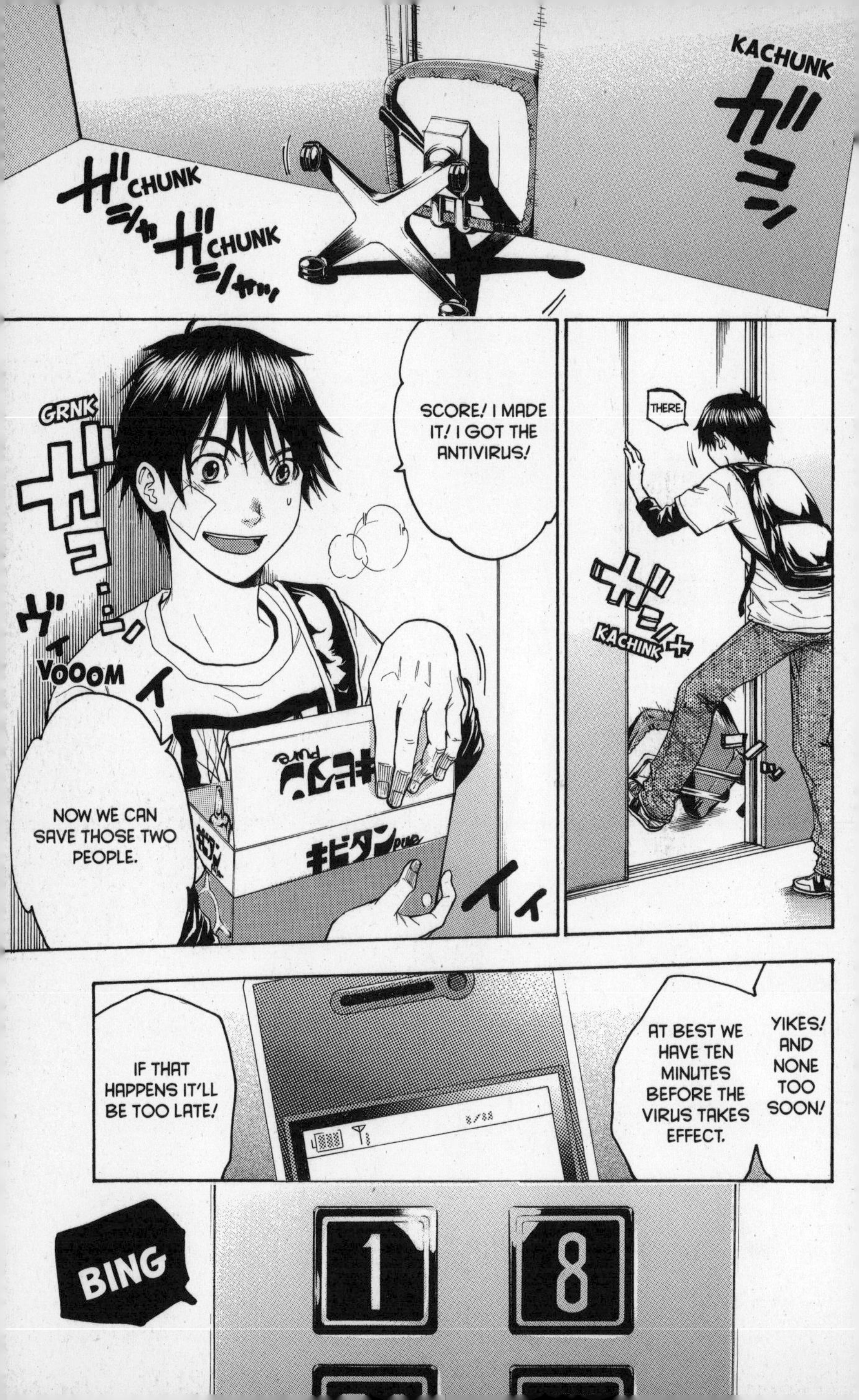
KACHUNK
CHUNK
CHUNK
THERE.
KACHINK
SCORE! I MADE IT! I GOT THE ANTIVIRUS!
GRNK
VOOOM
NOW WE CAN SAVE THOSE TWO PEOPLE.
YIKES! AND NONE TOO SOON!
AT BEST WE HAVE TEN MINUTES BEFORE THE VIRUS TAKES EFFECT.
IF THAT HAPPENS IT'LL BE TOO LATE!
BING

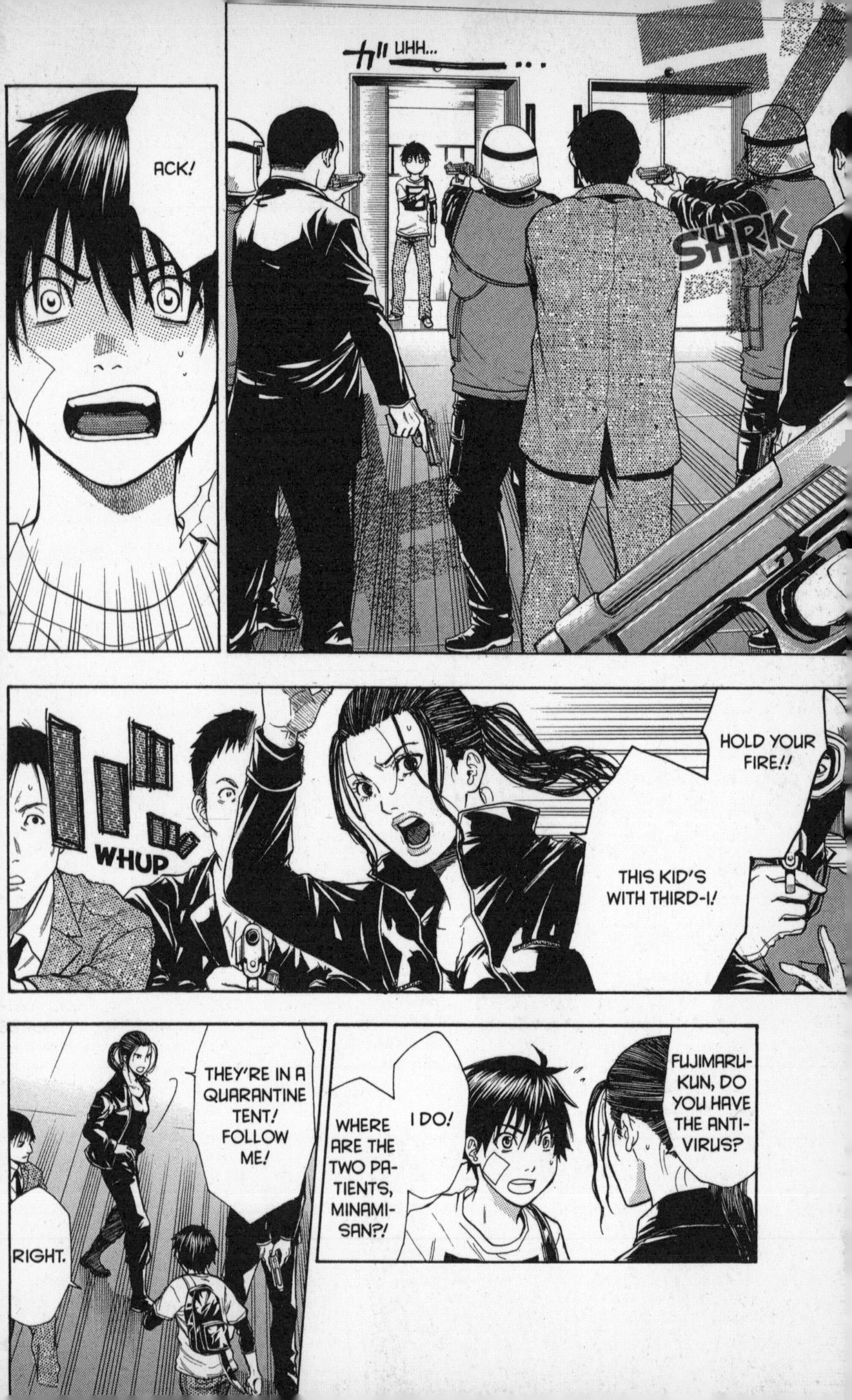
ガ UHH...
SHRK
ACK!
HOLD YOUR FIRE!!
THIS KID'S WITH THIRD-I!
WHUP
FUJIMARU-KUN, DO YOU HAVE THE ANTI-VIRUS?
I DO!
WHERE ARE THE TWO PATIENTS, MINAMI-SAN?!
THEY'RE IN A QUARANTINE TENT! FOLLOW ME!
RIGHT.

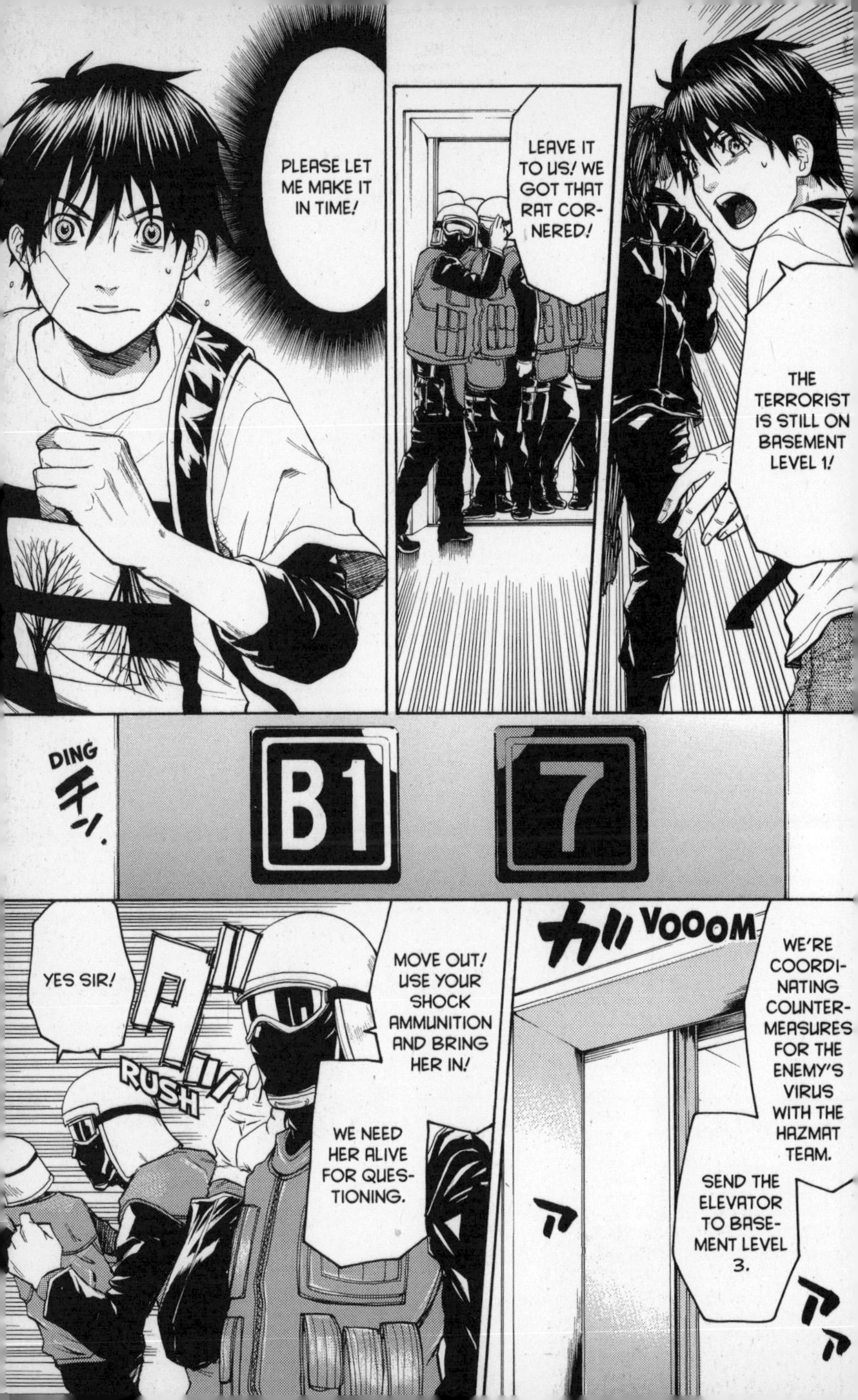
THE TERRORIST IS STILL ON BASEMENT LEVEL 1!
LEAVE IT TO US! WE GOT THAT RAT COR-NERED!
PLEASE LET ME MAKE IT IN TIME!
DING
B1
7
VOOOM
WE'RE COORDI-NATING COUNTER-MEASURES FOR THE ENEMY'S VIRUS WITH THE HAZMAT TEAM.
SEND THE ELEVATOR TO BASE-MENT LEVEL 3.
MOVE OUT! USE YOUR SHOCK AMMUNITION AND BRING HER IN!
WE NEED HER ALIVE FOR QUES-TIONING.
YES SIR!
RUSH

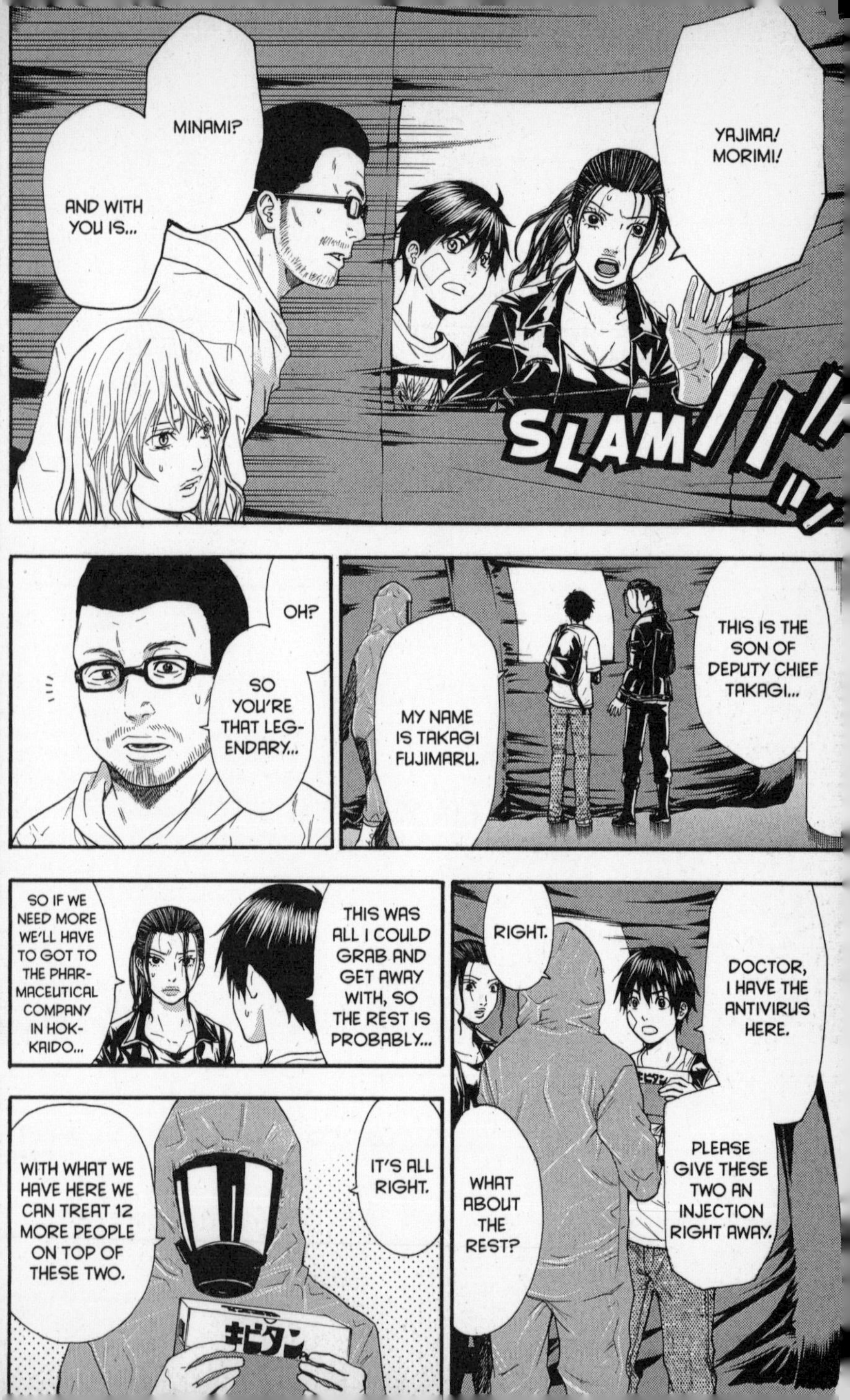
YAJIMA! MORIMI!
MINAMI?
AND WITH YOU IS...
SLAM
THIS IS THE SON OF DEPUTY CHIEF TAKAGI...
MY NAME IS TAKAGI FUJIMARU.
OH?
SO YOU'RE THAT LEG-ENDARY...
DOCTOR, I HAVE THE ANTIVIRUS HERE.
RIGHT.
PLEASE GIVE THESE TWO AN INJECTION RIGHT AWAY.
WHAT ABOUT THE REST?
THIS WAS ALL I COULD GRAB AND GET AWAY WITH, SO THE REST IS PROBABLY...
SO IF WE NEED MORE WE'LL HAVE TO GOT TO THE PHAR-MACEUTICAL COMPANY IN HOK-KAIDO...
IT'S ALL RIGHT.
WITH WHAT WE HAVE HERE WE CAN TREAT 12 MORE PEOPLE ON TOP OF THESE TWO.
キビタン

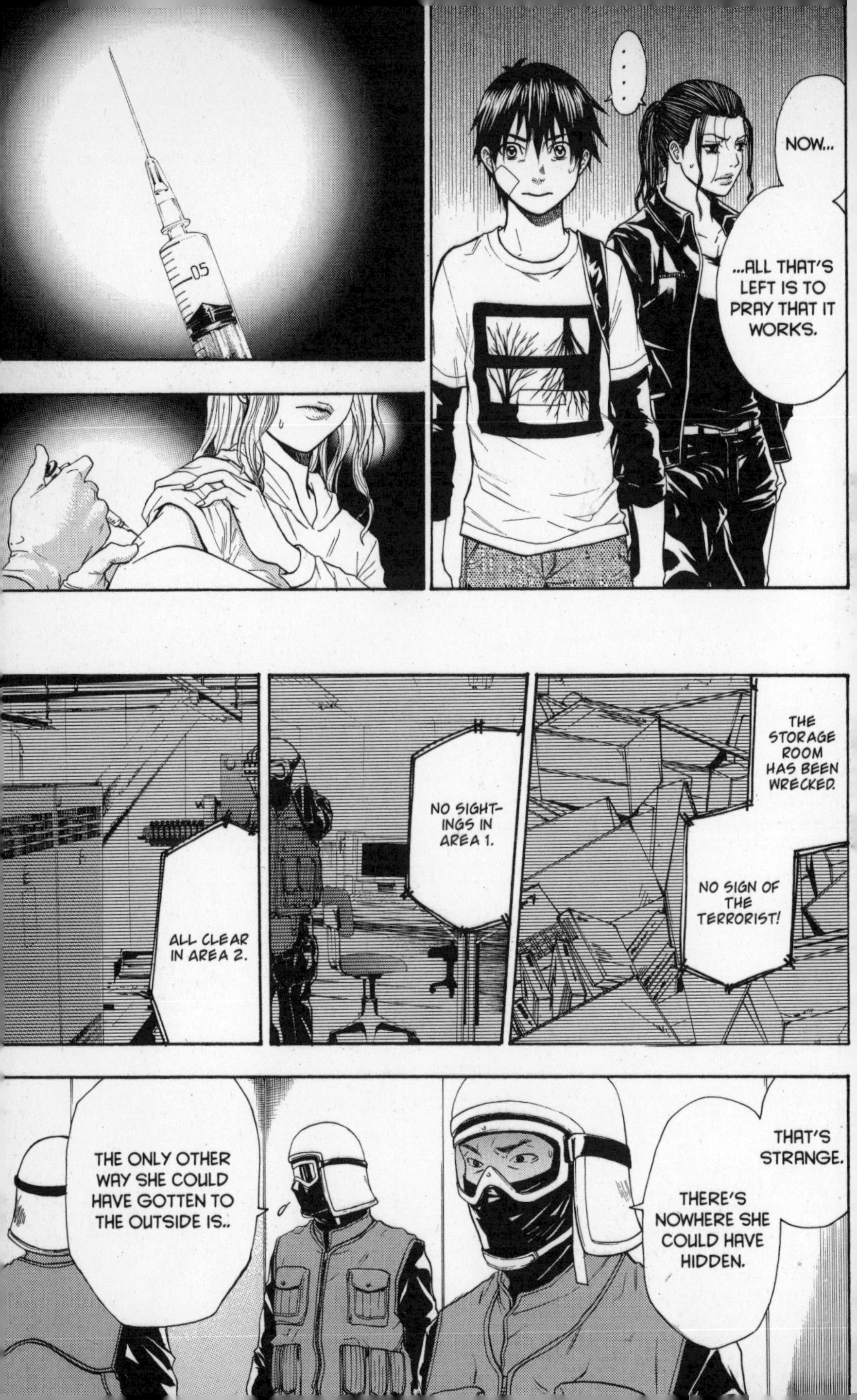
...
NOW...
...ALL THAT'S LEFT IS TO PRAY THAT IT WORKS.
0.5
THE STORAGE ROOM HAS BEEN WRECKED.
NO SIGN OF THE TERRORIST!
NO SIGHTINGS IN AREA 1.
ALL CLEAR IN AREA 2.
THAT'S STRANGE.
THERE'S NOWHERE SHE COULD HAVE HIDDEN.
THE ONLY OTHER WAY SHE COULD HAVE GOTTEN TO THE OUTSIDE IS..

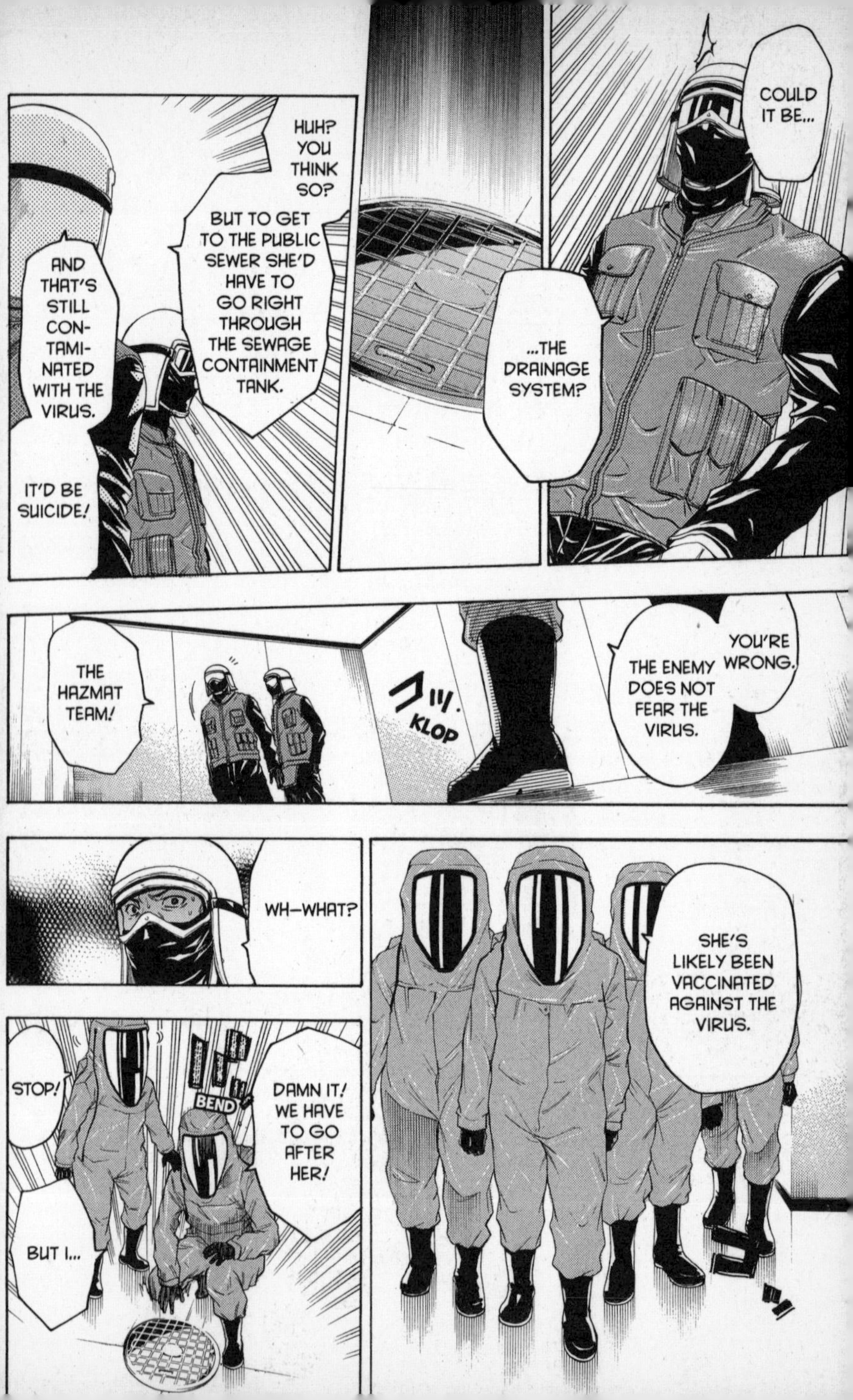
COULD IT BE...
...THE DRAINAGE SYSTEM?
HUH? YOU THINK SO?
BUT TO GET TO THE PUBLIC SEWER SHE'D HAVE TO GO RIGHT THROUGH THE SEWAGE CONTAINMENT TANK.
AND THAT'S STILL CONTAMINATED WITH THE VIRUS.
IT'D BE SUICIDE!
YOU'RE WRONG.
THE ENEMY DOES NOT FEAR THE VIRUS.
KLOP
THE HAZMAT TEAM!
SHE'S LIKELY BEEN VACCINATED AGAINST THE VIRUS.
WH—WHAT?
DAMN IT! WE HAVE TO GO AFTER HER!
BEND
STOP!
BUT I...

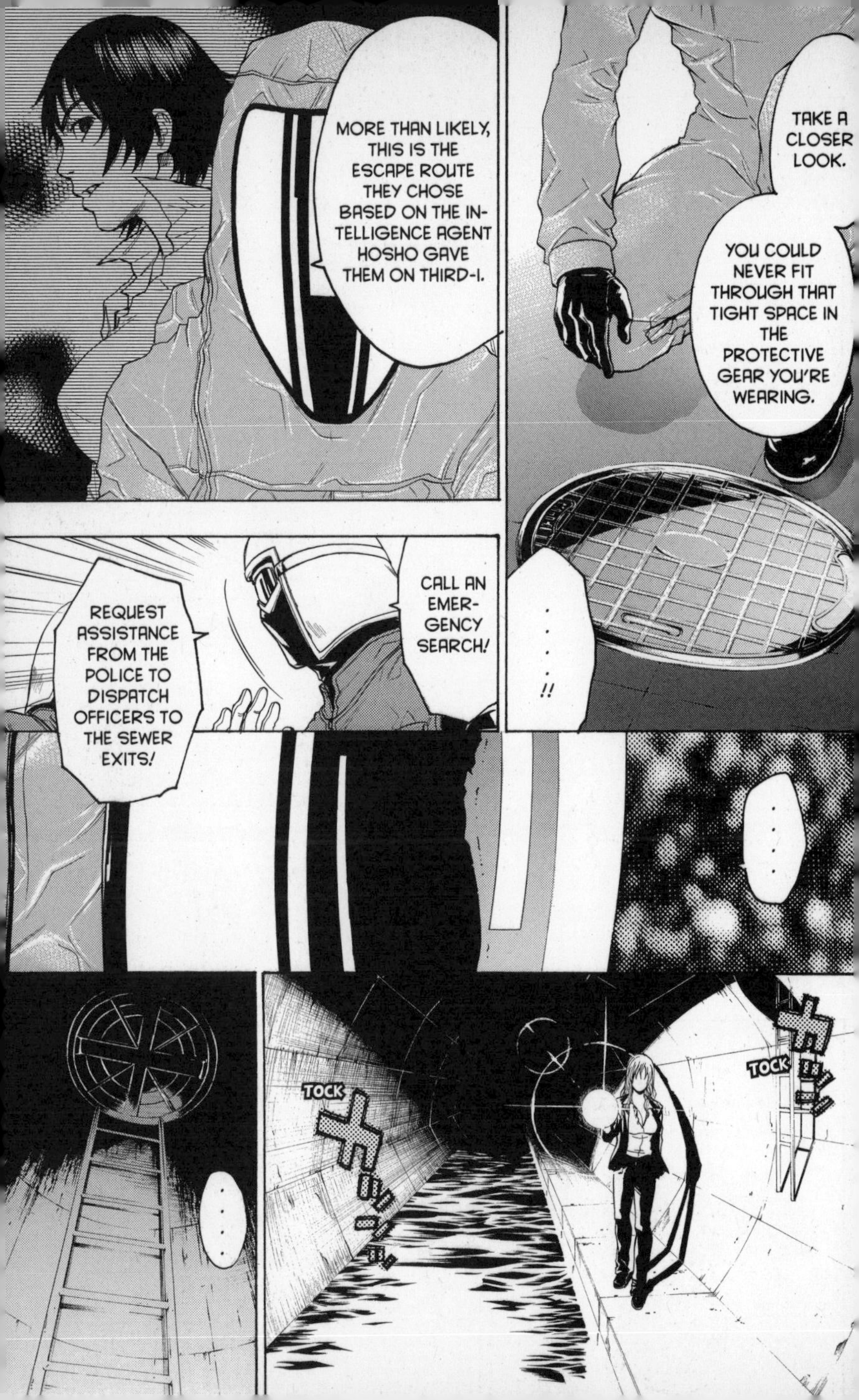
TAKE A CLOSER LOOK.
YOU COULD NEVER FIT THROUGH THAT TIGHT SPACE IN THE PROTECTIVE GEAR YOU'RE WEARING.
.....!!
MORE THAN LIKELY, THIS IS THE ESCAPE ROUTE THEY CHOSE BASED ON THE INTELLIGENCE AGENT HOSHO GAVE THEM ON THIRD-I.
CALL AN EMERGENCY SEARCH!
REQUEST ASSISTANCE FROM THE POLICE TO DISPATCH OFFICERS TO THE SEWER EXITS!
....
TOCK
TOCK
....

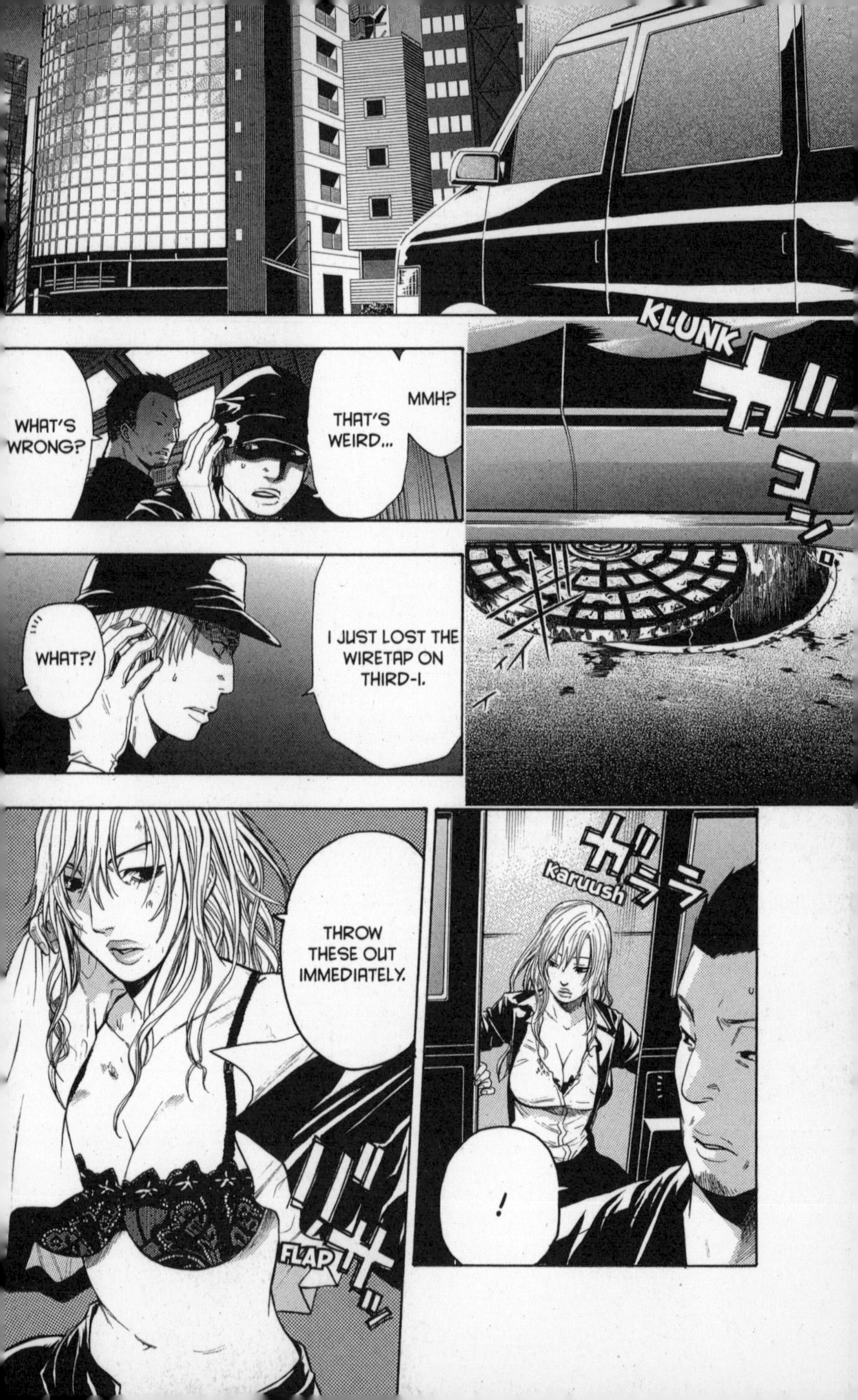
KLUNK
MMH? THAT'S WEIRD...
WHAT'S WRONG?
I JUST LOST THE WIRETAP ON THIRD-I.
WHAT?!
Karuush
!
THROW THESE OUT IMMEDIATELY.
FLAP

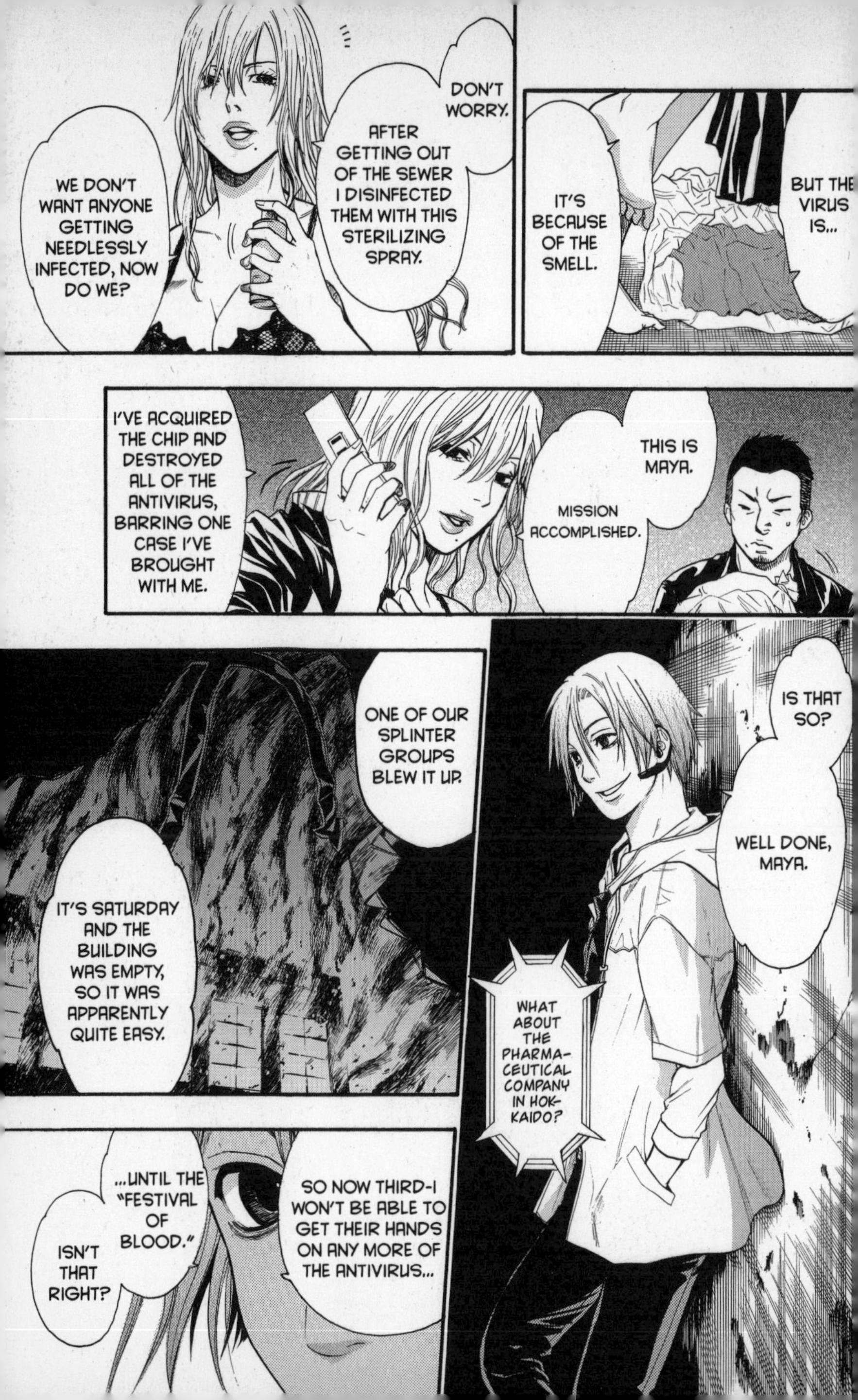
BUT THE VIRUS IS...
IT'S BECAUSE OF THE SMELL.
DON'T WORRY.
AFTER GETTING OUT OF THE SEWER I DISINFECTED THEM WITH THIS STERILIZING SPRAY.
WE DON'T WANT ANYONE GETTING NEEDLESSLY INFECTED, NOW DO WE?
THIS IS MAYA.
MISSION ACCOMPLISHED.
I'VE ACQUIRED THE CHIP AND DESTROYED ALL OF THE ANTIVIRUS, BARRING ONE CASE I'VE BROUGHT WITH ME.
IS THAT SO?
WELL DONE, MAYA.
WHAT ABOUT THE PHARMA-CEUTICAL COMPANY IN HOK-KAIDO?
ONE OF OUR SPLINTER GROUPS BLEW IT UP.
IT'S SATURDAY AND THE BUILDING WAS EMPTY, SO IT WAS APPARENTLY QUITE EASY.
SO NOW THIRD-I WON'T BE ABLE TO GET THEIR HANDS ON ANY MORE OF THE ANTIVIRUS...
...UNTIL THE "FESTIVAL OF BLOOD."
ISN'T THAT RIGHT?

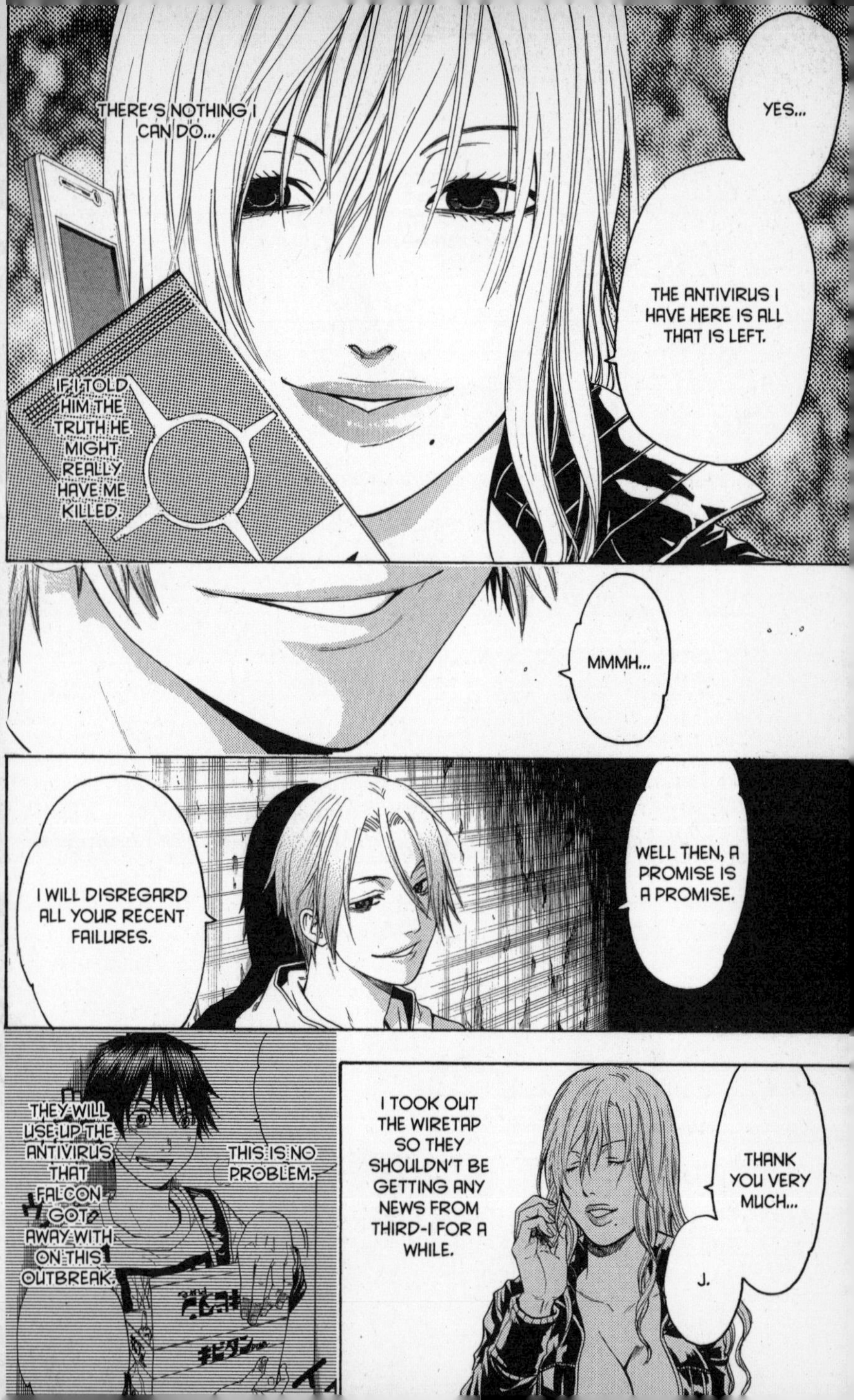
YES...
THE ANTIVIRUS I HAVE HERE IS ALL THAT IS LEFT.
THERE'S NOTHING I CAN DO...
IF I TOLD HIM THE TRUTH HE MIGHT REALLY HAVE ME KILLED.
MMMH...
WELL THEN, A PROMISE IS A PROMISE.
I WILL DISREGARD ALL YOUR RECENT FAILURES.
THANK YOU VERY MUCH...
J.
I TOOK OUT THE WIRETAP SO THEY SHOULDN'T BE GETTING ANY NEWS FROM THIRD-I FOR A WHILE.
THIS IS NO PROBLEM.
THEY WILL USE UP THE ANTIVIRUS THAT FALCON GOT AWAY WITH ON THIS OUTBREAK.

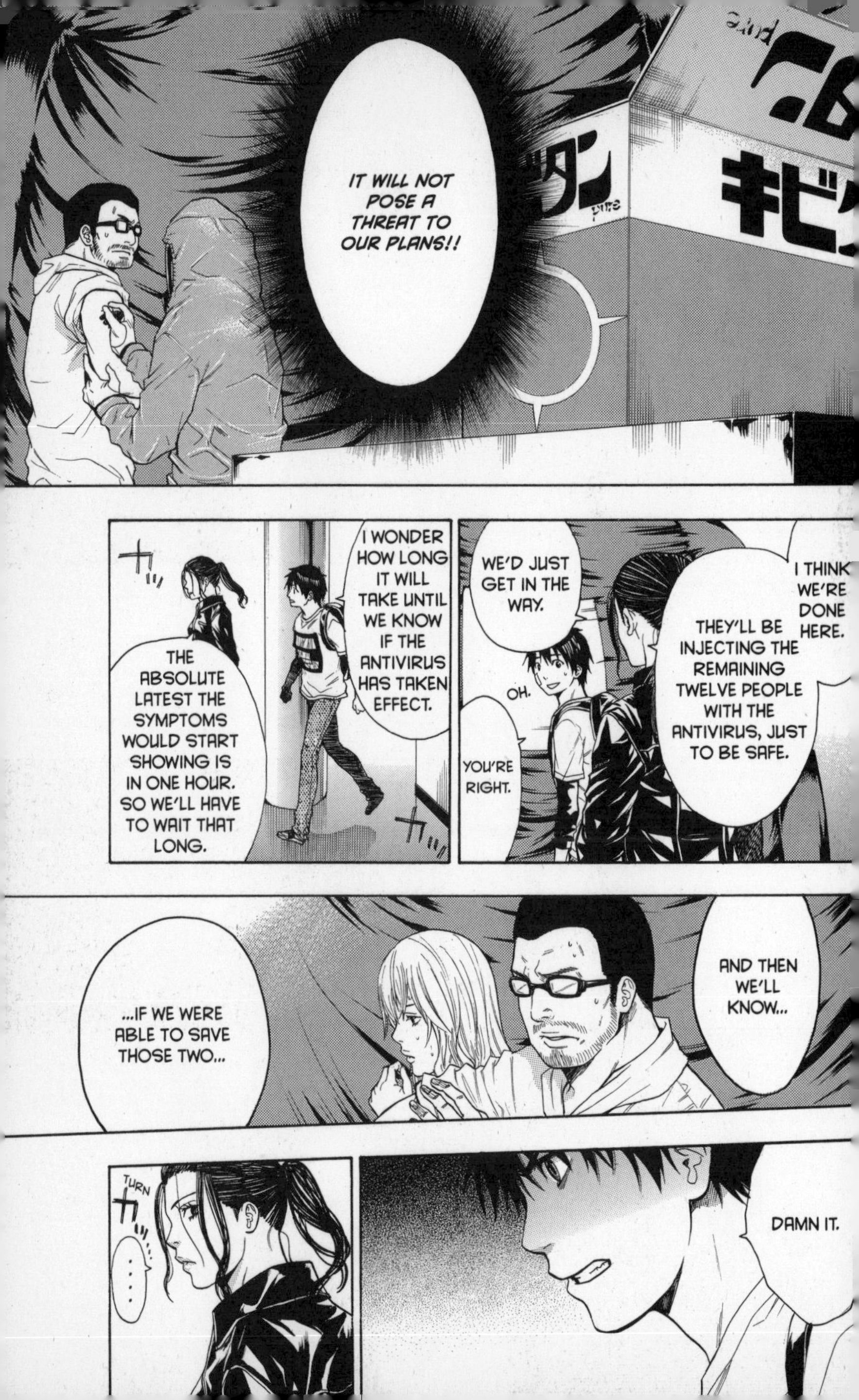
IT WILL NOT POSE A THREAT TO OUR PLANS!!
I THINK WE'RE DONE HERE.
THEY'LL BE INJECTING THE REMAINING TWELVE PEOPLE WITH THE ANTIVIRUS, JUST TO BE SAFE.
WE'D JUST GET IN THE WAY.
OH.
YOU'RE RIGHT.
I WONDER HOW LONG IT WILL TAKE UNTIL WE KNOW IF THE ANTIVIRUS HAS TAKEN EFFECT.
THE ABSOLUTE LATEST THE SYMPTOMS WOULD START SHOWING IS IN ONE HOUR. SO WE'LL HAVE TO WAIT THAT LONG.
AND THEN WE'LL KNOW...
...IF WE WERE ABLE TO SAVE THOSE TWO...
DAMN IT.
TURN
.....

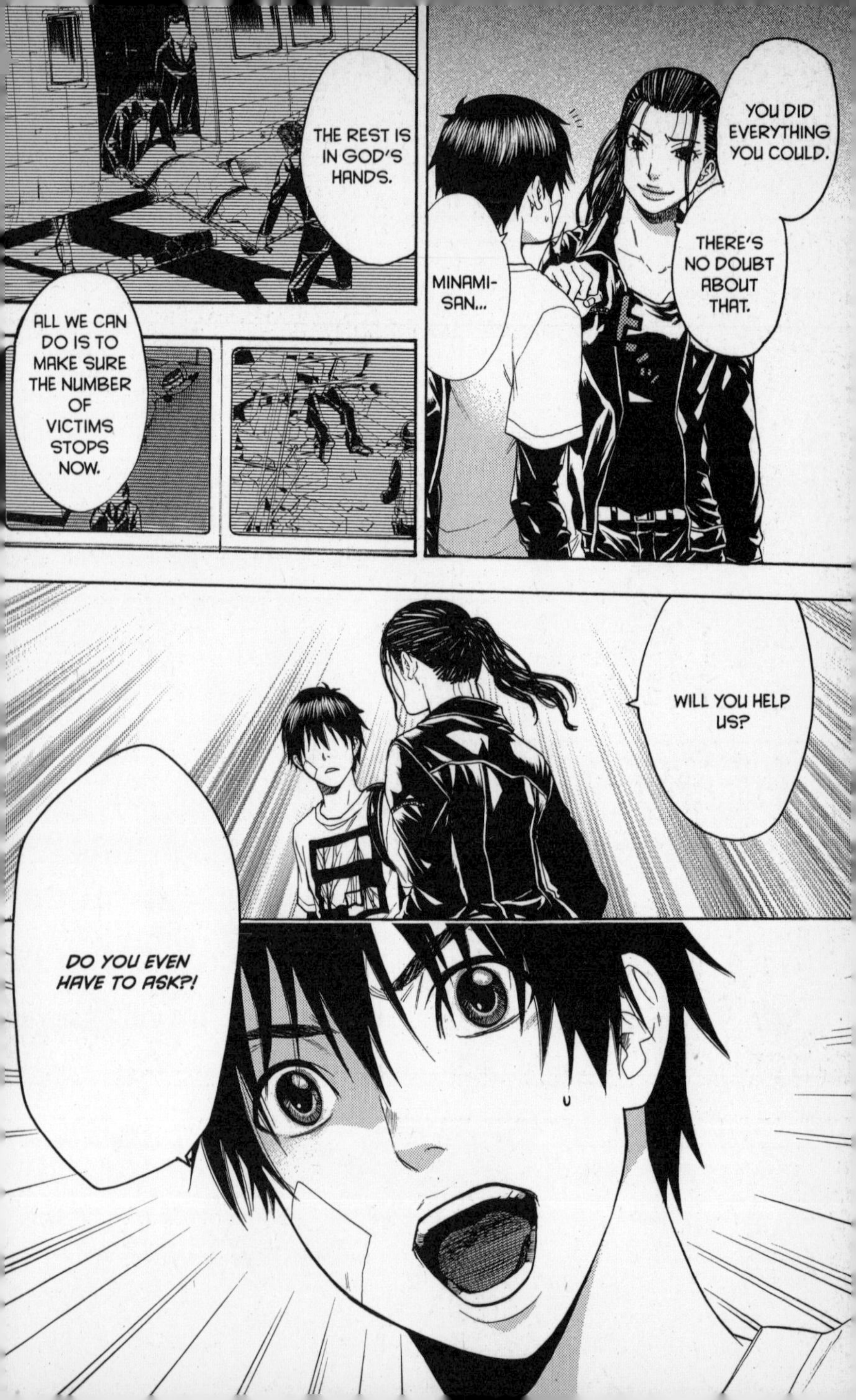
YOU DID EVERYTHING YOU COULD.
THERE'S NO DOUBT ABOUT THAT.
MINAMI-SAN...
THE REST IS IN GOD'S HANDS.
ALL WE CAN DO IS TO MAKE SURE THE NUMBER OF VICTIMS STOPS NOW.
WILL YOU HELP US?
DO YOU EVEN HAVE TO ASK?!

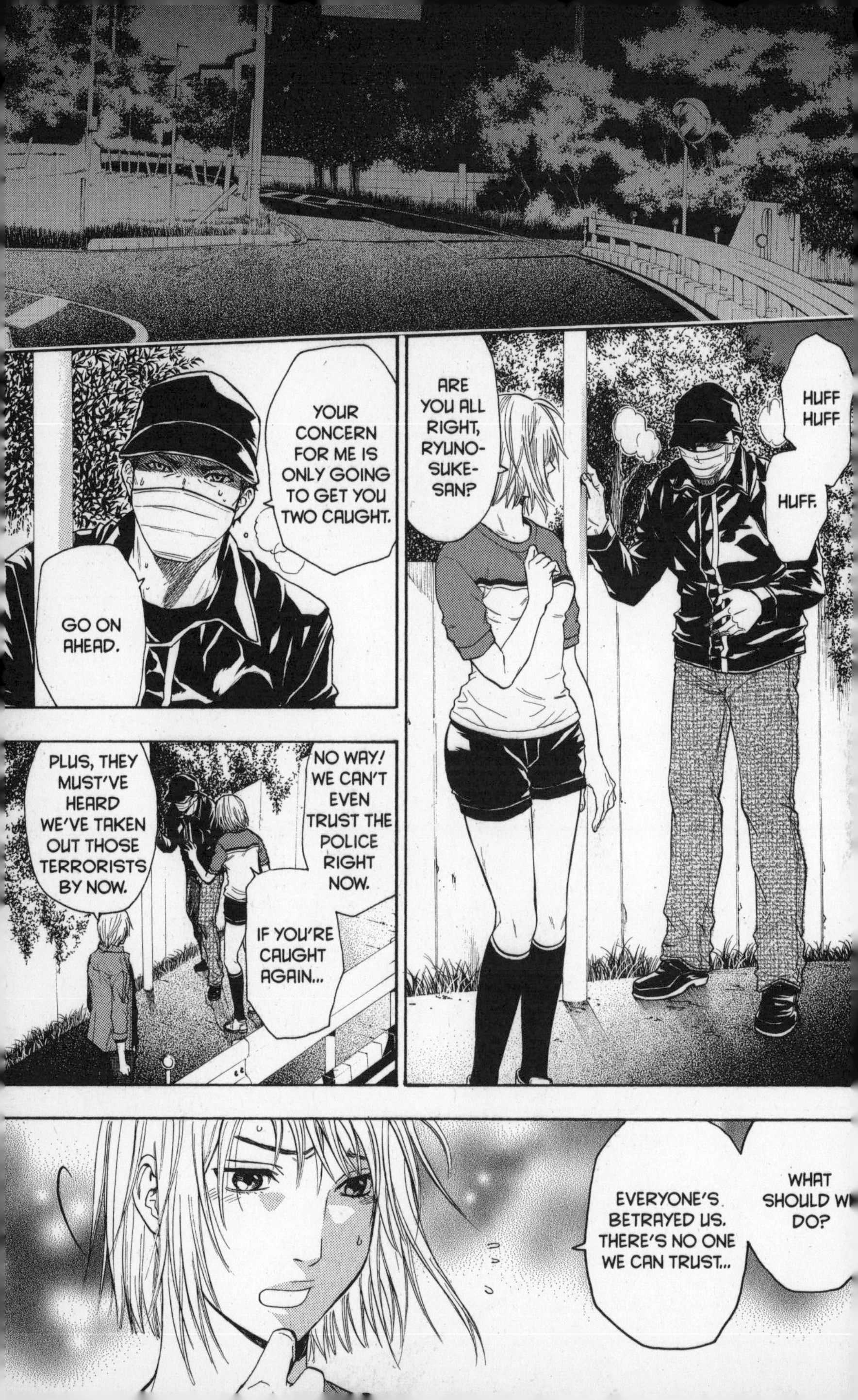
HUFF HUFF
HUFF.
ARE YOU ALL RIGHT, RYUNO-SUKE-SAN?
YOUR CONCERN FOR ME IS ONLY GOING TO GET YOU TWO CAUGHT.
GO ON AHEAD.
NO WAY! WE CAN'T EVEN TRUST THE POLICE RIGHT NOW.
IF YOU'RE CAUGHT AGAIN...
PLUS, THEY MUST'VE HEARD WE'VE TAKEN OUT THOSE TERRORISTS BY NOW.
WHAT SHOULD W DO?
EVERYONE'S BETRAYED US. THERE'S NO ONE WE CAN TRUST...

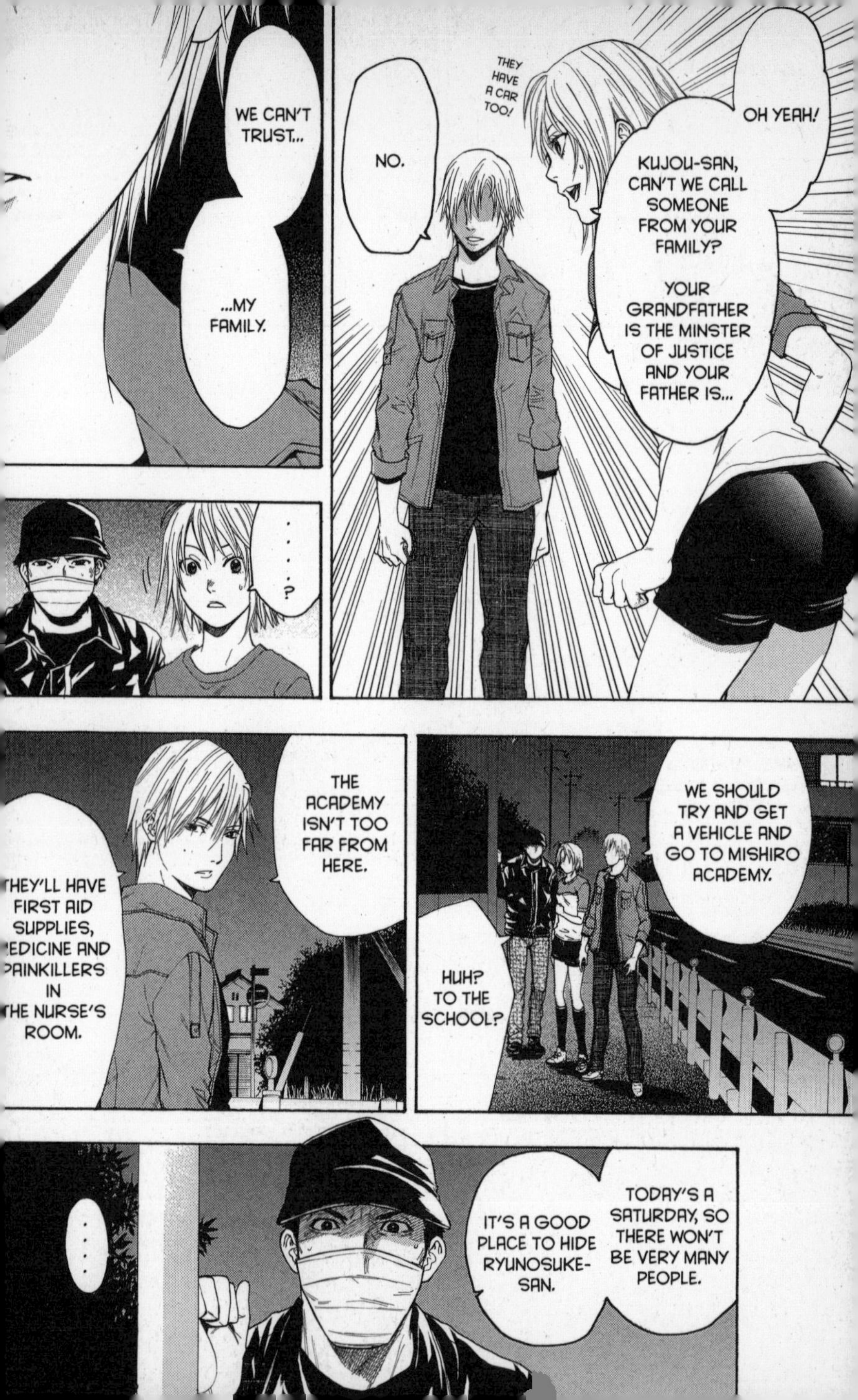
OH YEAH!
KUJOU-SAN, CAN'T WE CALL SOMEONE FROM YOUR FAMILY?
YOUR GRANDFATHER IS THE MINSTER OF JUSTICE AND YOUR FATHER IS...
THEY HAVE A CAR TOO!
NO.
WE CAN'T TRUST...
...MY FAMILY.
....?
WE SHOULD TRY AND GET A VEHICLE AND GO TO MISHIRO ACADEMY.
HUH? TO THE SCHOOL?
THE ACADEMY ISN'T TOO FAR FROM HERE.
THEY'LL HAVE FIRST AID SUPPLIES, EDICINE AND AINKILLERS IN HE NURSE'S ROOM.
TODAY'S A SATURDAY, SO THERE WON'T BE VERY MANY PEOPLE.
IT'S A GOOD PLACE TO HIDE RYUNOSUKE-SAN.
....

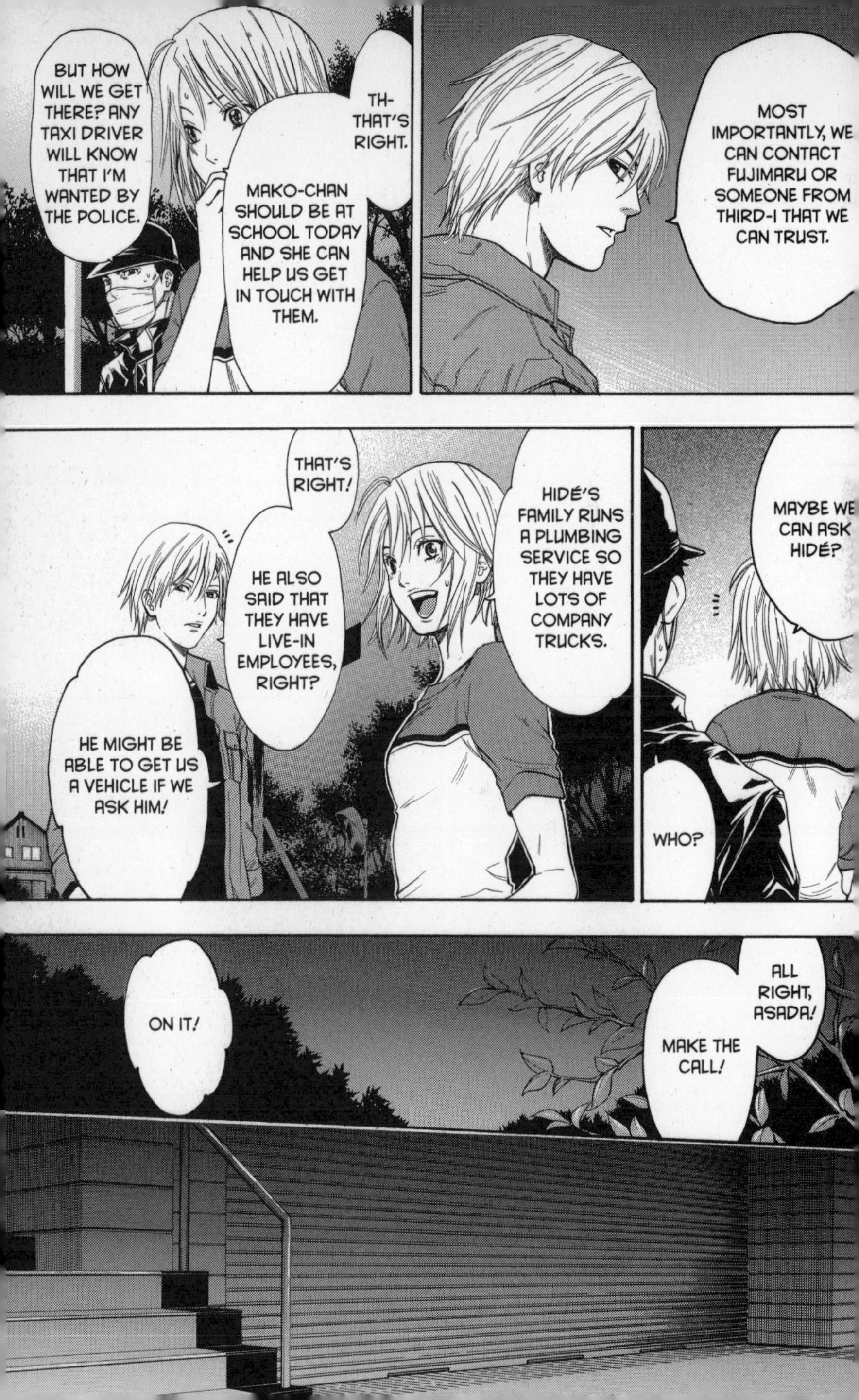
MOST IMPORTANTLY, WE CAN CONTACT FUJIMARU OR SOMEONE FROM THIRD-I THAT WE CAN TRUST.
TH- THAT'S RIGHT.
MAKO-CHAN SHOULD BE AT SCHOOL TODAY AND SHE CAN HELP US GET IN TOUCH WITH THEM.
BUT HOW WILL WE GET THERE? ANY TAXI DRIVER WILL KNOW THAT I'M WANTED BY THE POLICE.
MAYBE WE CAN ASK HIDÉ?
WHO?
HIDÉ'S FAMILY RUNS A PLUMBING SERVICE SO THEY HAVE LOTS OF COMPANY TRUCKS.
THAT'S RIGHT!
HE ALSO SAID THAT THEY HAVE LIVE-IN EMPLOYEES, RIGHT?
HE MIGHT BE ABLE TO GET US A VEHICLE IF WE ASK HIM!
ALL RIGHT, ASADA!
MAKE THE CALL!
ON IT!

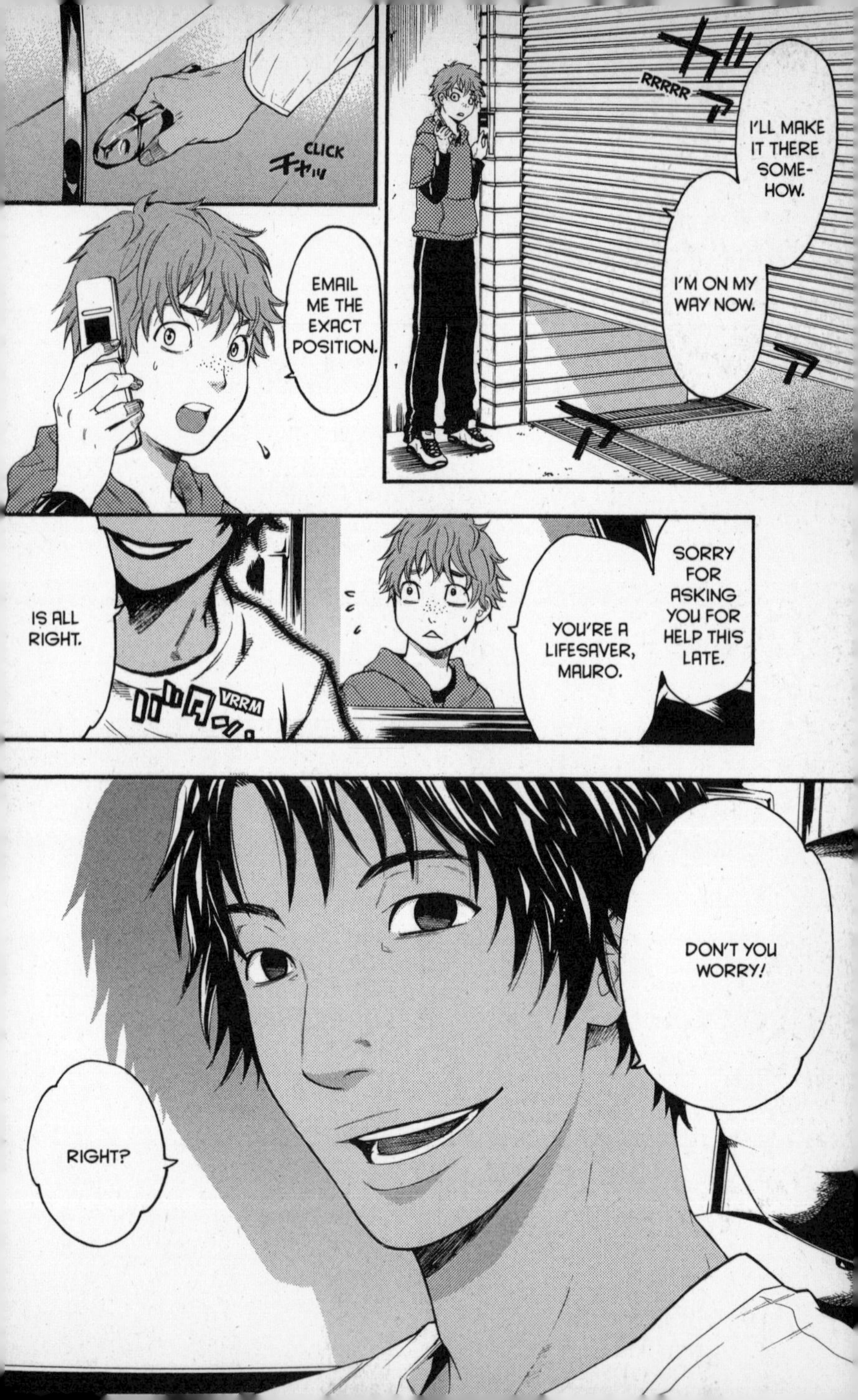
RRRRR
I'LL MAKE IT THERE SOME-HOW.
I'M ON MY WAY NOW.
CLICK
EMAIL ME THE EXACT POSITION.
SORRY FOR ASKING YOU FOR HELP THIS LATE.
YOU'RE A LIFESAVER, MAURO.
VRRM
IS ALL RIGHT.
DON'T YOU WORRY!
RIGHT?

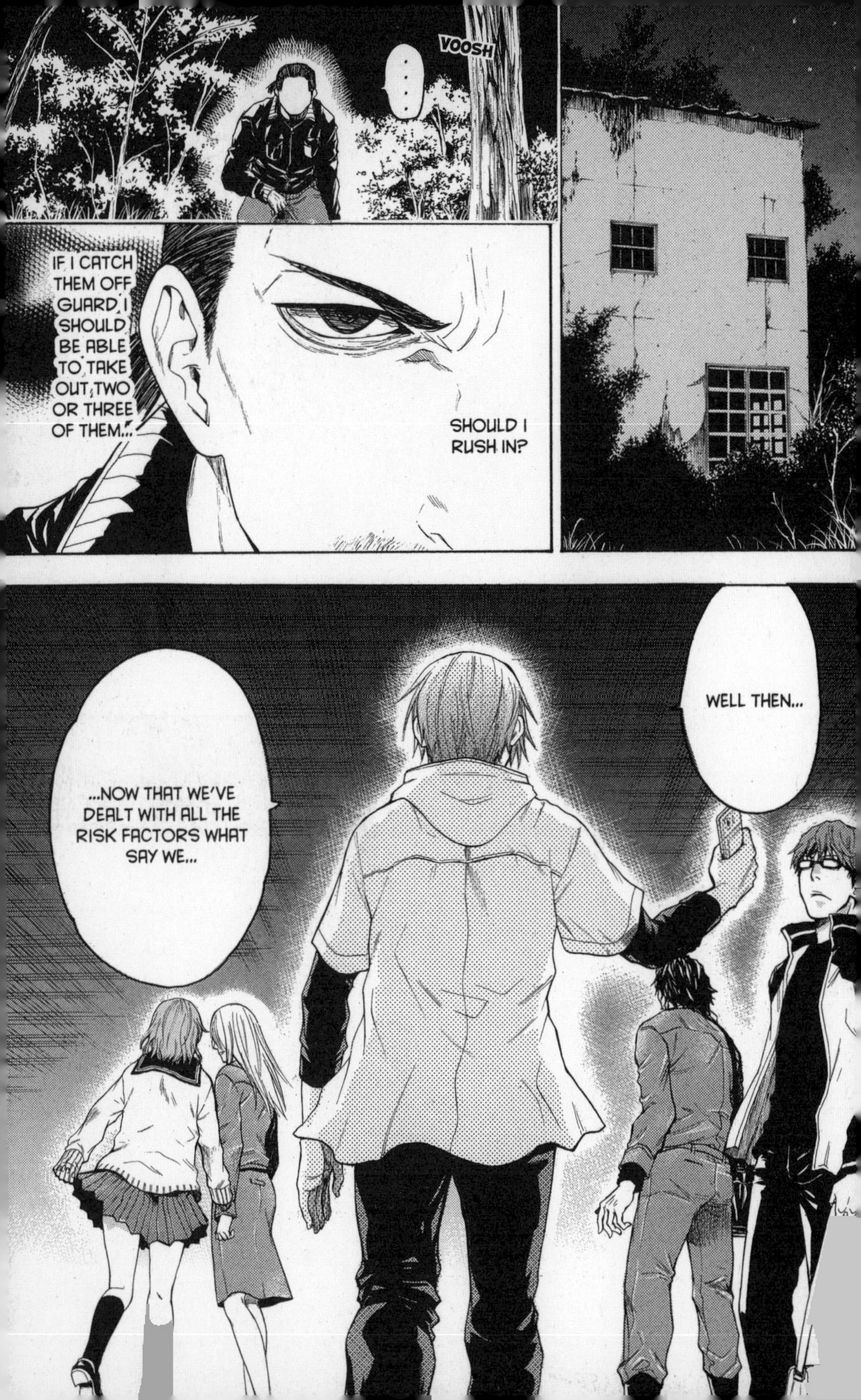
VOOSH
...
SHOULD I RUSH IN?
IF I CATCH THEM OFF GUARD I SHOULD BE ABLE TO TAKE OUT TWO OR THREE OF THEM...
WELL THEN...
...NOW THAT WE'VE DEALT WITH ALL THE RISK FACTORS WHAT SAY WE...

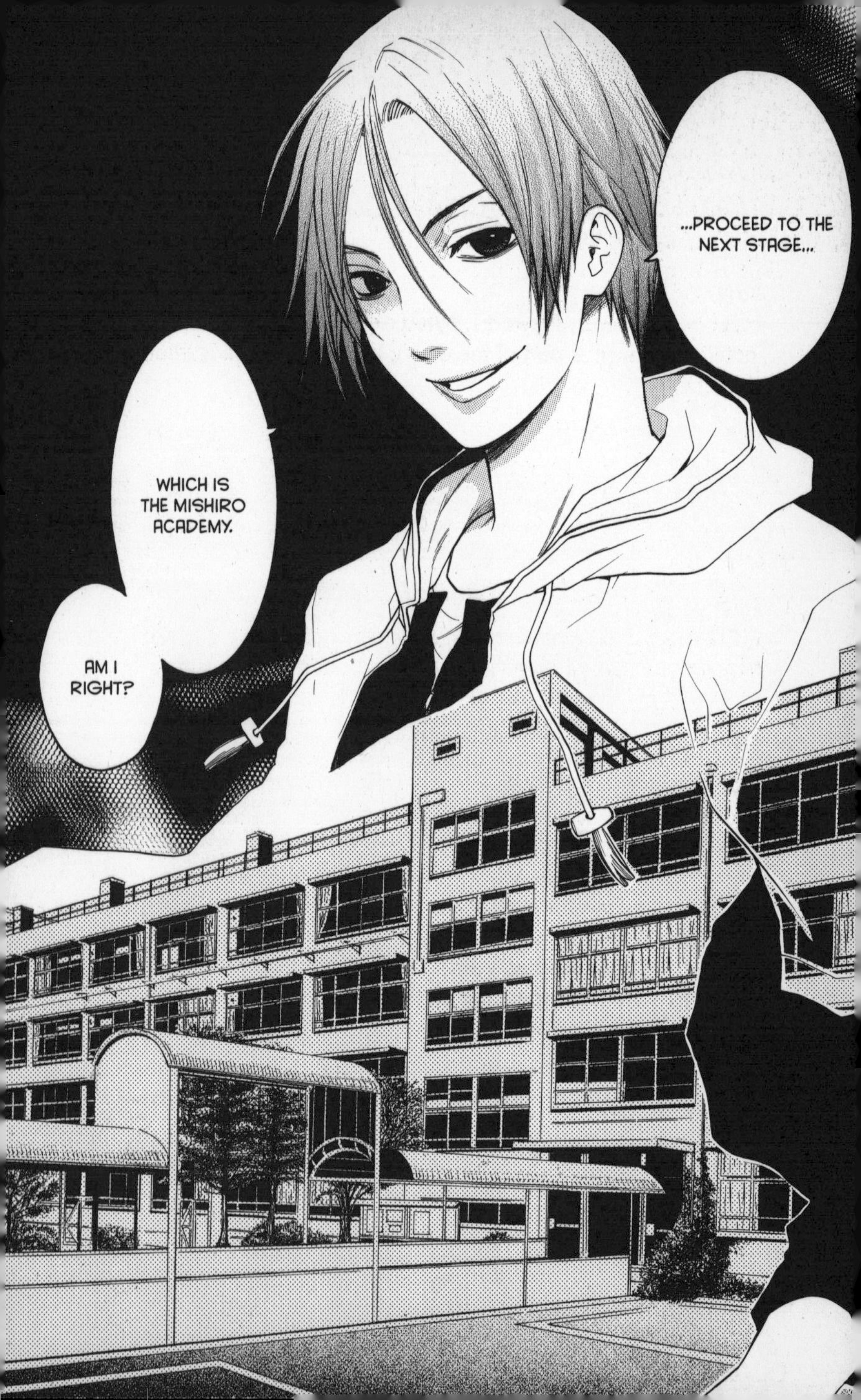
...PROCEED TO THE NEXT STAGE...
WHICH IS THE MISHIRO ACADEMY.
AM I RIGHT?

Bloody Monday

Glossary of Terms List 14

Page 110:
Fuse: In explosives, fireworks, pyrotechnic devices and military munitions, a fuse is part of the device that initiates the ignition or detonation.

Page 169:
PLC: Power Line Communication is the ability to connect to the internet to send and receive data via an electrical outlet.

Page 170:
Splitter: A device used as a filter and separate ADSL and telephone frequencies that are operating on the same line.

…いや
どーだろうな

ぱっと目に入った
ブービートラップの
信管に遅延タイマーが
見えたからな

Bloody Monday

Glossary of Terms List 15

Page 170:
AES: Advanced Encryption Standard is a method for the encryption of electronic data. It was established as the government standard for data encryption by the American National Institute for Standards and Technology (NIST).

Page 170:
DES: Data Encryption Standard is another method of electronic data encryption. Originally designed by IBM it was chosen as the official standard for the United States by NIST in 1977. It was later replaced by the more advanced AES encryption standard.

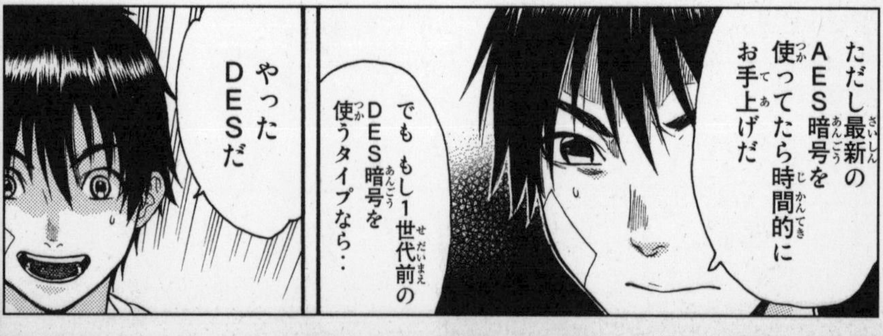
ただし最新のAES暗号を使ってたら時間的にお手上げだ
でももし1世代前のDES暗号を使うタイプなら…
やったDESだ

File 54: The true meaning.

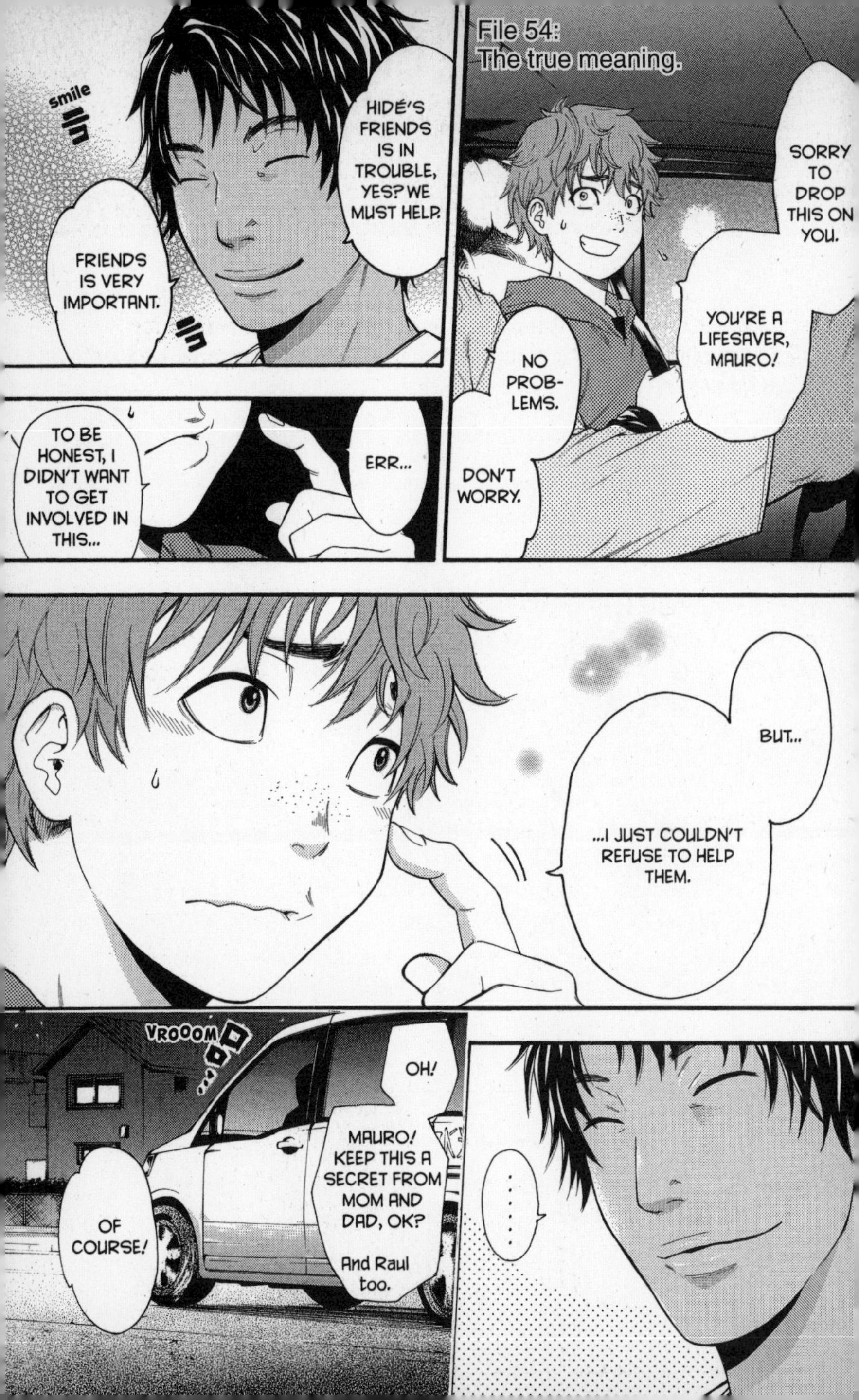
SORRY TO DROP THIS ON YOU.
YOU'RE A LIFESAVER, MAURO!
NO PROBLEMS.
DON'T WORRY.
smile
HIDÉ'S FRIENDS IS IN TROUBLE, YES? WE MUST HELP.
FRIENDS IS VERY IMPORTANT.
ERR...
TO BE HONEST, I DIDN'T WANT TO GET INVOLVED IN THIS...
BUT...
...I JUST COULDN'T REFUSE TO HELP THEM.
......
VROOOM
OH!
MAURO! KEEP THIS A SECRET FROM MOM AND DAD, OK?
And Raul too.
OF COURSE!

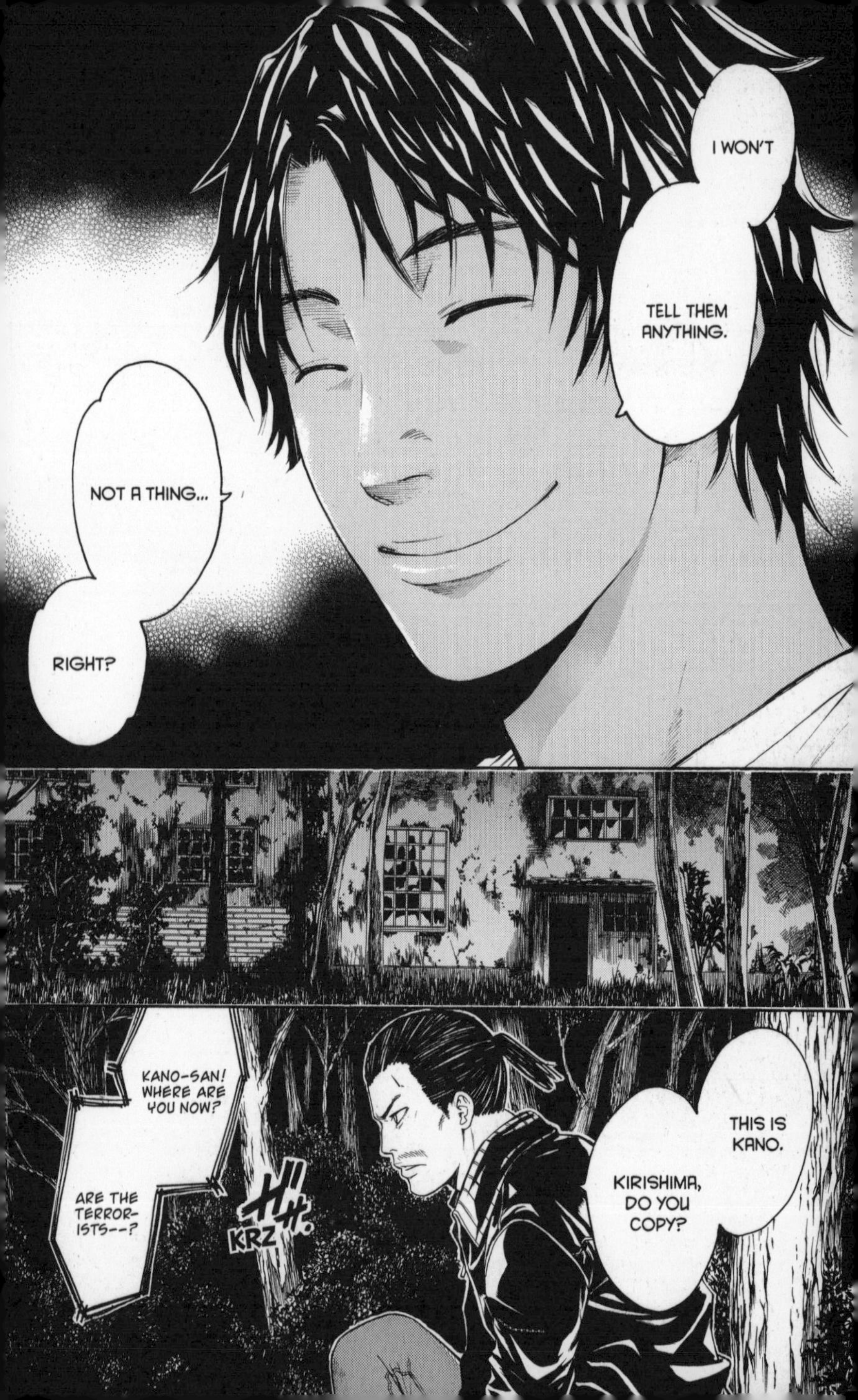
I WON'T
TELL THEM ANYTHING.
NOT A THING...
RIGHT?
THIS IS KANO.
KIRISHIMA, DO YOU COPY?
KRZ
KANO-SAN! WHERE ARE YOU NOW?
ARE THE TERROR-ISTS--?

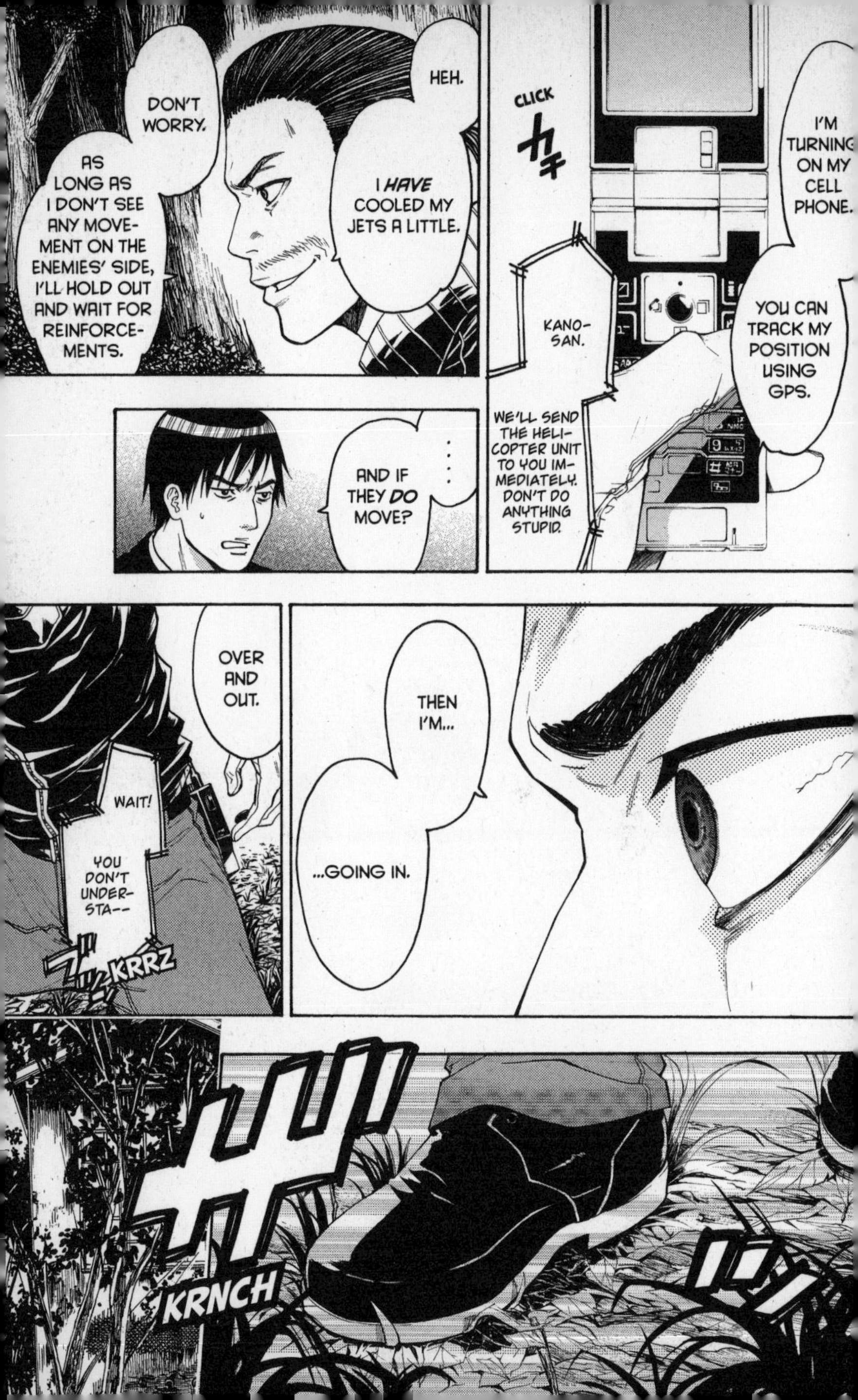
I'M TURNING ON MY CELL PHONE.
YOU CAN TRACK MY POSITION USING GPS.
CLICK
KANO-SAN.
WE'LL SEND THE HELICOPTER UNIT TO YOU IMMEDIATELY. DON'T DO ANYTHING STUPID.
HEH.
I *HAVE* COOLED MY JETS A LITTLE.
DON'T WORRY.
AS LONG AS I DON'T SEE ANY MOVEMENT ON THE ENEMIES' SIDE, I'LL HOLD OUT AND WAIT FOR REINFORCEMENTS.
....
AND IF THEY *DO* MOVE?
THEN I'M...
...GOING IN.
OVER AND OUT.
WAIT!
YOU DON'T UNDERSTA--
KRRZ
KRNCH

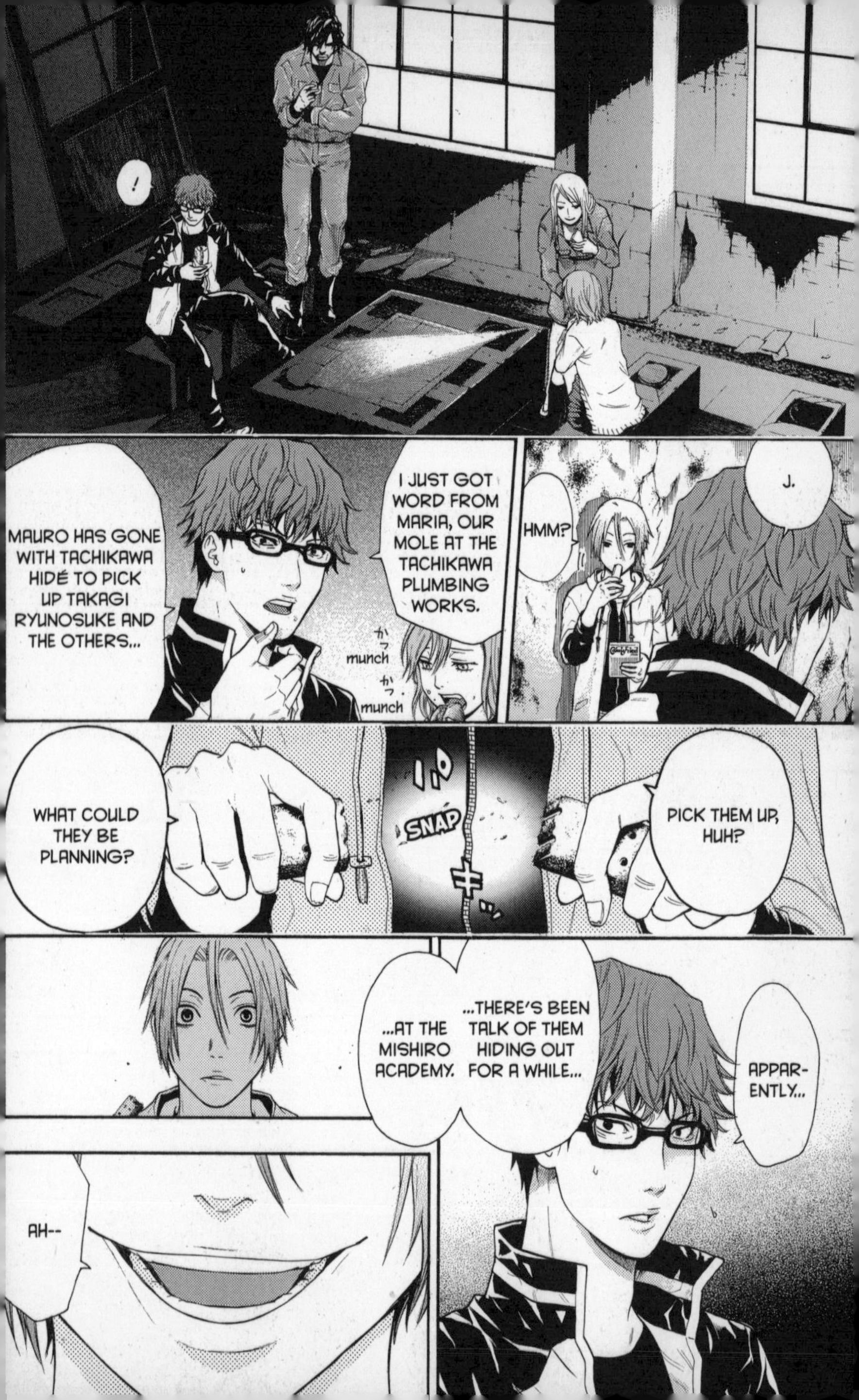

!
J.
HMM?
I JUST GOT WORD FROM MARIA, OUR MOLE AT THE TACHIKAWA PLUMBING WORKS.
MAURO HAS GONE WITH TACHIKAWA HIDÉ TO PICK UP TAKAGI RYUNOSUKE AND THE OTHERS...
かっ munch
かっ munch
PICK THEM UP, HUH?
SNAP
WHAT COULD THEY BE PLANNING?
APPAR-ENTLY...
...THERE'S BEEN TALK OF THEM HIDING OUT FOR A WHILE...
...AT THE MISHIRO ACADEMY.
AH--

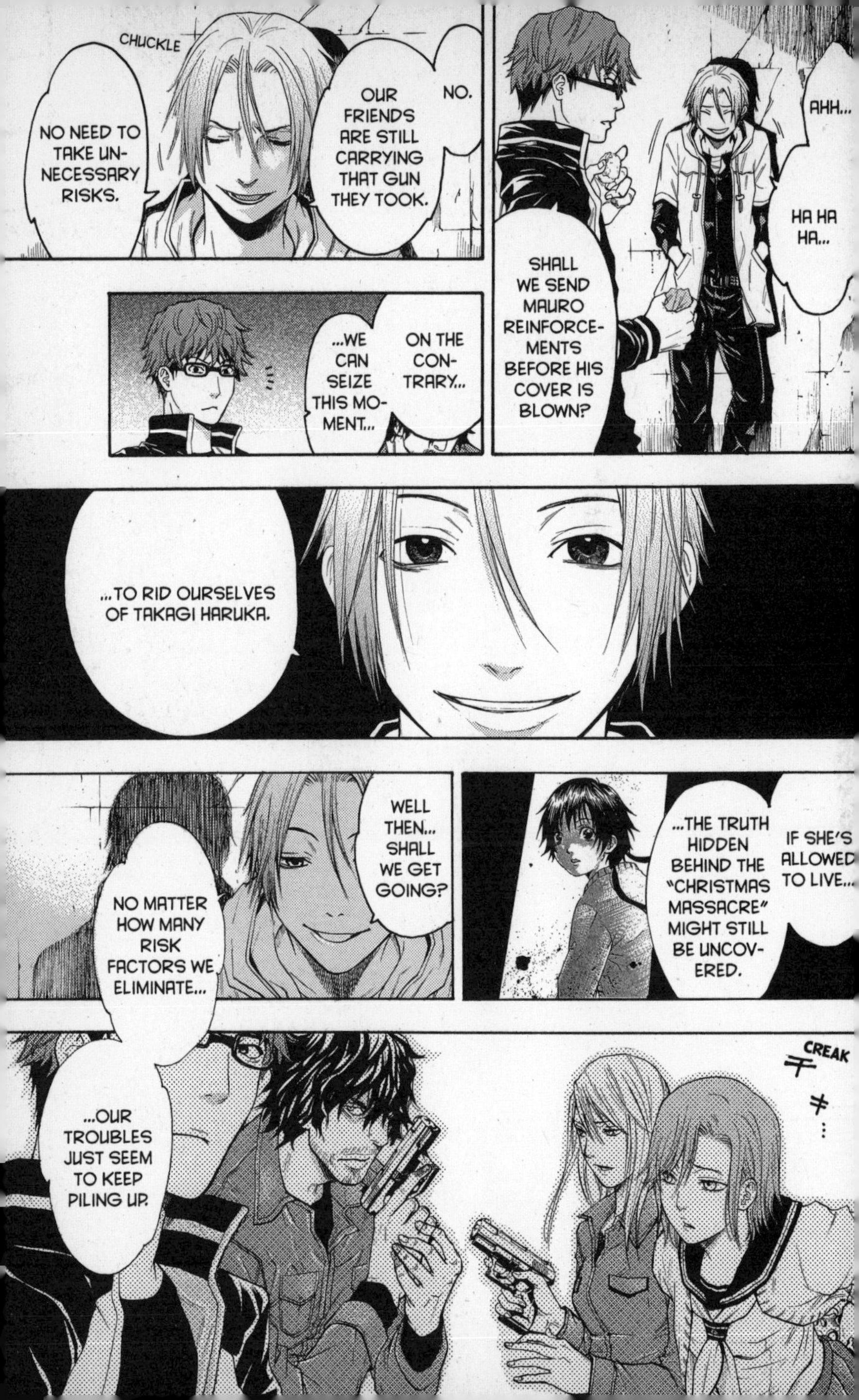
AHH...
HA HA HA...
SHALL WE SEND MAURO REINFORCEMENTS BEFORE HIS COVER IS BLOWN?
NO.
OUR FRIENDS ARE STILL CARRYING THAT GUN THEY TOOK.
CHUCKLE
NO NEED TO TAKE UNNECESSARY RISKS.
ON THE CONTRARY...
...WE CAN SEIZE THIS MOMENT...
...TO RID OURSELVES OF TAKAGI HARUKA.
IF SHE'S ALLOWED TO LIVE...
...THE TRUTH HIDDEN BEHIND THE "CHRISTMAS MASSACRE" MIGHT STILL BE UNCOVERED.
WELL THEN... SHALL WE GET GOING?
NO MATTER HOW MANY RISK FACTORS WE ELIMINATE...
CREAK
...OUR TROUBLES JUST SEEM TO KEEP PILING UP.

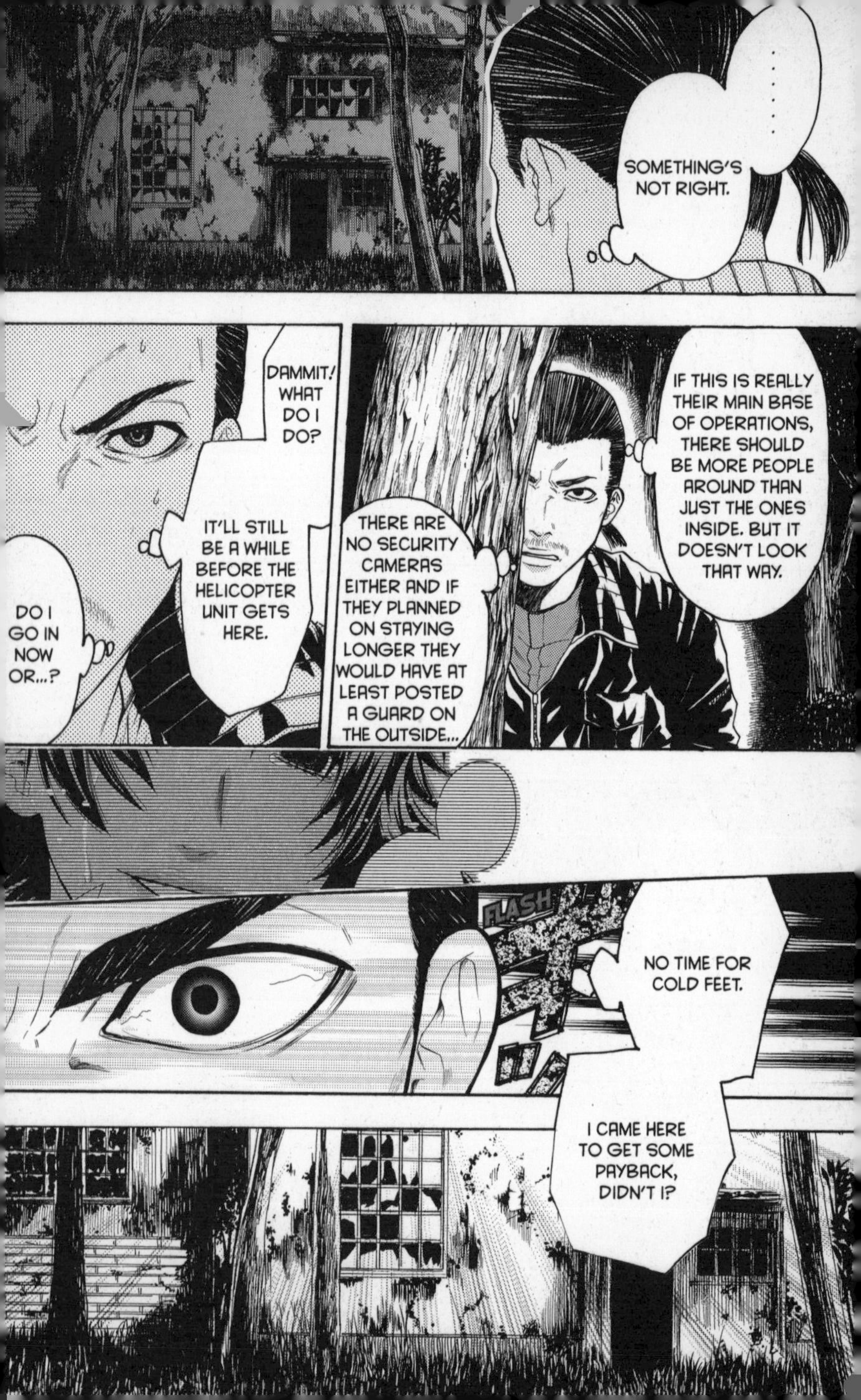
SOMETHING'S NOT RIGHT.
IF THIS IS REALLY THEIR MAIN BASE OF OPERATIONS, THERE SHOULD BE MORE PEOPLE AROUND THAN JUST THE ONES INSIDE. BUT IT DOESN'T LOOK THAT WAY.
THERE ARE NO SECURITY CAMERAS EITHER AND IF THEY PLANNED ON STAYING LONGER THEY WOULD HAVE AT LEAST POSTED A GUARD ON THE OUTSIDE...
DAMMIT! WHAT DO I DO?
IT'LL STILL BE A WHILE BEFORE THE HELICOPTER UNIT GETS HERE.
DO I GO IN NOW OR...?
FLASH
NO TIME FOR COLD FEET.
I CAME HERE TO GET SOME PAYBACK, DIDN'T I?

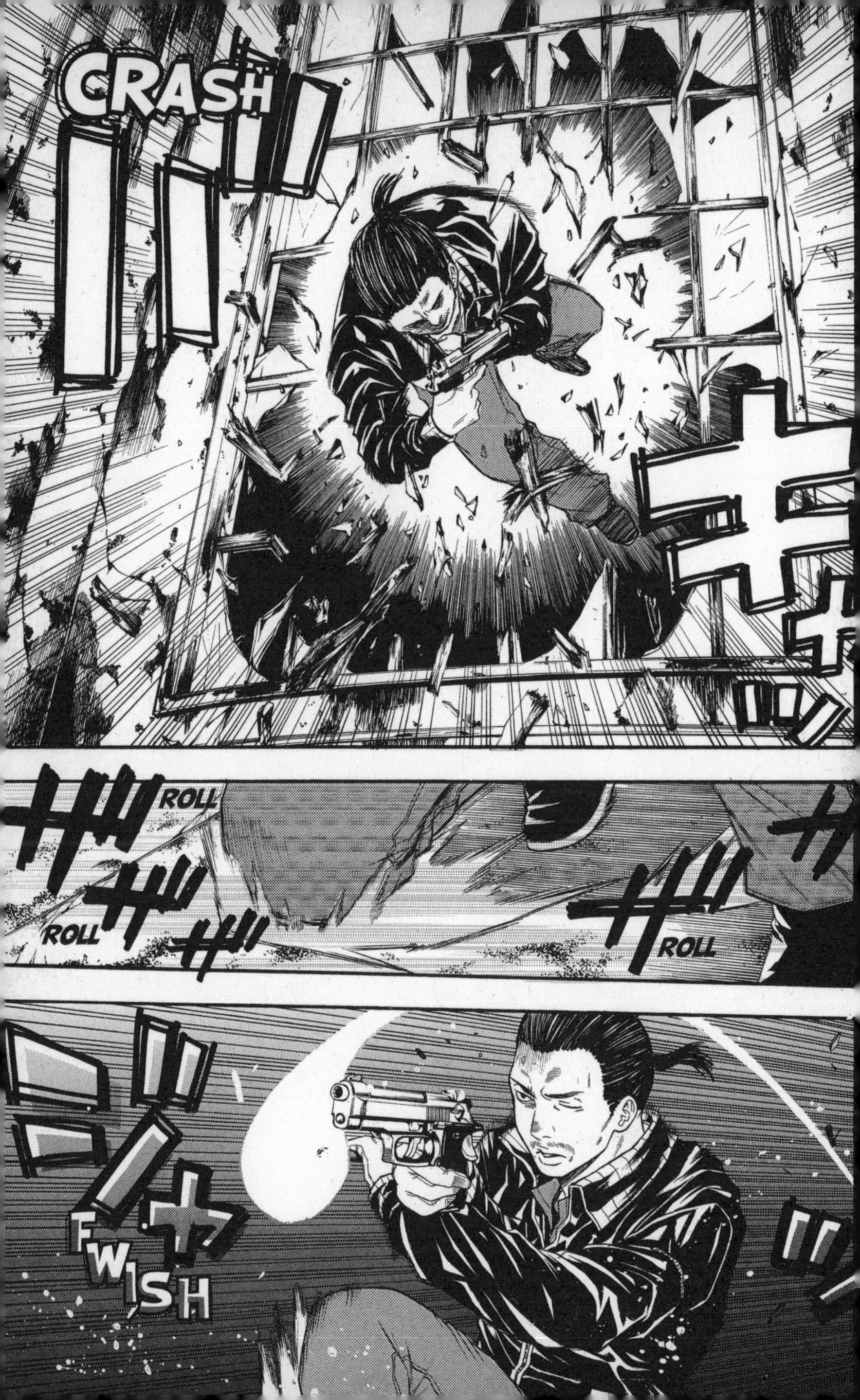
CRASH
ROLL
ROLL
ROLL
FWISH

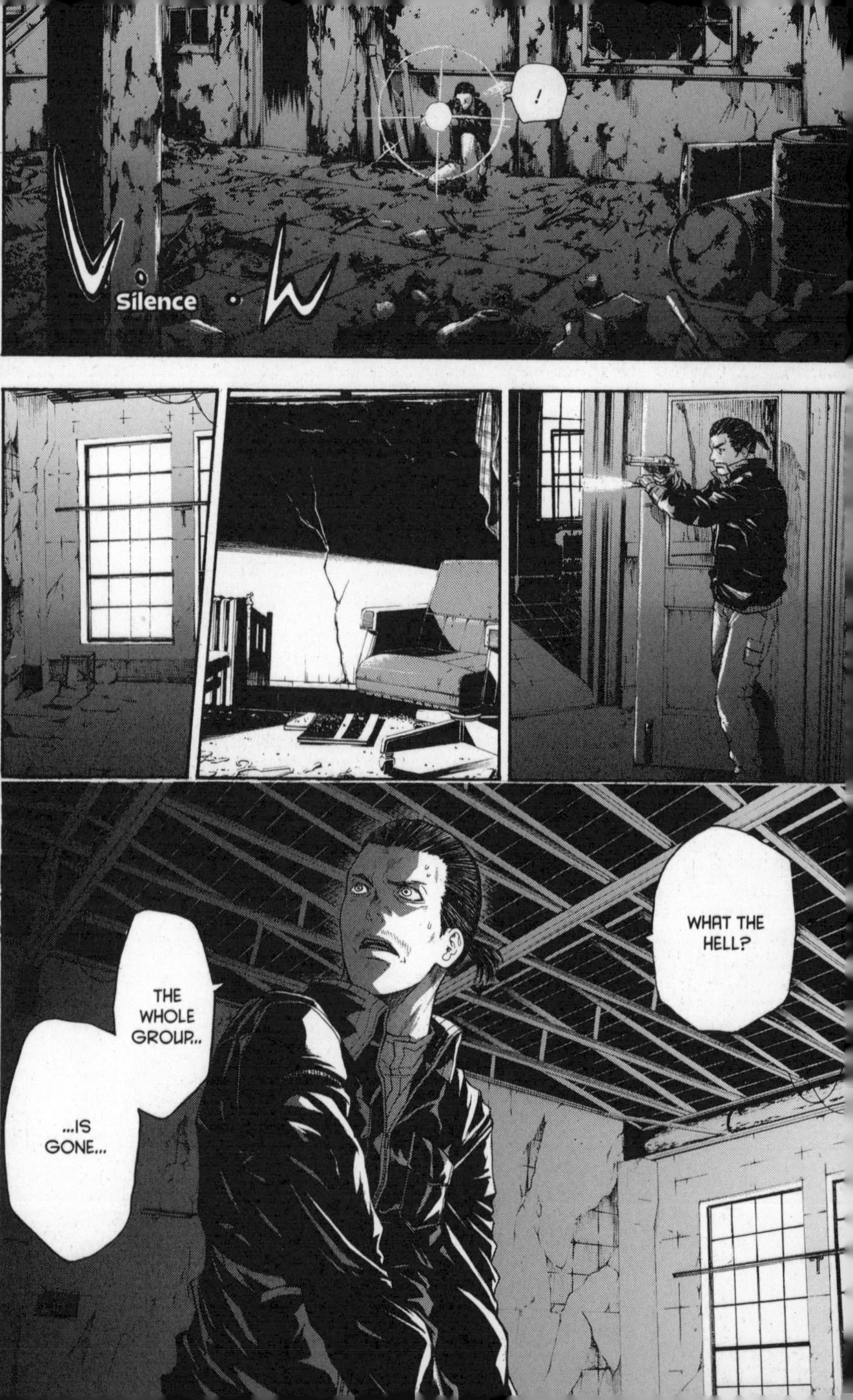
!
Silence
WHAT THE HELL?
THE WHOLE GROUP...
...IS GONE...

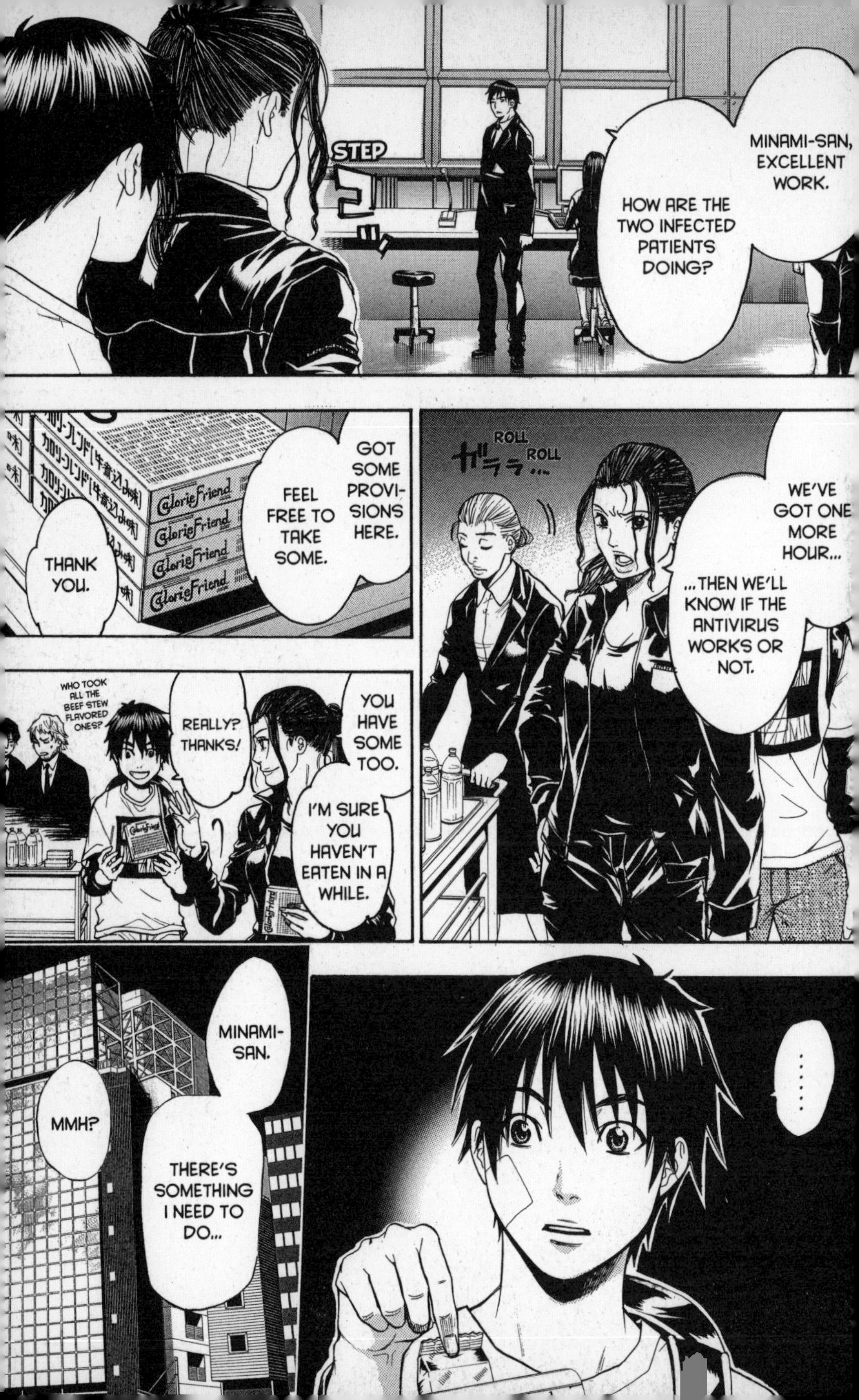
MINAMI-SAN, EXCELLENT WORK.
HOW ARE THE TWO INFECTED PATIENTS DOING?
STEP
ROLL ROLL
WE'VE GOT ONE MORE HOUR...
...THEN WE'LL KNOW IF THE ANTIVIRUS WORKS OR NOT.
GOT SOME PROVISIONS HERE.
FEEL FREE TO TAKE SOME.
CalorieFriend
THANK YOU.
YOU HAVE SOME TOO.
I'M SURE YOU HAVEN'T EATEN IN A WHILE.
REALLY? THANKS!
WHO TOOK ALL THE BEEF STEW FLAVORED ONES?
......
MINAMI-SAN.
MMH?
THERE'S SOMETHING I NEED TO DO...

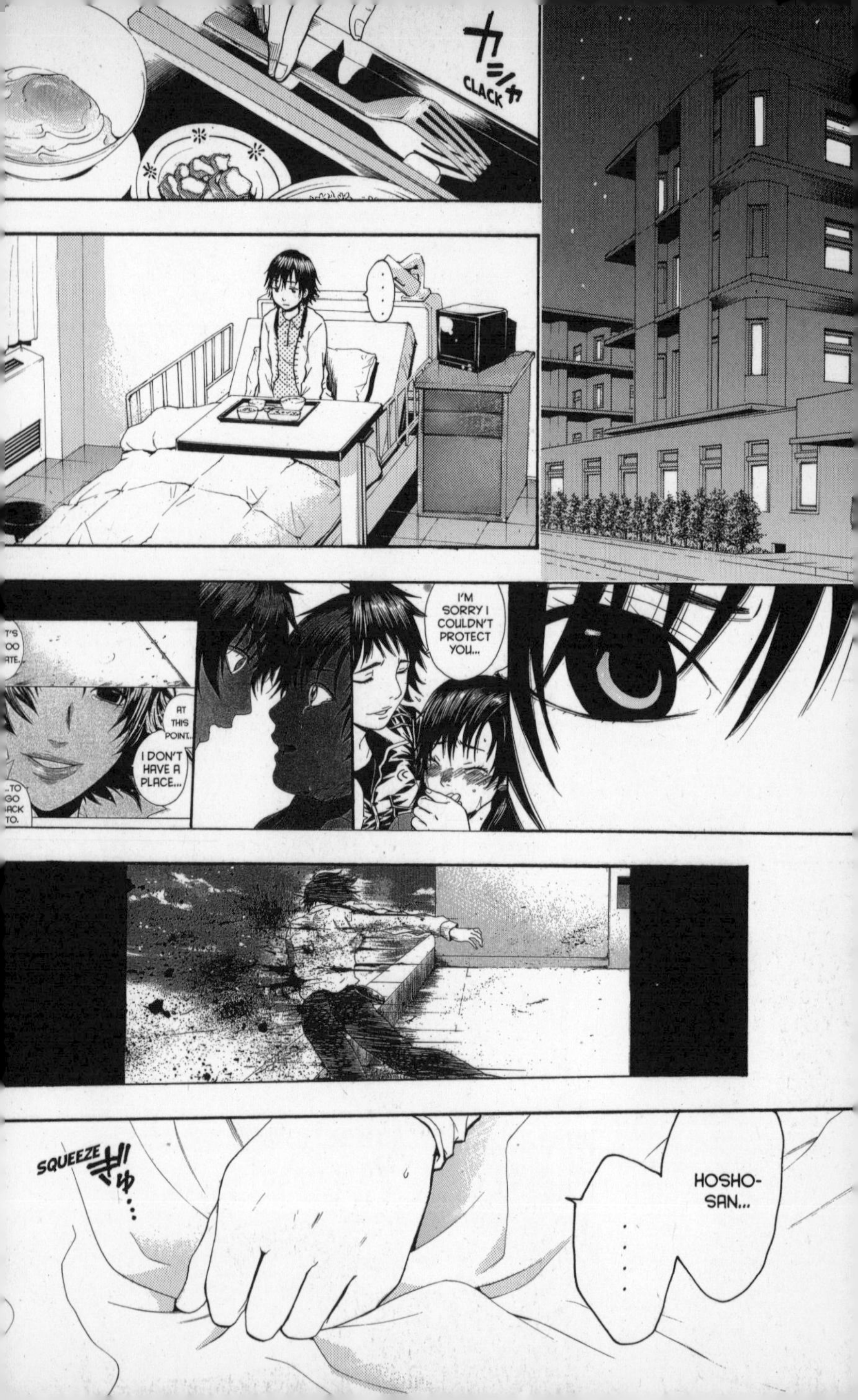

カシャ
CLACK
...
I'M SORRY I COULDN'T PROTECT YOU...
AT THIS POINT...
I DON'T HAVE A PLACE...
T'S OO ATE.
..TO GO ACK TO.
HOSHO-SAN...
....
SQUEEZE
ぎゅ...

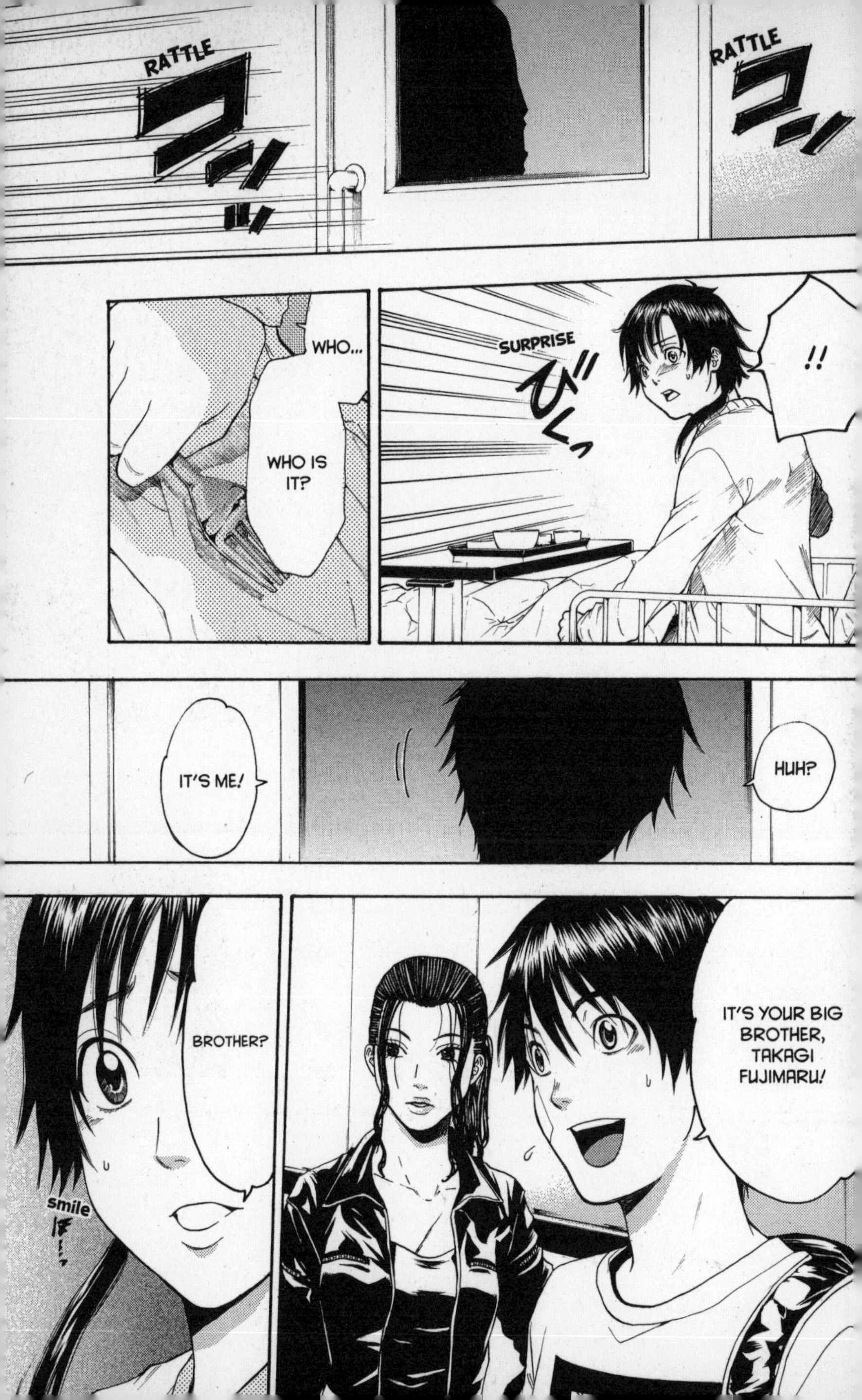
RATTLE
RATTLE
!!
SURPRISE
WHO...
WHO IS IT?
HUH?
IT'S ME!
IT'S YOUR BIG BROTHER, TAKAGI FUJIMARU!
BROTHER?
smile

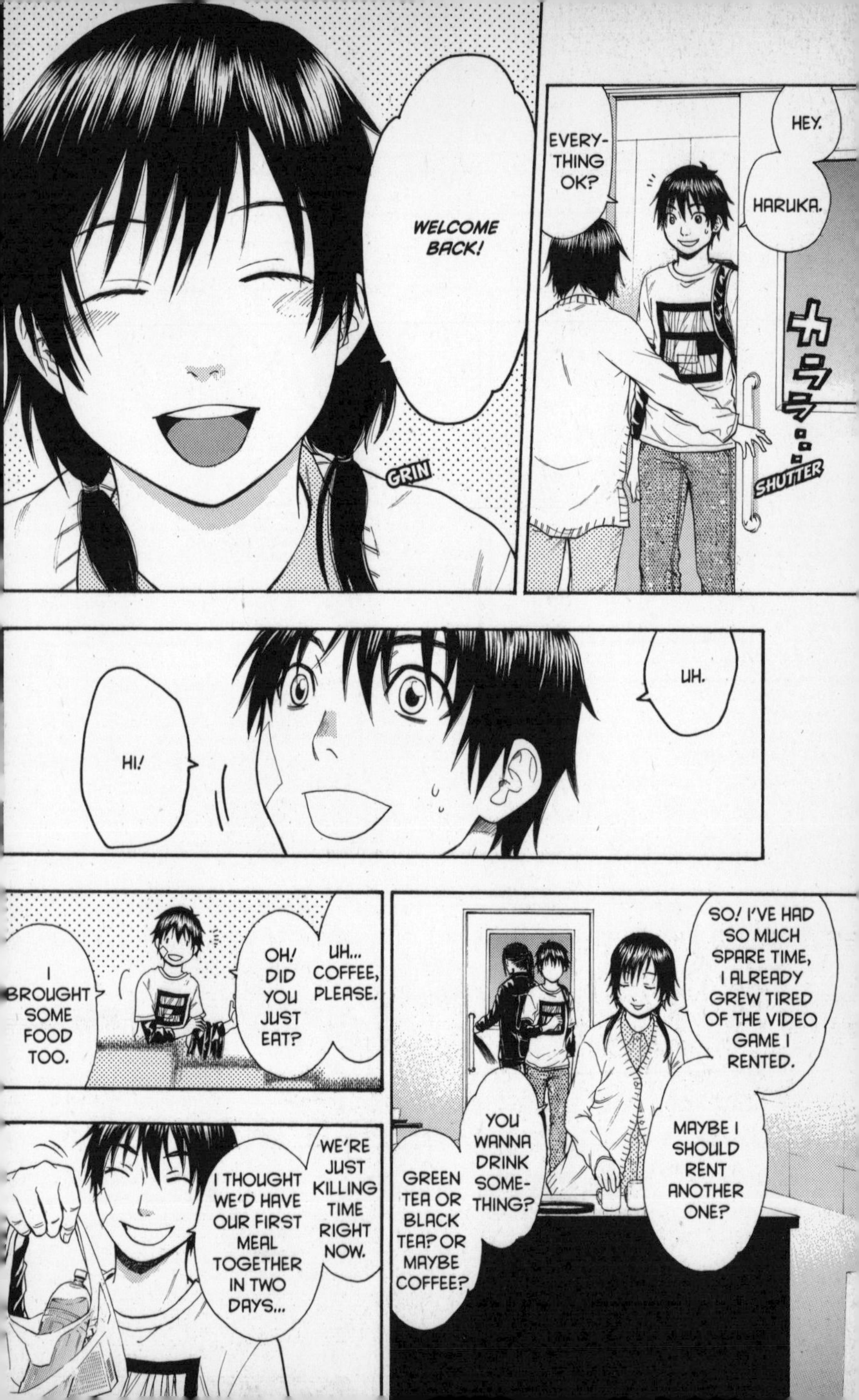
HEY.
HARUKA.
EVERY-THING OK?
カララ…
SHUTTER
WELCOME BACK!
GRIN
UH.
HI!
SO! I'VE HAD SO MUCH SPARE TIME, I ALREADY GREW TIRED OF THE VIDEO GAME I RENTED.
MAYBE I SHOULD RENT ANOTHER ONE?
YOU WANNA DRINK SOME-THING?
GREEN TEA OR BLACK TEA? OR MAYBE COFFEE?
UH... COFFEE, PLEASE.
OH! DID YOU JUST EAT?
I BROUGHT SOME FOOD TOO.
WE'RE JUST KILLING TIME RIGHT NOW.
I THOUGHT WE'D HAVE OUR FIRST MEAL TOGETHER IN TWO DAYS...

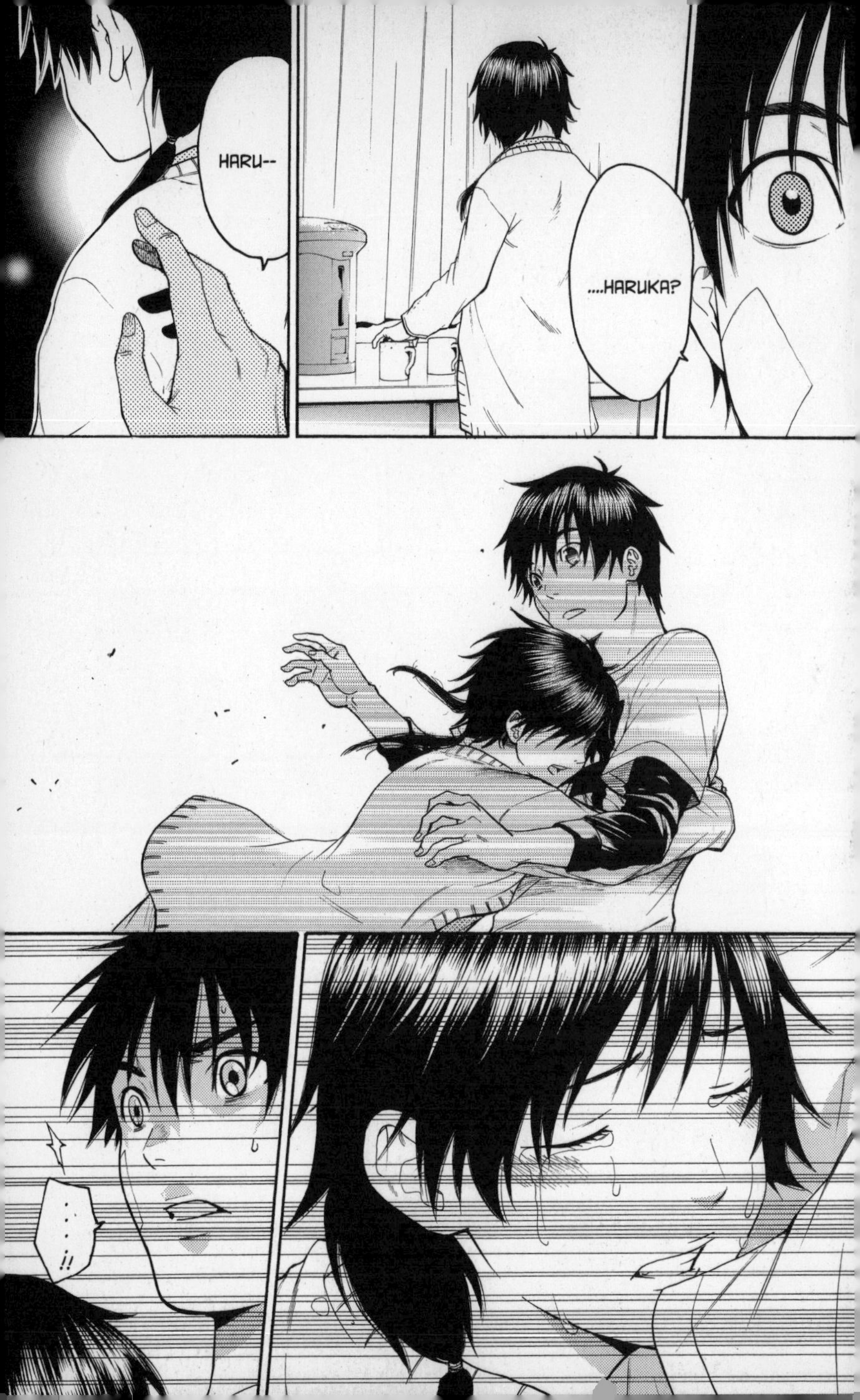
....HARUKA?
HARU--
...!!

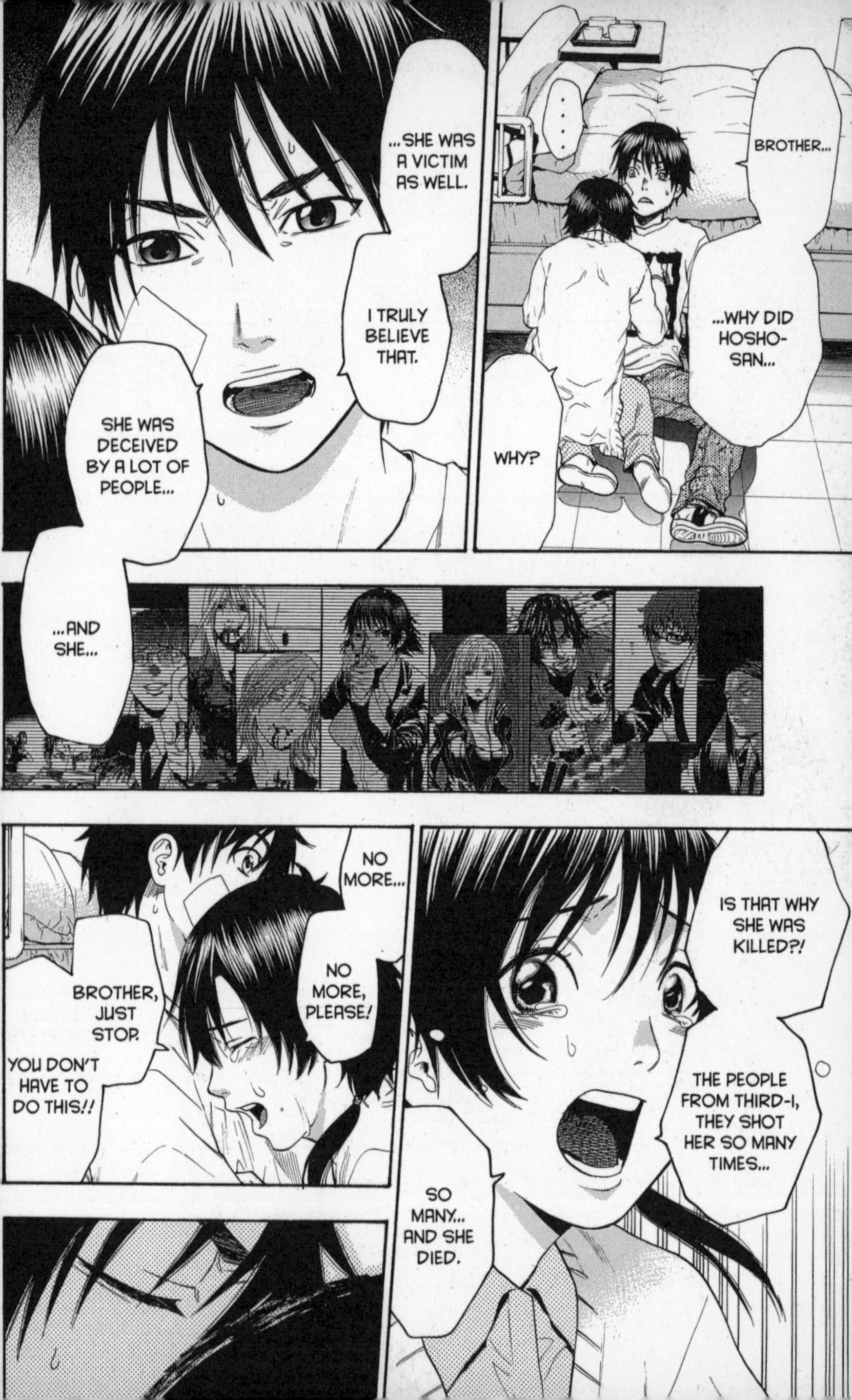
BROTHER...
....
...WHY DID HOSHO-SAN...
WHY?
...SHE WAS A VICTIM AS WELL.
I TRULY BELIEVE THAT.
SHE WAS DECEIVED BY A LOT OF PEOPLE...
...AND SHE...
IS THAT WHY SHE WAS KILLED?!
THE PEOPLE FROM THIRD-I, THEY SHOT HER SO MANY TIMES...
SO MANY... AND SHE DIED.
NO MORE...
NO MORE, PLEASE!
BROTHER, JUST STOP.
YOU DON'T HAVE TO DO THIS!!

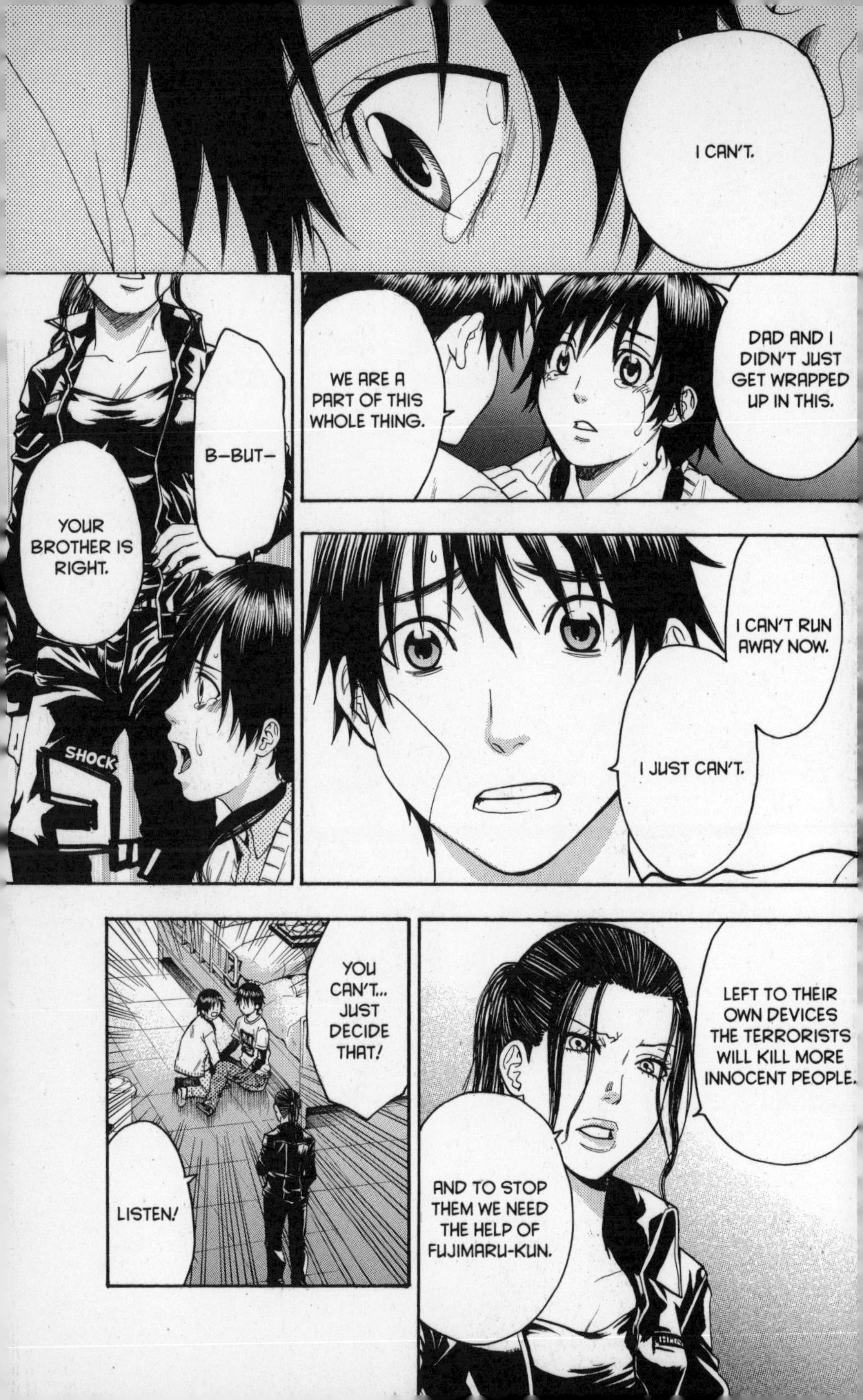
I CAN'T.
DAD AND I DIDN'T JUST GET WRAPPED UP IN THIS.
WE ARE A PART OF THIS WHOLE THING.
I CAN'T RUN AWAY NOW.
I JUST CAN'T.
B—BUT—
YOUR BROTHER IS RIGHT.
SHOCK
LEFT TO THEIR OWN DEVICES THE TERRORISTS WILL KILL MORE INNOCENT PEOPLE.
AND TO STOP THEM WE NEED THE HELP OF FUJIMARU-KUN.
YOU CAN'T... JUST DECIDE THAT!
LISTEN!

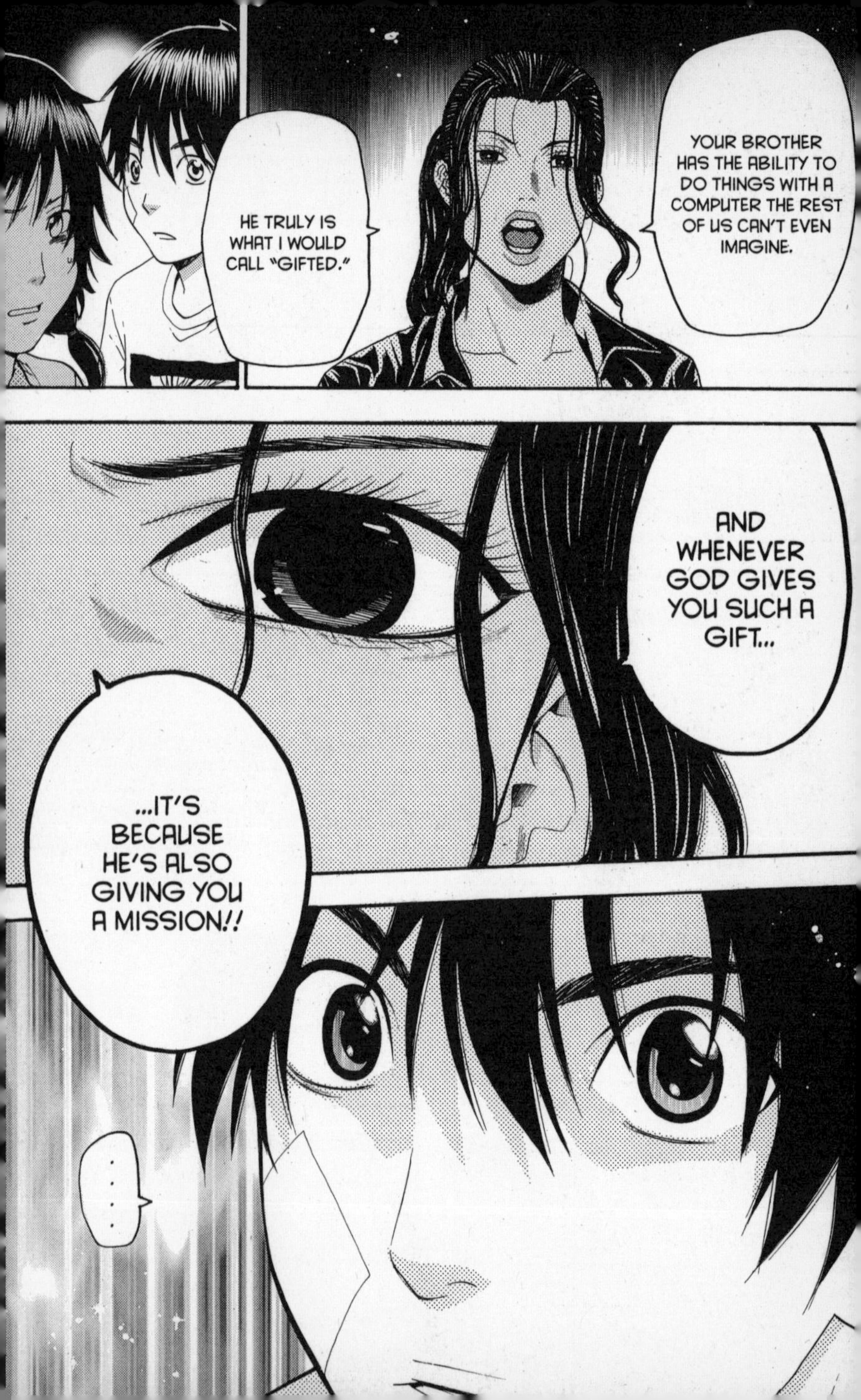
YOUR BROTHER HAS THE ABILITY TO DO THINGS WITH A COMPUTER THE REST OF US CAN'T EVEN IMAGINE.
HE TRULY IS WHAT I WOULD CALL "GIFTED."
AND WHENEVER GOD GIVES YOU SUCH A GIFT...
...IT'S BECAUSE HE'S ALSO GIVING YOU A MISSION!!
.....

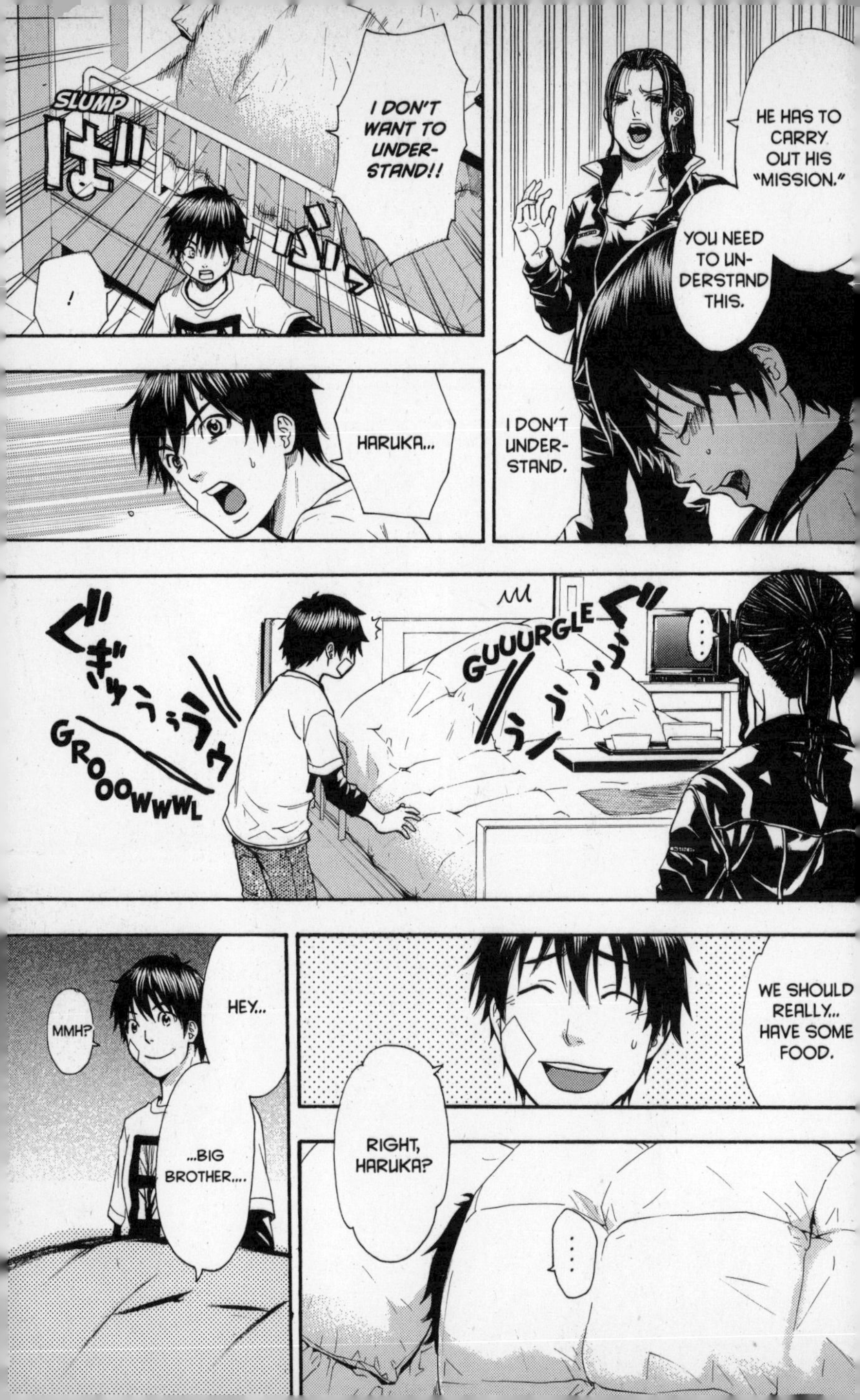
HE HAS TO CARRY OUT HIS "MISSION."
YOU NEED TO UNDERSTAND THIS.
I DON'T UNDERSTAND.
SLUMP
I DON'T WANT TO UNDERSTAND!!
!
HARUKA...
GUUURGLE
...
GROOOWWWL
WE SHOULD REALLY... HAVE SOME FOOD.
RIGHT, HARUKA?
....
HEY...
MMH?
...BIG BROTHER....

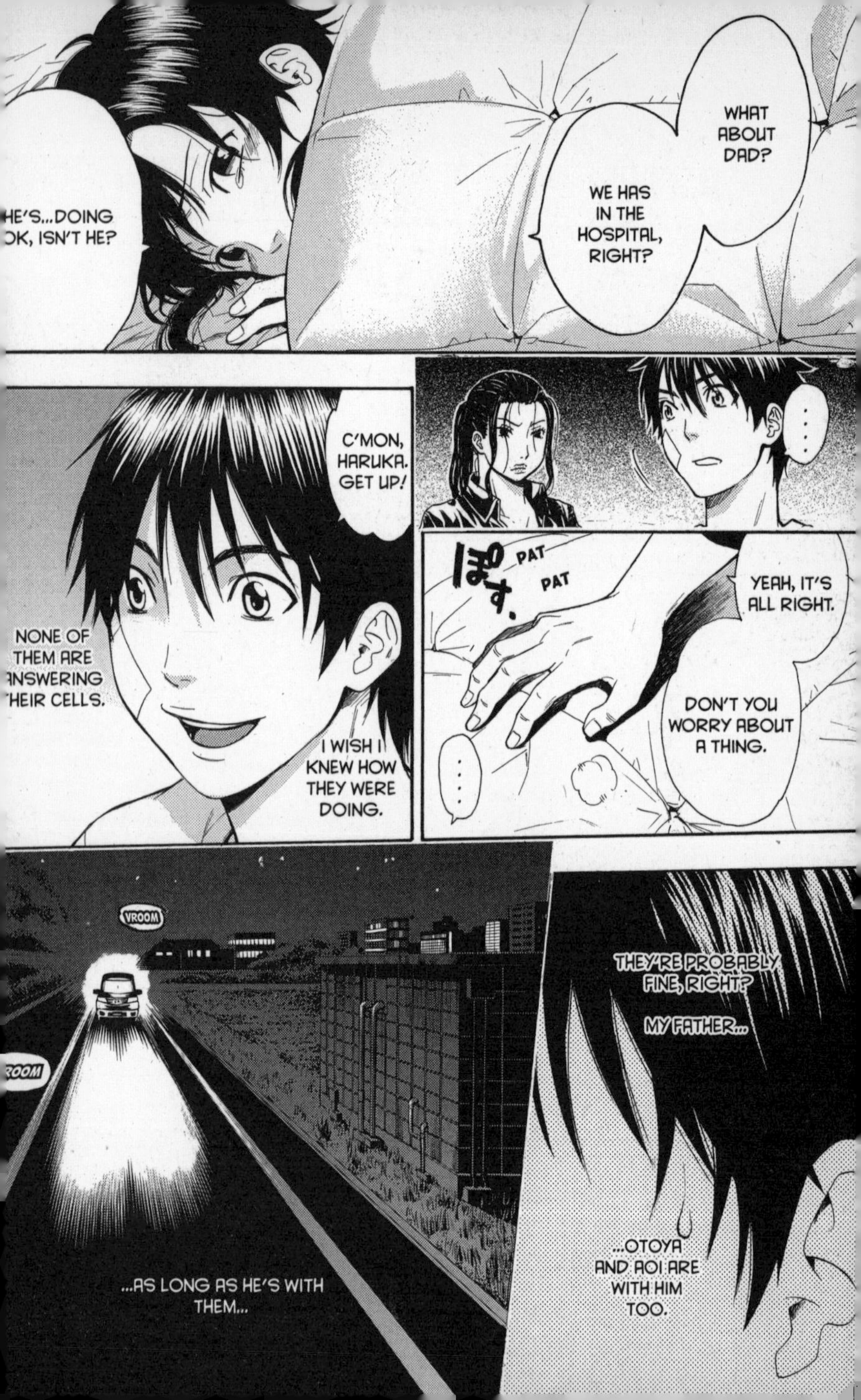
WHAT ABOUT DAD?
WE HAS IN THE HOSPITAL, RIGHT?
HE'S...DOING OK, ISN'T HE?
...
ぽす。
PAT
PAT
YEAH, IT'S ALL RIGHT.
DON'T YOU WORRY ABOUT A THING.
...
C'MON, HARUKA. GET UP!
I WISH I KNEW HOW THEY WERE DOING.
NONE OF THEM ARE ANSWERING THEIR CELLS.
THEY'RE PROBABLY FINE, RIGHT?
MY FATHER...
...OTOYA AND AOI ARE WITH HIM TOO.
VROOM
ROOM
...AS LONG AS HE'S WITH THEM...

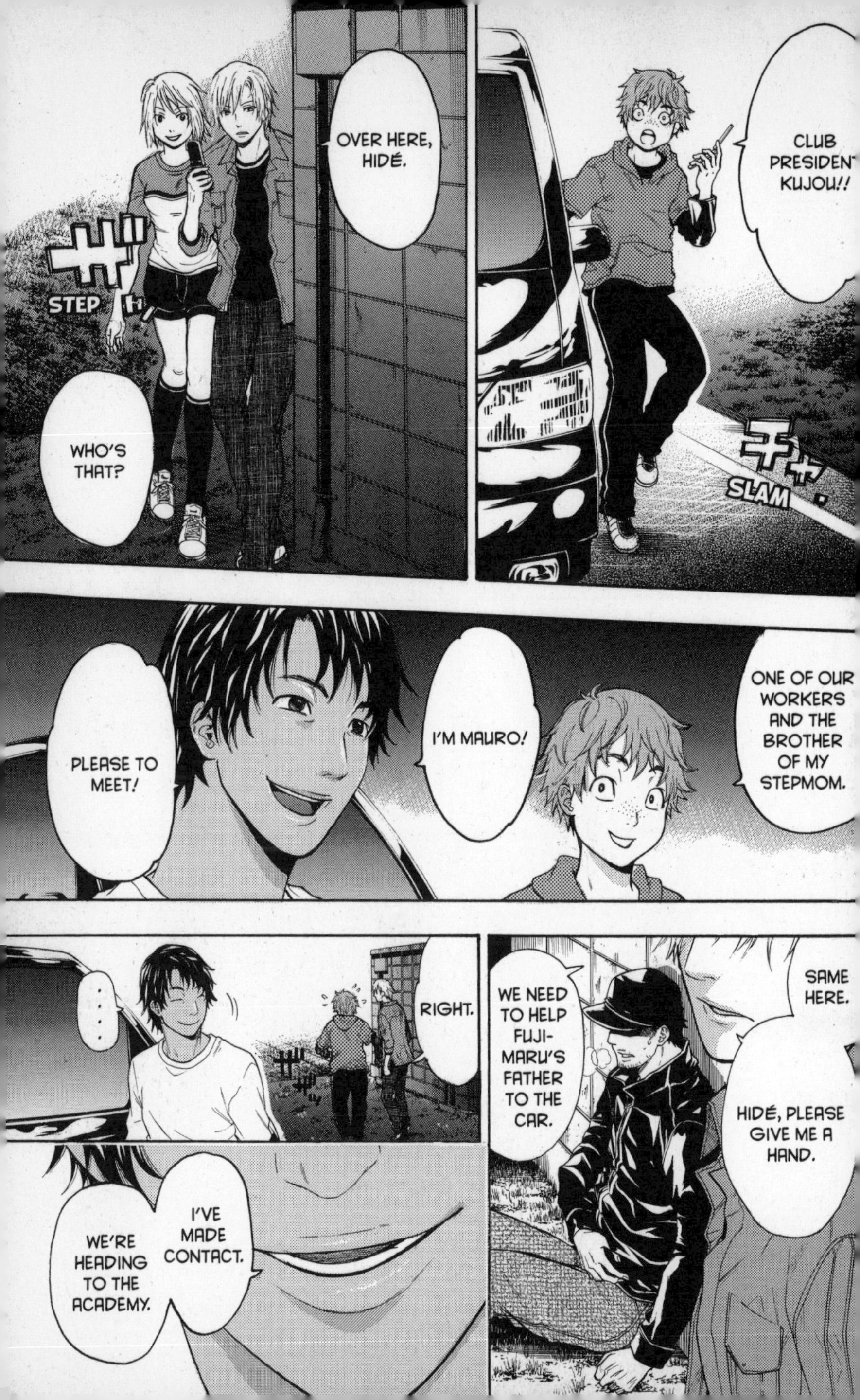
CLUB PRESIDEN KUJOU!!
SLAM
OVER HERE, HIDÉ.
STEP
WHO'S THAT?
ONE OF OUR WORKERS AND THE BROTHER OF MY STEPMOM.
I'M MAURO!
PLEASE TO MEET!
SAME HERE.
WE NEED TO HELP FUJI-MARU'S FATHER TO THE CAR.
HIDÉ, PLEASE GIVE ME A HAND.
RIGHT.
. . . .
I'VE MADE CONTACT.
WE'RE HEADING TO THE ACADEMY.

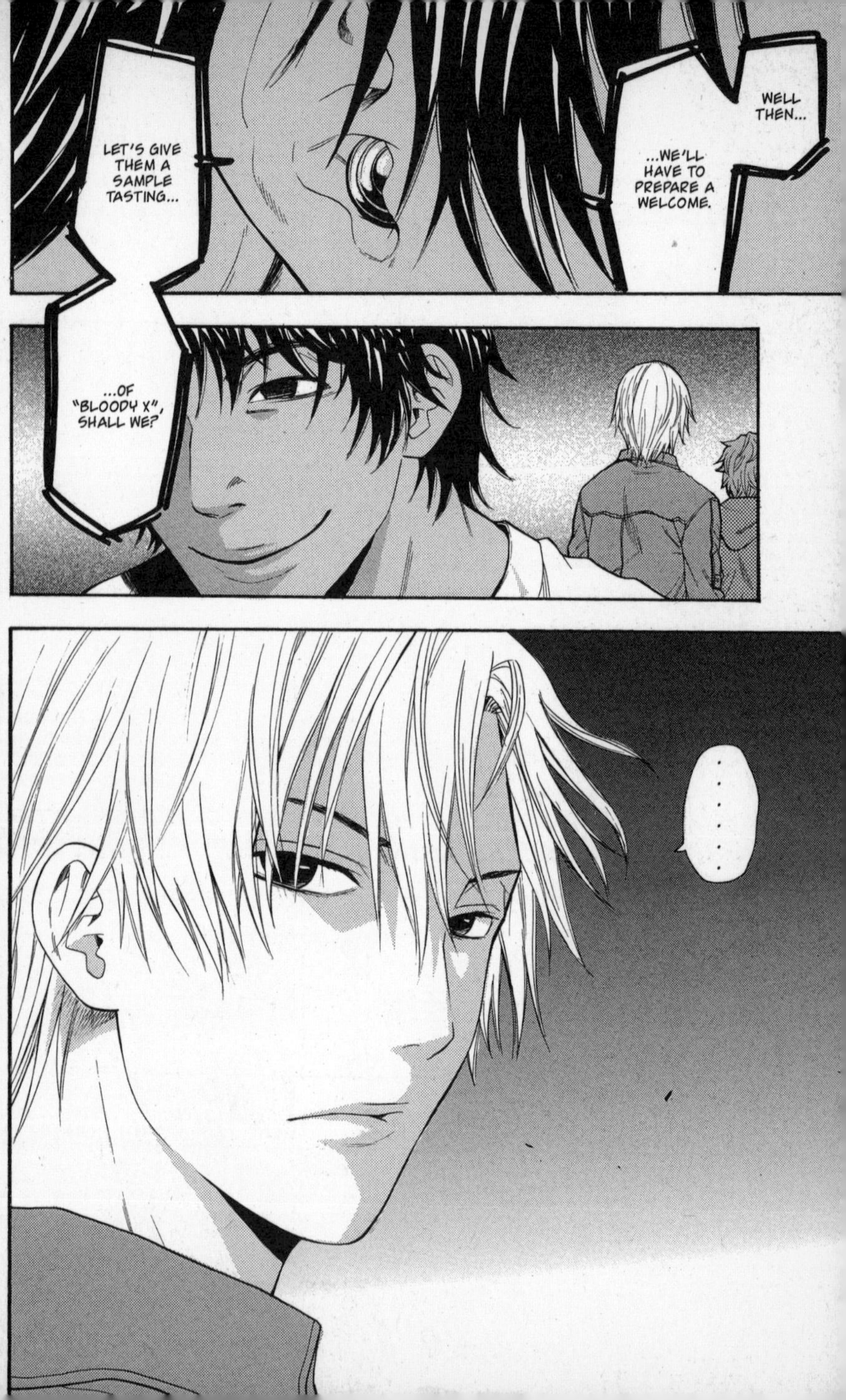
WELL THEN...
...WE'LL HAVE TO PREPARE A WELCOME.
LET'S GIVE THEM A SAMPLE TASTING...
...OF "BLOODY X", SHALL WE?
......

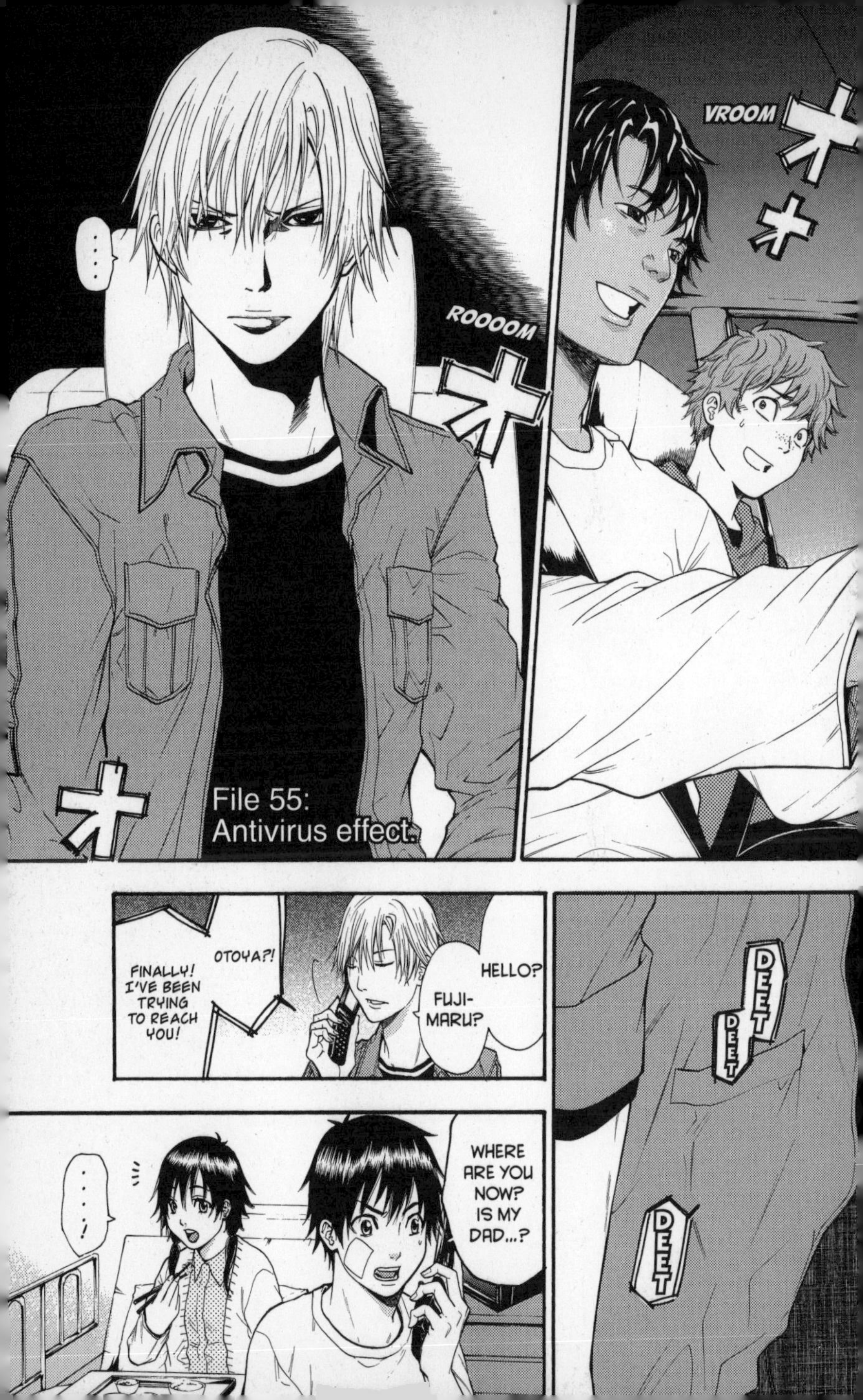
VROOM
ROOOOM
. . . .
File 55:
Antivirus effect.
DEET
DEET
DEET
HELLO?
FUJI-MARU?
OTOYA?!
FINALLY! I'VE BEEN TRYING TO REACH YOU!
WHERE ARE YOU NOW? IS MY DAD...?
. . . !

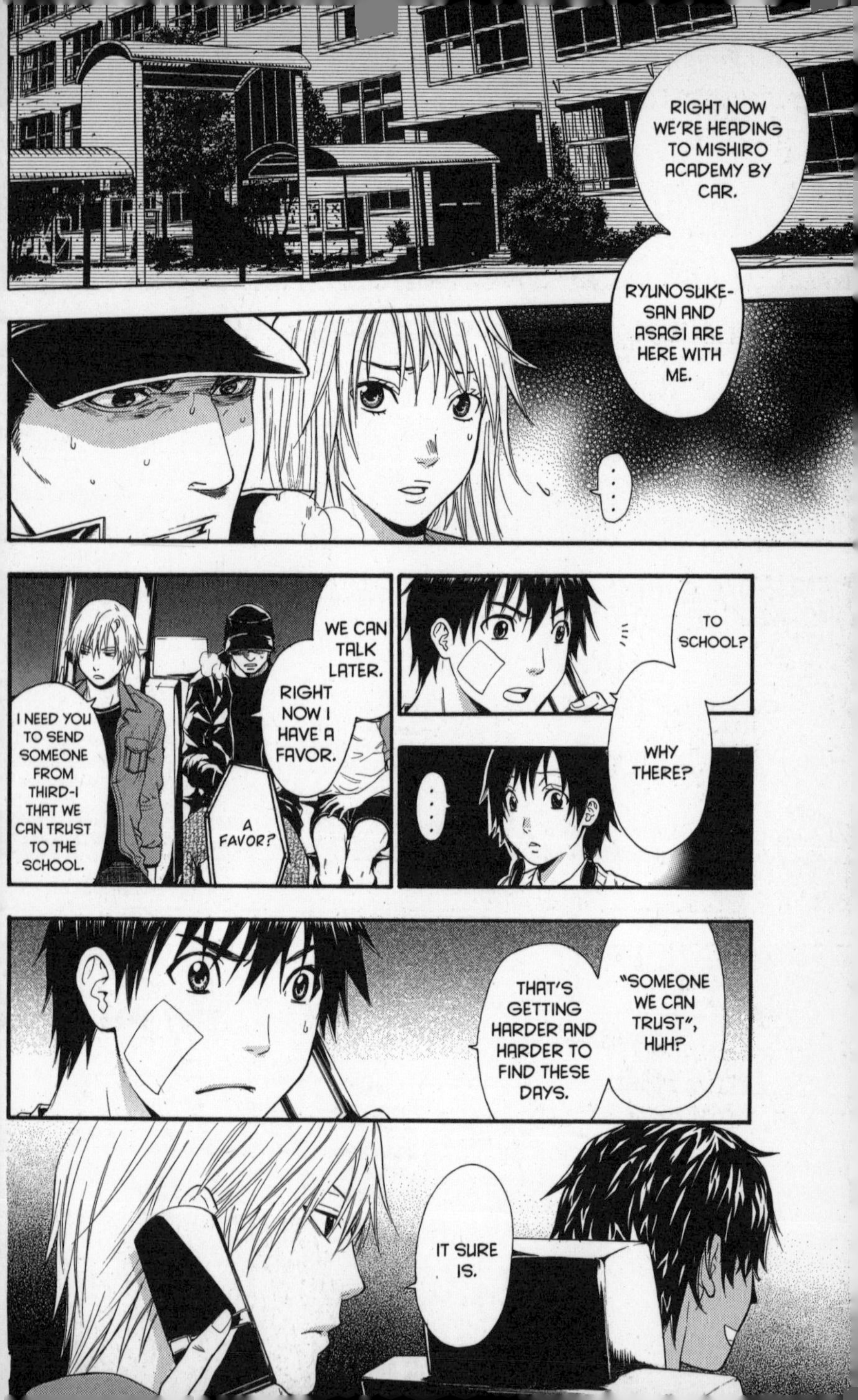
RIGHT NOW WE'RE HEADING TO MISHIRO ACADEMY BY CAR.
RYUNOSUKE-SAN AND ASAGI ARE HERE WITH ME.
...
TO SCHOOL?
WHY THERE?
...
WE CAN TALK LATER.
RIGHT NOW I HAVE A FAVOR.
A FAVOR?
I NEED YOU TO SEND SOMEONE FROM THIRD-I THAT WE CAN TRUST TO THE SCHOOL.
"SOMEONE WE CAN TRUST", HUH?
THAT'S GETTING HARDER AND HARDER TO FIND THESE DAYS.
IT SURE IS.

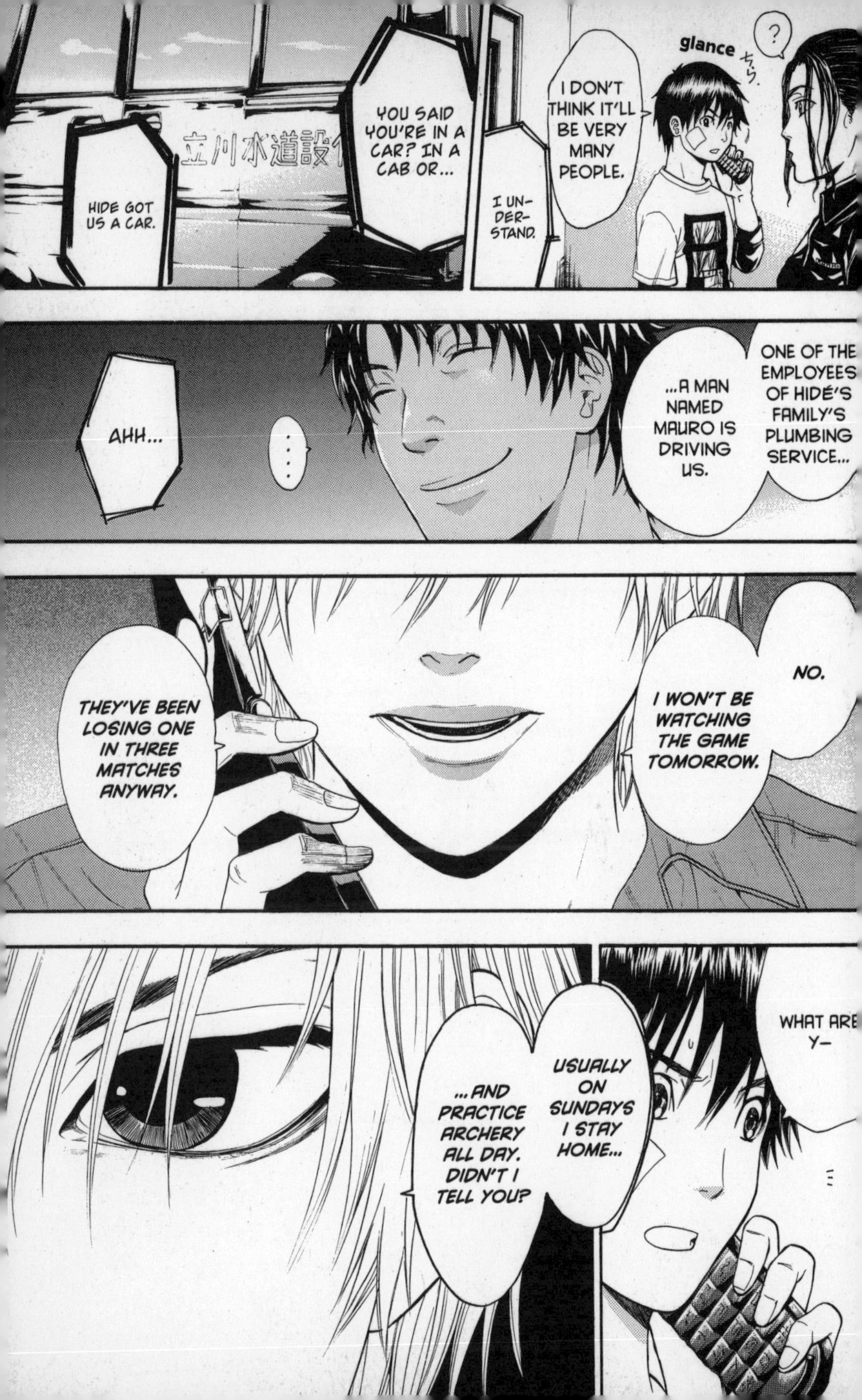
?
glance
I DON'T THINK IT'LL BE VERY MANY PEOPLE.
I UNDERSTAND.
YOU SAID YOU'RE IN A CAR? IN A CAB OR...
立川水道設
HIDE GOT US A CAR.
ONE OF THE EMPLOYEES OF HIDÉ'S FAMILY'S PLUMBING SERVICE...
...A MAN NAMED MAURO IS DRIVING US.
....
AHH...
NO.
I WON'T BE WATCHING THE GAME TOMORROW.
THEY'VE BEEN LOSING ONE IN THREE MATCHES ANYWAY.
WHAT ARE Y—
USUALLY ON SUNDAYS I STAY HOME...
...AND PRACTICE ARCHERY ALL DAY. DIDN'T I TELL YOU?

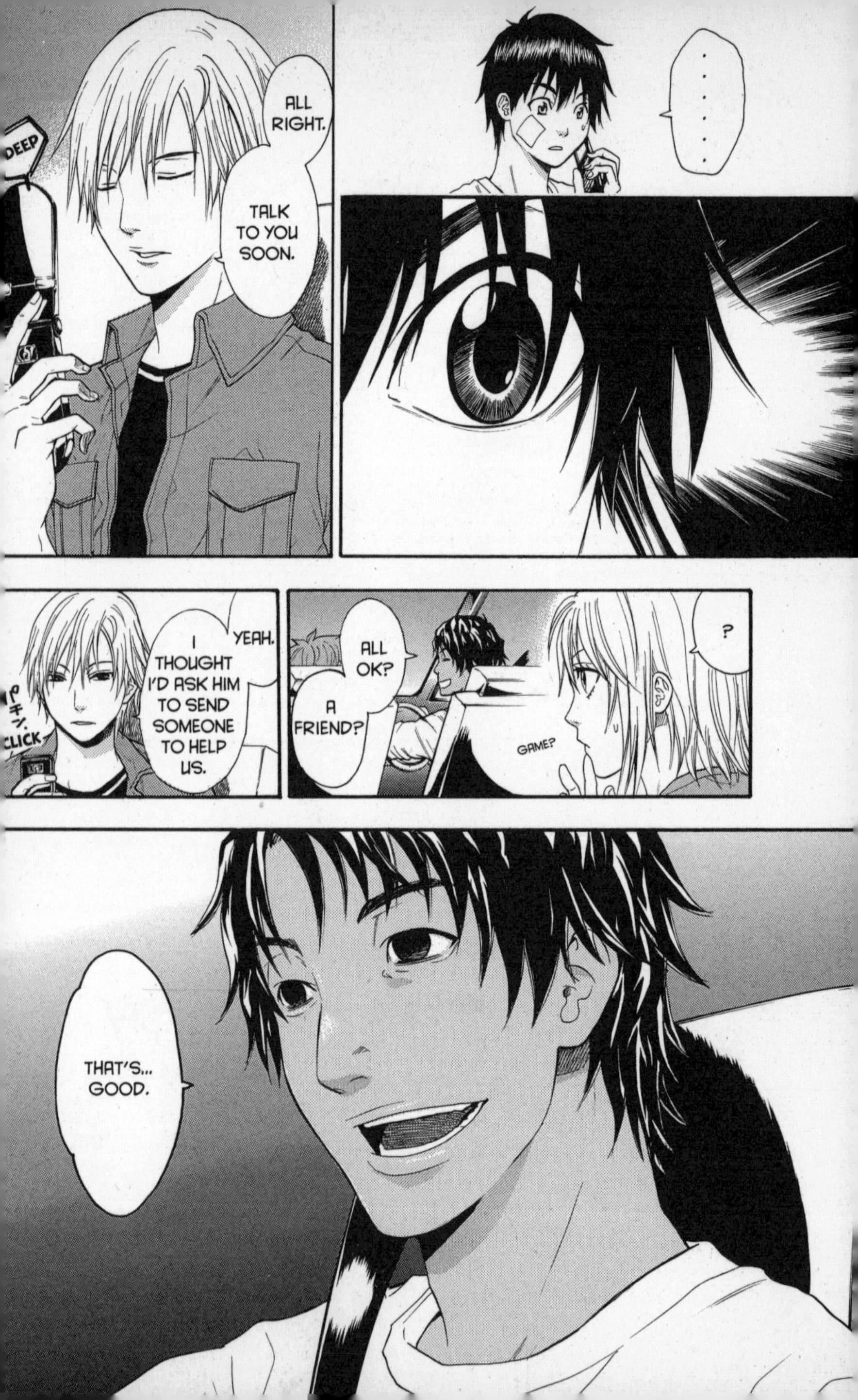
.....
ALL RIGHT.
TALK TO YOU SOON.
DEEP
?
GAME?
ALL OK?
A FRIEND?
YEAH.
I THOUGHT I'D ASK HIM TO SEND SOMEONE TO HELP US.
パチン
CLICK
THAT'S... GOOD.

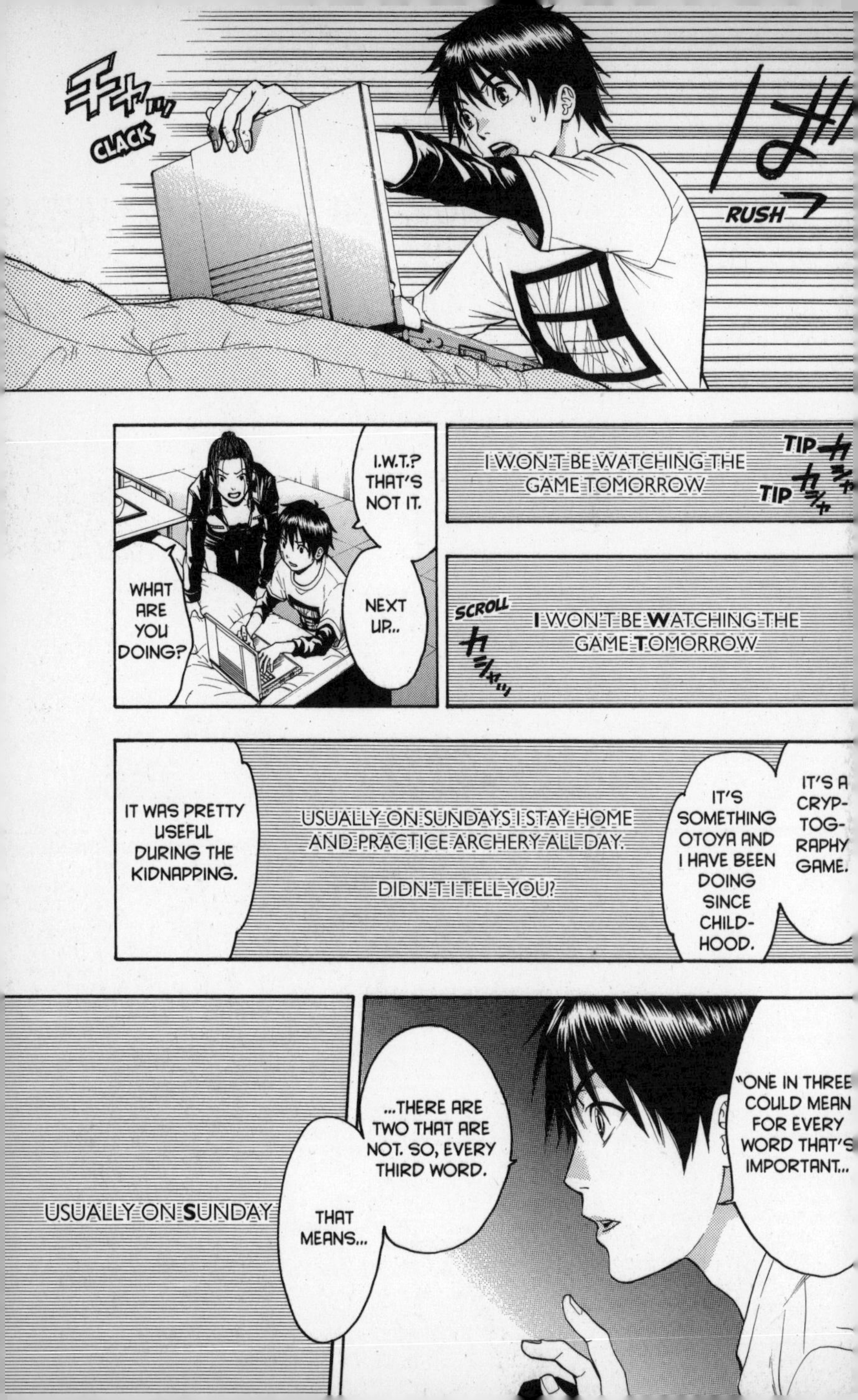
RUSH
CLACK
I WON'T BE WATCHING THE GAME TOMORROW
TIP
TIP
SCROLL
I WON'T BE WATCHING THE GAME TOMORROW
I.W.T.? THAT'S NOT IT.
NEXT UP...
WHAT ARE YOU DOING?
IT'S A CRYPTOGRAPHY GAME.
IT'S SOMETHING OTOYA AND I HAVE BEEN DOING SINCE CHILDHOOD.
USUALLY ON SUNDAYS I STAY HOME AND PRACTICE ARCHERY ALL DAY.
DIDN'T I TELL YOU?
IT WAS PRETTY USEFUL DURING THE KIDNAPPING.
"ONE IN THREE COULD MEAN FOR EVERY WORD THAT'S IMPORTANT...
...THERE ARE TWO THAT ARE NOT. SO, EVERY THIRD WORD.
THAT MEANS...
USUALLY ON SUNDAY

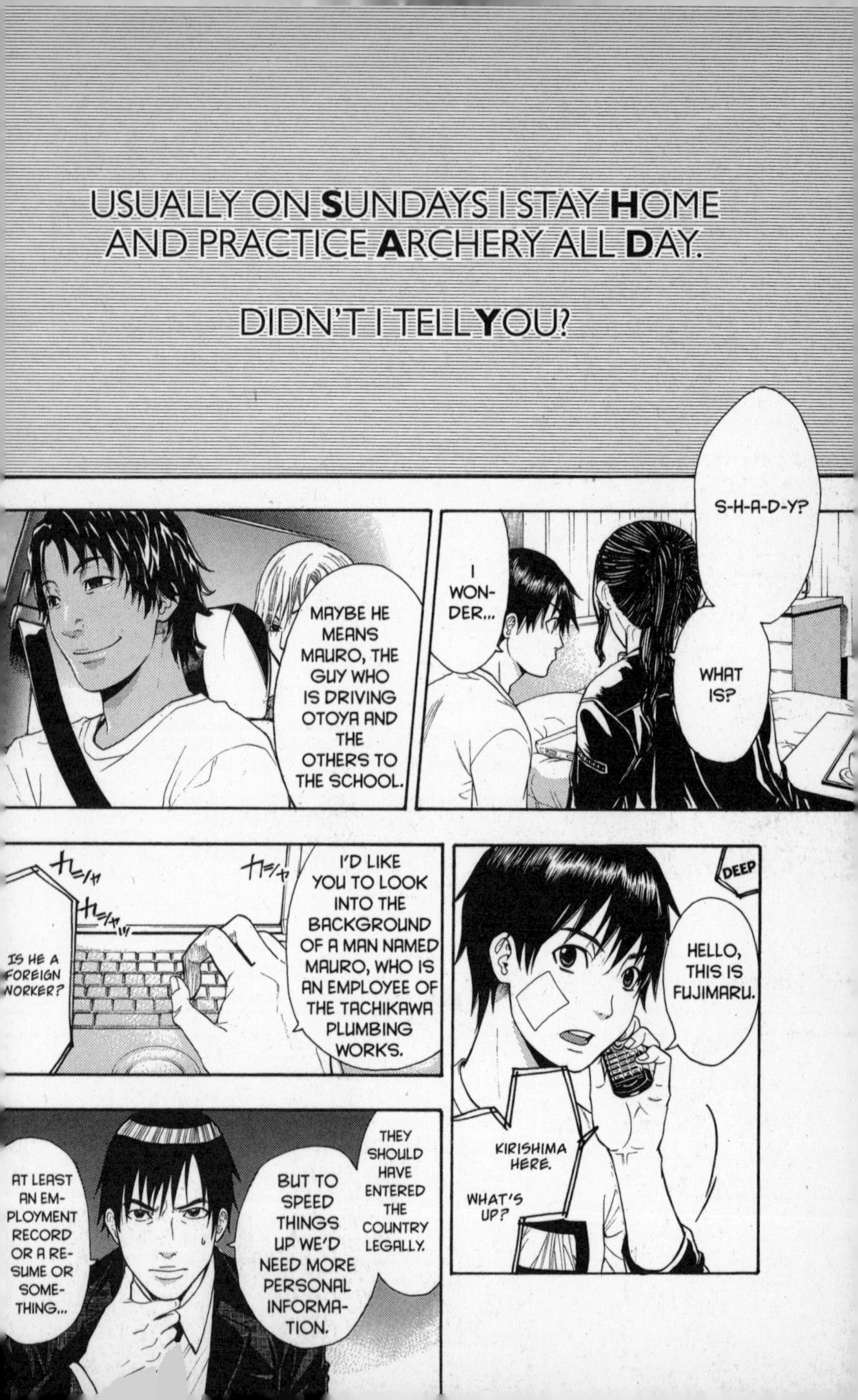
USUALLY ON SUNDAYS I STAY HOME AND PRACTICE ARCHERY ALL DAY.
DIDN'T I TELL YOU?
S-H-A-D-Y?
WHAT IS?
I WONDER...
MAYBE HE MEANS MAURO, THE GUY WHO IS DRIVING OTOYA AND THE OTHERS TO THE SCHOOL.
DEEP
HELLO, THIS IS FUJIMARU.
KIRISHIMA HERE.
WHAT'S UP?
カチャ
I'D LIKE YOU TO LOOK INTO THE BACKGROUND OF A MAN NAMED MAURO, WHO IS AN EMPLOYEE OF THE TACHIKAWA PLUMBING WORKS.
カチャ
カチャ
IS HE A FOREIGN WORKER?
THEY SHOULD HAVE ENTERED THE COUNTRY LEGALLY.
BUT TO SPEED THINGS UP WE'D NEED MORE PERSONAL INFORMATION.
AT LEAST AN EMPLOYMENT RECORD OR A RESUME OR SOMETHING...

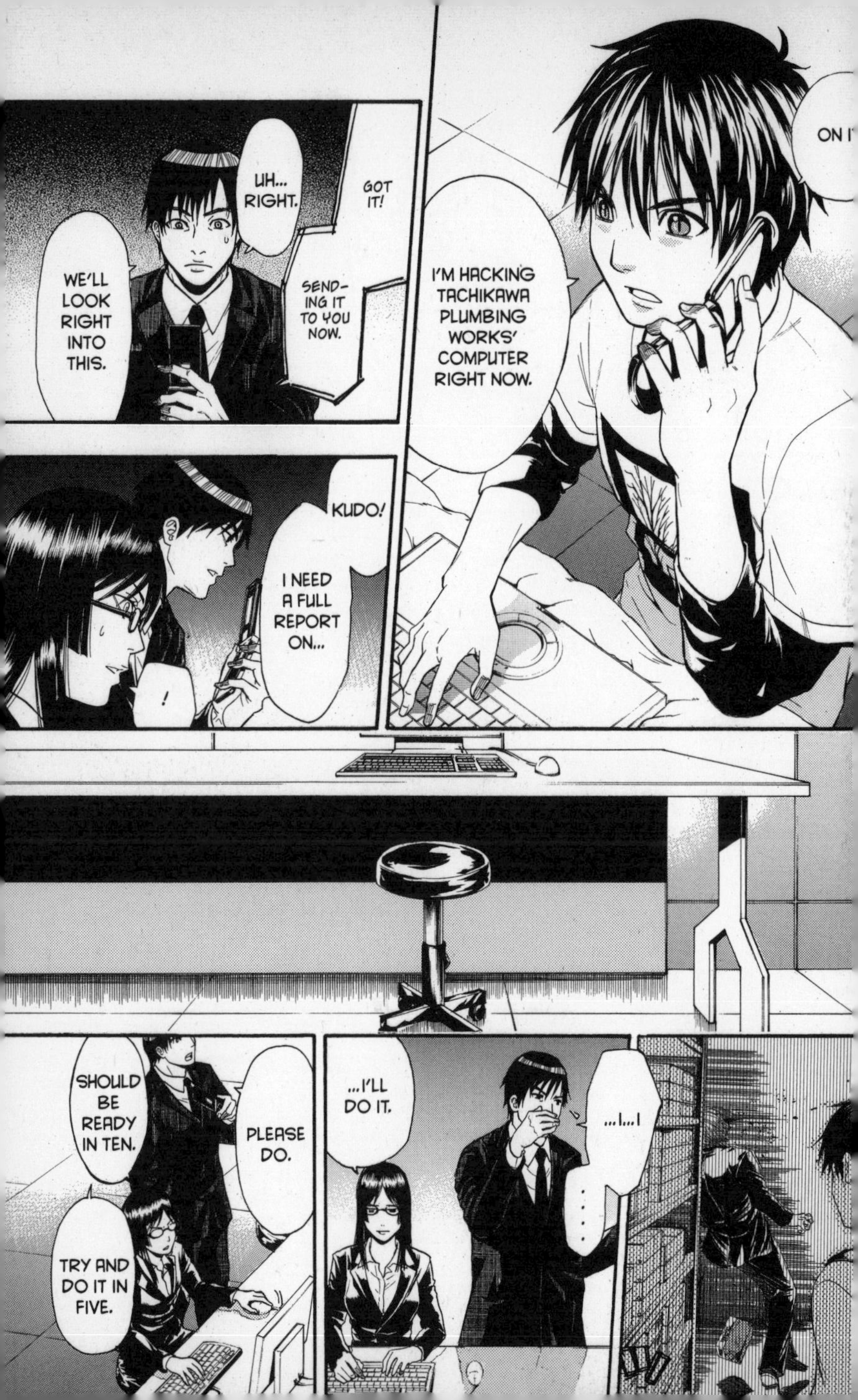
ON I'
I'M HACKING TACHIKAWA PLUMBING WORKS' COMPUTER RIGHT NOW.
GOT IT!
SENDING IT TO YOU NOW.
UH... RIGHT.
WE'LL LOOK RIGHT INTO THIS.
KUDO!
I NEED A FULL REPORT ON...
!
...I...I
......
...I'LL DO IT.
PLEASE DO.
SHOULD BE READY IN TEN.
TRY AND DO IT IN FIVE.

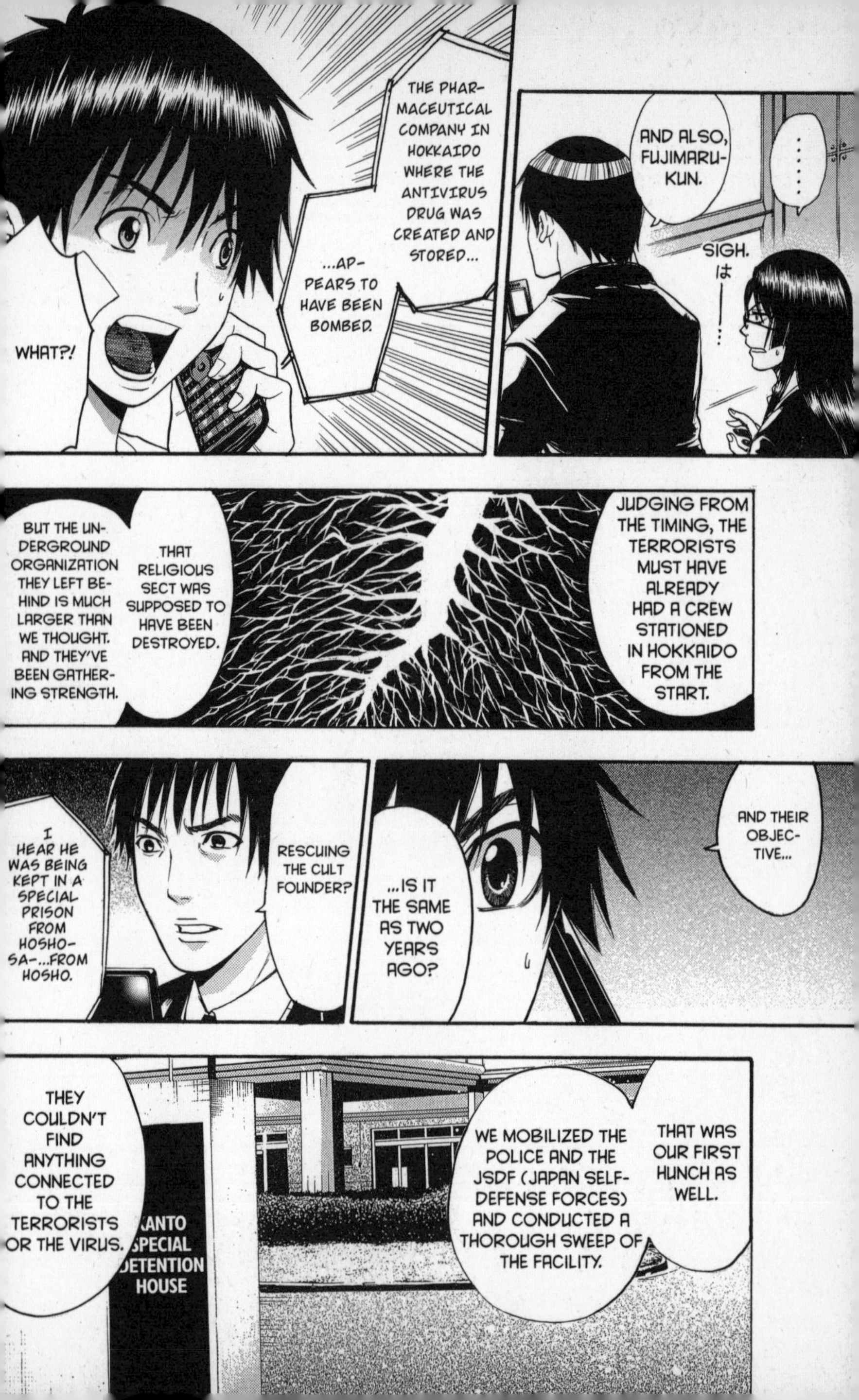
AND ALSO, FUJIMARU-KUN.
....
SIGH.
は—!
THE PHARMACEUTICAL COMPANY IN HOKKAIDO WHERE THE ANTIVIRUS DRUG WAS CREATED AND STORED...
...APPEARS TO HAVE BEEN BOMBED.
WHAT?!
JUDGING FROM THE TIMING, THE TERRORISTS MUST HAVE ALREADY HAD A CREW STATIONED IN HOKKAIDO FROM THE START.
THAT RELIGIOUS SECT WAS SUPPOSED TO HAVE BEEN DESTROYED.
BUT THE UNDERGROUND ORGANIZATION THEY LEFT BEHIND IS MUCH LARGER THAN WE THOUGHT. AND THEY'VE BEEN GATHERING STRENGTH.
AND THEIR OBJECTIVE...
...IS IT THE SAME AS TWO YEARS AGO?
RESCUING THE CULT FOUNDER?
I HEAR HE WAS BEING KEPT IN A SPECIAL PRISON FROM HOSHOSA-...FROM HOSHO.
THAT WAS OUR FIRST HUNCH AS WELL.
WE MOBILIZED THE POLICE AND THE JSDF (JAPAN SELF-DEFENSE FORCES) AND CONDUCTED A THOROUGH SWEEP OF THE FACILITY.
KANTO SPECIAL DETENTION HOUSE
THEY COULDN'T FIND ANYTHING CONNECTED TO THE TERRORISTS OR THE VIRUS.

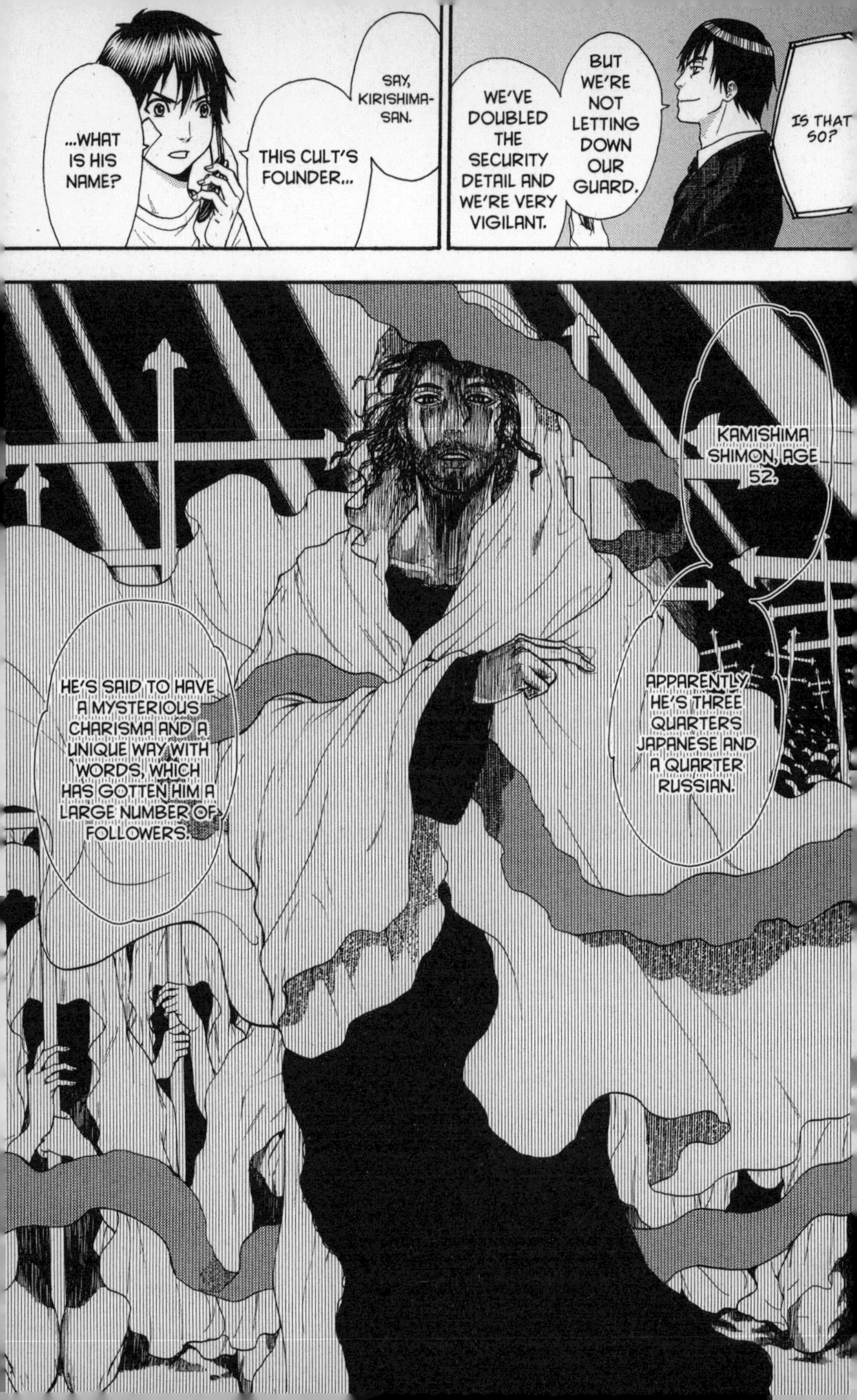
IS THAT SO?
BUT WE'RE NOT LETTING DOWN OUR GUARD.
WE'VE DOUBLED THE SECURITY DETAIL AND WE'RE VERY VIGILANT.
SAY, KIRISHIMA-SAN.
THIS CULT'S FOUNDER...
...WHAT IS HIS NAME?
KAMISHIMA SHIMON, AGE 52.
APPARENTLY HE'S THREE QUARTERS JAPANESE AND A QUARTER RUSSIAN.
HE'S SAID TO HAVE A MYSTERIOUS CHARISMA AND A UNIQUE WAY WITH WORDS, WHICH HAS GOTTEN HIM A LARGE NUMBER OF FOLLOWERS.

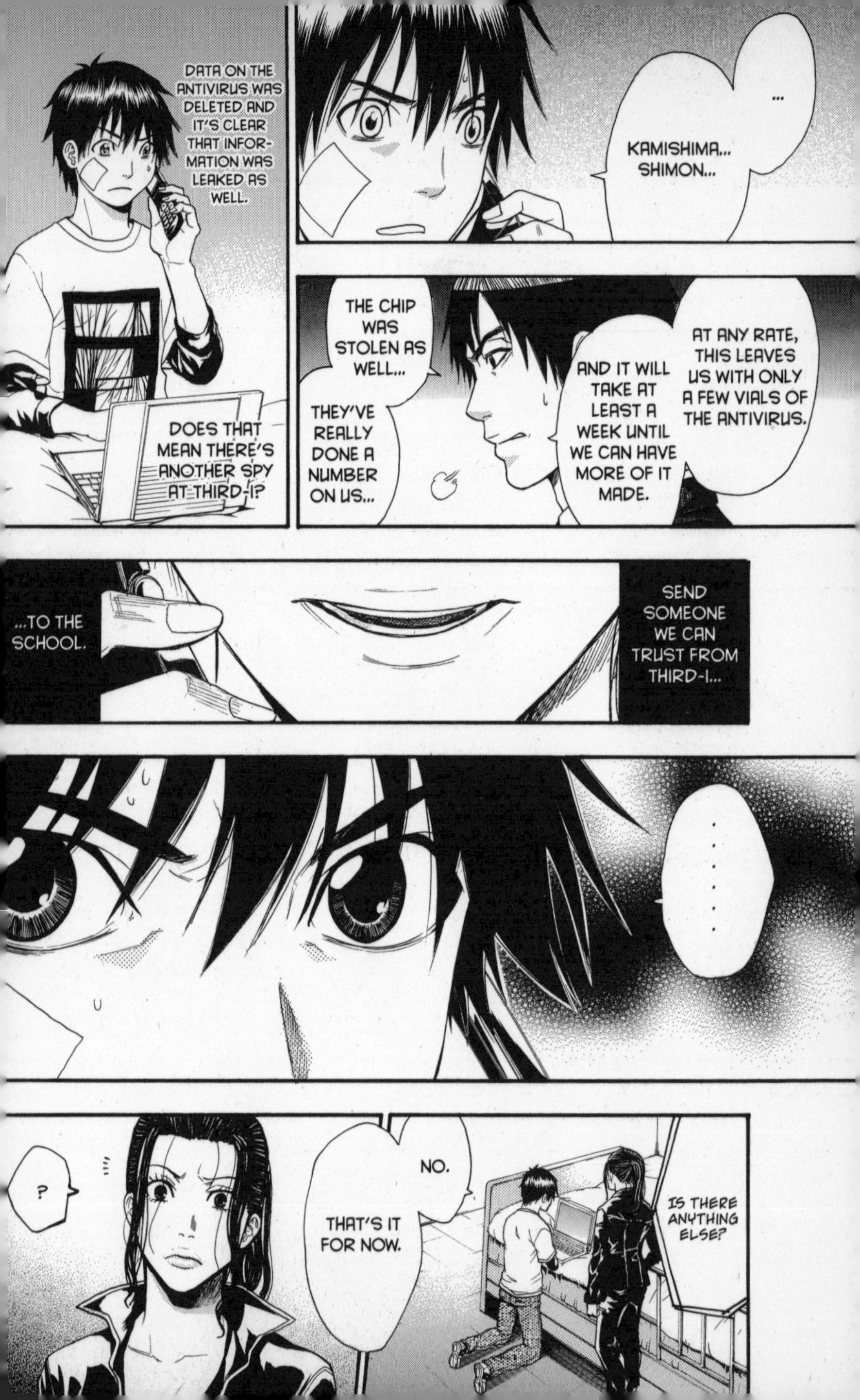
...
KAMISHIMA... SHIMON...
AT ANY RATE, THIS LEAVES US WITH ONLY A FEW VIALS OF THE ANTIVIRUS.
AND IT WILL TAKE AT LEAST A WEEK UNTIL WE CAN HAVE MORE OF IT MADE.
THE CHIP WAS STOLEN AS WELL...
THEY'VE REALLY DONE A NUMBER ON US...
DATA ON THE ANTIVIRUS WAS DELETED AND IT'S CLEAR THAT INFORMATION WAS LEAKED AS WELL.
DOES THAT MEAN THERE'S ANOTHER SPY AT THIRD-I?
SEND SOMEONE WE CAN TRUST FROM THIRD-I...
...TO THE SCHOOL.
......
IS THERE ANYTHING ELSE?
NO.
THAT'S IT FOR NOW.
?

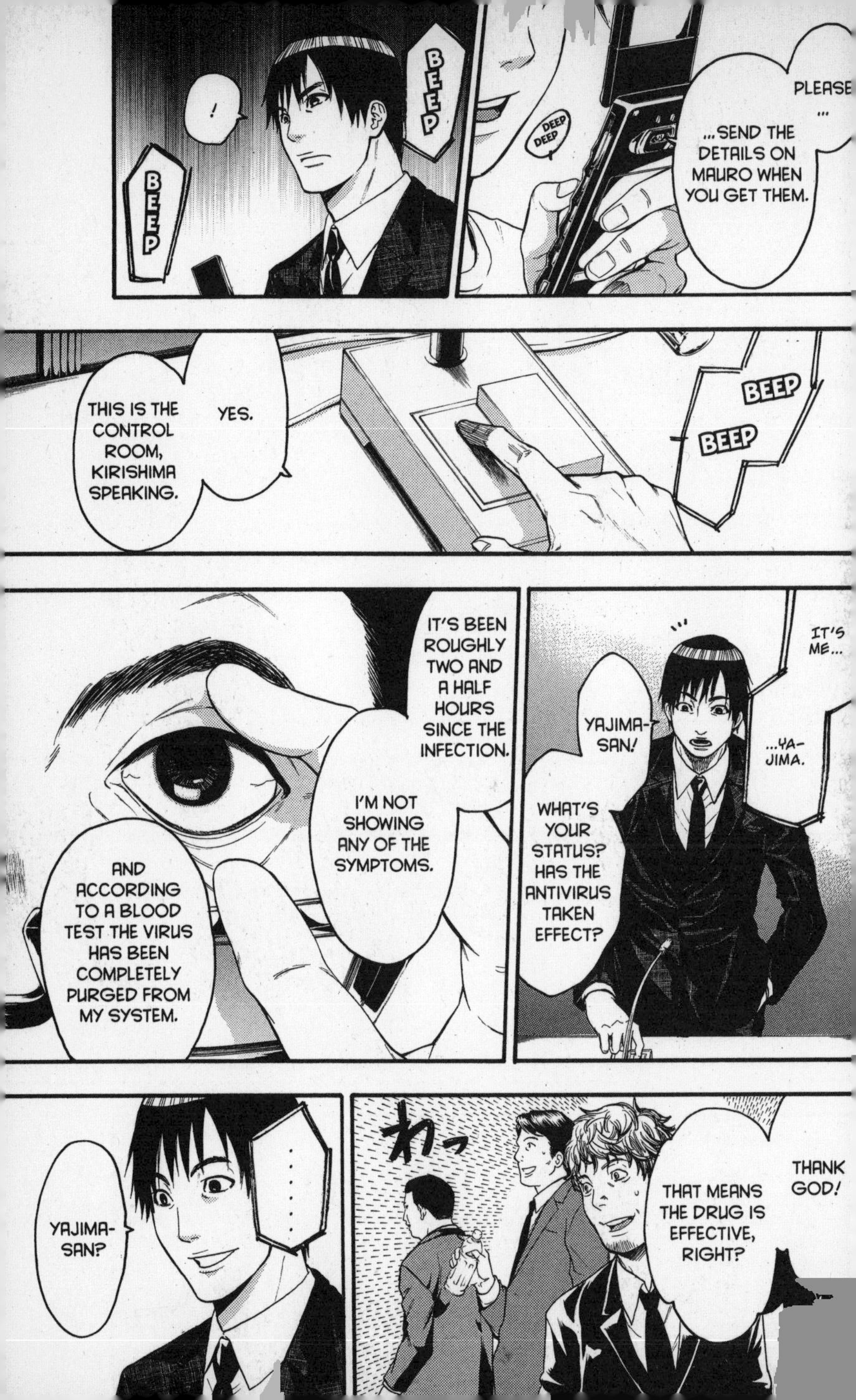
PLEASE ...
...SEND THE DETAILS ON MAURO WHEN YOU GET THEM.
DEEP DEEP
BEEP
BEEP
!
BEEP
BEEP
YES.
THIS IS THE CONTROL ROOM, KIRISHIMA SPEAKING.
IT'S ME...
...YA-JIMA.
YAJIMA-SAN!
WHAT'S YOUR STATUS? HAS THE ANTIVIRUS TAKEN EFFECT?
IT'S BEEN ROUGHLY TWO AND A HALF HOURS SINCE THE INFECTION.
I'M NOT SHOWING ANY OF THE SYMPTOMS.
AND ACCORDING TO A BLOOD TEST THE VIRUS HAS BEEN COMPLETELY PURGED FROM MY SYSTEM.
THANK GOD!
THAT MEANS THE DRUG IS EFFECTIVE, RIGHT?
わっ
......
YAJIMA-SAN?

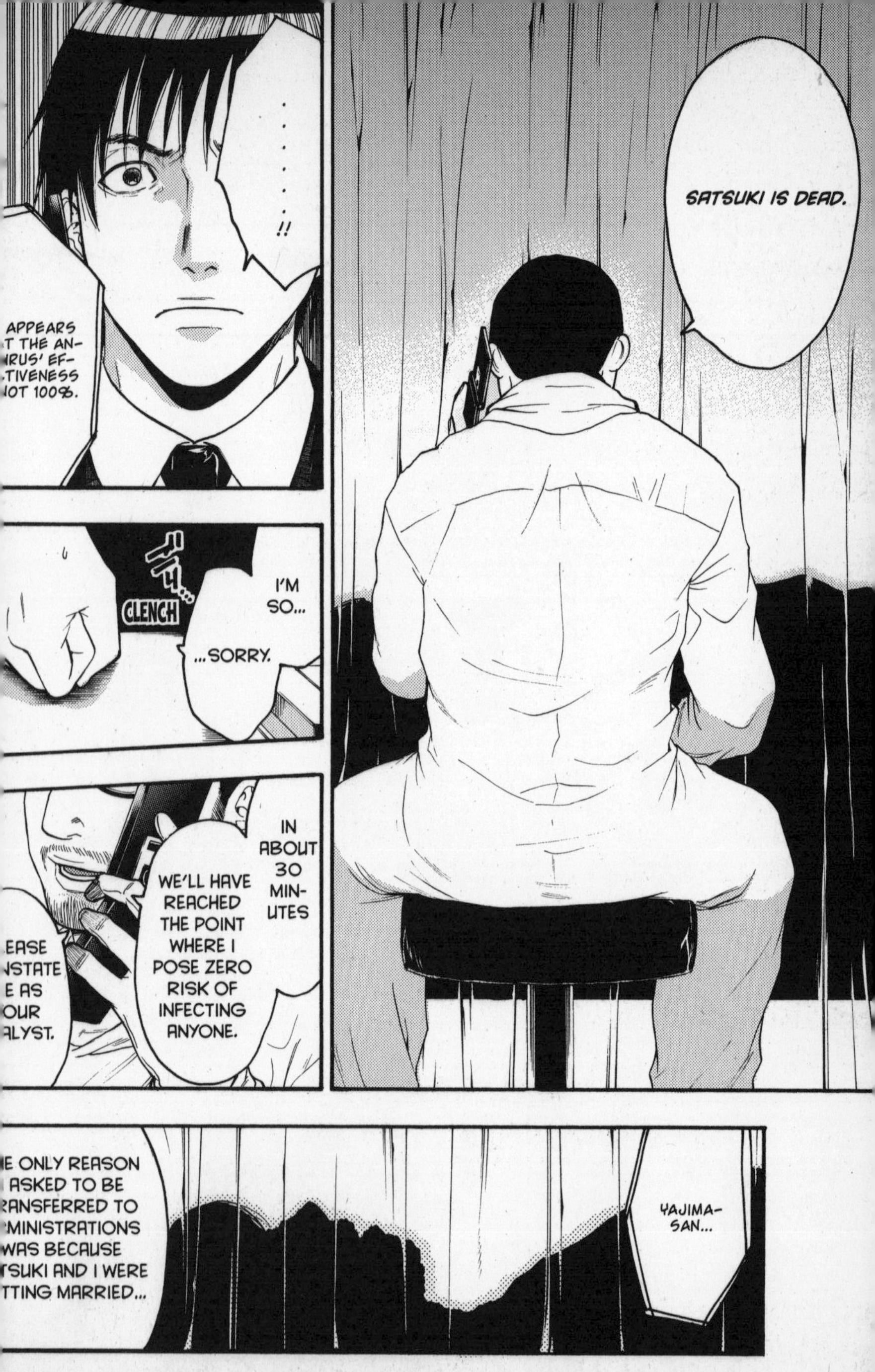
SATSUKI IS DEAD.
......!!
APPEARS T THE AN- IRUS' EF- TIVENESS OT 100%.
CLENCH
I'M SO...
...SORRY.
IN ABOUT 30 MIN- UTES
WE'LL HAVE REACHED THE POINT WHERE I POSE ZERO RISK OF INFECTING ANYONE.
EASE NSTATE E AS OUR ALYST.
YAJIMA-SAN...
E ONLY REASON ASKED TO BE RANSFERRED TO MINISTRATIONS WAS BECAUSE TSUKI AND I WERE TTING MARRIED...

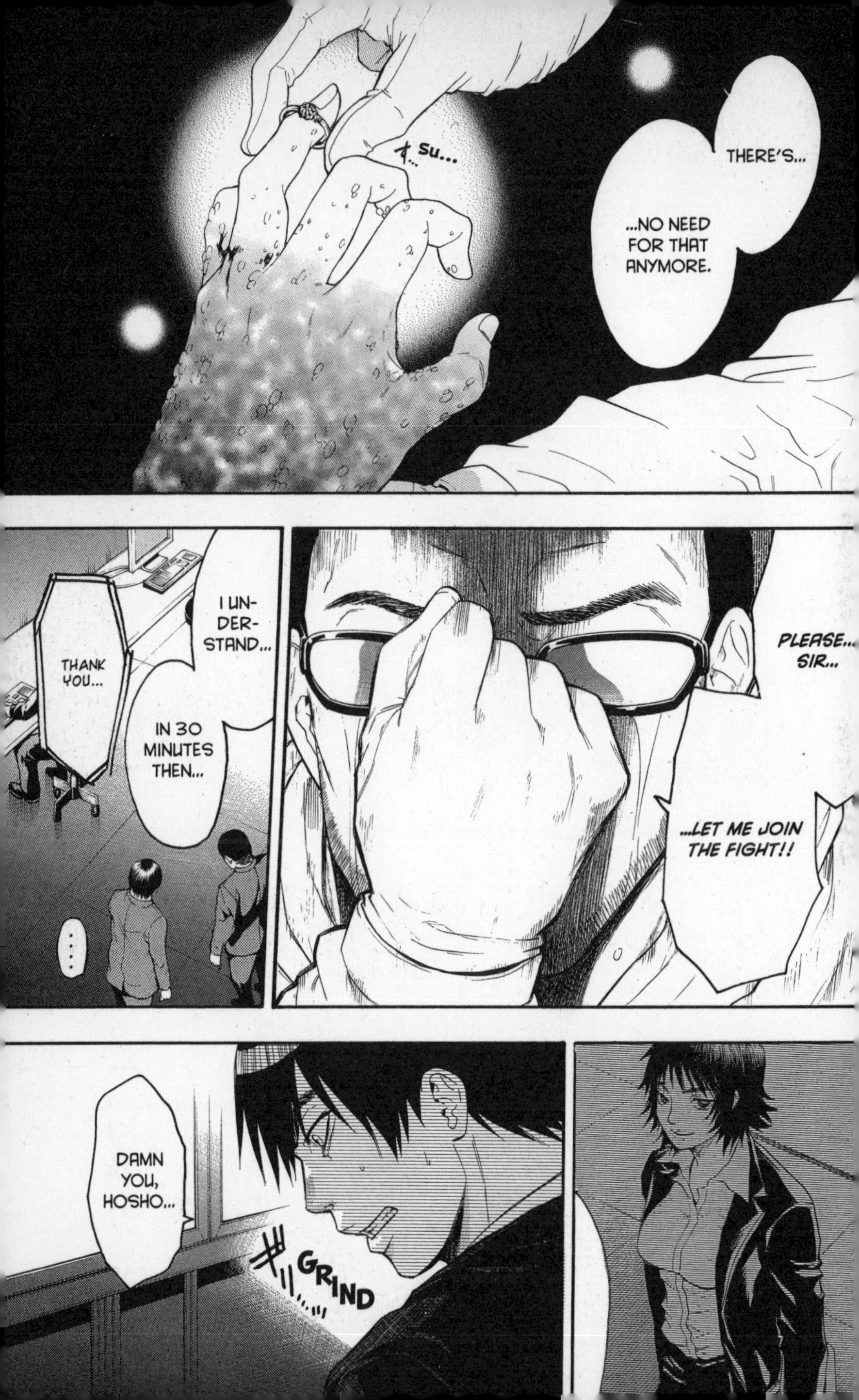
THERE'S...
...NO NEED FOR THAT ANYMORE.
す SU...
PLEASE... SIR...
...LET ME JOIN THE FIGHT!!
I UN-DER-STAND...
IN 30 MINUTES THEN...
THANK YOU...
...
DAMN YOU, HOSHO...
GRIND

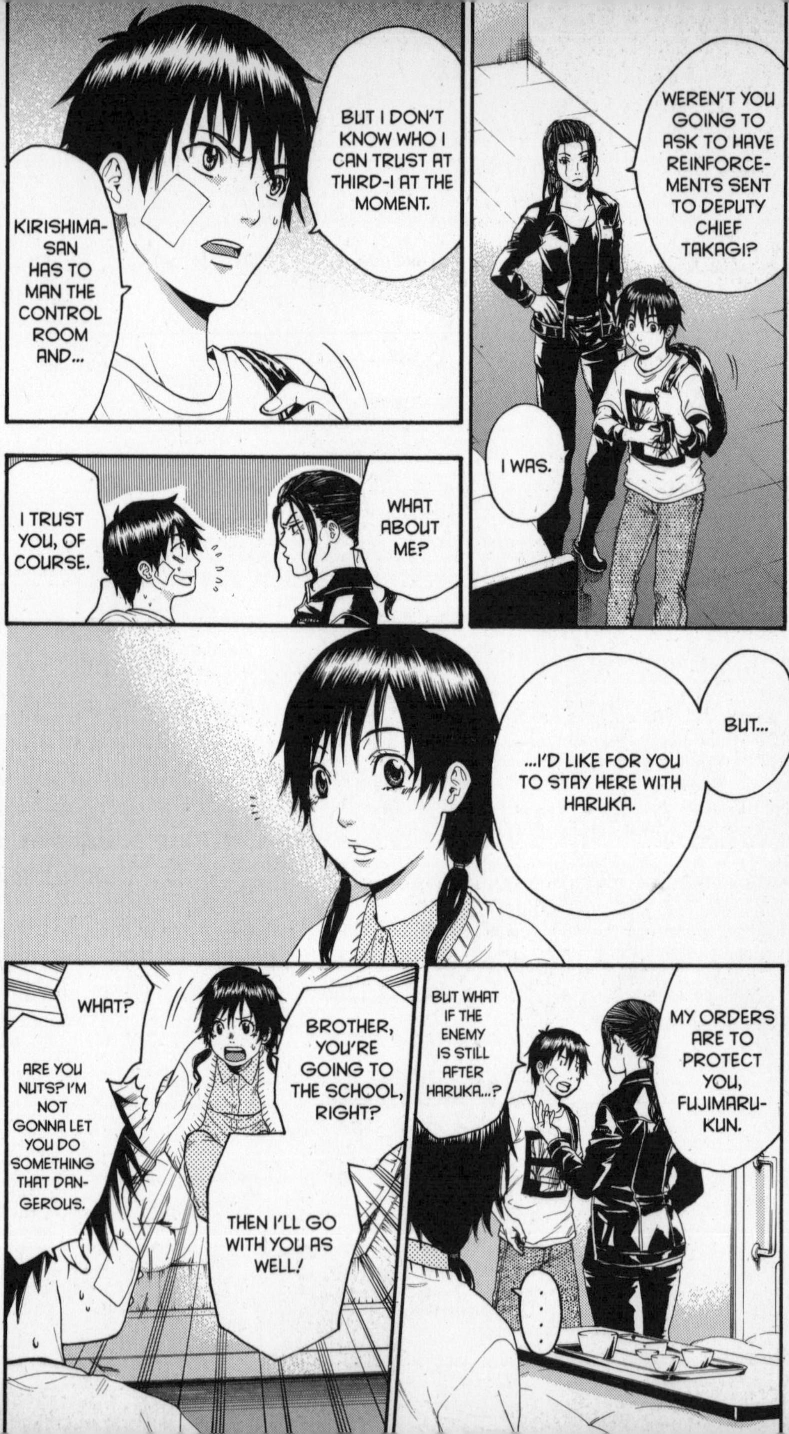
WEREN'T YOU GOING TO ASK TO HAVE REINFORCE-MENTS SENT TO DEPUTY CHIEF TAKAGI?
I WAS.
BUT I DON'T KNOW WHO I CAN TRUST AT THIRD-I AT THE MOMENT.
KIRISHIMA-SAN HAS TO MAN THE CONTROL ROOM AND...
WHAT ABOUT ME?
I TRUST YOU, OF COURSE.
BUT...
...I'D LIKE FOR YOU TO STAY HERE WITH HARUKA.
MY ORDERS ARE TO PROTECT YOU, FUJIMARU-KUN.
BUT WHAT IF THE ENEMY IS STILL AFTER HARUKA...?
...
BROTHER, YOU'RE GOING TO THE SCHOOL, RIGHT?
THEN I'LL GO WITH YOU AS WELL!
WHAT?
ARE YOU NUTS? I'M NOT GONNA LET YOU DO SOMETHING THAT DAN-GEROUS.

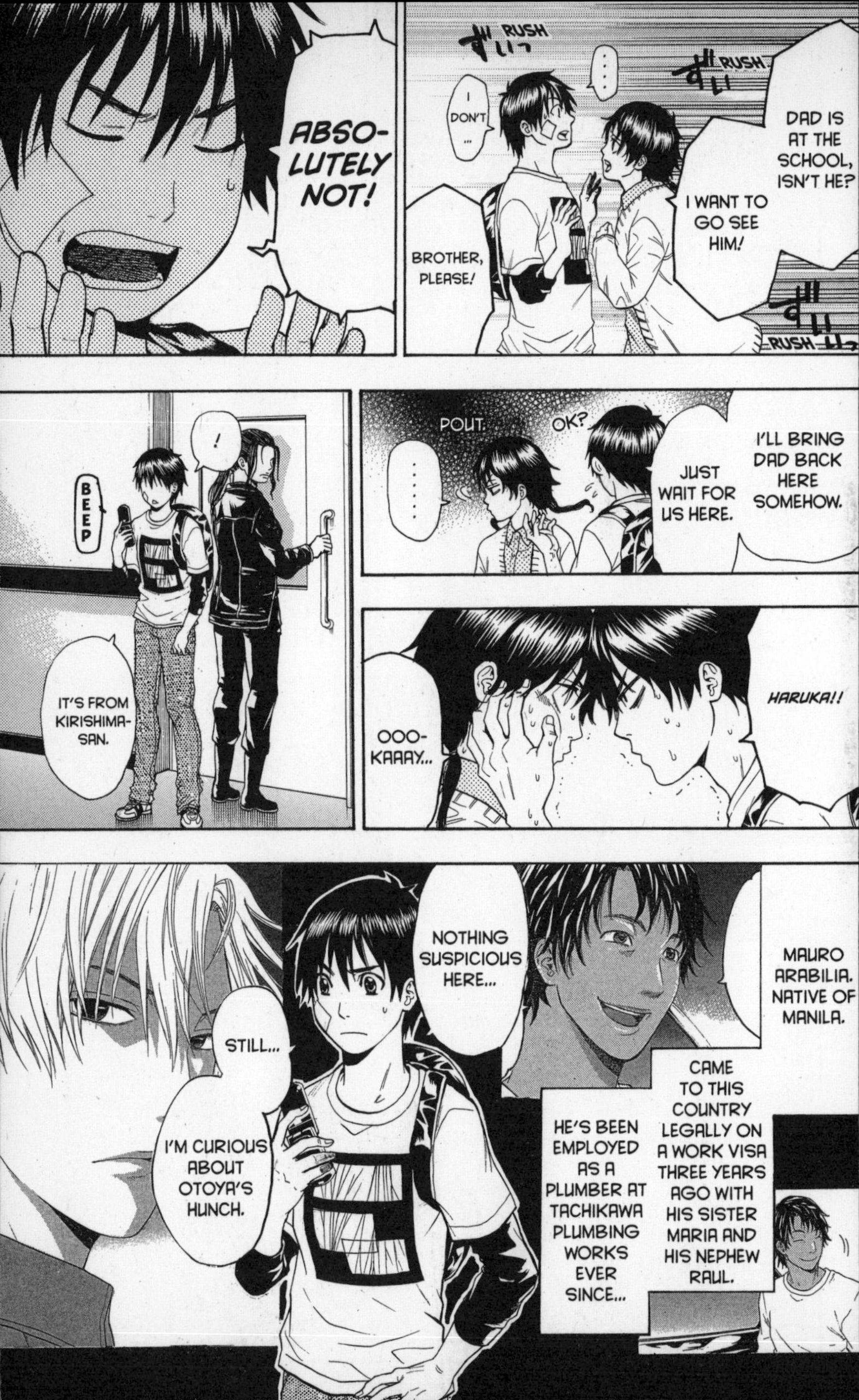

RUSH
DAD IS AT THE SCHOOL, ISN'T HE?
I WANT TO GO SEE HIM!
...
RUSH
I DON'T ...
BROTHER, PLEASE!
RUSH
ABSO-LUTELY NOT!
I'LL BRING DAD BACK HERE SOMEHOW.
JUST WAIT FOR US HERE.
OK?
POUT.
......
HARUKA!!
OOO-KAAAY...
!
BEEP
IT'S FROM KIRISHIMA-SAN.
MAURO ARABILIA. NATIVE OF MANILA.
CAME TO THIS COUNTRY LEGALLY ON A WORK VISA THREE YEARS AGO WITH HIS SISTER MARIA AND HIS NEPHEW RAUL.
HE'S BEEN EMPLOYED AS A PLUMBER AT TACHIKAWA PLUMBING WORKS EVER SINCE...
NOTHING SUSPICIOUS HERE...
STILL...
I'M CURIOUS ABOUT OTOYA'S HUNCH.

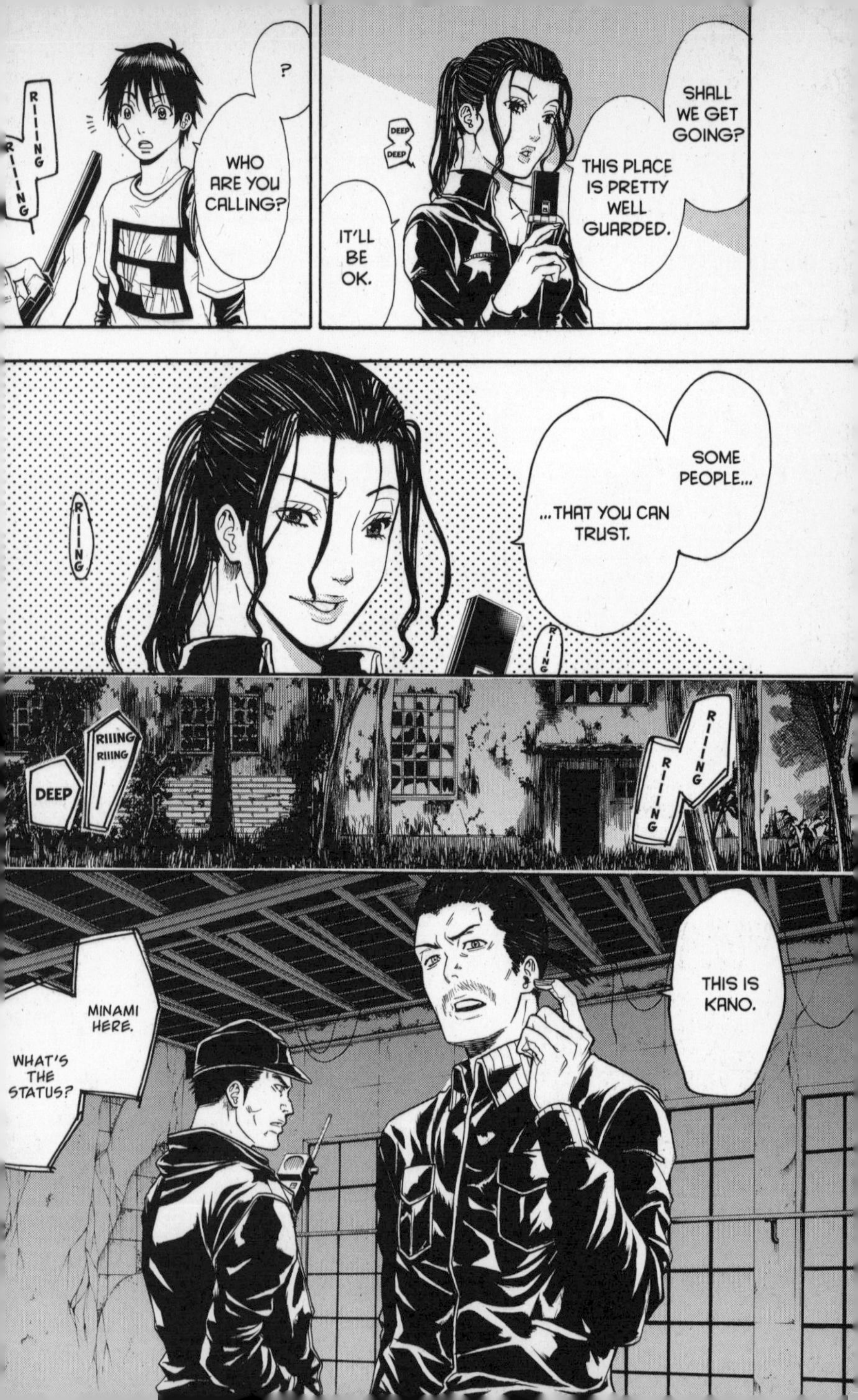
SHALL WE GET GOING?
THIS PLACE IS PRETTY WELL GUARDED.
DEEP DEEP
IT'LL BE OK.
?
WHO ARE YOU CALLING?
RIIING RIIING
SOME PEOPLE...
...THAT YOU CAN TRUST.
RIIING
RIIING
RIIING RIIING
RIIING RIIING
DEEP
THIS IS KANO.
MINAMI HERE.
WHAT'S THE STATUS?

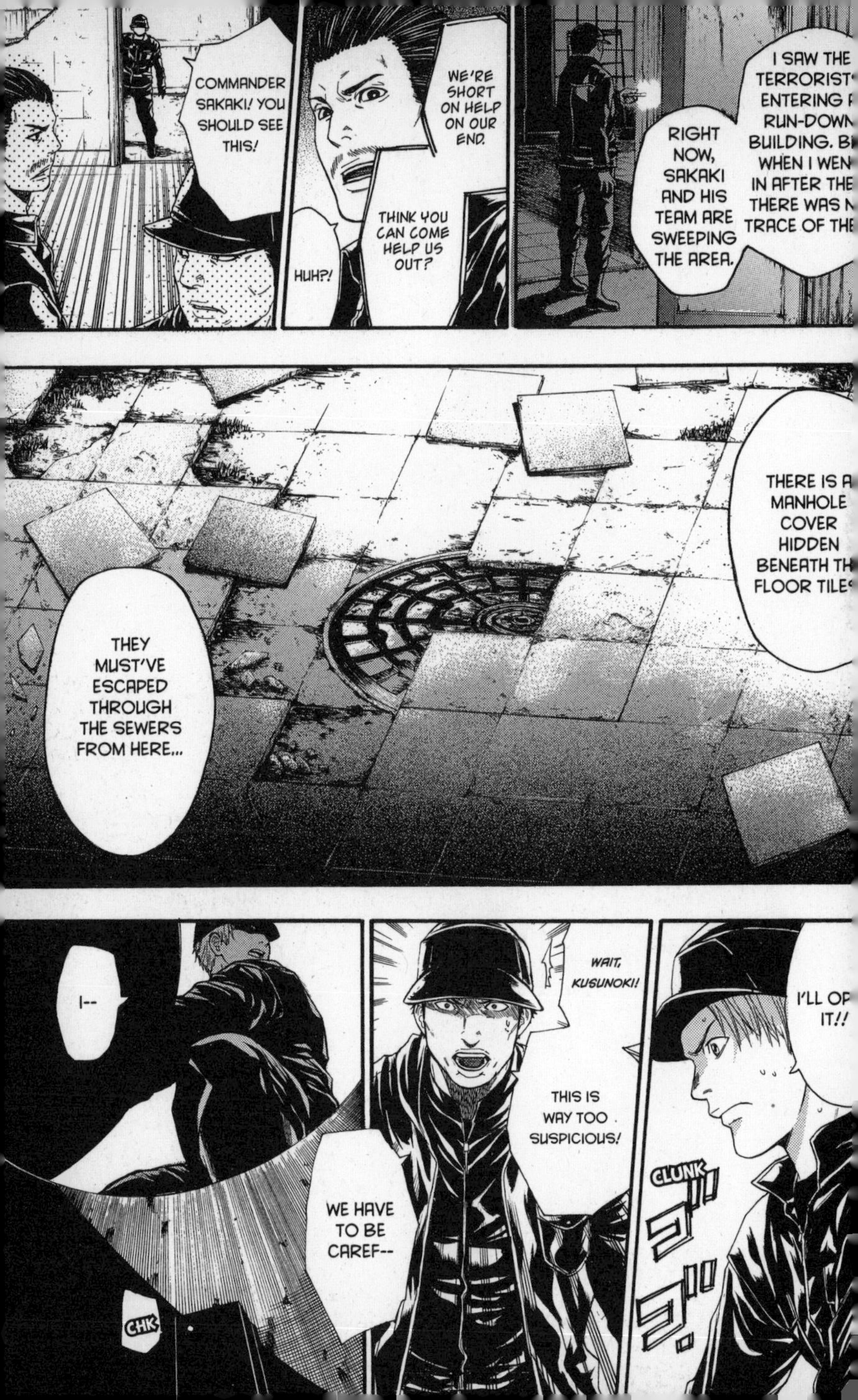
I SAW THE TERRORIST ENTERING RUN-DOWN BUILDING. B WHEN I WEN IN AFTER THE THERE WAS N TRACE OF THE
RIGHT NOW, SAKAKI AND HIS TEAM ARE SWEEPING THE AREA.
WE'RE SHORT ON HELP ON OUR END.
THINK YOU CAN COME HELP US OUT?
HUH?!
COMMANDER SAKAKI! YOU SHOULD SEE THIS!
THERE IS A MANHOLE COVER HIDDEN BENEATH TH FLOOR TILE
THEY MUST'VE ESCAPED THROUGH THE SEWERS FROM HERE...
I'LL OP IT!!
CLUNK
WAIT, KUSUNOKI!
THIS IS WAY TOO SUSPICIOUS!
WE HAVE TO BE CAREF--
I--
CHK

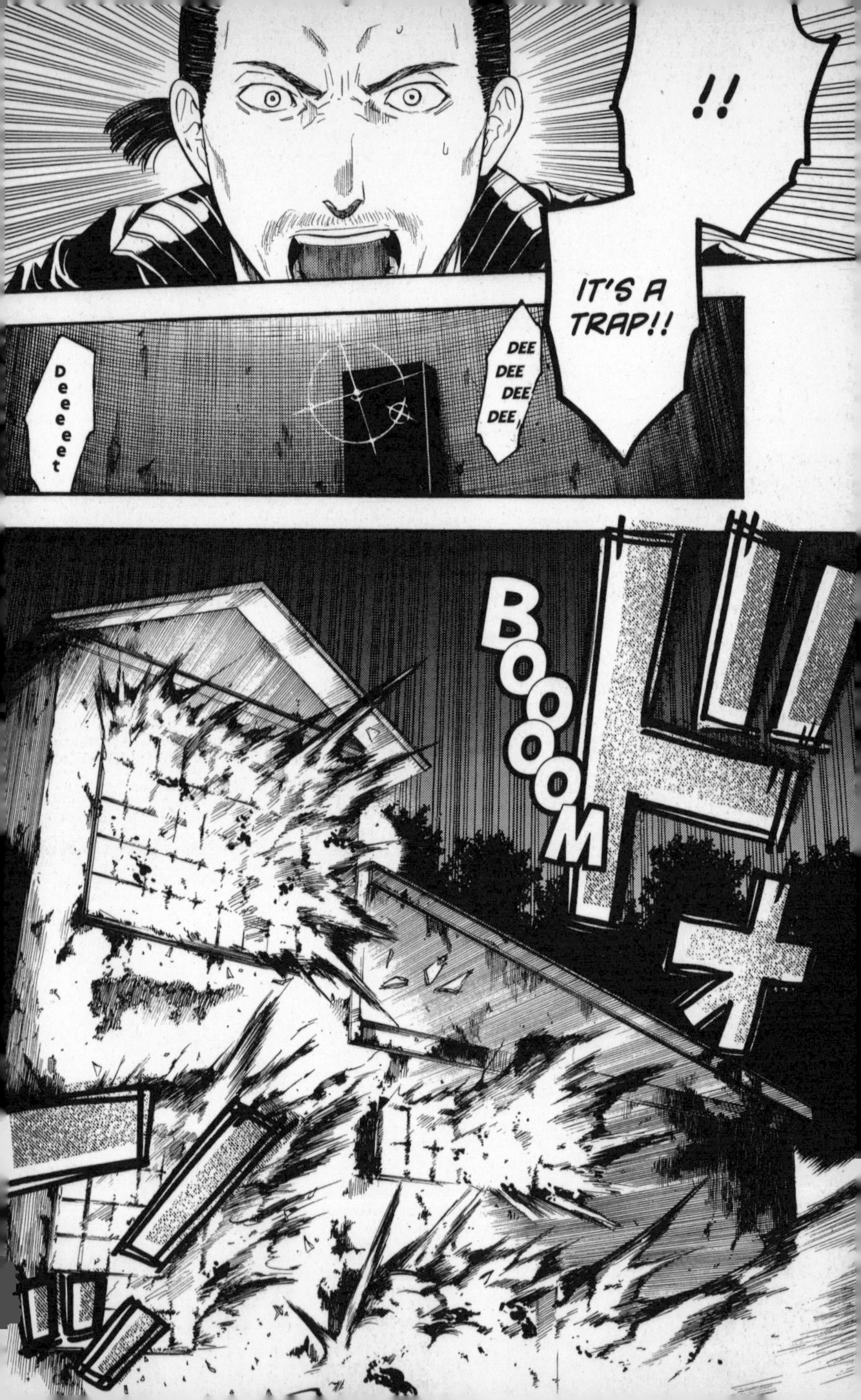
!!
IT'S A TRAP!!
DEE DEE DEE DEE
Deeeeet
BOOOOM

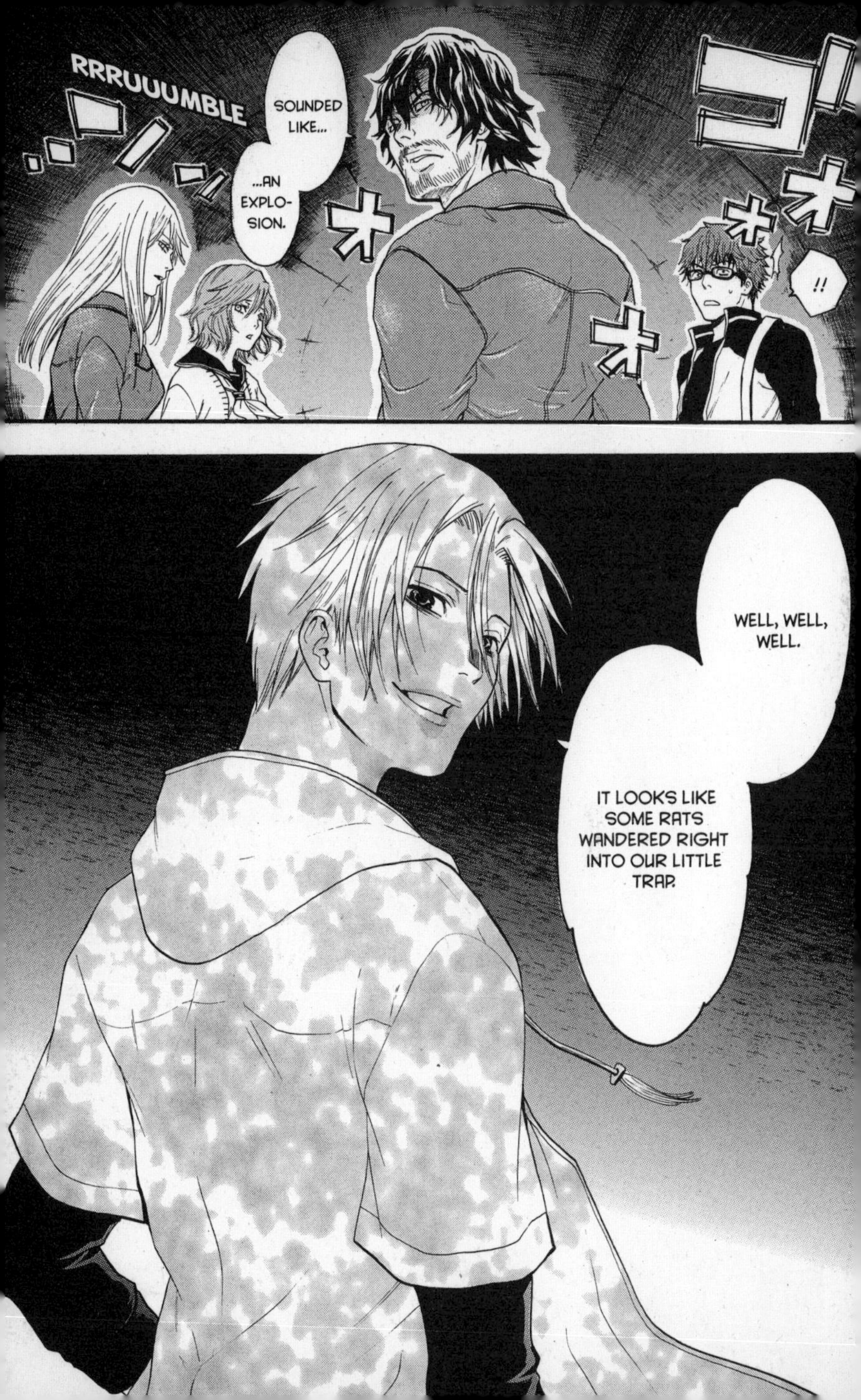
ゴオオオ
!!
SOUNDED LIKE...
...AN EXPLO-SION.
RRRUUUMBLE
WELL, WELL, WELL.
IT LOOKS LIKE SOME RATS WANDERED RIGHT INTO OUR LITTLE TRAP.

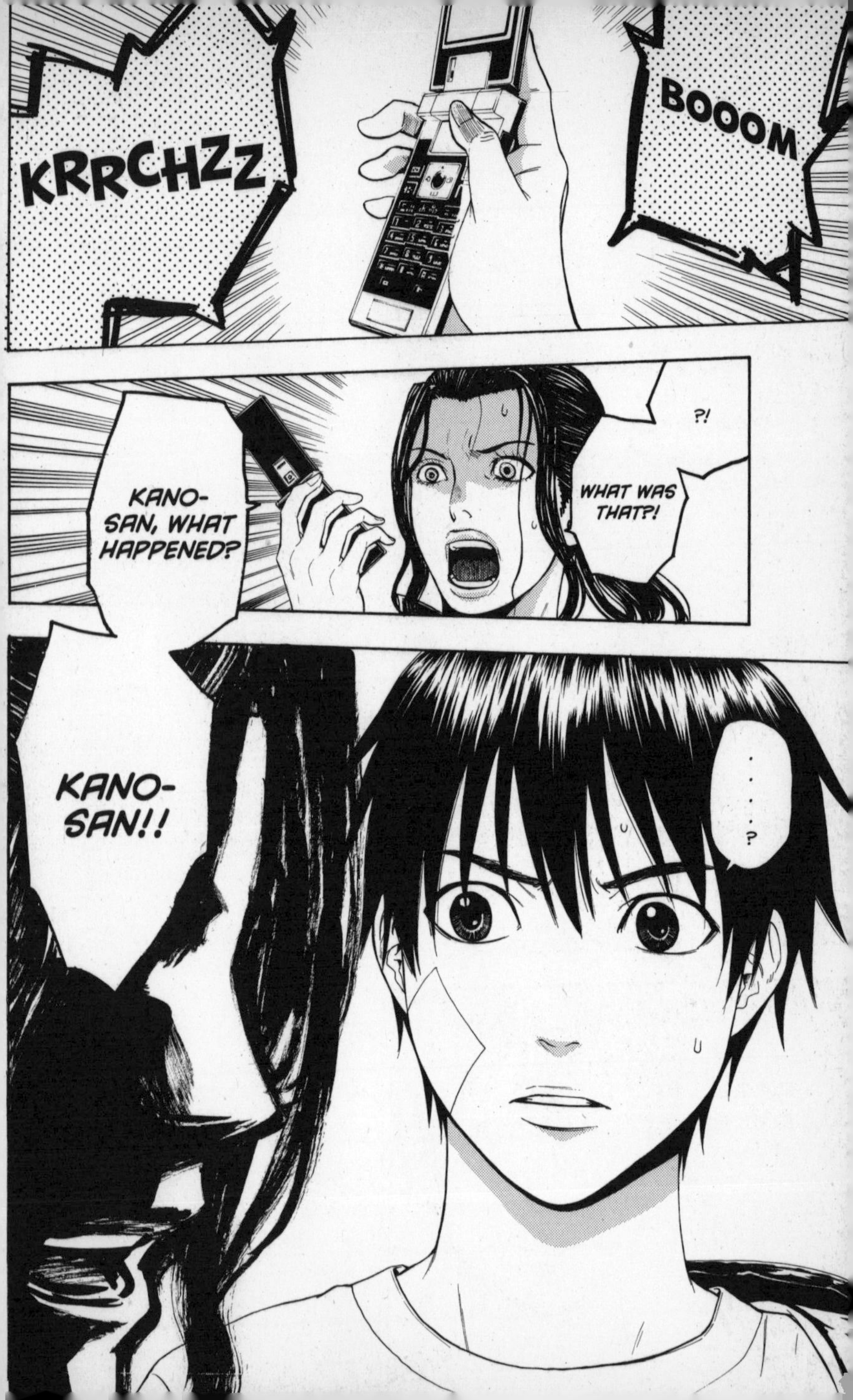
BOOOM
KRRCHZZ
?!
WHAT WAS THAT?!
KANO-SAN, WHAT HAPPENED?
....?
KANO-SAN!!

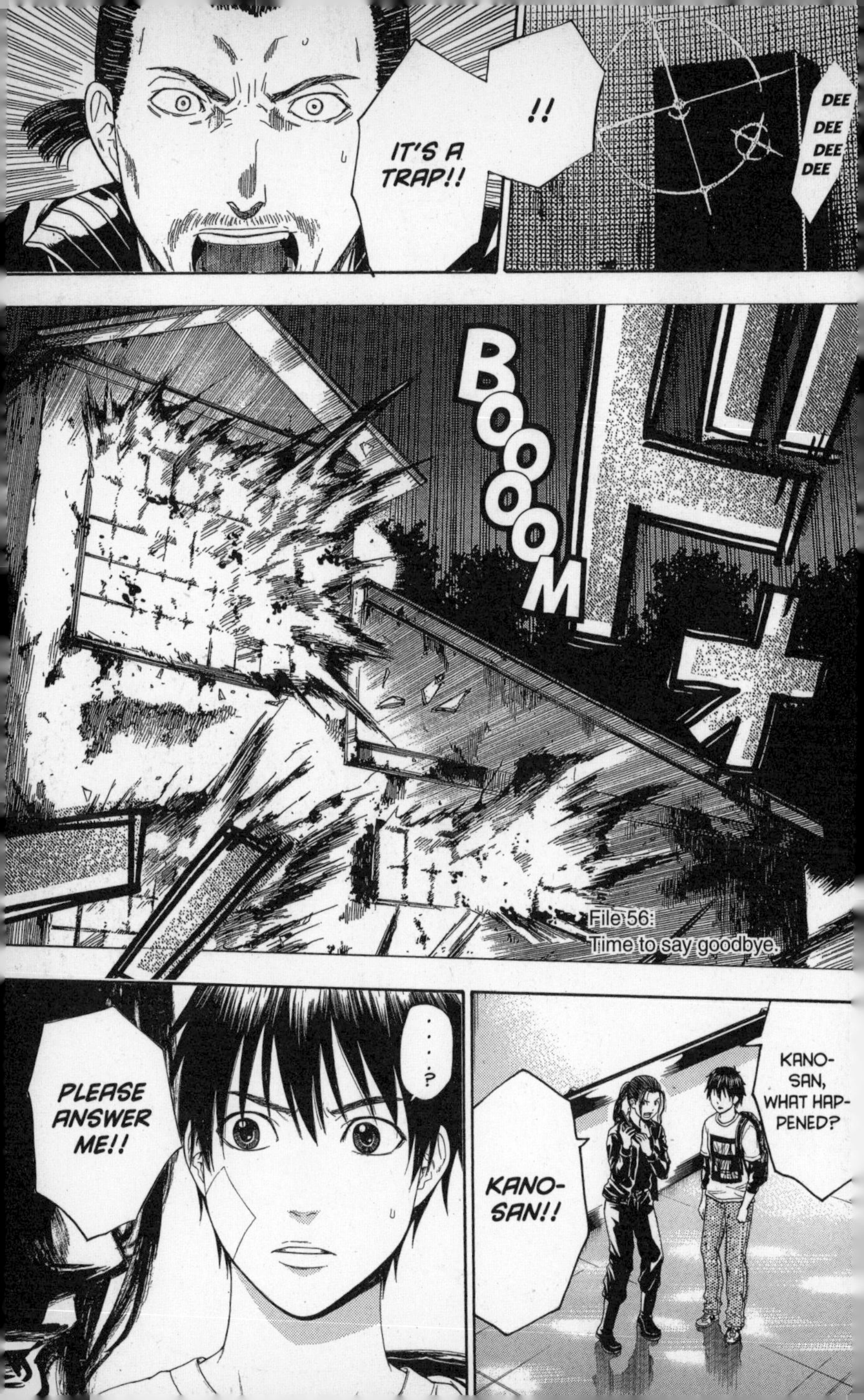
DEE DEE DEE DEE
!!
IT'S A TRAP!!
BOOOOM
File 56:
Time to say goodbye.
KANO-SAN, WHAT HAPPENED?
KANO-SAN!!
...?
PLEASE ANSWER ME!!

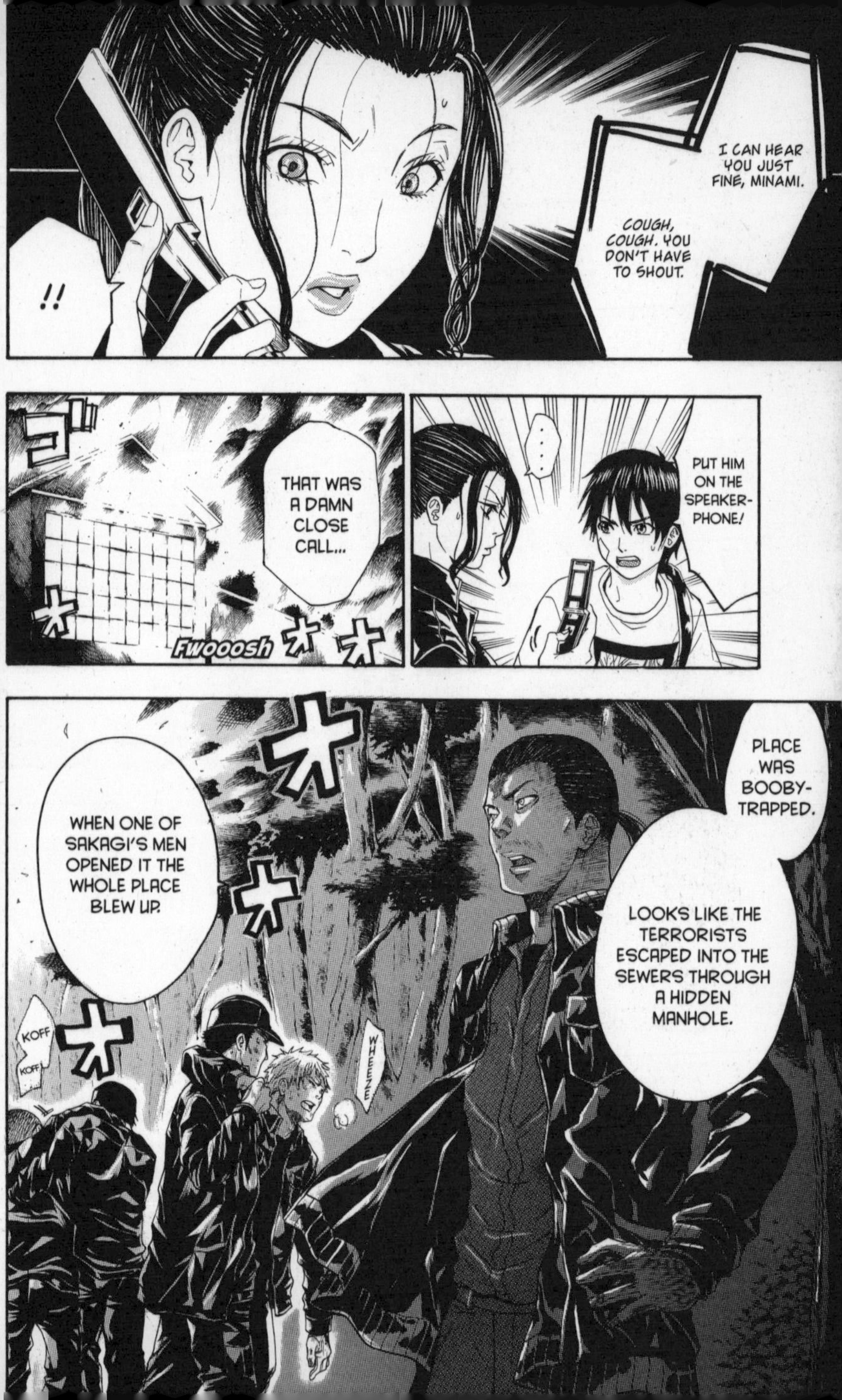
I CAN HEAR YOU JUST FINE, MINAMI.
COUGH, COUGH. YOU DON'T HAVE TO SHOUT.
!!
PUT HIM ON THE SPEAKER-PHONE!
...
THAT WAS A DAMN CLOSE CALL...
Fwooosh
PLACE WAS BOOBY-TRAPPED.
LOOKS LIKE THE TERRORISTS ESCAPED INTO THE SEWERS THROUGH A HIDDEN MANHOLE.
WHEN ONE OF SAKAGI'S MEN OPENED IT THE WHOLE PLACE BLEW UP.
WHEEZE
KOFF KOFF

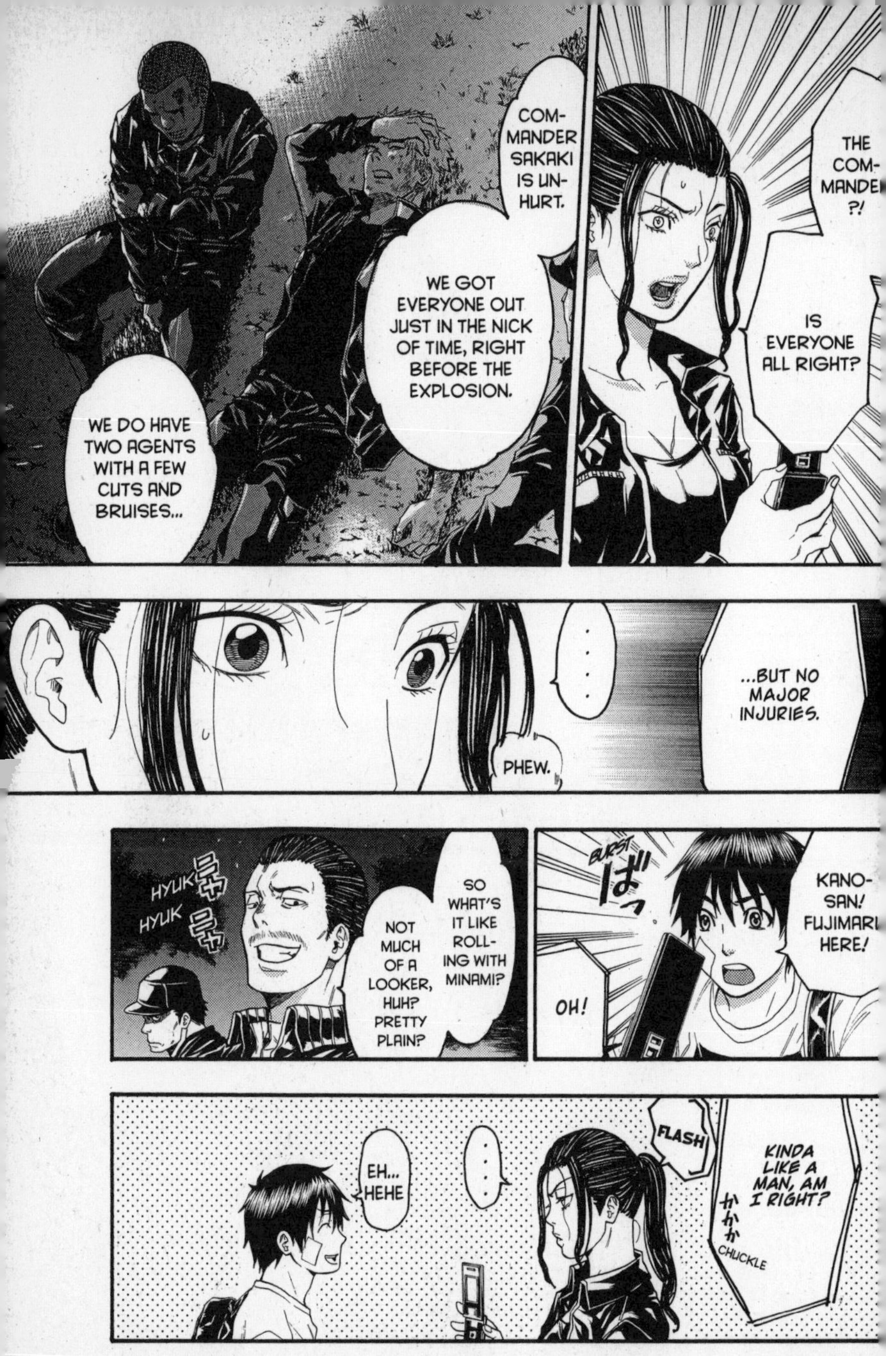
THE COM-MANDE ?!
IS EVERYONE ALL RIGHT?
COM-MANDER SAKAKI IS UN-HURT.
WE GOT EVERYONE OUT JUST IN THE NICK OF TIME, RIGHT BEFORE THE EXPLOSION.
WE DO HAVE TWO AGENTS WITH A FEW CUTS AND BRUISES...
...BUT NO MAJOR INJURIES.
...
PHEW.
KANO-SAN! FUJIMAR HERE!
BURST
OH!
SO WHAT'S IT LIKE ROLL-ING WITH MINAMI?
NOT MUCH OF A LOOKER, HUH? PRETTY PLAIN?
HYUK HYUK
KINDA LIKE A MAN, AM I RIGHT?
CHUCKLE
FLASH
...
EH... HEHE

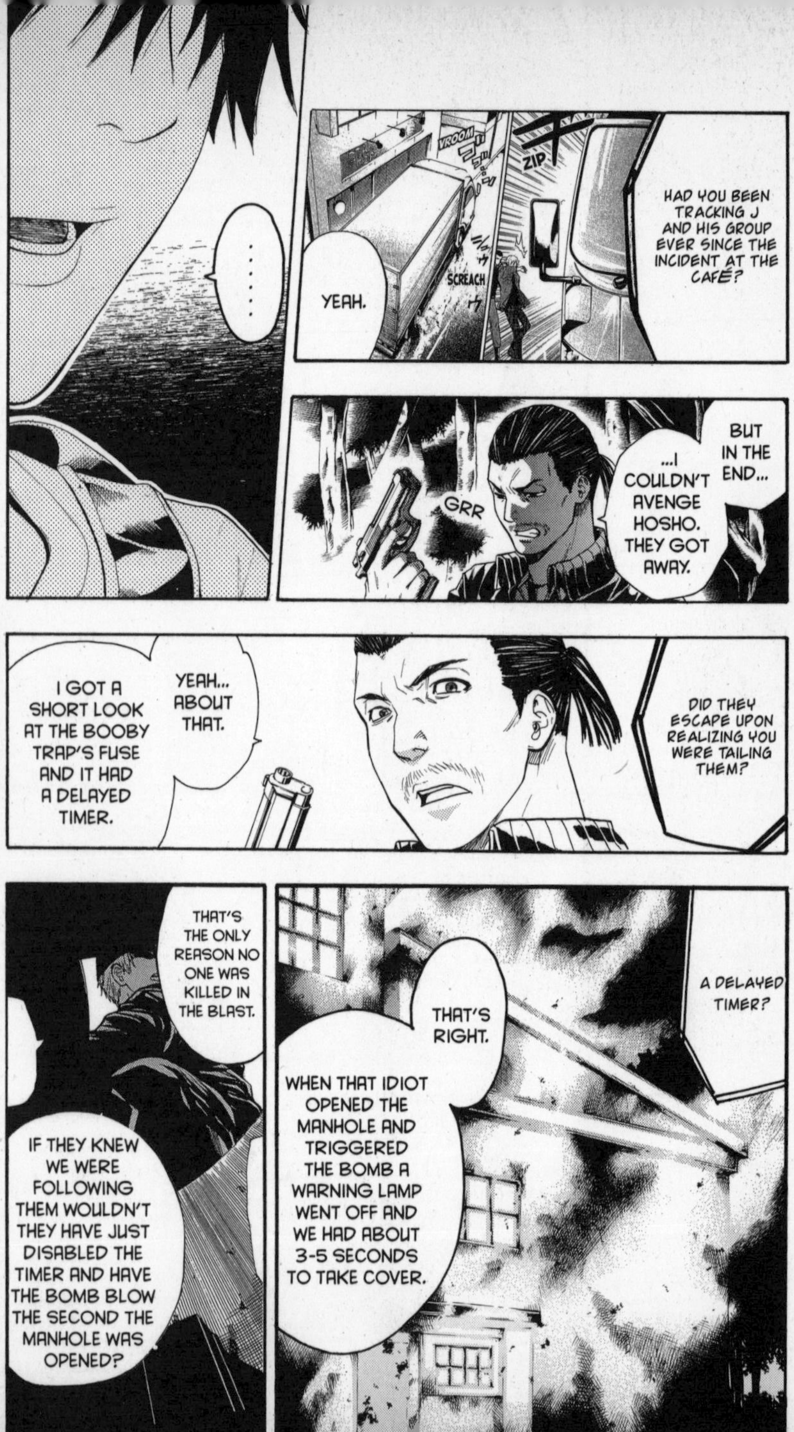
HAD YOU BEEN TRACKING J AND HIS GROUP EVER SINCE THE INCIDENT AT THE CAFÉ?
ZIP
VROOM
SCREACH
YEAH.
BUT IN THE END...
...I COULDN'T AVENGE HOSHO. THEY GOT AWAY.
GRR
......
DID THEY ESCAPE UPON REALIZING YOU WERE TAILING THEM?
YEAH... ABOUT THAT.
I GOT A SHORT LOOK AT THE BOOBY TRAP'S FUSE AND IT HAD A DELAYED TIMER.
A DELAYED TIMER?
THAT'S RIGHT.
WHEN THAT IDIOT OPENED THE MANHOLE AND TRIGGERED THE BOMB A WARNING LAMP WENT OFF AND WE HAD ABOUT 3-5 SECONDS TO TAKE COVER.
THAT'S THE ONLY REASON NO ONE WAS KILLED IN THE BLAST.
IF THEY KNEW WE WERE FOLLOWING THEM WOULDN'T THEY HAVE JUST DISABLED THE TIMER AND HAVE THE BOMB BLOW THE SECOND THE MANHOLE WAS OPENED?

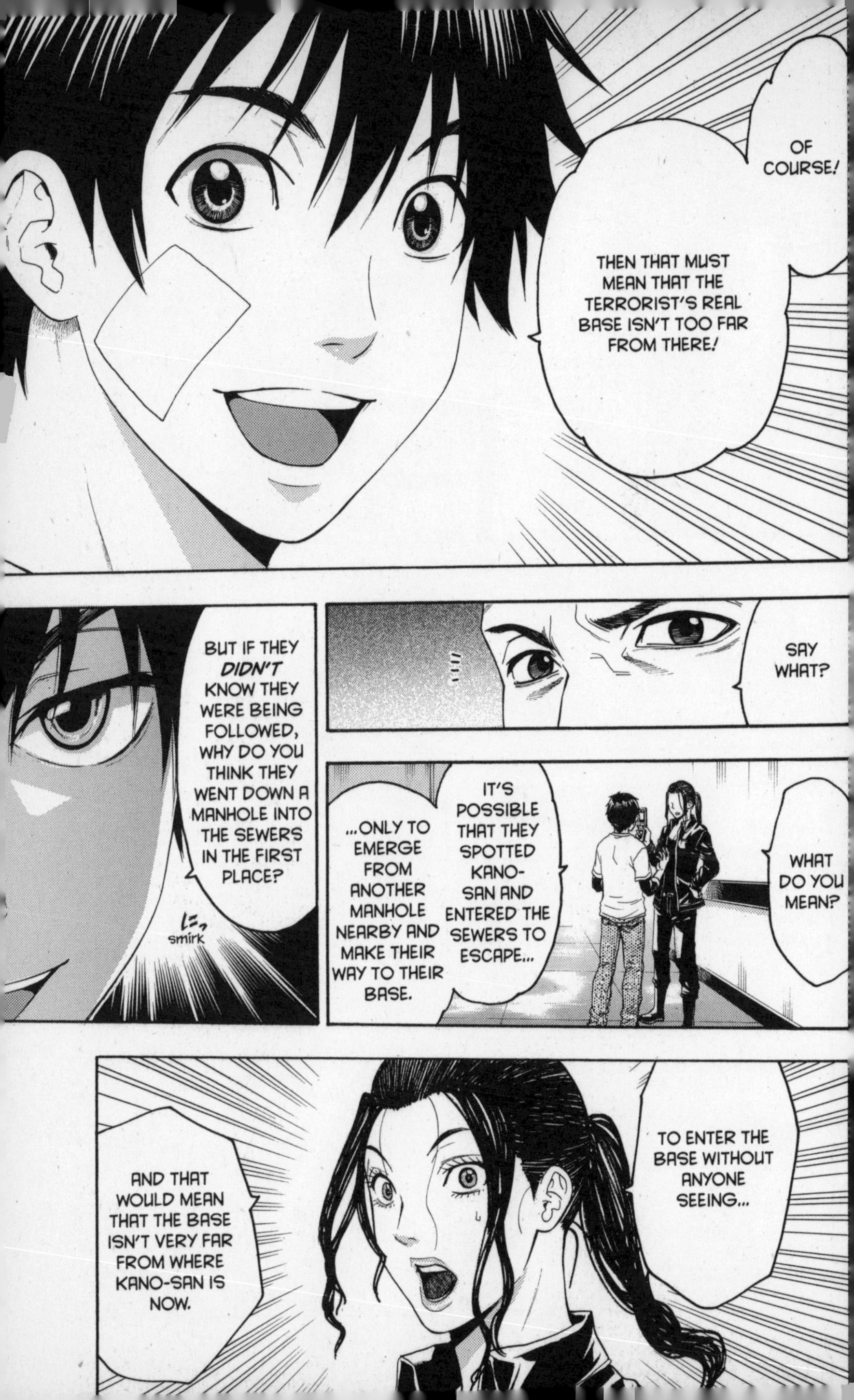

OF COURSE!
THEN THAT MUST MEAN THAT THE TERRORIST'S REAL BASE ISN'T TOO FAR FROM THERE!
SAY WHAT?
WHAT DO YOU MEAN?
IT'S POSSIBLE THAT THEY SPOTTED KANO-SAN AND ENTERED THE SEWERS TO ESCAPE...
...ONLY TO EMERGE FROM ANOTHER MANHOLE NEARBY AND MAKE THEIR WAY TO THEIR BASE.
BUT IF THEY *DIDN'T* KNOW THEY WERE BEING FOLLOWED, WHY DO YOU THINK THEY WENT DOWN A MANHOLE INTO THE SEWERS IN THE FIRST PLACE?
smirk
TO ENTER THE BASE WITHOUT ANYONE SEEING...
AND THAT WOULD MEAN THAT THE BASE ISN'T VERY FAR FROM WHERE KANO-SAN IS NOW.

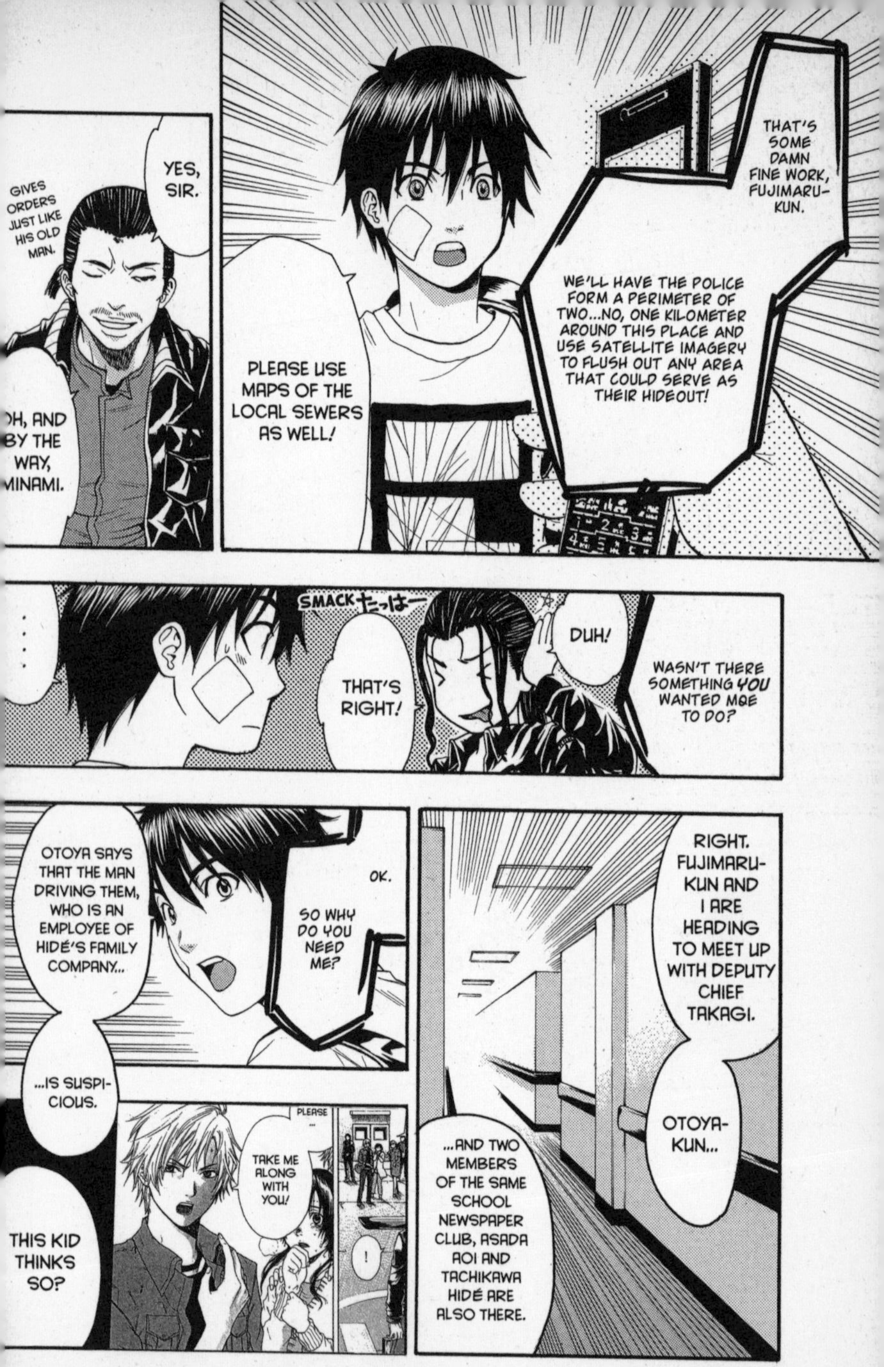
THAT'S SOME DAMN FINE WORK, FUJIMARU-KUN.
WE'LL HAVE THE POLICE FORM A PERIMETER OF TWO...NO, ONE KILOMETER AROUND THIS PLACE AND USE SATELLITE IMAGERY TO FLUSH OUT ANY AREA THAT COULD SERVE AS THEIR HIDEOUT!
PLEASE USE MAPS OF THE LOCAL SEWERS AS WELL!
YES, SIR.
GIVES ORDERS JUST LIKE HIS OLD MAN.
OH, AND BY THE WAY, MINAMI.
WASN'T THERE SOMETHING *YOU* WANTED MQE TO DO?
DUH!
SMACK
THAT'S RIGHT!
.....
RIGHT. FUJIMARU-KUN AND I ARE HEADING TO MEET UP WITH DEPUTY CHIEF TAKAGI.
OTOYA-KUN...
...AND TWO MEMBERS OF THE SAME SCHOOL NEWSPAPER CLUB, ASADA AOI AND TACHIKAWA HIDÉ ARE ALSO THERE.
OK.
SO WHY DO YOU NEED ME?
OTOYA SAYS THAT THE MAN DRIVING THEM, WHO IS AN EMPLOYEE OF HIDÉ'S FAMILY COMPANY...
...IS SUSPICIOUS.
PLEASE...
TAKE ME ALONG WITH YOU!
!
THIS KID THINKS SO?

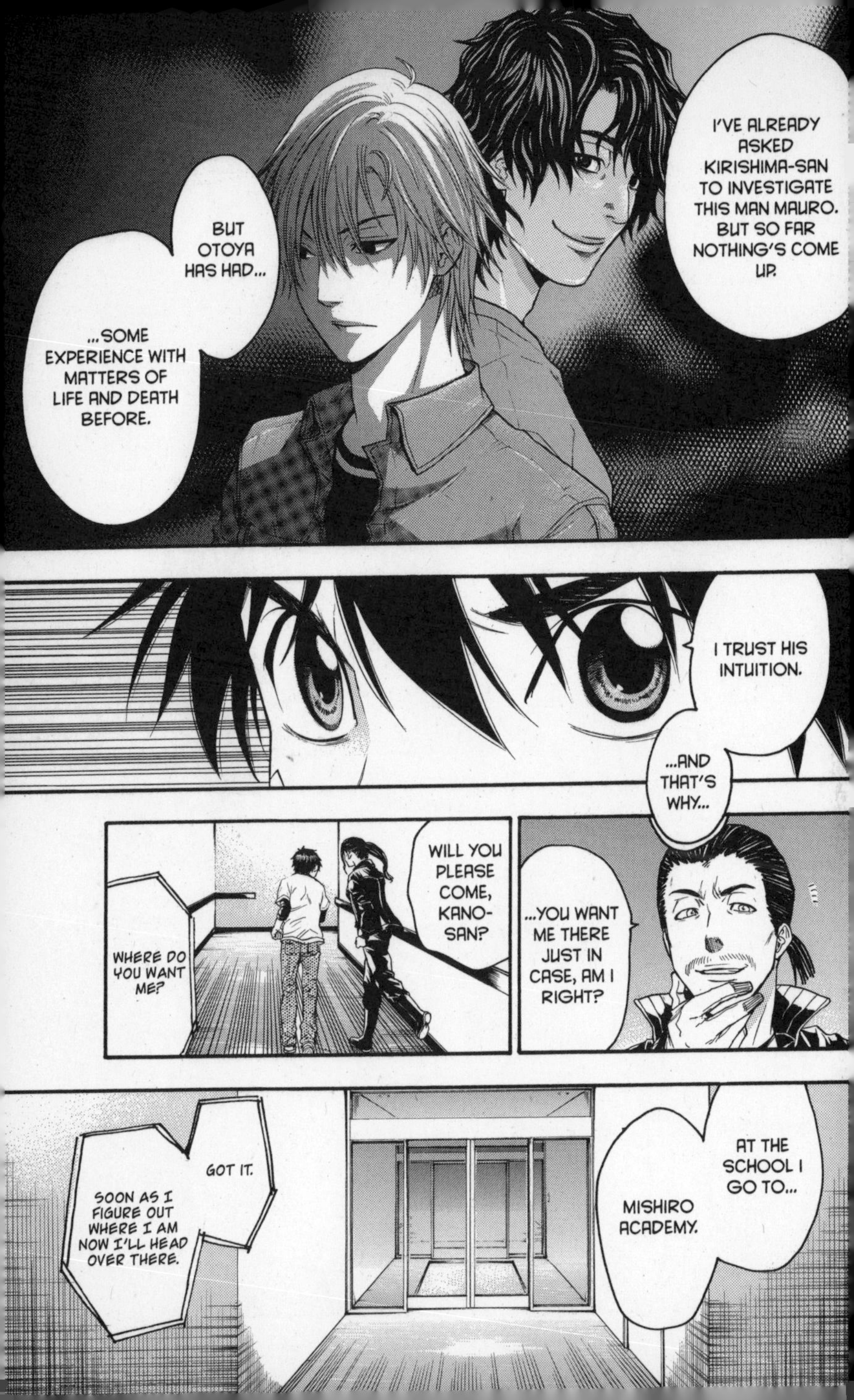
I'VE ALREADY ASKED KIRISHIMA-SAN TO INVESTIGATE THIS MAN MAURO. BUT SO FAR NOTHING'S COME UP.
BUT OTOYA HAS HAD...
...SOME EXPERIENCE WITH MATTERS OF LIFE AND DEATH BEFORE.
I TRUST HIS INTUITION.
...AND THAT'S WHY...
...YOU WANT ME THERE JUST IN CASE, AM I RIGHT?
WILL YOU PLEASE COME, KANO-SAN?
WHERE DO YOU WANT ME?
AT THE SCHOOL I GO TO...
MISHIRO ACADEMY.
GOT IT.
SOON AS I FIGURE OUT WHERE I AM NOW I'LL HEAD OVER THERE.

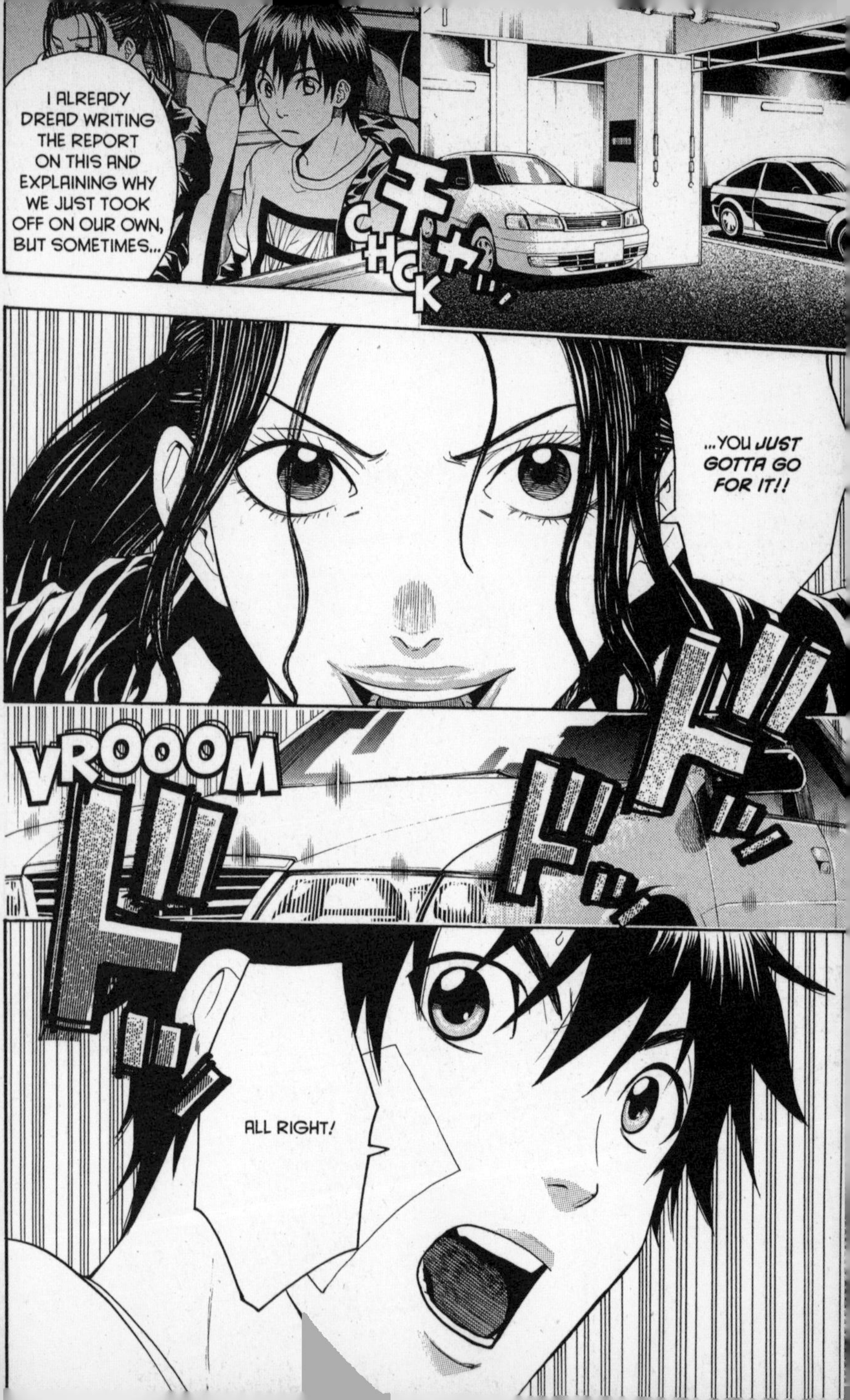
CHCK
I ALREADY DREAD WRITING THE REPORT ON THIS AND EXPLAINING WHY WE JUST TOOK OFF ON OUR OWN, BUT SOMETIMES...
...YOU JUST GOTTA GO FOR IT!!
VROOOM
ALL RIGHT!

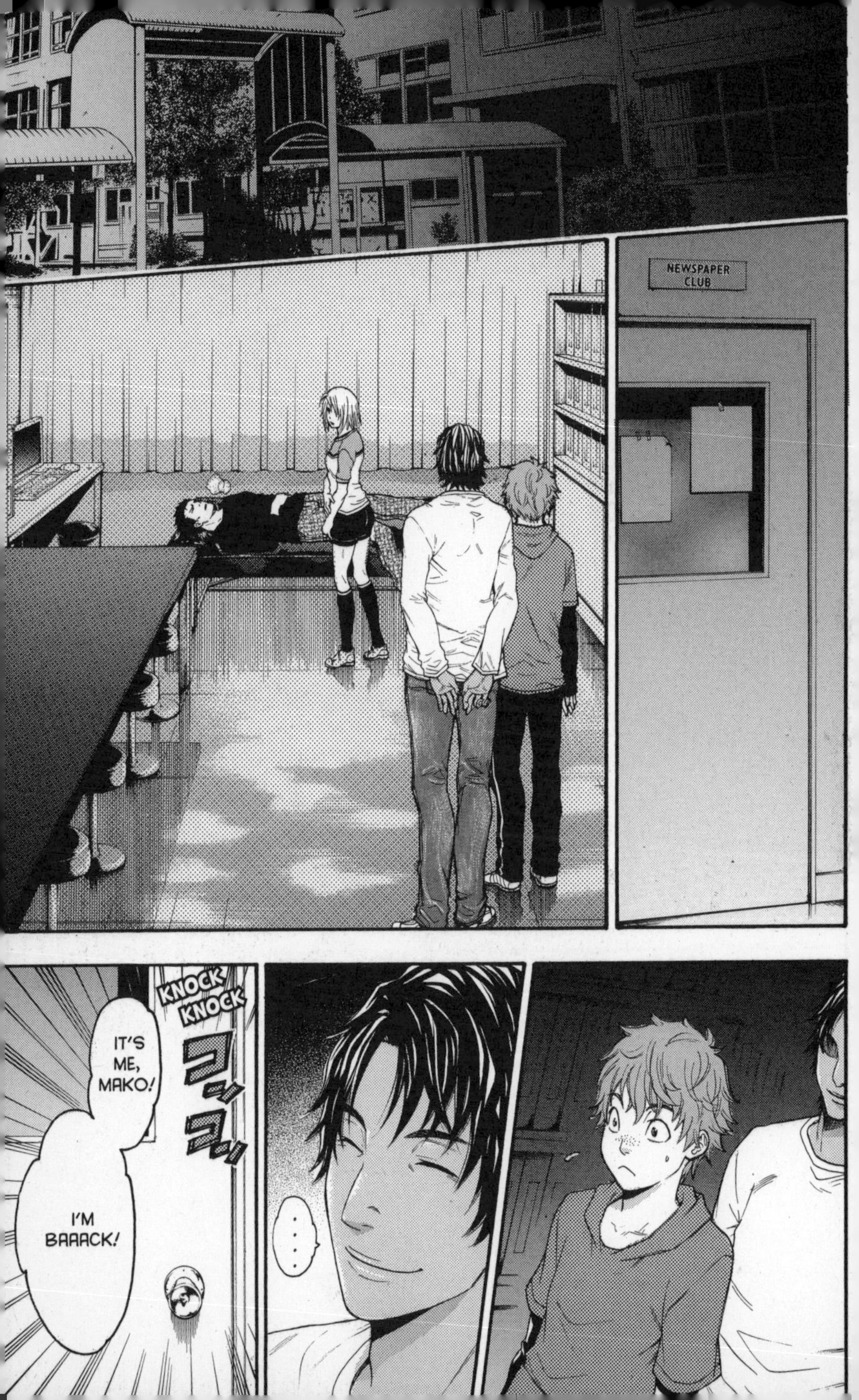
NEWSPAPER CLUB
. . . .
KNOCK KNOCK
IT'S ME, MAKO!
I'M BAAACK!

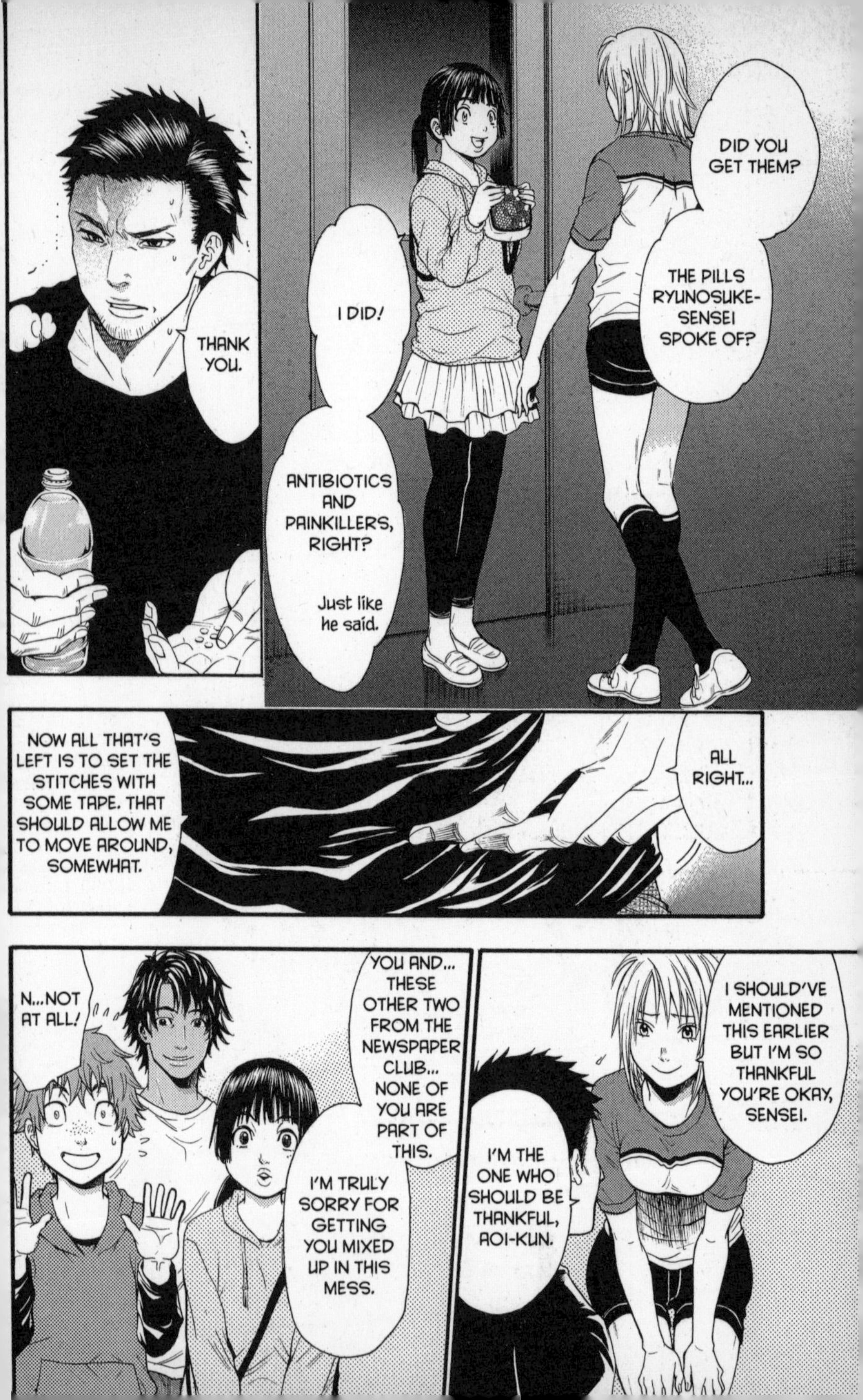
DID YOU GET THEM?
THE PILLS RYUNOSUKE-SENSEI SPOKE OF?
I DID!
ANTIBIOTICS AND PAINKILLERS, RIGHT?
Just like he said.
THANK YOU.
ALL RIGHT...
NOW ALL THAT'S LEFT IS TO SET THE STITCHES WITH SOME TAPE. THAT SHOULD ALLOW ME TO MOVE AROUND, SOMEWHAT.
I SHOULD'VE MENTIONED THIS EARLIER BUT I'M SO THANKFUL YOU'RE OKAY, SENSEI.
I'M THE ONE WHO SHOULD BE THANKFUL, AOI-KUN.
YOU AND... THESE OTHER TWO FROM THE NEWSPAPER CLUB... NONE OF YOU ARE PART OF THIS.
I'M TRULY SORRY FOR GETTING YOU MIXED UP IN THIS MESS.
N...NOT AT ALL!

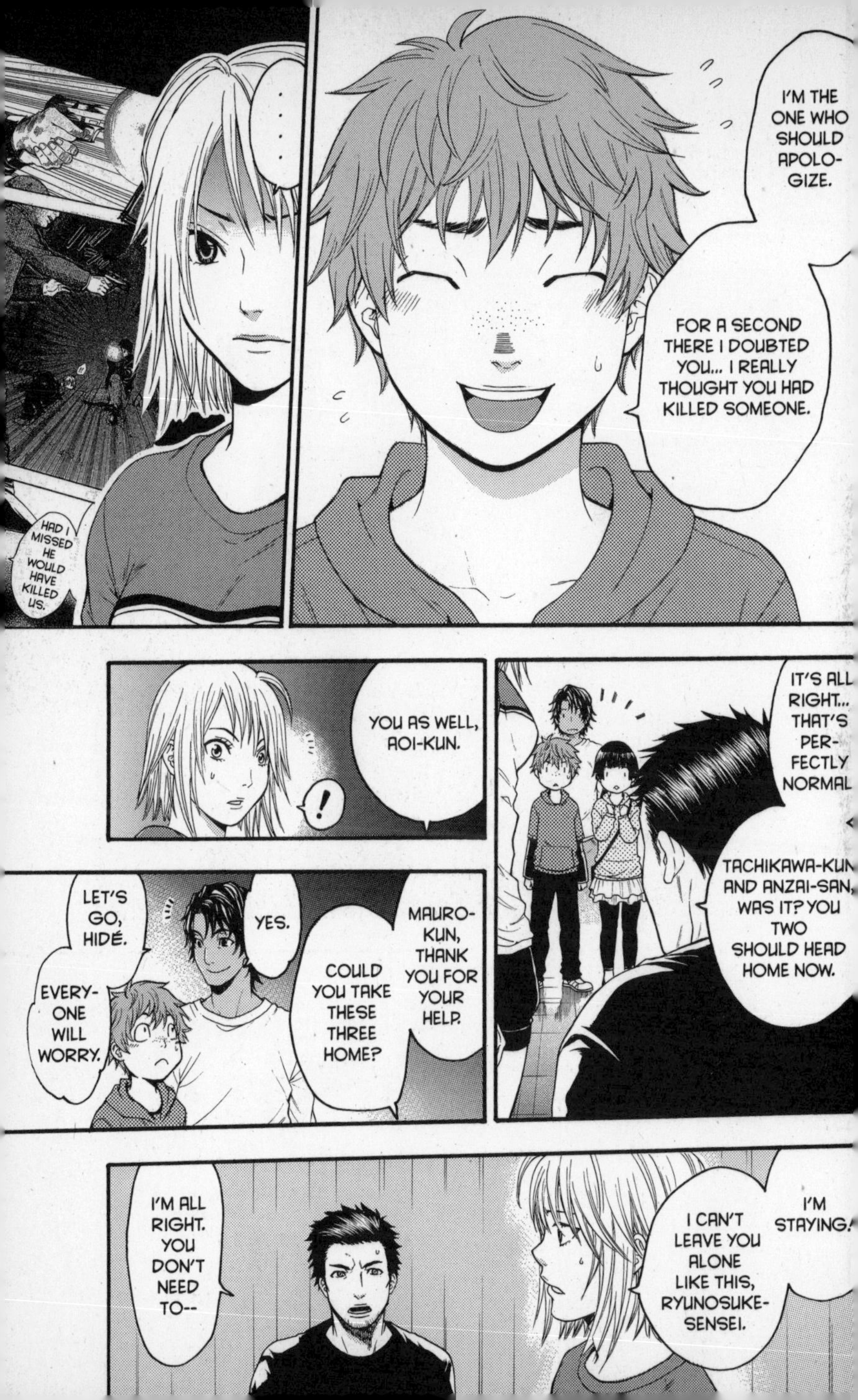
I'M THE ONE WHO SHOULD APOLOGIZE.
FOR A SECOND THERE I DOUBTED YOU... I REALLY THOUGHT YOU HAD KILLED SOMEONE.
...
HAD I MISSED HE WOULD HAVE KILLED US.
IT'S ALL RIGHT... THAT'S PERFECTLY NORMAL
TACHIKAWA-KUN AND ANZAI-SAN, WAS IT? YOU TWO SHOULD HEAD HOME NOW.
YOU AS WELL, AOI-KUN.
!
MAURO-KUN, THANK YOU FOR YOUR HELP.
COULD YOU TAKE THESE THREE HOME?
YES.
LET'S GO, HIDÉ.
EVERYONE WILL WORRY.
I'M STAYING!
I CAN'T LEAVE YOU ALONE LIKE THIS, RYUNOSUKE-SENSEI.
I'M ALL RIGHT. YOU DON'T NEED TO--

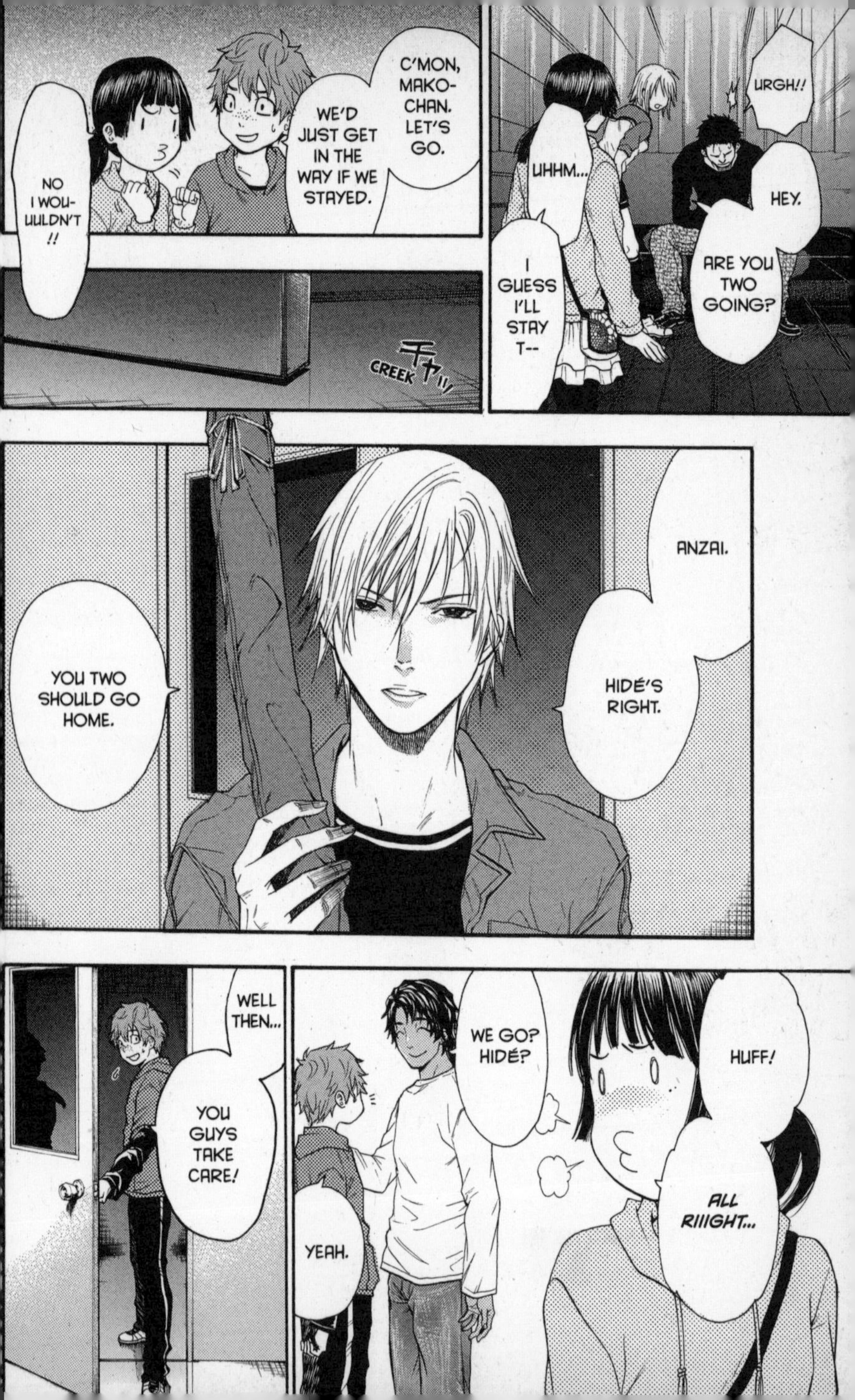
URGH!!
HEY.
ARE YOU TWO GOING?
UHHM...
I GUESS I'LL STAY T--
C'MON, MAKO-CHAN. LET'S GO.
WE'D JUST GET IN THE WAY IF WE STAYED.
NO I WOU-UULDN'T!!
チャ
CREEK
ANZAI.
HIDÉ'S RIGHT.
YOU TWO SHOULD GO HOME.
HUFF!
WE GO? HIDÉ?
ALL RIIIGHT...
YEAH.
WELL THEN...
YOU GUYS TAKE CARE!

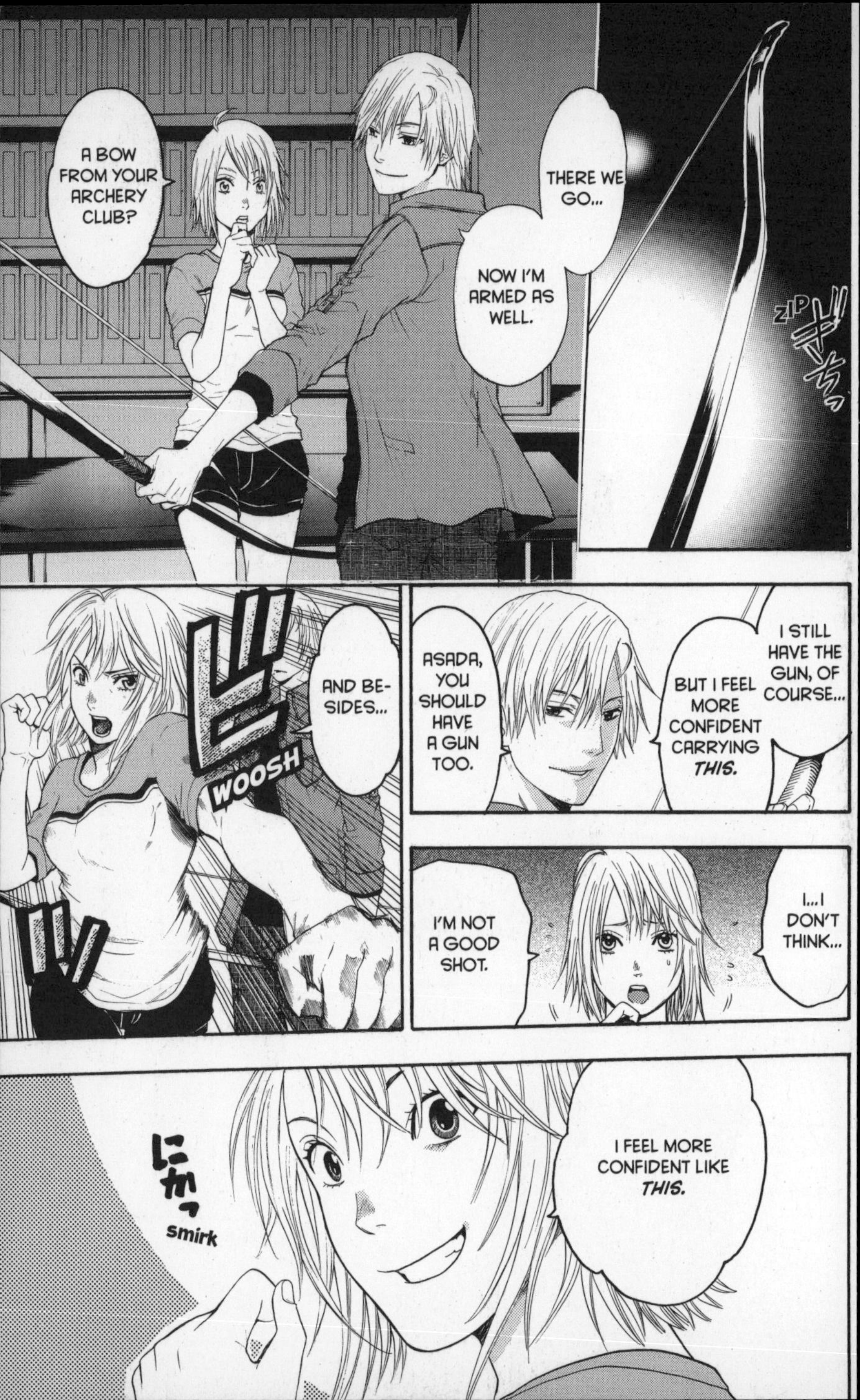
ギちっ
ZIP
THERE WE GO...
NOW I'M ARMED AS WELL.
A BOW FROM YOUR ARCHERY CLUB?
I STILL HAVE THE GUN, OF COURSE...
BUT I FEEL MORE CONFIDENT CARRYING *THIS.*
ASADA, YOU SHOULD HAVE A GUN TOO.
I...I DON'T THINK...
I'M NOT A GOOD SHOT.
AND BE-SIDES...
ビッ
WOOSH
I FEEL MORE CONFIDENT LIKE *THIS.*
にかっ
smirk

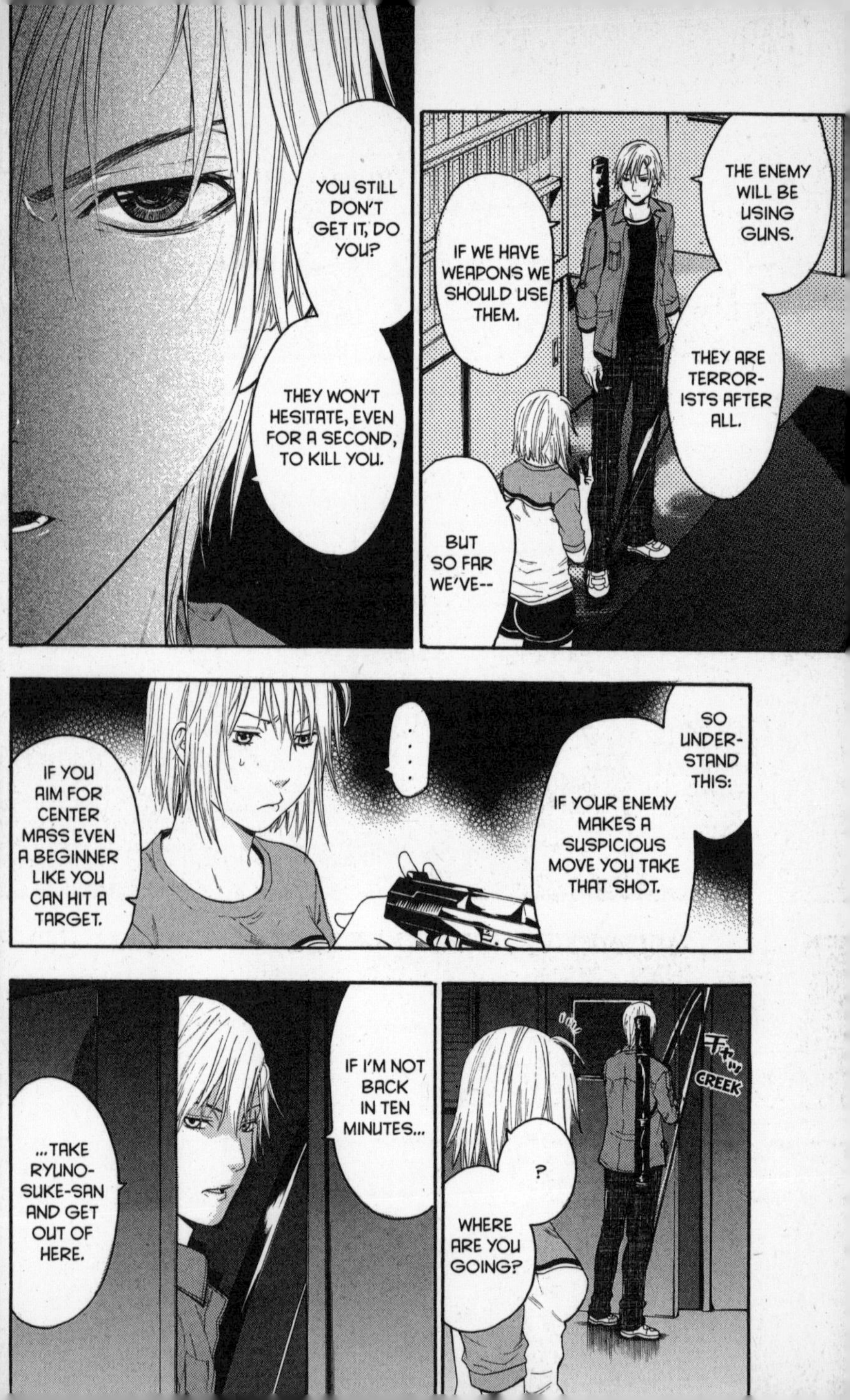
THE ENEMY WILL BE USING GUNS.
THEY ARE TERRORISTS AFTER ALL.
IF WE HAVE WEAPONS WE SHOULD USE THEM.
BUT SO FAR WE'VE--
YOU STILL DON'T GET IT, DO YOU?
THEY WON'T HESITATE, EVEN FOR A SECOND, TO KILL YOU.
SO UNDERSTAND THIS:
IF YOUR ENEMY MAKES A SUSPICIOUS MOVE YOU TAKE THAT SHOT.
....
IF YOU AIM FOR CENTER MASS EVEN A BEGINNER LIKE YOU CAN HIT A TARGET.
CREEK
?
WHERE ARE YOU GOING?
IF I'M NOT BACK IN TEN MINUTES...
...TAKE RYUNOSUKE-SAN AND GET OUT OF HERE.

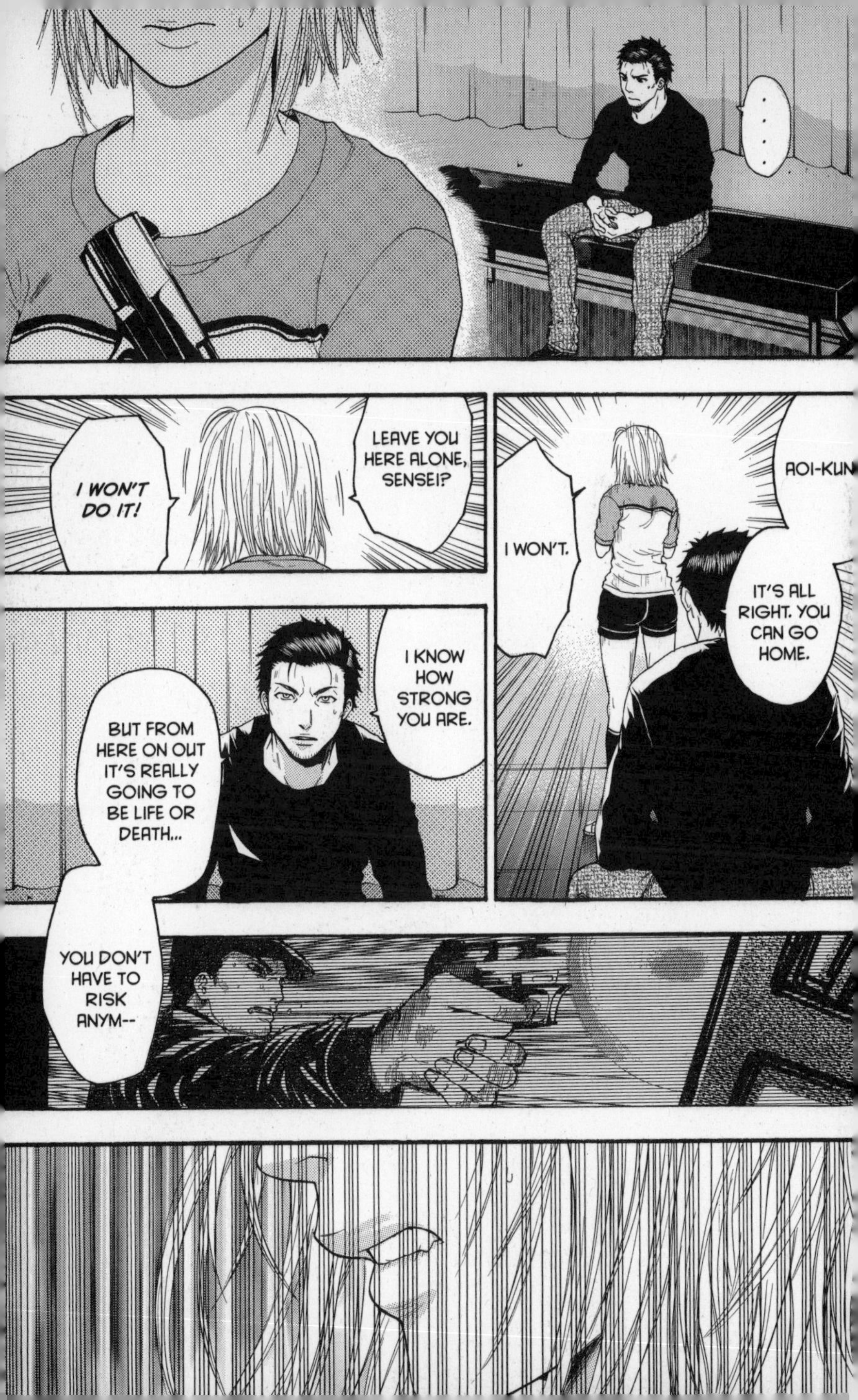
AOI-KUN
IT'S ALL RIGHT. YOU CAN GO HOME.
I WON'T.
LEAVE YOU HERE ALONE, SENSEI?
I WON'T DO IT!
I KNOW HOW STRONG YOU ARE.
BUT FROM HERE ON OUT IT'S REALLY GOING TO BE LIFE OR DEATH...
YOU DON'T HAVE TO RISK ANYM--

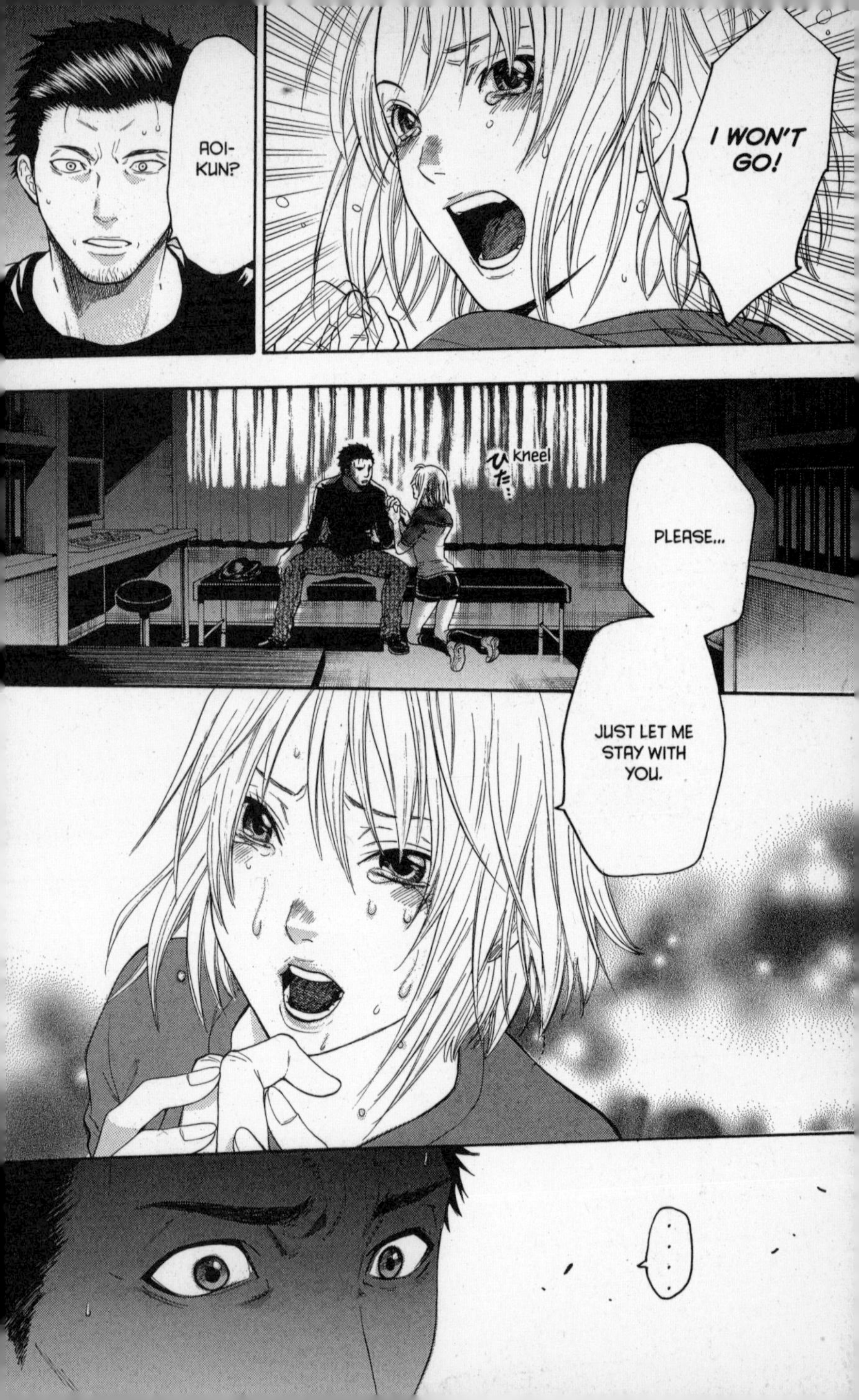
I WON'T GO!
AOI-KUN?
ひた…
kneel
PLEASE...
JUST LET ME STAY WITH YOU.
...

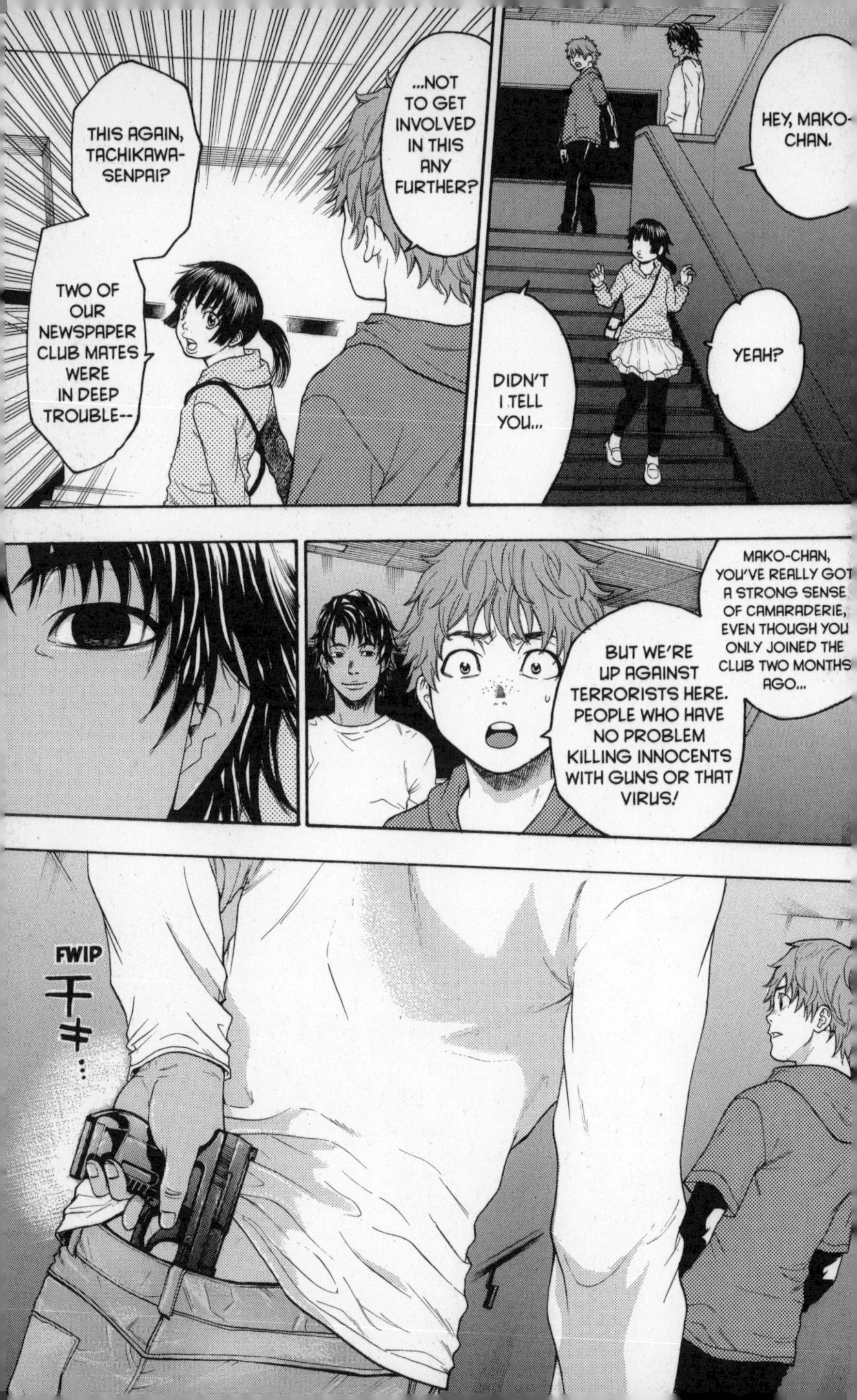
HEY, MAKO-CHAN.
YEAH?
DIDN'T I TELL YOU...
...NOT TO GET INVOLVED IN THIS ANY FURTHER?
THIS AGAIN, TACHIKAWA-SENPAI?
TWO OF OUR NEWSPAPER CLUB MATES WERE IN DEEP TROUBLE--
MAKO-CHAN, YOU'VE REALLY GOT A STRONG SENSE OF CAMARADERIE, EVEN THOUGH YOU ONLY JOINED THE CLUB TWO MONTHS AGO...
BUT WE'RE UP AGAINST TERRORISTS HERE. PEOPLE WHO HAVE NO PROBLEM KILLING INNOCENTS WITH GUNS OR THAT VIRUS!
FWIP

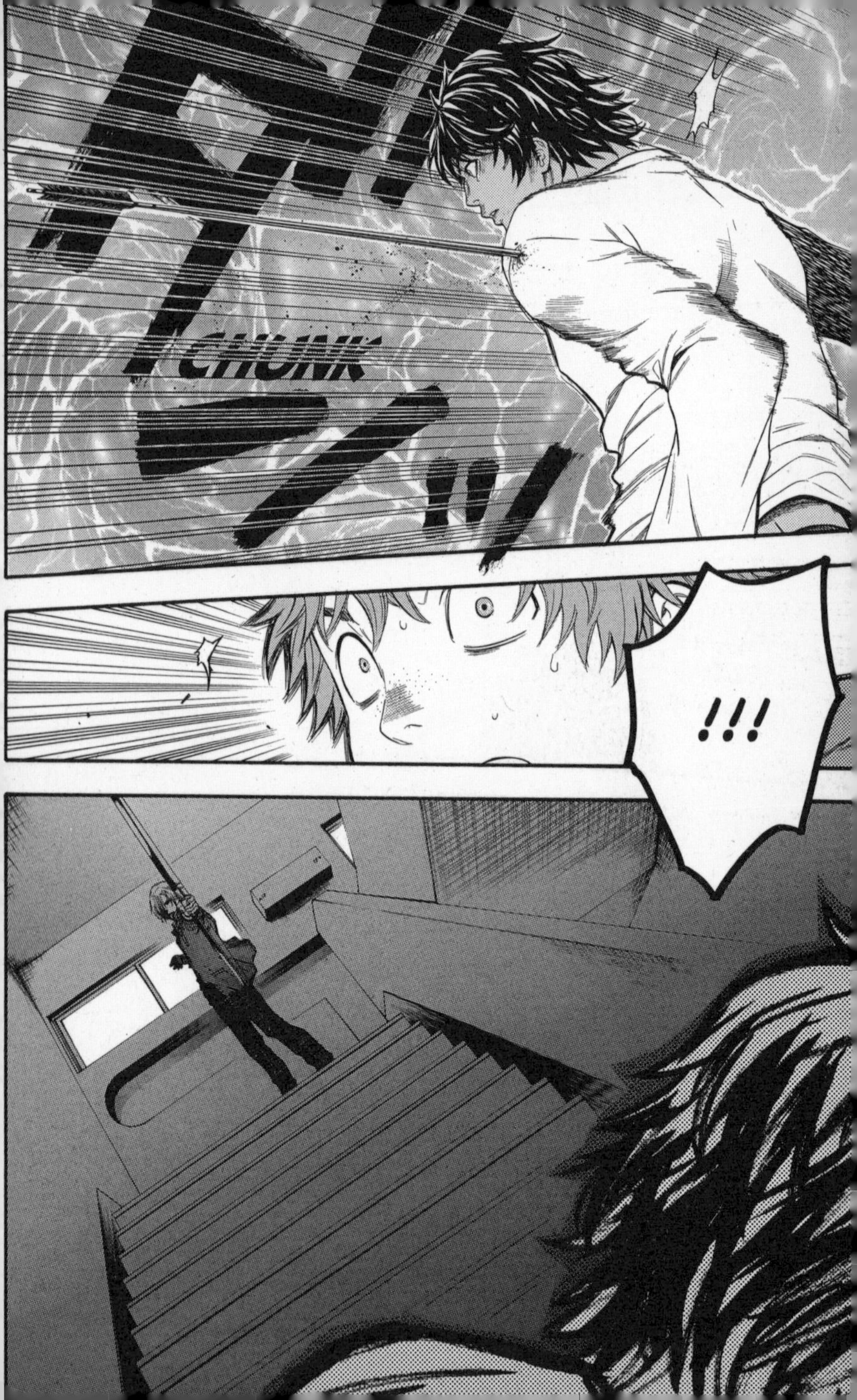
CHUNK
!!!

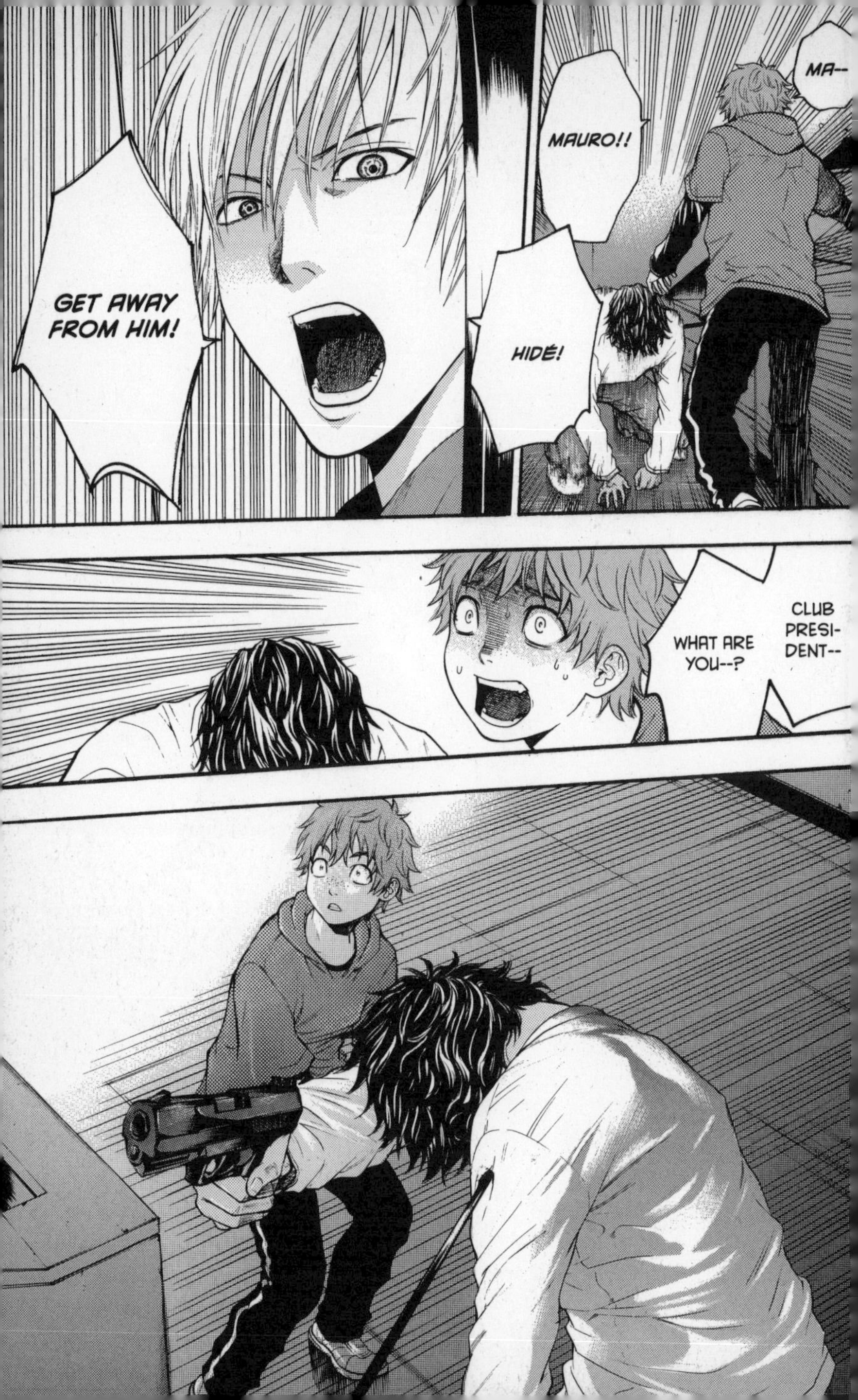
MA--
MAURO!!
HIDÉ!
GET AWAY FROM HIM!
CLUB PRESI-DENT--
WHAT ARE YOU--?

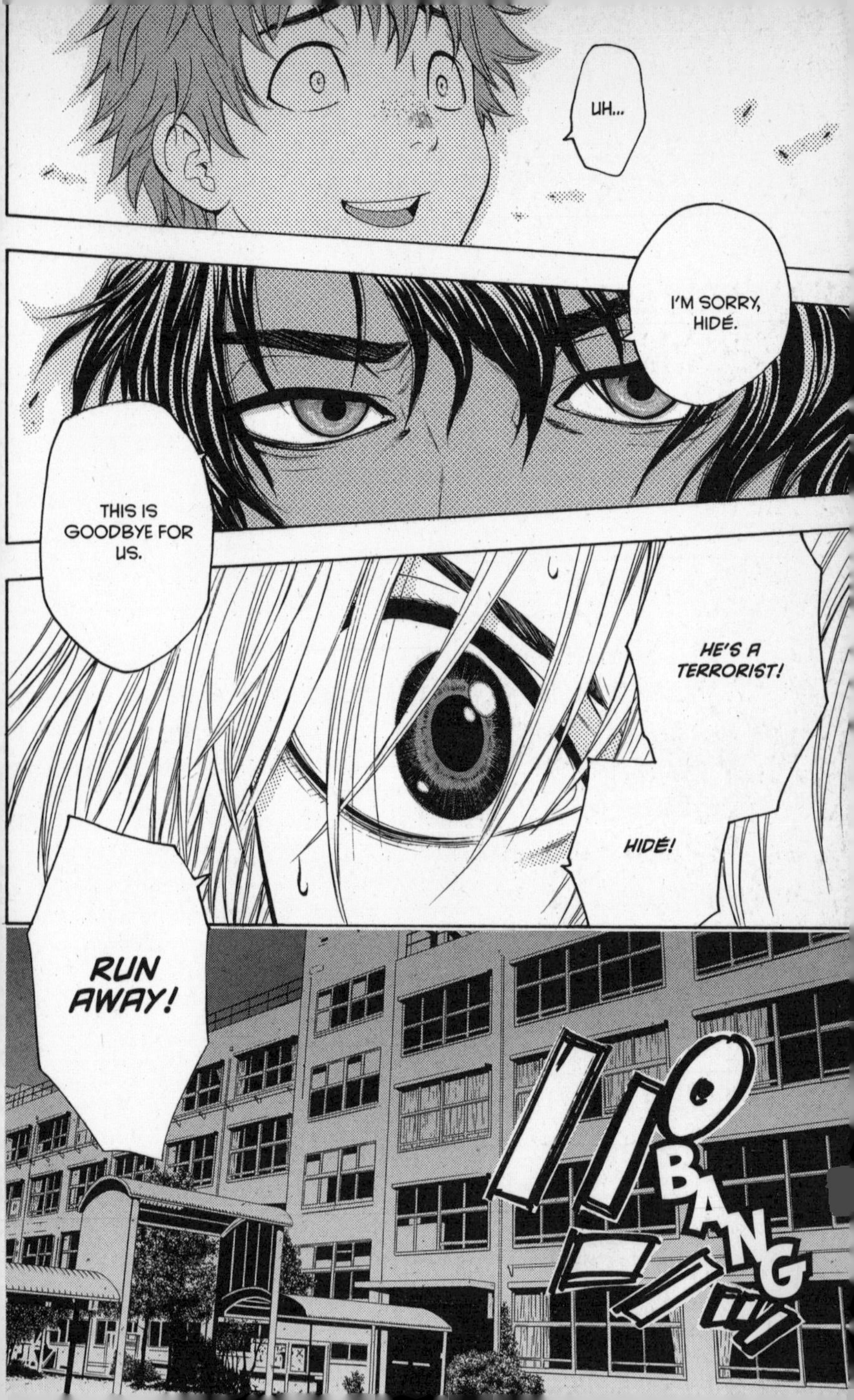

UH...
I'M SORRY, HIDÉ.
THIS IS GOODBYE FOR US.
HE'S A TERRORIST!
HIDÉ!
RUN AWAY!
BANG

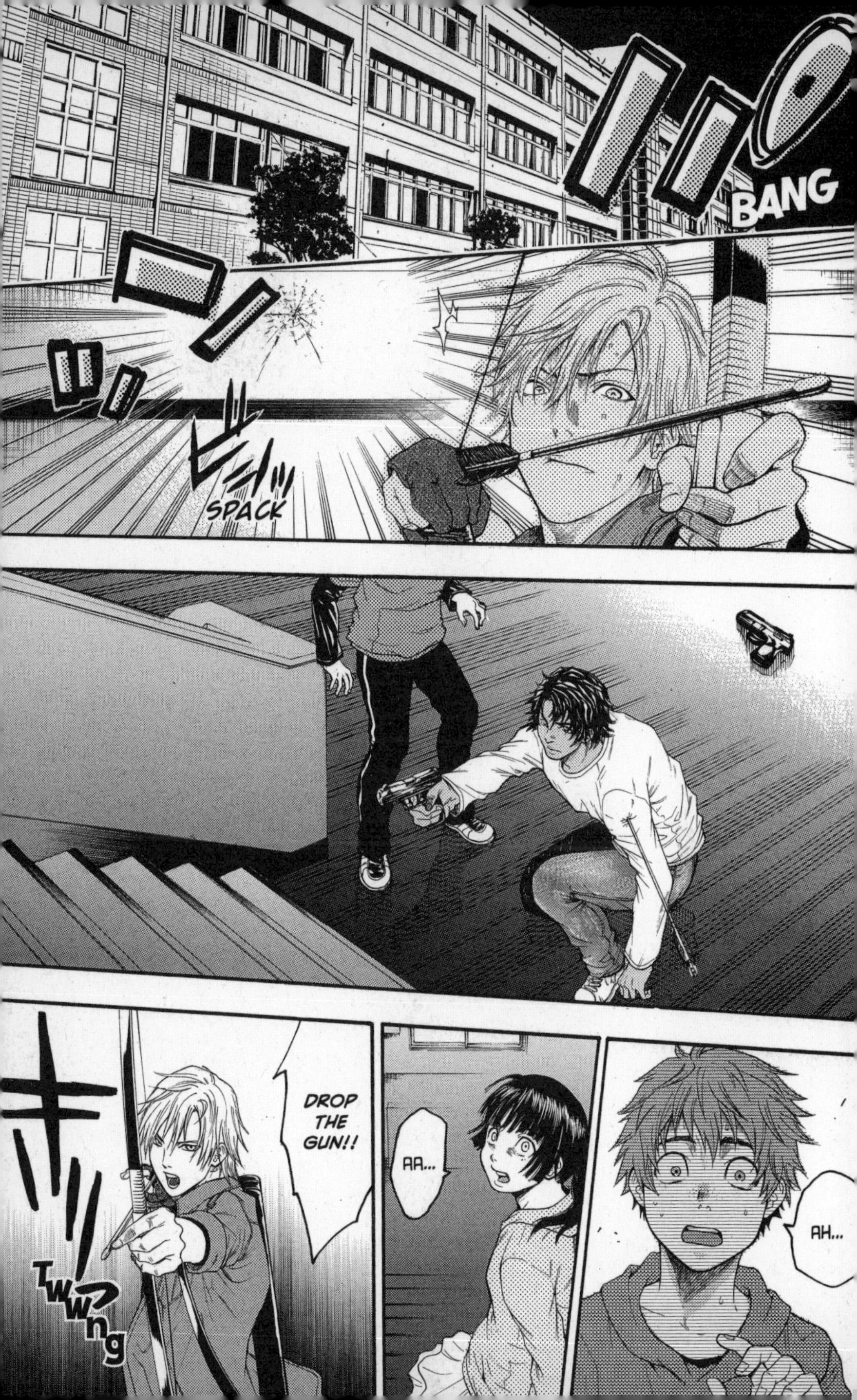
BANG
SPACK
AH...
AA...
DROP THE GUN!!
TWWng

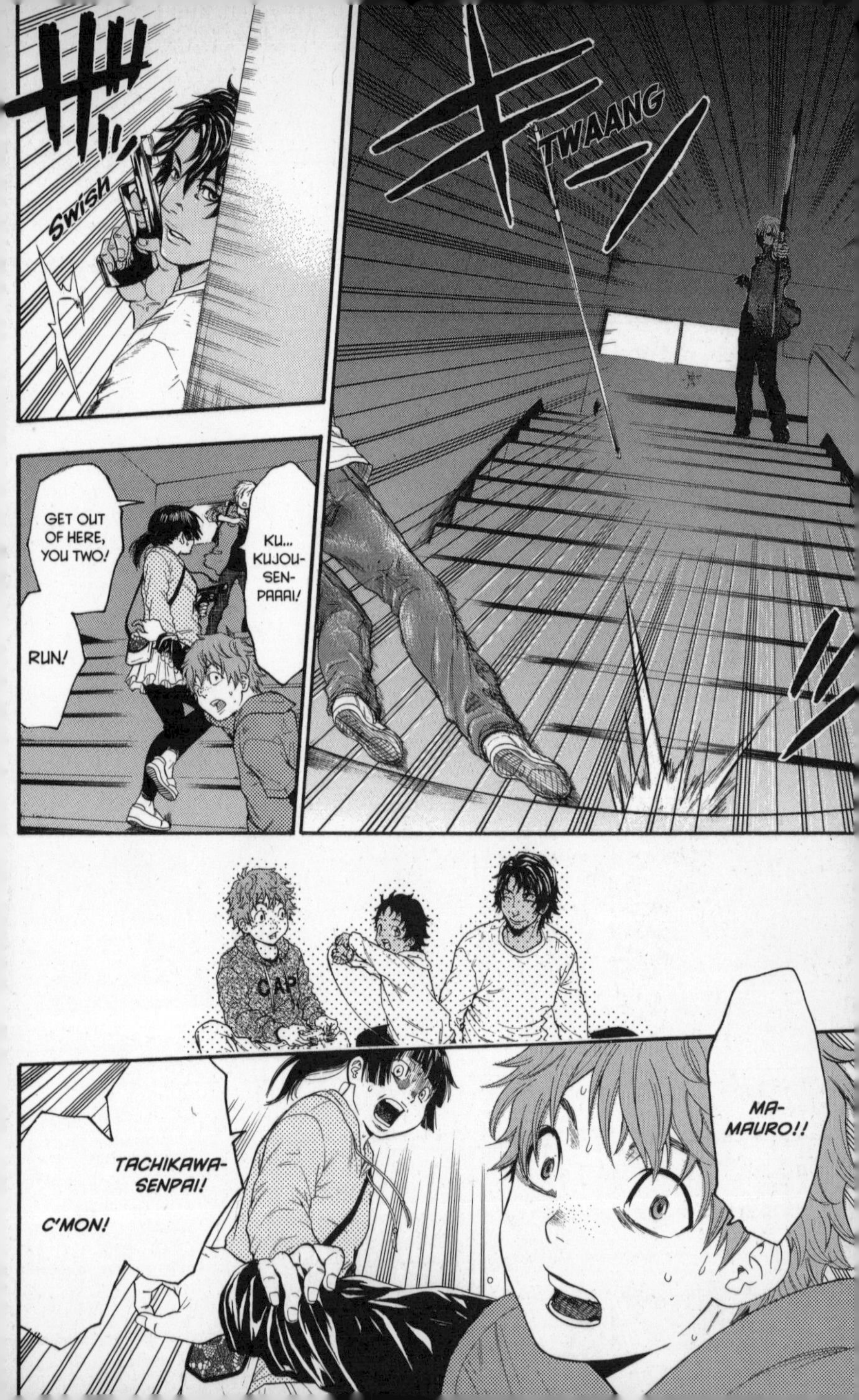
TWAANG
Swish
KU... KUJOU-SENPAAAI!
GET OUT OF HERE, YOU TWO!
RUN!
CAP
MA-MAURO!!
TACHIKAWA-SENPAI!
C'MON!

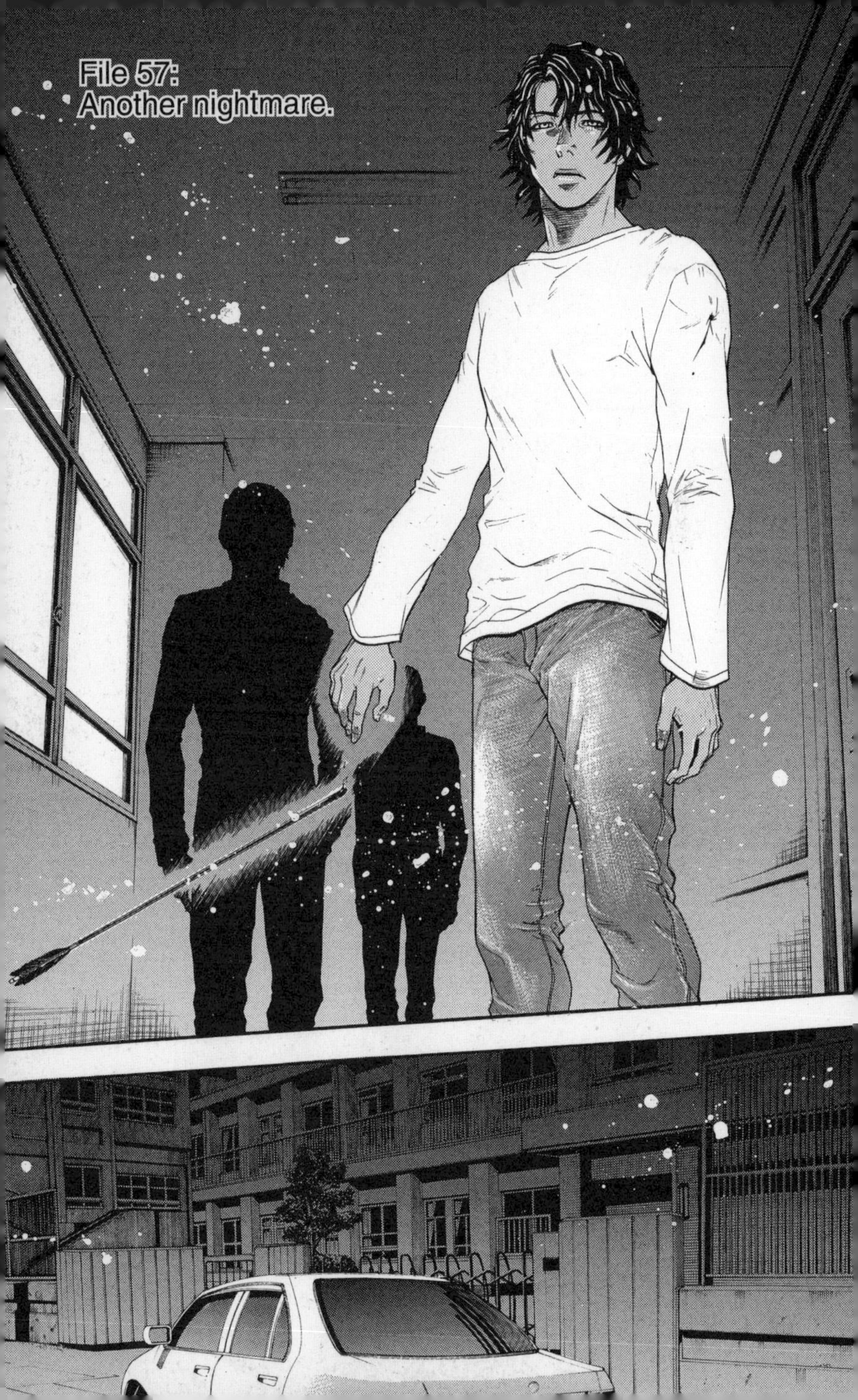
File 57:
Another nightmare.

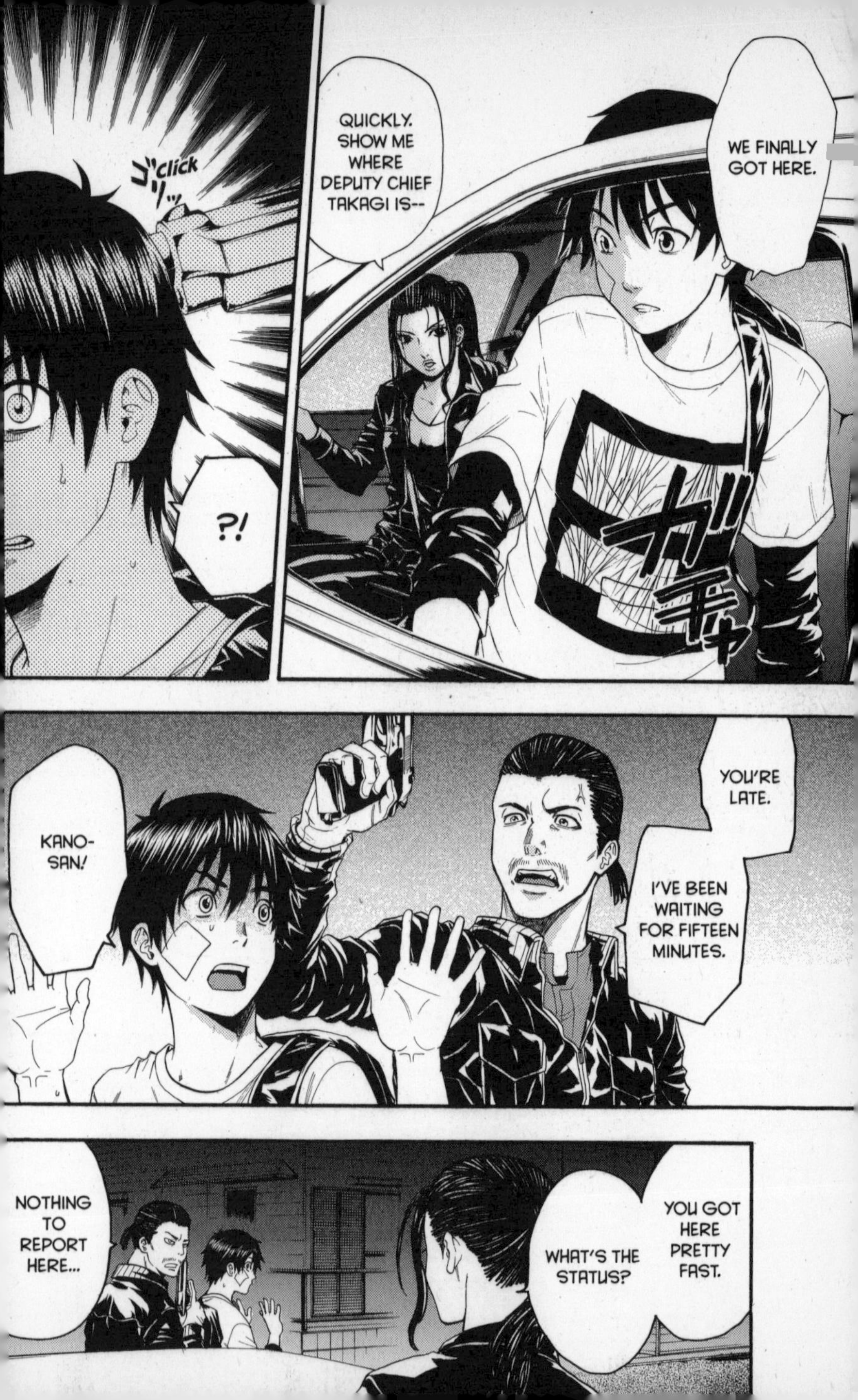
WE FINALLY GOT HERE.
QUICKLY. SHOW ME WHERE DEPUTY CHIEF TAKAGI IS--
click
?!
YOU'RE LATE.
I'VE BEEN WAITING FOR FIFTEEN MINUTES.
KANO-SAN!
YOU GOT HERE PRETTY FAST.
WHAT'S THE STATUS?
NOTHING TO REPORT HERE...

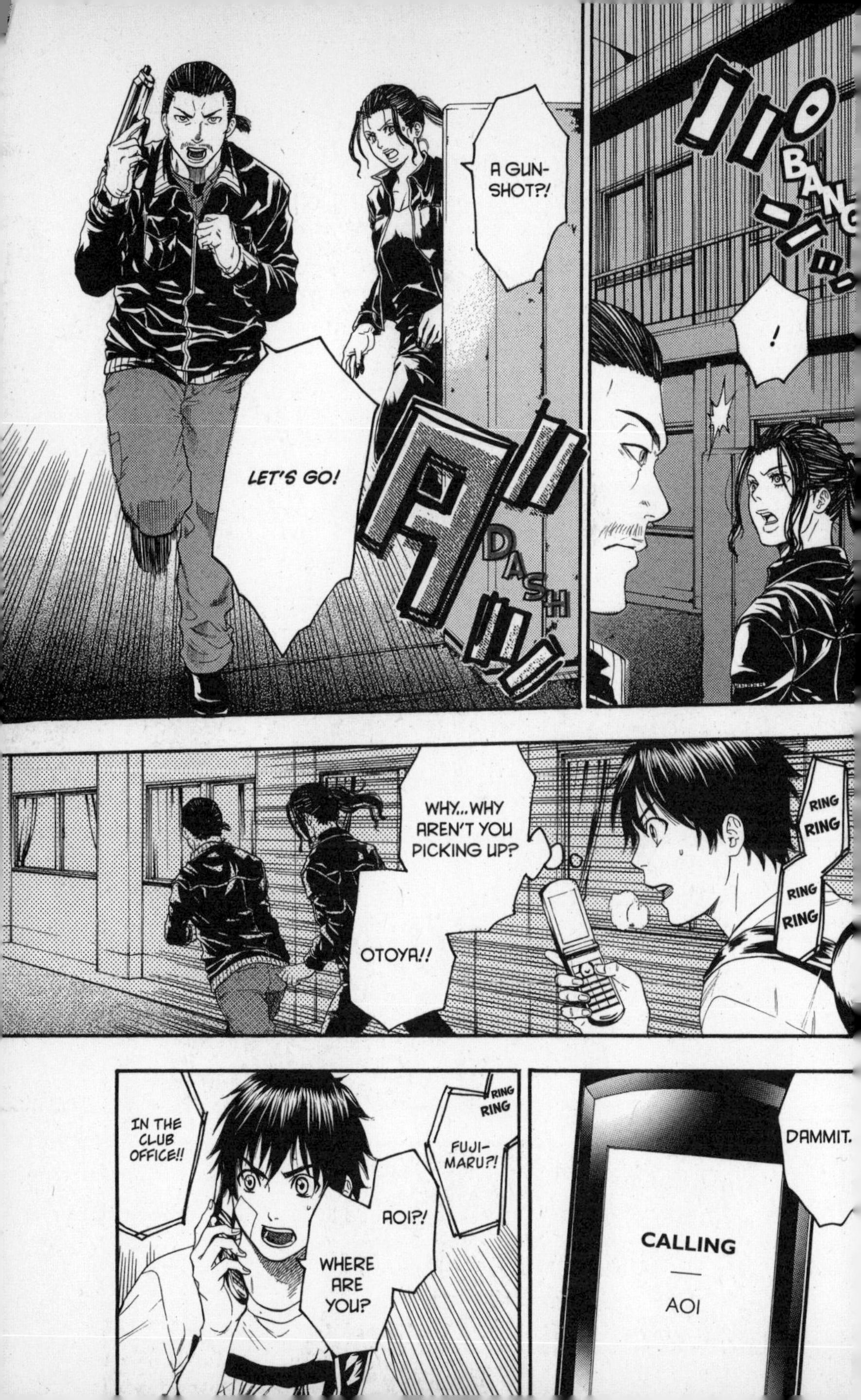
BANG
!
A GUN-SHOT?!
LET'S GO!
DASH
RING RING
RING RING
WHY...WHY AREN'T YOU PICKING UP?
OTOYA!!
DAMMIT.
CALLING
AOI
RING RING
FUJI-MARU?!
AOI?!
WHERE ARE YOU?
IN THE CLUB OFFICE!!

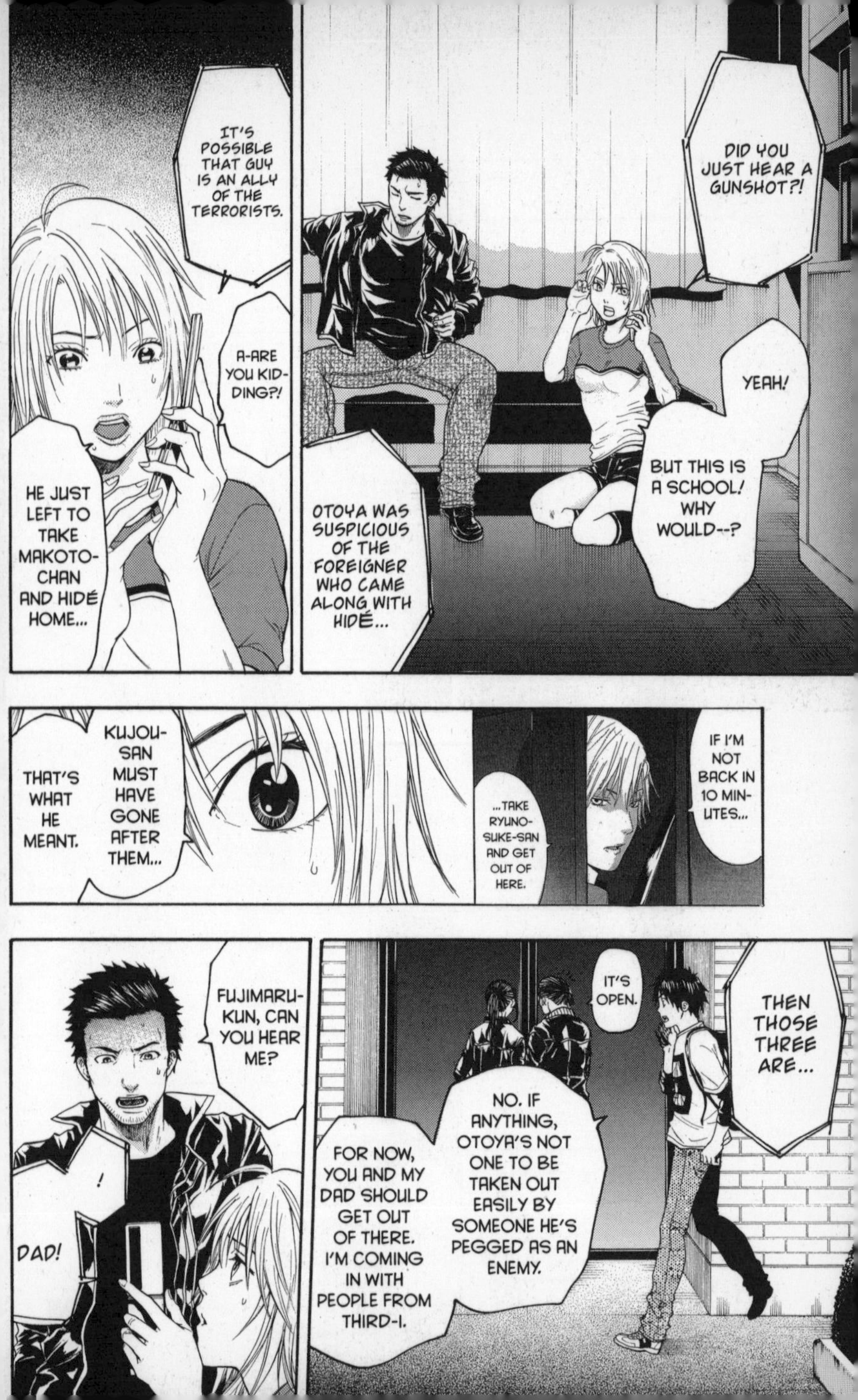
DID YOU JUST HEAR A GUNSHOT?!
YEAH!
BUT THIS IS A SCHOOL! WHY WOULD--?
OTOYA WAS SUSPICIOUS OF THE FOREIGNER WHO CAME ALONG WITH HIDÉ...
IT'S POSSIBLE THAT GUY IS AN ALLY OF THE TERRORISTS.
A-ARE YOU KIDDING?!
HE JUST LEFT TO TAKE MAKOTO-CHAN AND HIDÉ HOME...
IF I'M NOT BACK IN 10 MINUTES...
...TAKE RYUNOSUKE-SAN AND GET OUT OF HERE.
KUJOU-SAN MUST HAVE GONE AFTER THEM...
THAT'S WHAT HE MEANT.
THEN THOSE THREE ARE...
IT'S OPEN.
NO. IF ANYTHING, OTOYA'S NOT ONE TO BE TAKEN OUT EASILY BY SOMEONE HE'S PEGGED AS AN ENEMY.
FOR NOW, YOU AND MY DAD SHOULD GET OUT OF THERE. I'M COMING IN WITH PEOPLE FROM THIRD-I.
FUJIMARU-KUN, CAN YOU HEAR ME?
!
DAD!

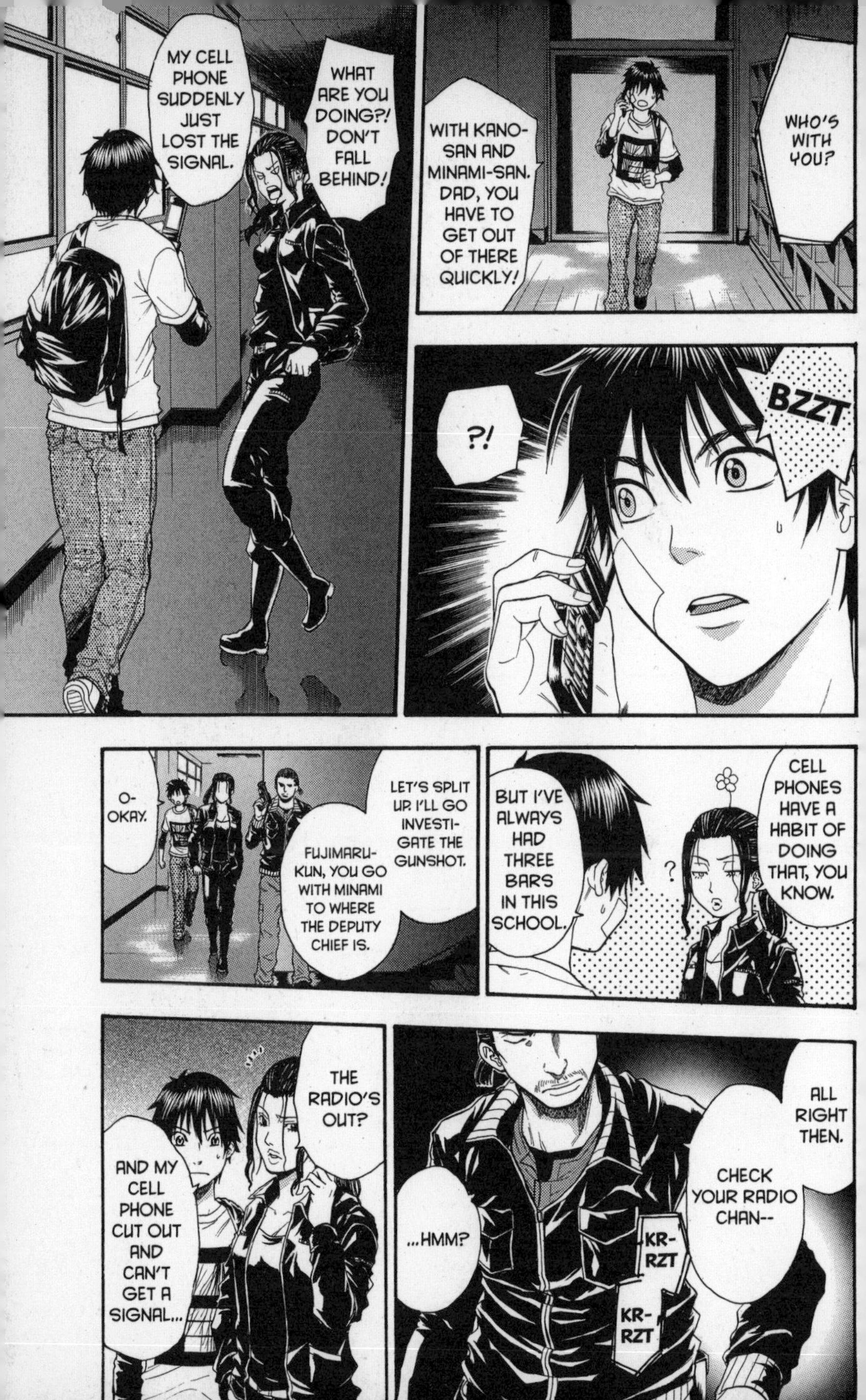
WHO'S WITH YOU?
WITH KANO-SAN AND MINAMI-SAN. DAD, YOU HAVE TO GET OUT OF THERE QUICKLY!
BZZT
?!
WHAT ARE YOU DOING?! DON'T FALL BEHIND!
MY CELL PHONE SUDDENLY JUST LOST THE SIGNAL.
CELL PHONES HAVE A HABIT OF DOING THAT, YOU KNOW.
?
BUT I'VE ALWAYS HAD THREE BARS IN THIS SCHOOL.
LET'S SPLIT UP. I'LL GO INVESTI-GATE THE GUNSHOT.
FUJIMARU-KUN, YOU GO WITH MINAMI TO WHERE THE DEPUTY CHIEF IS.
O-OKAY.
ALL RIGHT THEN.
CHECK YOUR RADIO CHAN--
KR-RZT
KR-RZT
...HMM?
THE RADIO'S OUT?
AND MY CELL PHONE CUT OUT AND CAN'T GET A SIGNAL...

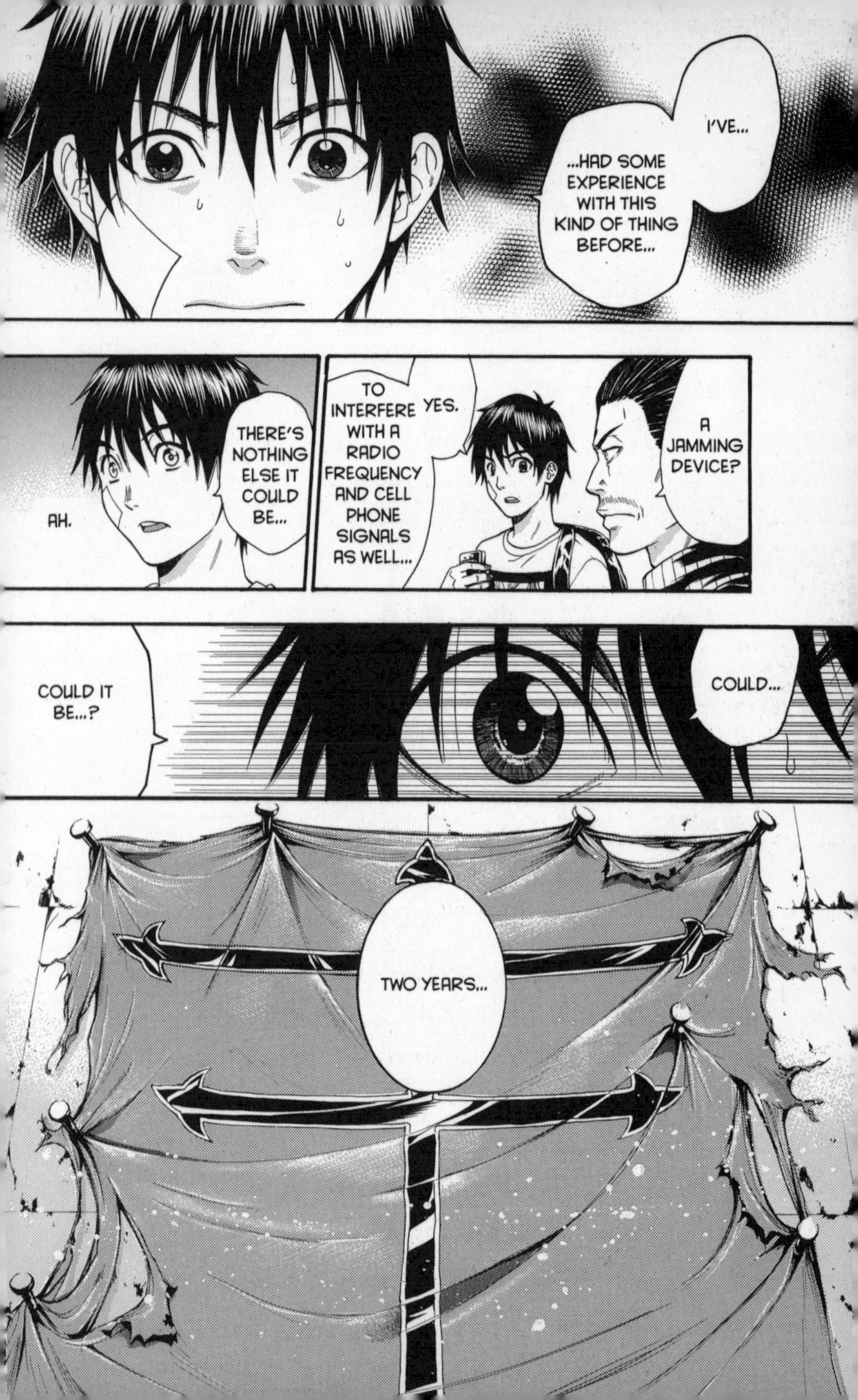
I'VE...
...HAD SOME EXPERIENCE WITH THIS KIND OF THING BEFORE...
A JAMMING DEVICE?
YES.
TO INTERFERE WITH A RADIO FREQUENCY AND CELL PHONE SIGNALS AS WELL...
THERE'S NOTHING ELSE IT COULD BE...
AH.
COULD...
COULD IT BE...?
TWO YEARS...

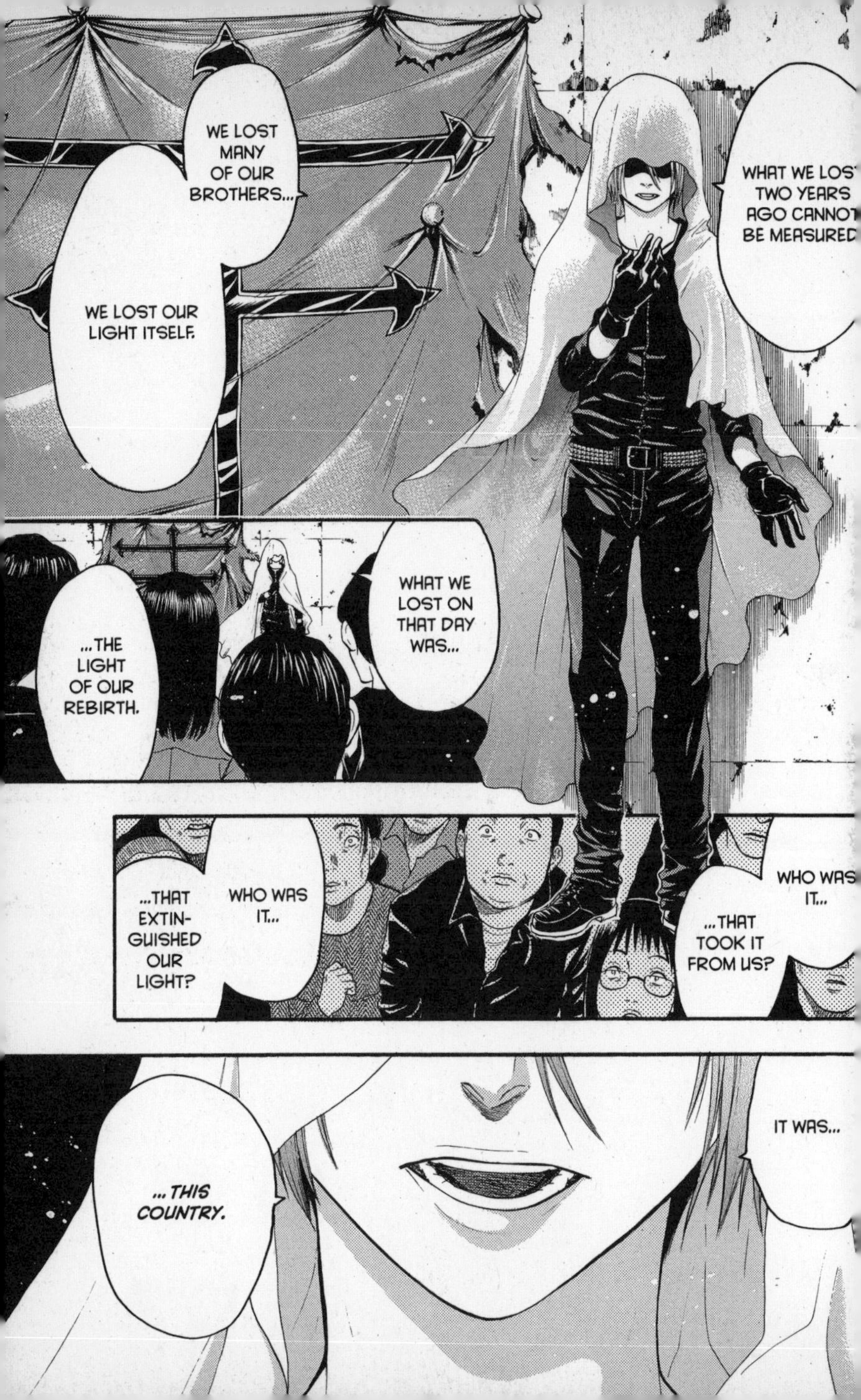
WHAT WE LOST TWO YEARS AGO CANNOT BE MEASURED
WE LOST MANY OF OUR BROTHERS...
WE LOST OUR LIGHT ITSELF.
WHAT WE LOST ON THAT DAY WAS...
...THE LIGHT OF OUR REBIRTH.
WHO WAS IT...
...THAT TOOK IT FROM US?
WHO WAS IT...
...THAT EXTINGUISHED OUR LIGHT?
IT WAS...
...THIS COUNTRY.

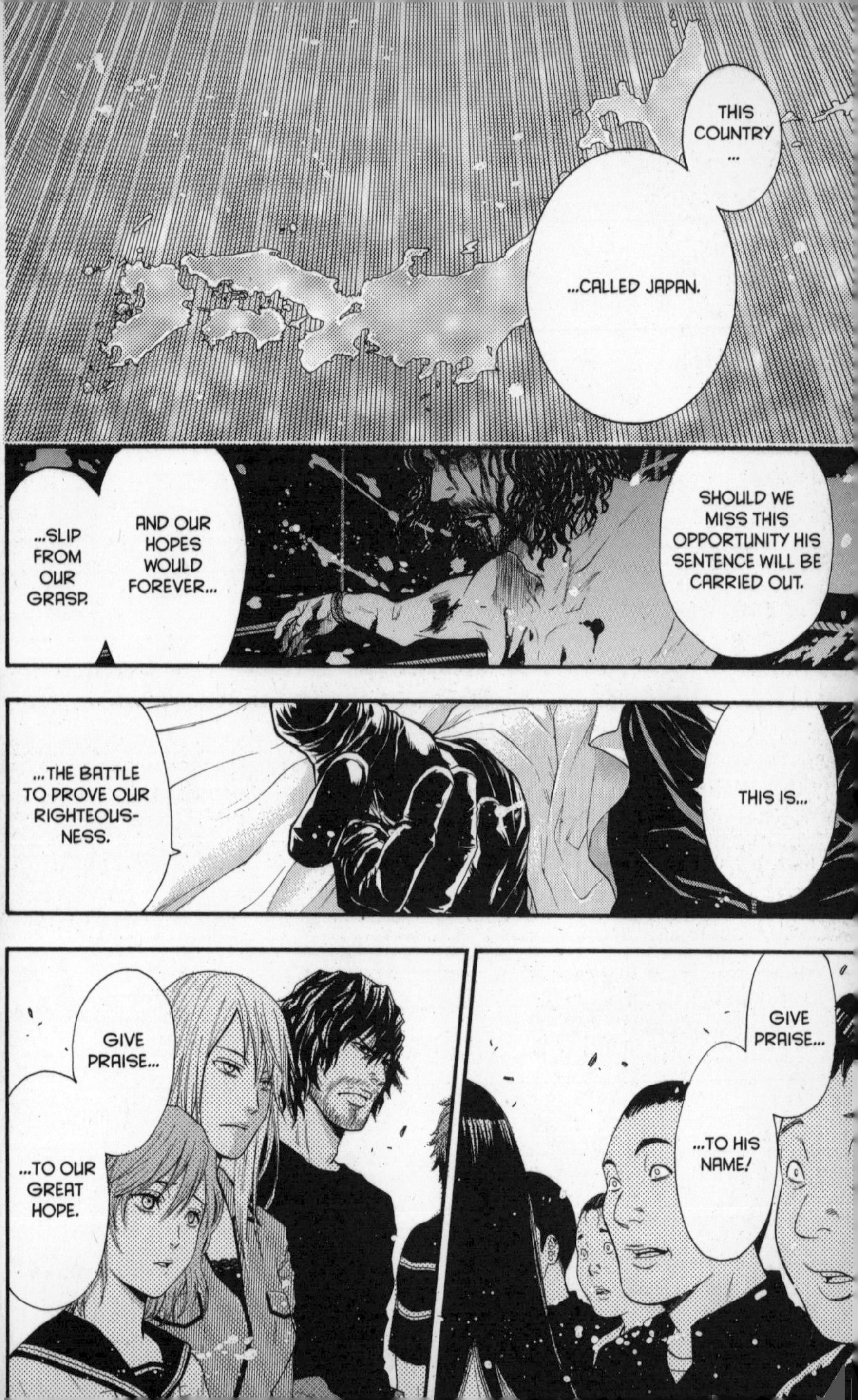
THIS COUNTRY ...
...CALLED JAPAN.
SHOULD WE MISS THIS OPPORTUNITY HIS SENTENCE WILL BE CARRIED OUT.
AND OUR HOPES WOULD FOREVER...
...SLIP FROM OUR GRASP.
THIS IS...
...THE BATTLE TO PROVE OUR RIGHTEOUSNESS.
GIVE PRAISE...
...TO HIS NAME!
GIVE PRAISE...
...TO OUR GREAT HOPE.

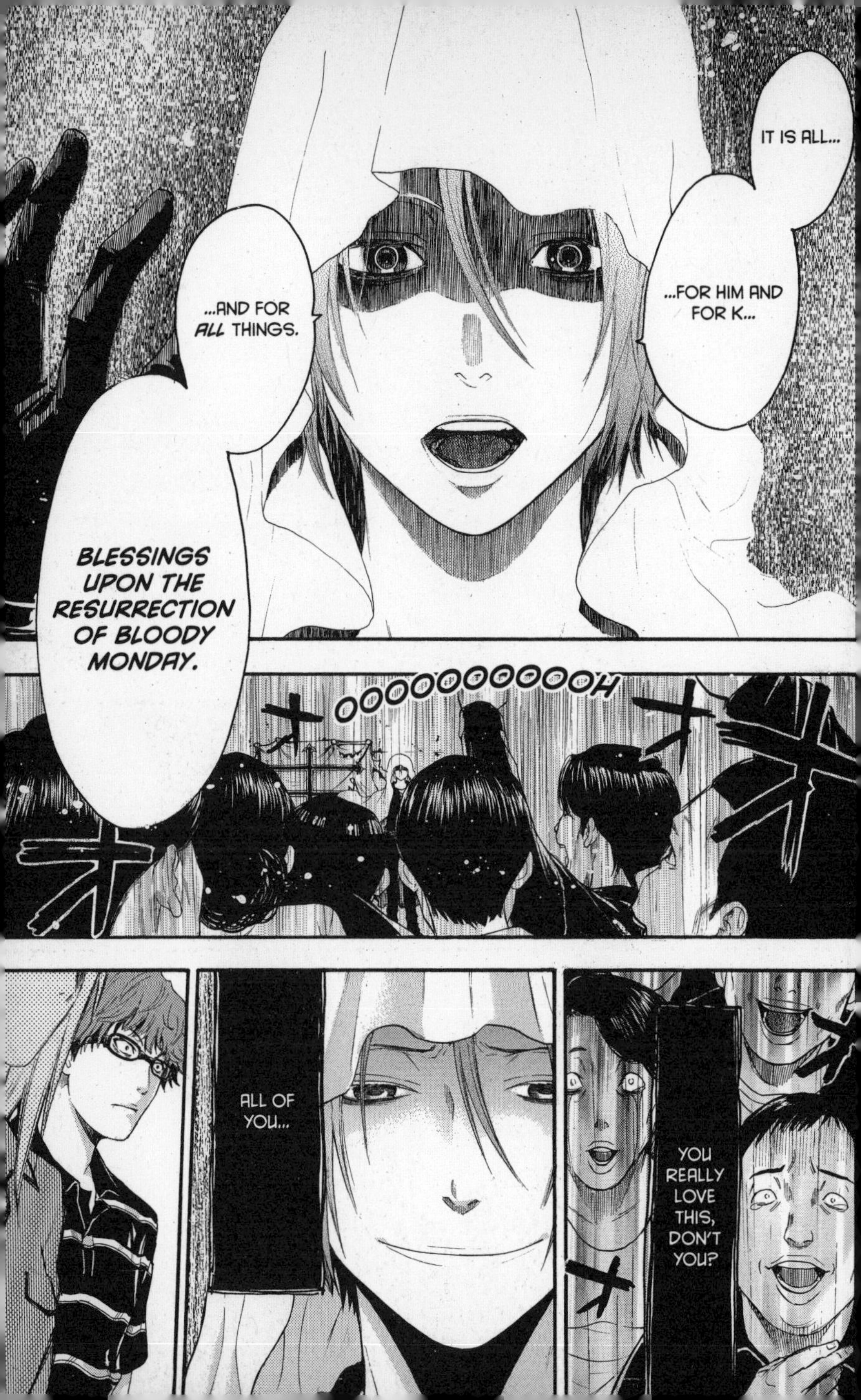
IT IS ALL...
...FOR HIM AND FOR K...
...AND FOR *ALL* THINGS.
BLESSINGS UPON THE RESURRECTION OF BLOODY MONDAY.
OOOOOOOOOOOH
YOU REALLY LOVE THIS, DON'T YOU?
ALL OF YOU...

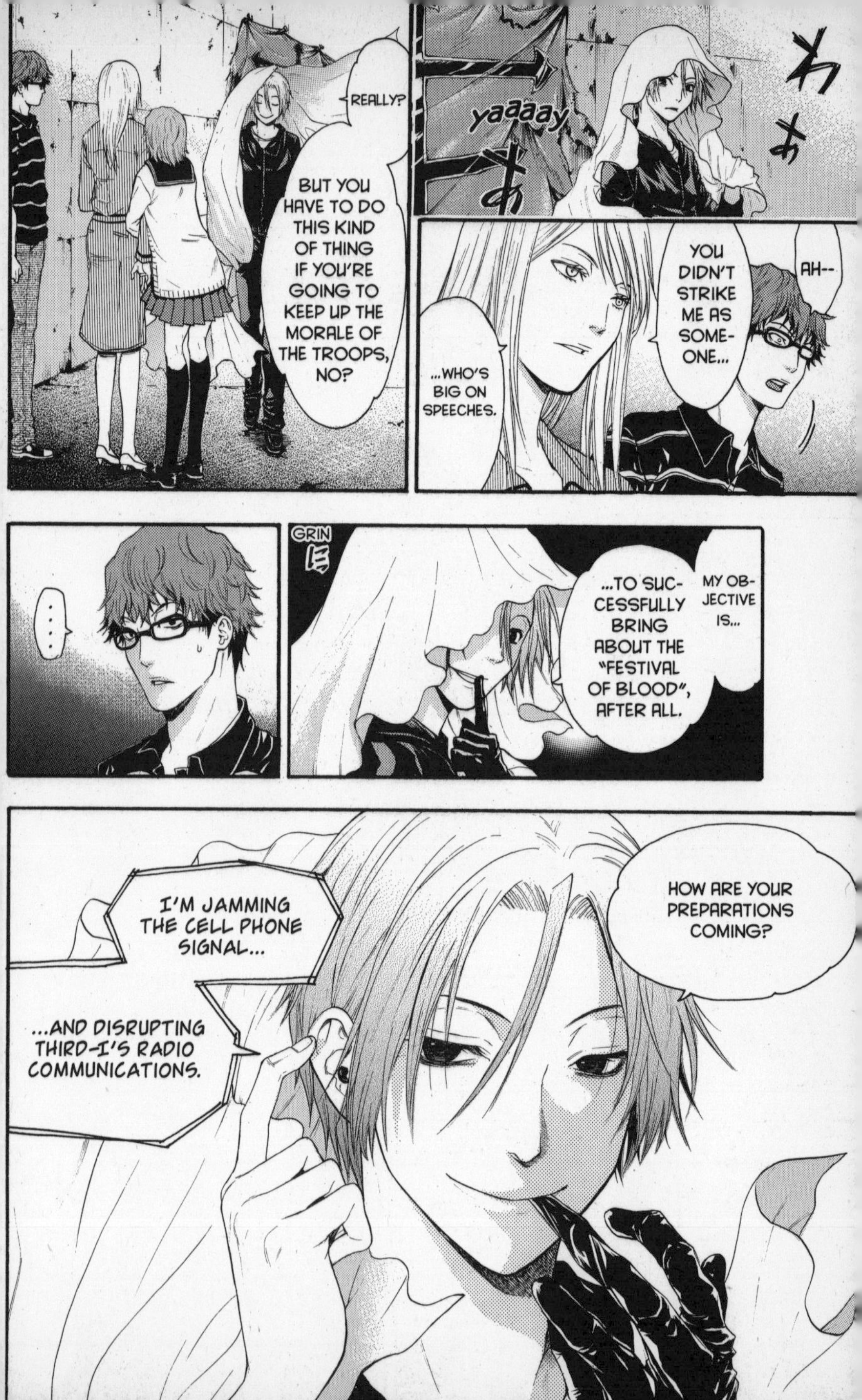

わぁ
yaaaay
AH--
YOU DIDN'T STRIKE ME AS SOME-ONE...
...WHO'S BIG ON SPEECHES.
REALLY?
BUT YOU HAVE TO DO THIS KIND OF THING IF YOU'RE GOING TO KEEP UP THE MORALE OF THE TROOPS, NO?
MY OBJECTIVE IS...
...TO SUCCESSFULLY BRING ABOUT THE "FESTIVAL OF BLOOD", AFTER ALL.
GRIN
....
HOW ARE YOUR PREPARATIONS COMING?
I'M JAMMING THE CELL PHONE SIGNAL...
...AND DISRUPTING THIRD-I'S RADIO COMMUNICATIONS.

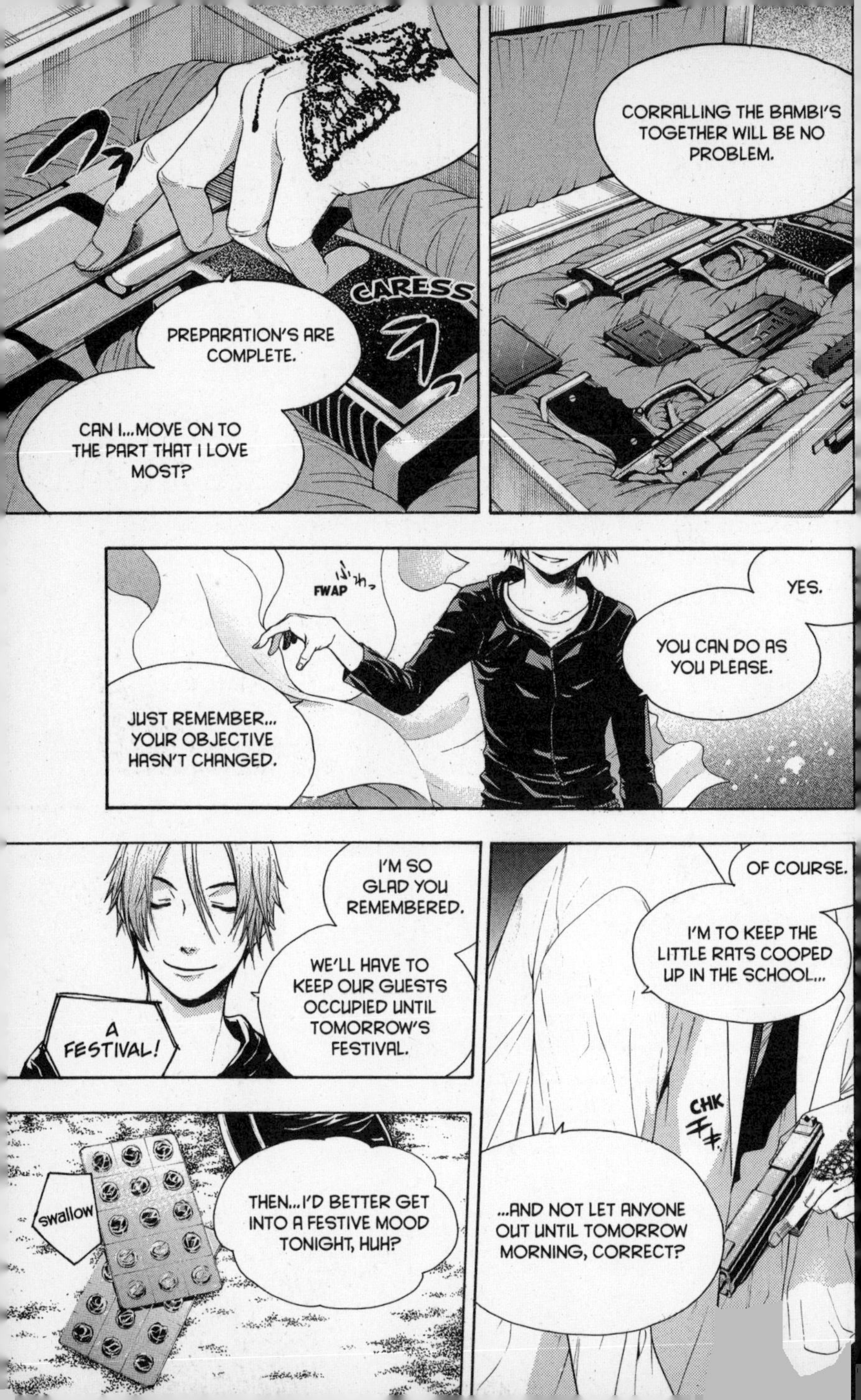
CORRALLING THE BAMBI'S TOGETHER WILL BE NO PROBLEM.
CARESS
PREPARATION'S ARE COMPLETE.
CAN I...MOVE ON TO THE PART THAT I LOVE MOST?
YES.
YOU CAN DO AS YOU PLEASE.
FWAP
JUST REMEMBER... YOUR OBJECTIVE HASN'T CHANGED.
OF COURSE.
I'M TO KEEP THE LITTLE RATS COOPED UP IN THE SCHOOL...
CHK
...AND NOT LET ANYONE OUT UNTIL TOMORROW MORNING, CORRECT?
I'M SO GLAD YOU REMEMBERED.
WE'LL HAVE TO KEEP OUR GUESTS OCCUPIED UNTIL TOMORROW'S FESTIVAL.
A FESTIVAL!
THEN...I'D BETTER GET INTO A FESTIVE MOOD TONIGHT, HUH?
swallow

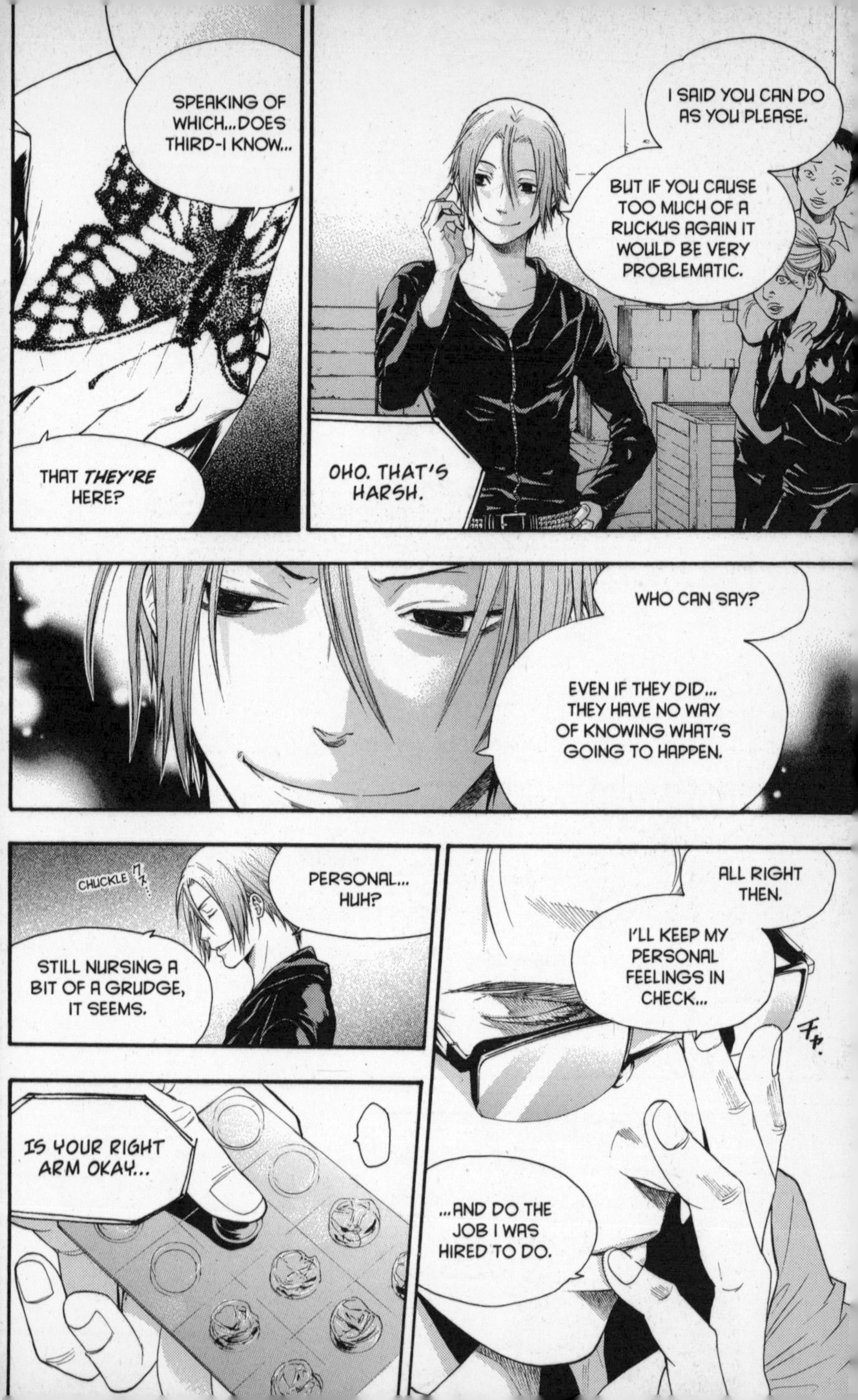
I SAID YOU CAN DO AS YOU PLEASE.
BUT IF YOU CAUSE TOO MUCH OF A RUCKUS AGAIN IT WOULD BE VERY PROBLEMATIC.
OHO. THAT'S HARSH.
SPEAKING OF WHICH...DOES THIRD-I KNOW...
THAT *THEY'RE* HERE?
WHO CAN SAY?
EVEN IF THEY DID... THEY HAVE NO WAY OF KNOWING WHAT'S GOING TO HAPPEN.
ALL RIGHT THEN.
I'LL KEEP MY PERSONAL FEELINGS IN CHECK...
...AND DO THE JOB I WAS HIRED TO DO.
PERSONAL... HUH?
CHUCKLE
STILL NURSING A BIT OF A GRUDGE, IT SEEMS.
IS YOUR RIGHT ARM OKAY...

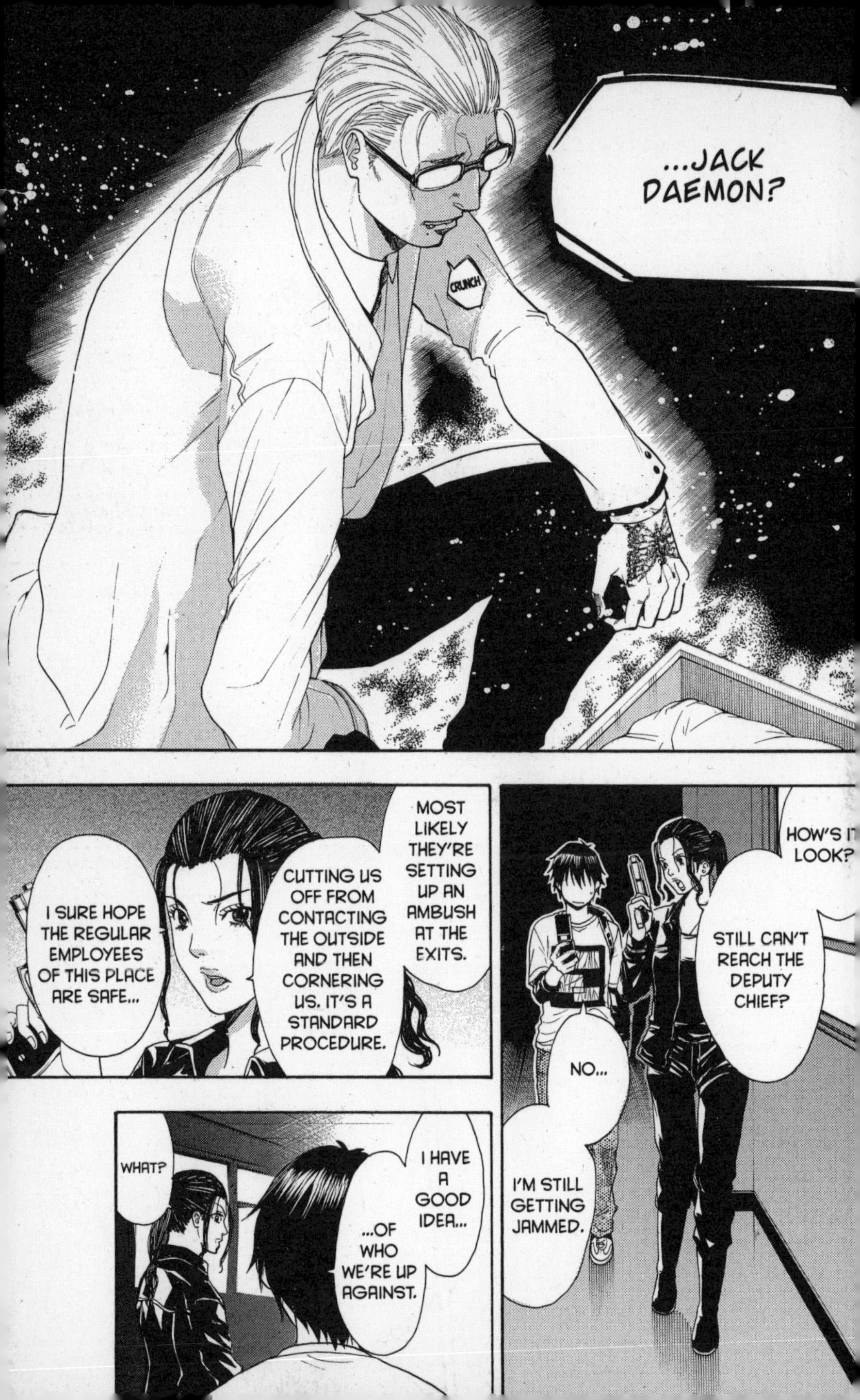
...JACK DAEMON?
CRUNCH
HOW'S IT LOOK?
STILL CAN'T REACH THE DEPUTY CHIEF?
NO...
I'M STILL GETTING JAMMED.
MOST LIKELY THEY'RE SETTING UP AN AMBUSH AT THE EXITS.
CUTTING US OFF FROM CONTACTING THE OUTSIDE AND THEN CORNERING US. IT'S A STANDARD PROCEDURE.
I SURE HOPE THE REGULAR EMPLOYEES OF THIS PLACE ARE SAFE...
I HAVE A GOOD IDEA...
...OF WHO WE'RE UP AGAINST.
WHAT?

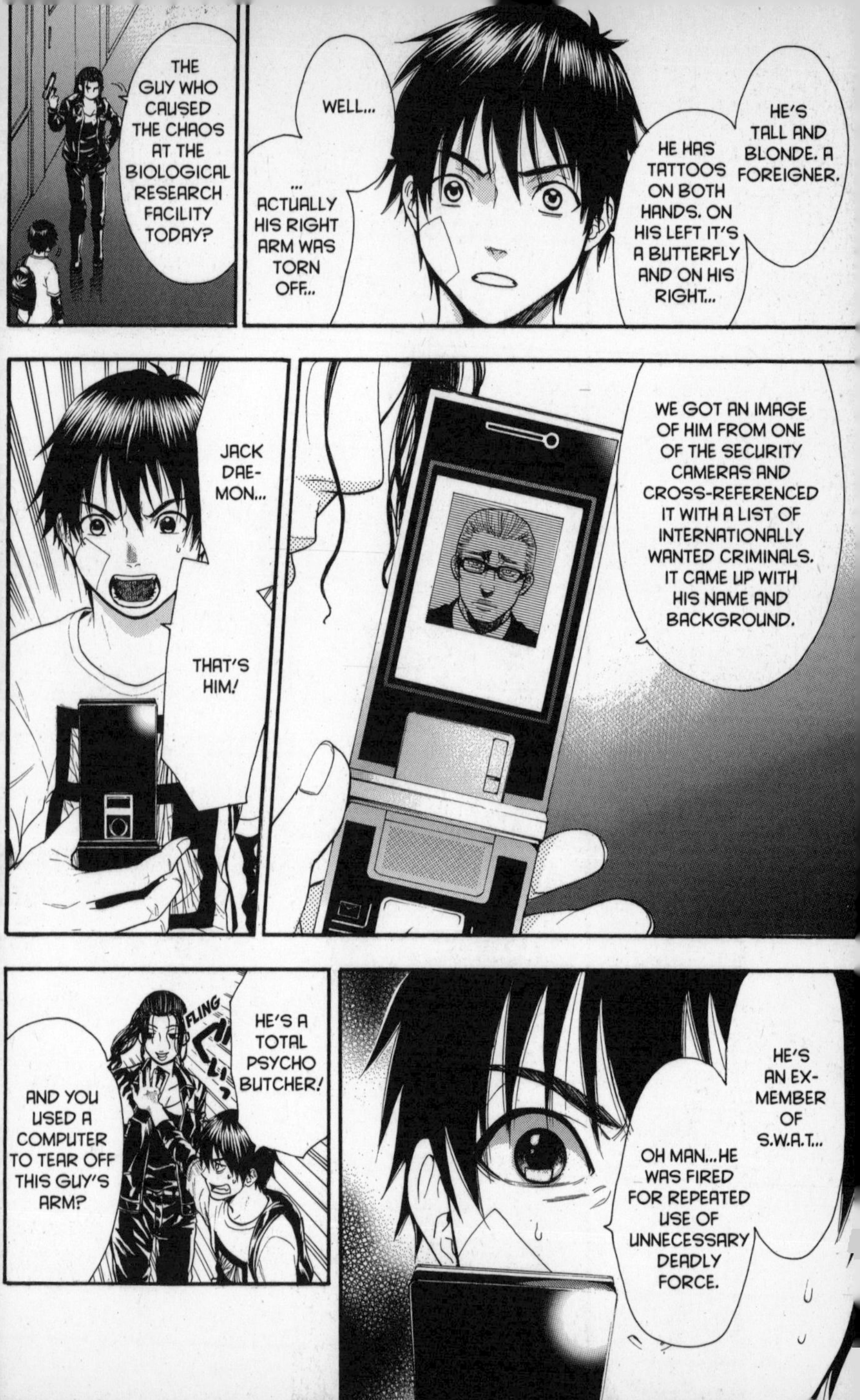
HE'S TALL AND BLONDE. A FOREIGNER.
HE HAS TATTOOS ON BOTH HANDS. ON HIS LEFT IT'S A BUTTERFLY AND ON HIS RIGHT...
WELL...
...ACTUALLY HIS RIGHT ARM WAS TORN OFF...
THE GUY WHO CAUSED THE CHAOS AT THE BIOLOGICAL RESEARCH FACILITY TODAY?
WE GOT AN IMAGE OF HIM FROM ONE OF THE SECURITY CAMERAS AND CROSS-REFERENCED IT WITH A LIST OF INTERNATIONALLY WANTED CRIMINALS. IT CAME UP WITH HIS NAME AND BACKGROUND.
JACK DAE-MON...
THAT'S HIM!
HE'S AN EX-MEMBER OF S.W.A.T...
OH MAN...HE WAS FIRED FOR REPEATED USE OF UNNECESSARY DEADLY FORCE.
HE'S A TOTAL PSYCHO BUTCHER!
FLING
AND YOU USED A COMPUTER TO TEAR OFF THIS GUY'S ARM?

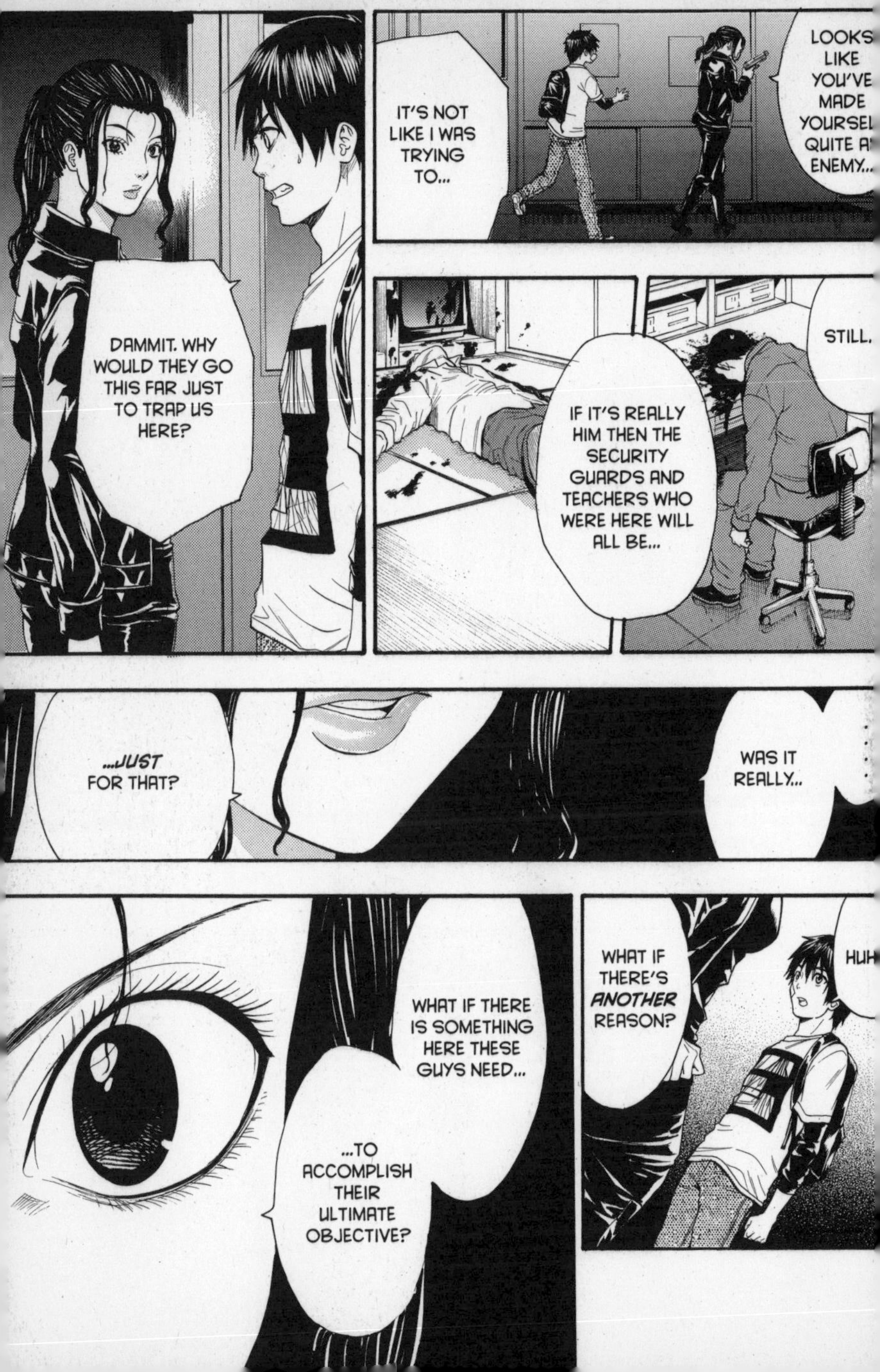
LOOKS LIKE YOU'VE MADE YOURSEL QUITE A ENEMY...
IT'S NOT LIKE I WAS TRYING TO...
STILL.
IF IT'S REALLY HIM THEN THE SECURITY GUARDS AND TEACHERS WHO WERE HERE WILL ALL BE...
DAMMIT. WHY WOULD THEY GO THIS FAR JUST TO TRAP US HERE?
WAS IT REALLY...
...JUST FOR THAT?
HUH
WHAT IF THERE'S ANOTHER REASON?
WHAT IF THERE IS SOMETHING HERE THESE GUYS NEED...
...TO ACCOMPLISH THEIR ULTIMATE OBJECTIVE?

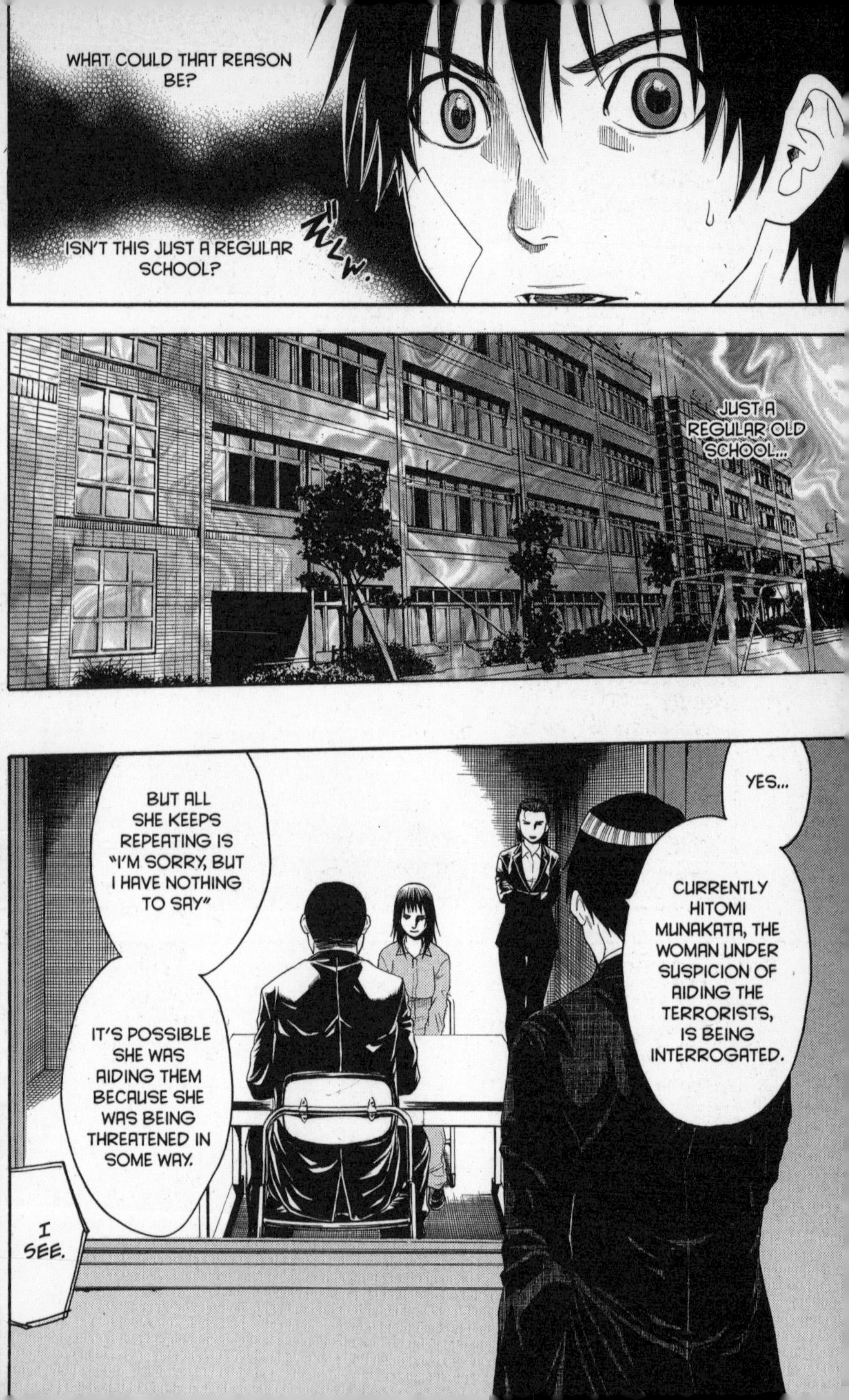
WHAT COULD THAT REASON BE?
ISN'T THIS JUST A REGULAR SCHOOL?
JUST A REGULAR OLD SCHOOL...
YES...
CURRENTLY HITOMI MUNAKATA, THE WOMAN UNDER SUSPICION OF AIDING THE TERRORISTS, IS BEING INTERROGATED.
BUT ALL SHE KEEPS REPEATING IS "I'M SORRY, BUT I HAVE NOTHING TO SAY"
IT'S POSSIBLE SHE WAS AIDING THEM BECAUSE SHE WAS BEING THREATENED IN SOME WAY.
I SEE.

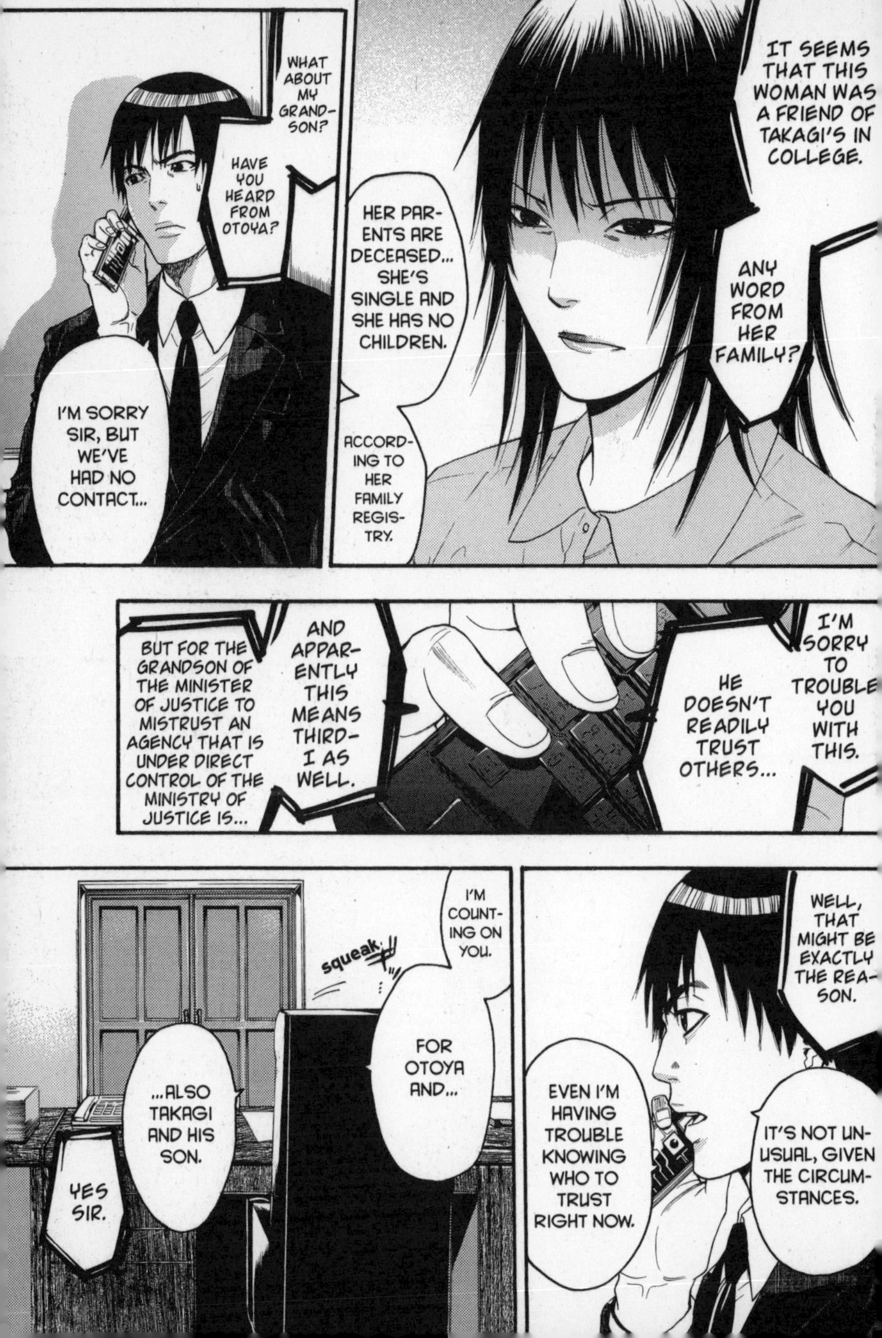
IT SEEMS THAT THIS WOMAN WAS A FRIEND OF TAKAGI'S IN COLLEGE.
ANY WORD FROM HER FAMILY?
HER PARENTS ARE DECEASED... SHE'S SINGLE AND SHE HAS NO CHILDREN.
ACCORDING TO HER FAMILY REGISTRY.
WHAT ABOUT MY GRANDSON?
HAVE YOU HEARD FROM OTOYA?
I'M SORRY SIR, BUT WE'VE HAD NO CONTACT...
I'M SORRY TO TROUBLE YOU WITH THIS.
HE DOESN'T READILY TRUST OTHERS...
AND APPARENTLY THIS MEANS THIRD-I AS WELL.
BUT FOR THE GRANDSON OF THE MINISTER OF JUSTICE TO MISTRUST AN AGENCY THAT IS UNDER DIRECT CONTROL OF THE MINISTRY OF JUSTICE IS...
WELL, THAT MIGHT BE EXACTLY THE REASON.
IT'S NOT UNUSUAL, GIVEN THE CIRCUMSTANCES.
EVEN I'M HAVING TROUBLE KNOWING WHO TO TRUST RIGHT NOW.
I'M COUNTING ON YOU.
squeak
FOR OTOYA AND...
...ALSO TAKAGI AND HIS SON.
YES SIR.

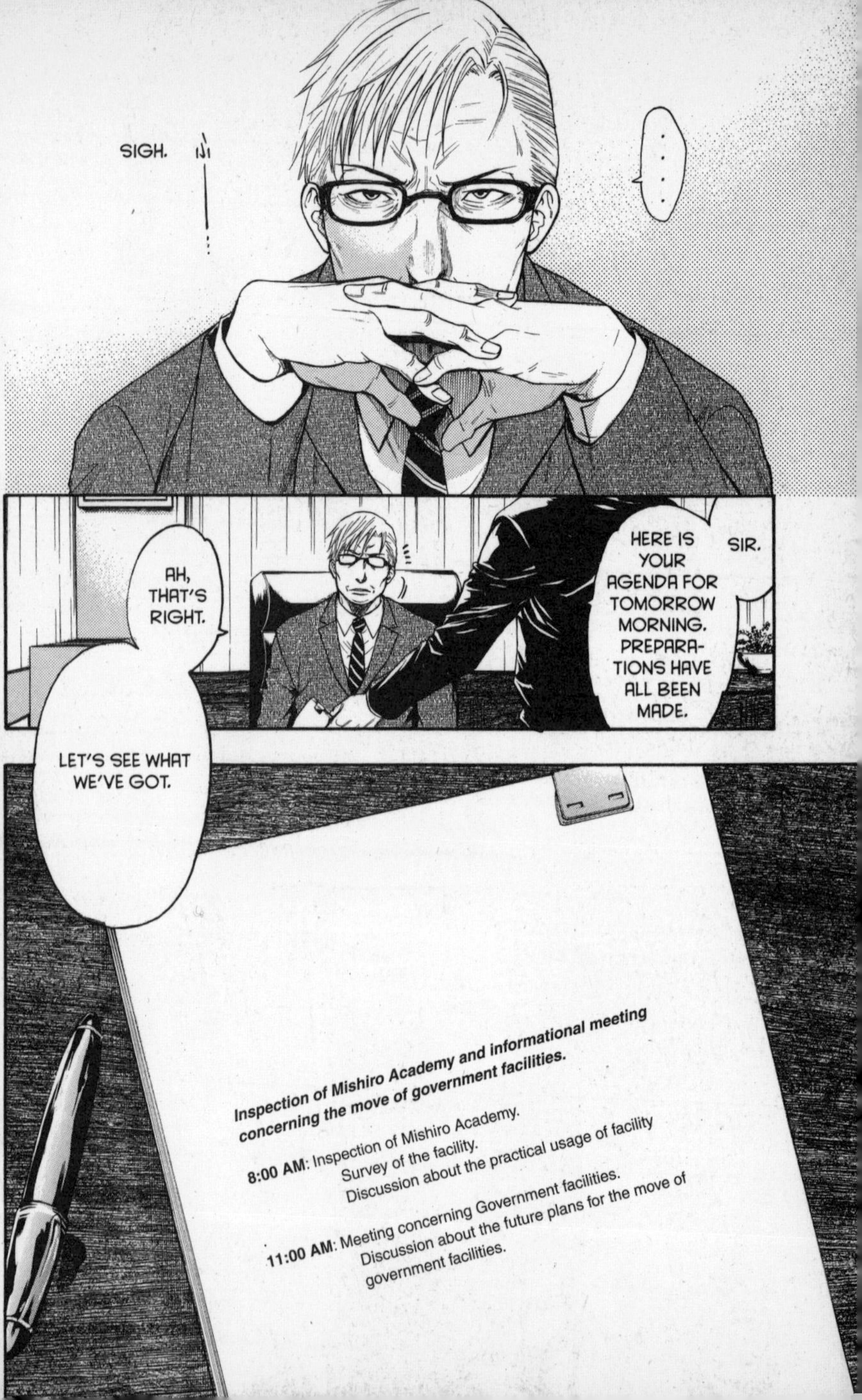
. . . .
SIGH.
SIR.
HERE IS YOUR AGENDA FOR TOMORROW MORNING. PREPARATIONS HAVE ALL BEEN MADE.
AH, THAT'S RIGHT.
LET'S SEE WHAT WE'VE GOT.
Inspection of Mishiro Academy and informational meeting concerning the move of government facilities.
8:00 AM: Inspection of Mishiro Academy.
Survey of the facility.
Discussion about the practical usage of facility
11:00 AM: Meeting concerning Government facilities.
Discussion about the future plans for the move of government facilities.

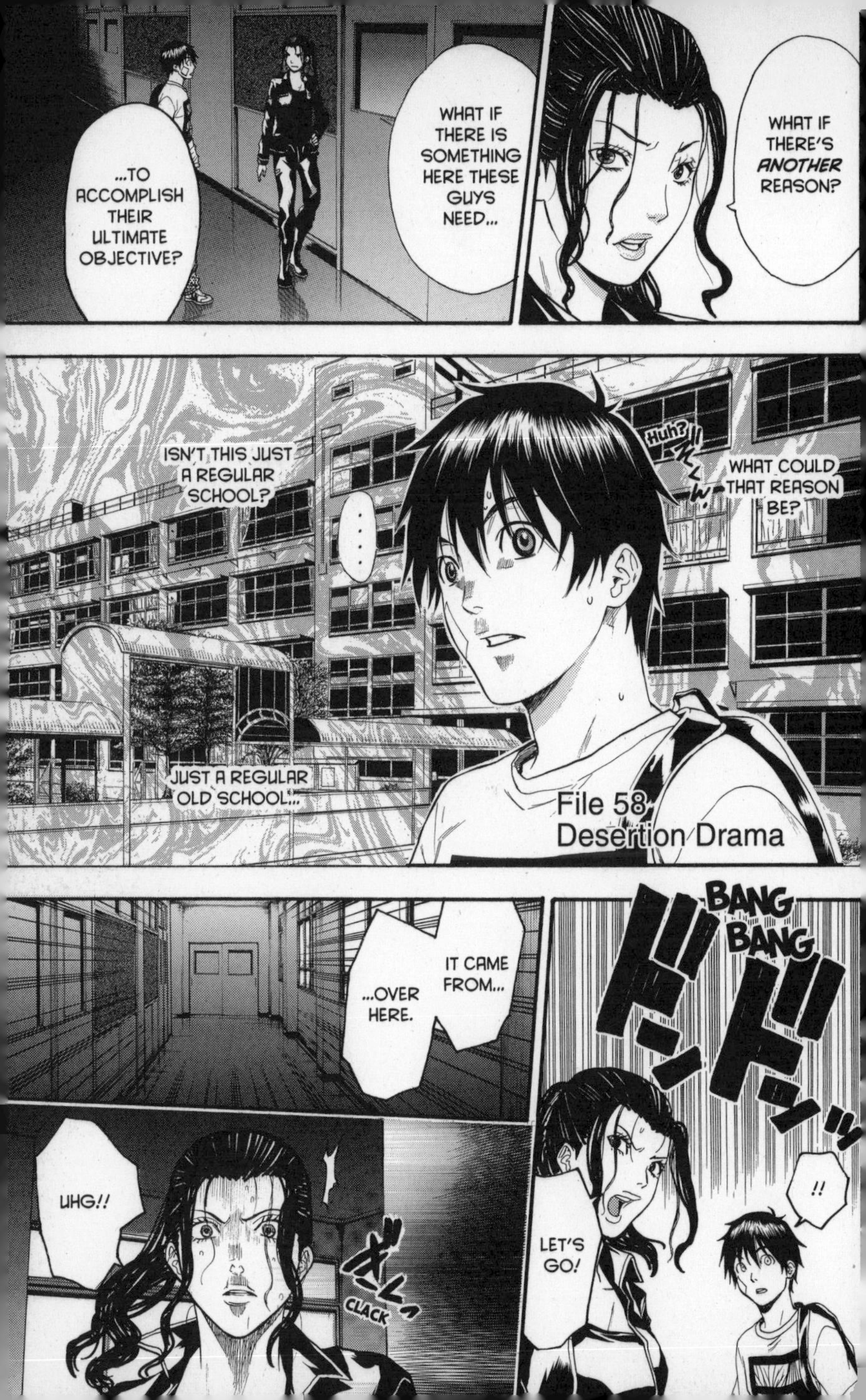
WHAT IF THERE'S ANOTHER REASON?
WHAT IF THERE IS SOMETHING HERE THESE GUYS NEED...
...TO ACCOMPLISH THEIR ULTIMATE OBJECTIVE?
Huh?
WHAT COULD THAT REASON BE?
....
ISN'T THIS JUST A REGULAR SCHOOL?
JUST A REGULAR OLD SCHOOL...
File 58 Desertion Drama
BANG BANG
!!
LET'S GO!
IT CAME FROM...
...OVER HERE.
CLACK
UHG!!

WHAT IS IT?

MINAMI-SAN?

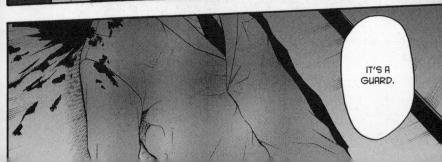

IT'S A GUARD.

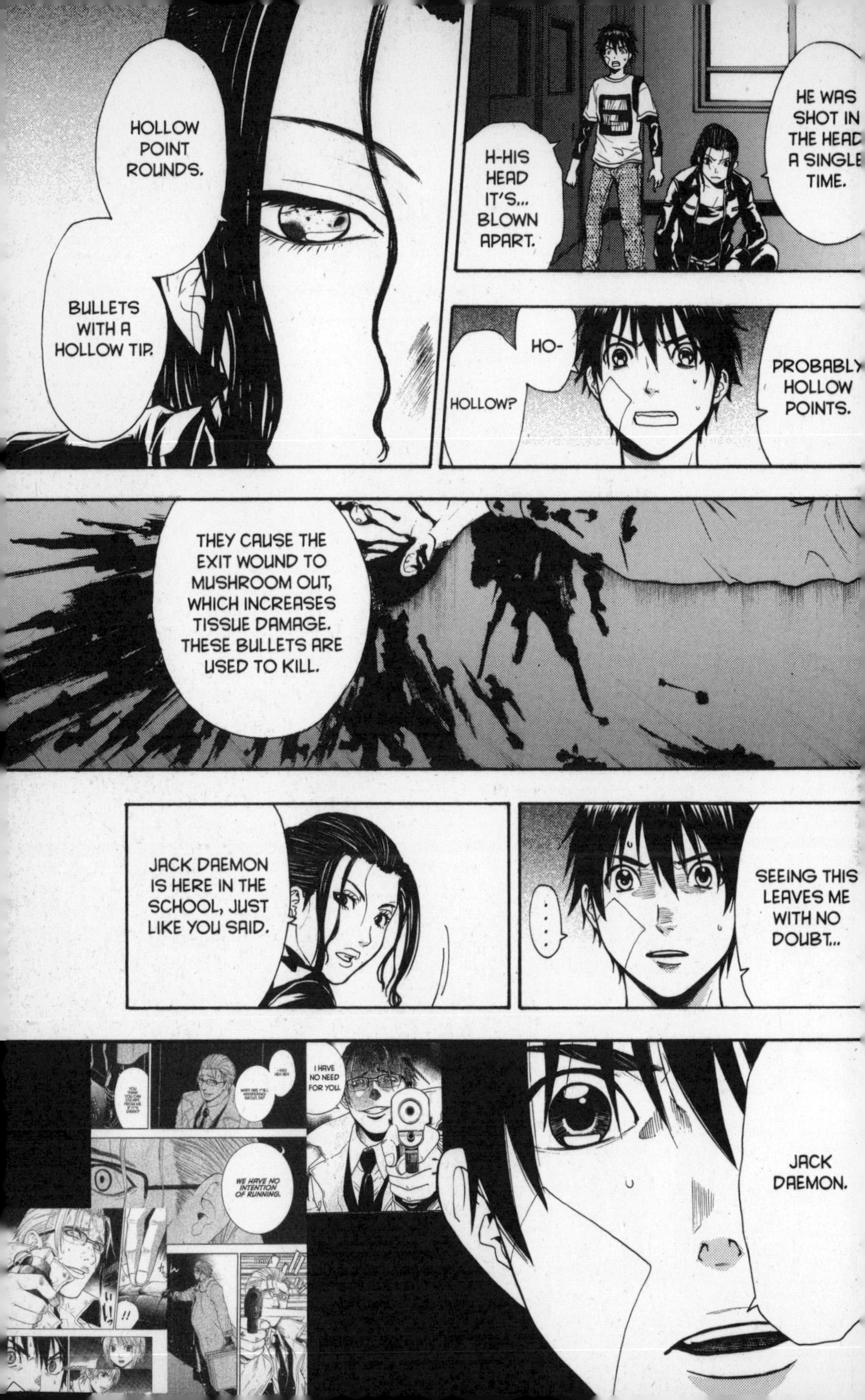
HE WAS SHOT IN THE HEAD A SINGLE TIME.
H-HIS HEAD IT'S... BLOWN APART.
PROBABLY HOLLOW POINTS.
HO-
HOLLOW?
HOLLOW POINT ROUNDS.
BULLETS WITH A HOLLOW TIP.
THEY CAUSE THE EXIT WOUND TO MUSHROOM OUT, WHICH INCREASES TISSUE DAMAGE. THESE BULLETS ARE USED TO KILL.
SEEING THIS LEAVES ME WITH NO DOUBT...
....
JACK DAEMON IS HERE IN THE SCHOOL, JUST LIKE YOU SAID.
JACK DAEMON.
I HAVE NO NEED FOR YOU.
WE HAVE NO INTENTION OF RUNNING.
WHIRL
!!

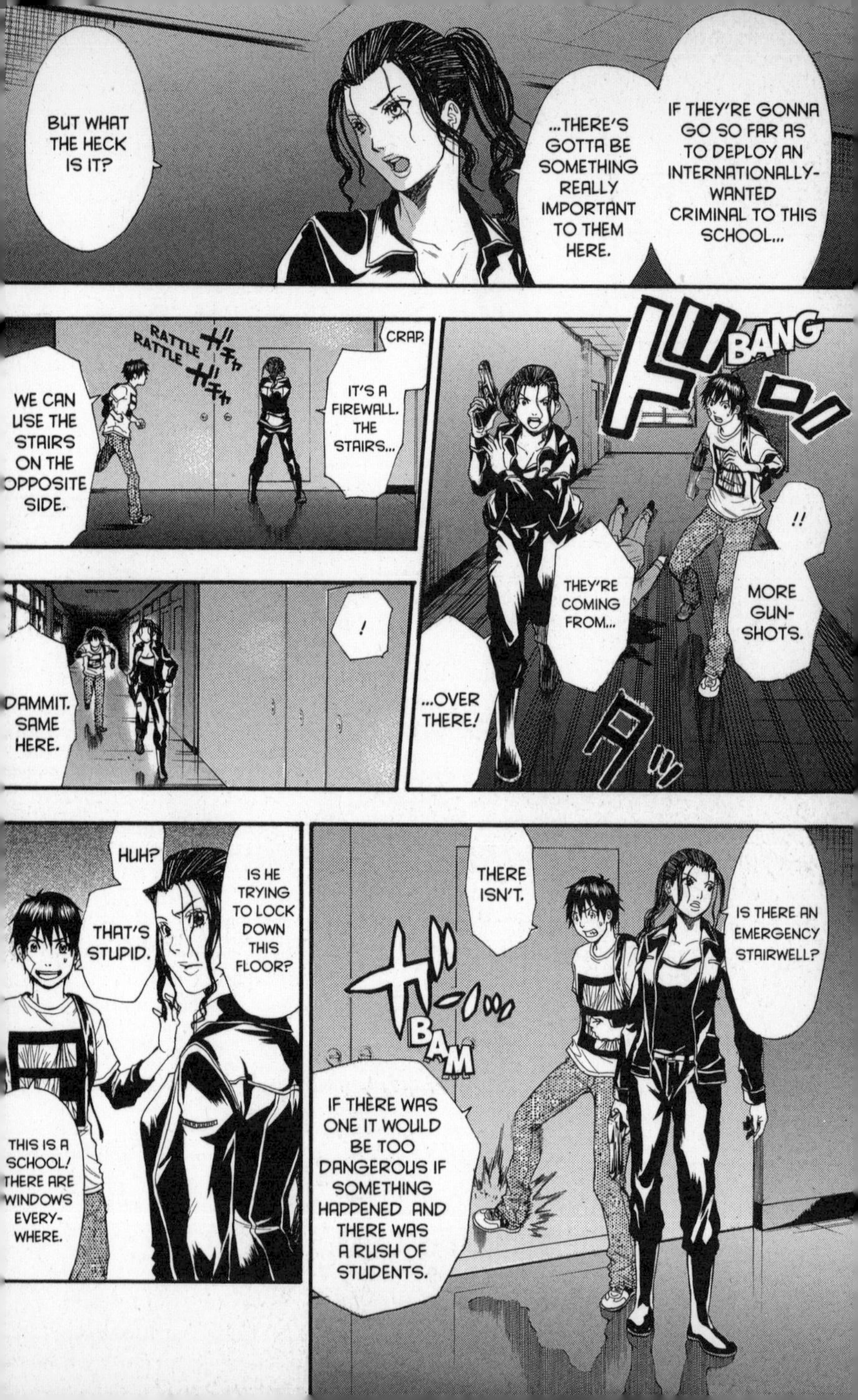
IF THEY'RE GONNA GO SO FAR AS TO DEPLOY AN INTERNATIONALLY-WANTED CRIMINAL TO THIS SCHOOL...
...THERE'S GOTTA BE SOMETHING REALLY IMPORTANT TO THEM HERE.
BUT WHAT THE HECK IS IT?
BANG
!!
MORE GUN-SHOTS.
THEY'RE COMING FROM...
...OVER THERE!
CRAP.
IT'S A FIREWALL. THE STAIRS...
RATTLE RATTLE
WE CAN USE THE STAIRS ON THE OPPOSITE SIDE.
!
DAMMIT. SAME HERE.
IS THERE AN EMERGENCY STAIRWELL?
THERE ISN'T.
BAM
IF THERE WAS ONE IT WOULD BE TOO DANGEROUS IF SOMETHING HAPPENED AND THERE WAS A RUSH OF STUDENTS.
IS HE TRYING TO LOCK DOWN THIS FLOOR?
HUH?
THAT'S STUPID.
THIS IS A SCHOOL! THERE ARE WINDOWS EVERY-WHERE.

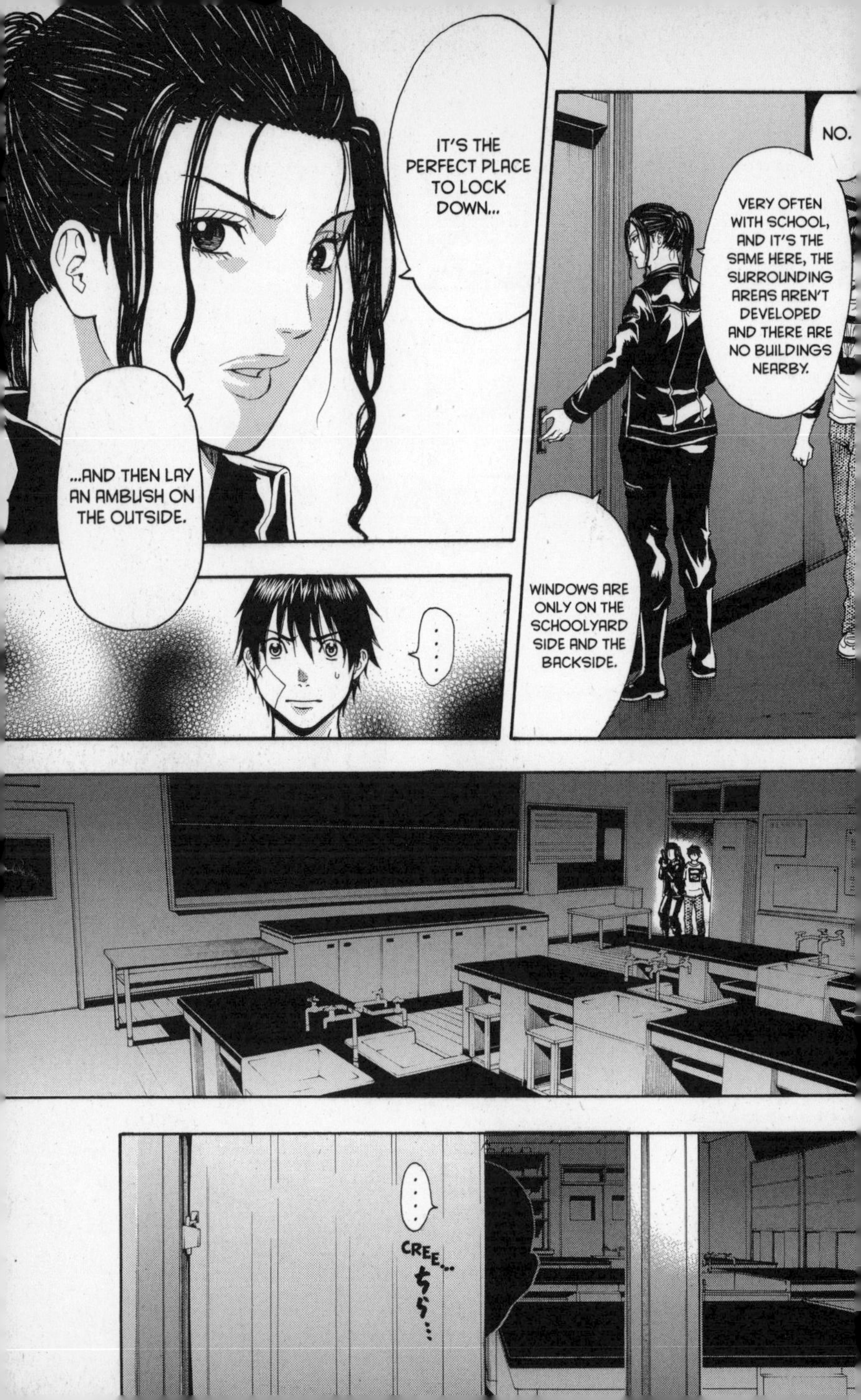
NO.
VERY OFTEN WITH SCHOOL, AND IT'S THE SAME HERE, THE SURROUNDING AREAS AREN'T DEVELOPED AND THERE ARE NO BUILDINGS NEARBY.
WINDOWS ARE ONLY ON THE SCHOOLYARD SIDE AND THE BACKSIDE.
IT'S THE PERFECT PLACE TO LOCK DOWN...
...AND THEN LAY AN AMBUSH ON THE OUTSIDE.
....
....
CREE...
ちら...

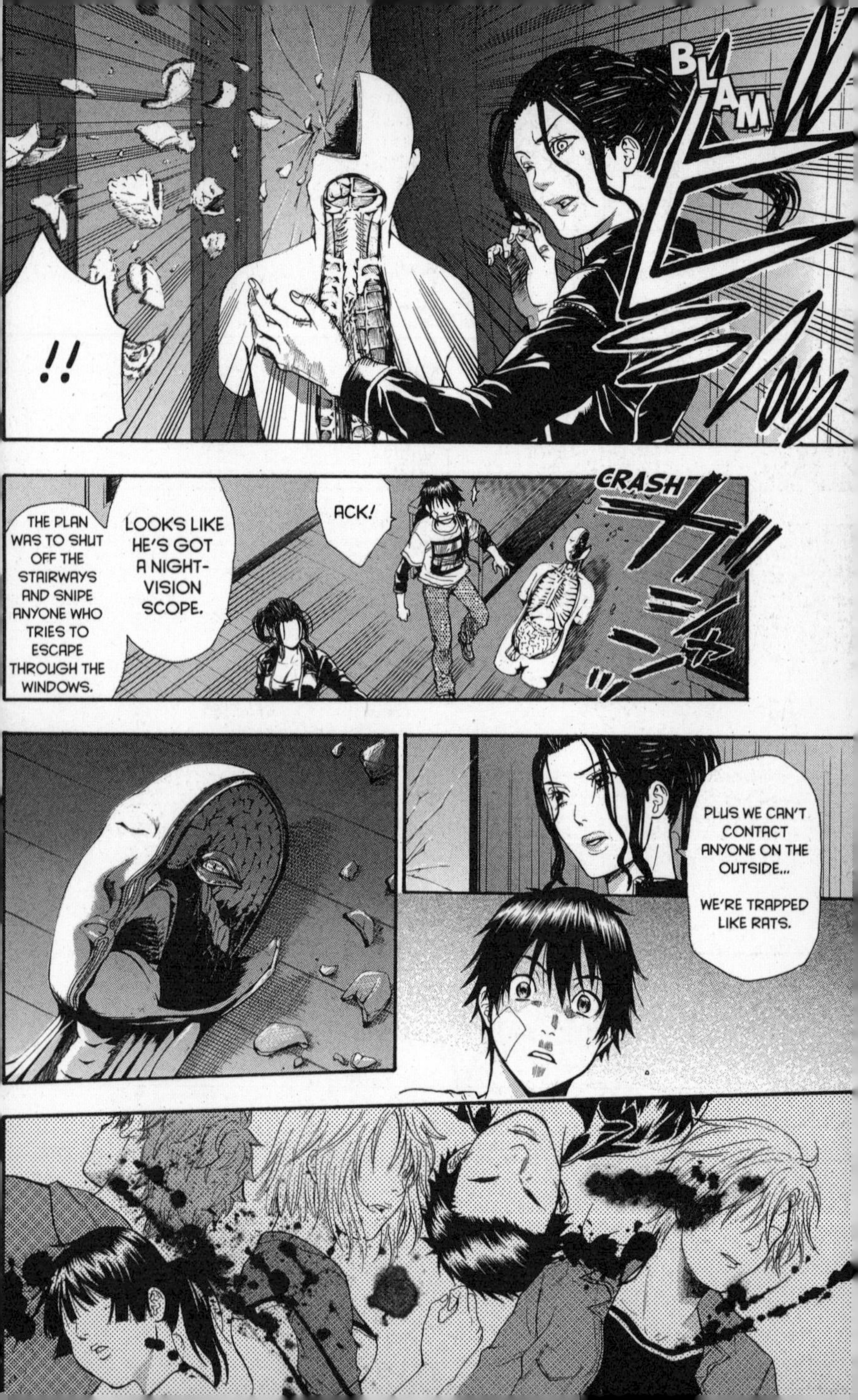
BLAM
!!
CRASH
ACK!
LOOKS LIKE HE'S GOT A NIGHT-VISION SCOPE.
THE PLAN WAS TO SHUT OFF THE STAIRWAYS AND SNIPE ANYONE WHO TRIES TO ESCAPE THROUGH THE WINDOWS.
PLUS WE CAN'T CONTACT ANYONE ON THE OUTSIDE...
WE'RE TRAPPED LIKE RATS.

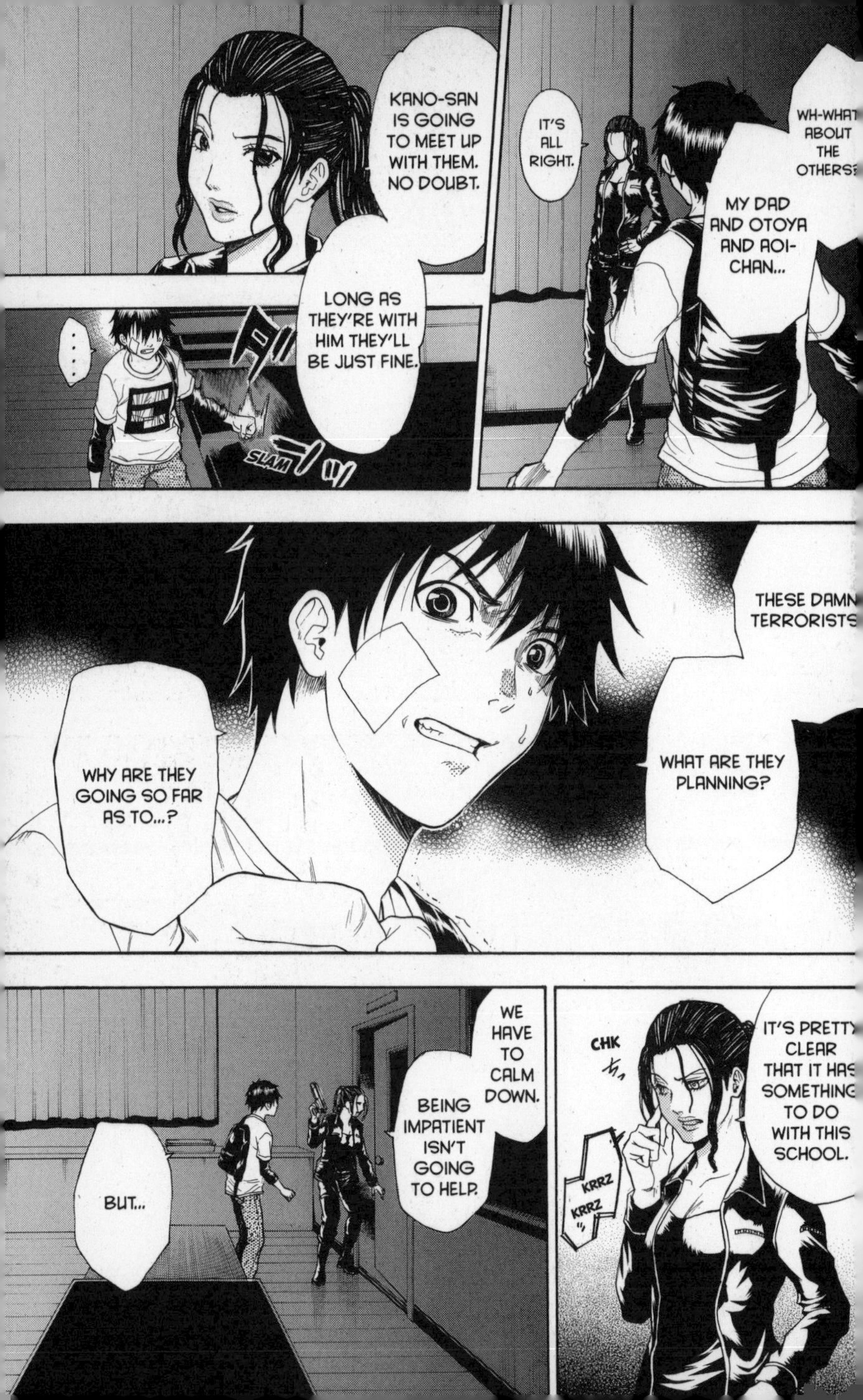
WH-WHAT ABOUT THE OTHERS?
MY DAD AND OTOYA AND AOI-CHAN...
IT'S ALL RIGHT.
KANO-SAN IS GOING TO MEET UP WITH THEM. NO DOUBT.
LONG AS THEY'RE WITH HIM THEY'LL BE JUST FINE.
...
SLAM
THESE DAMN TERRORISTS
WHAT ARE THEY PLANNING?
WHY ARE THEY GOING SO FAR AS TO...?
IT'S PRETTY CLEAR THAT IT HAS SOMETHING TO DO WITH THIS SCHOOL.
CHK
KRRZ
KRRZ
WE HAVE TO CALM DOWN.
BEING IMPATIENT ISN'T GOING TO HELP.
BUT...

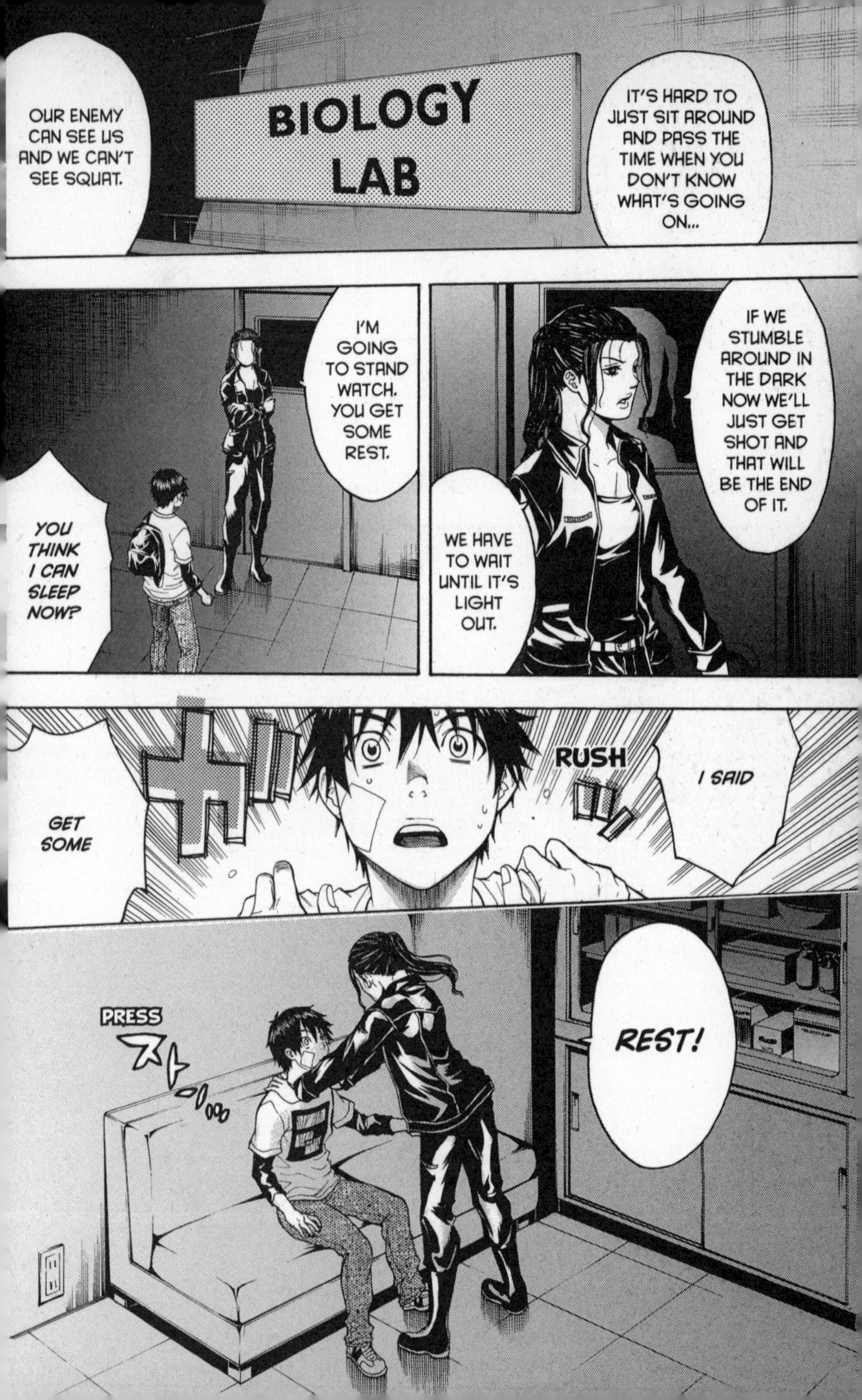
BIOLOGY LAB
IT'S HARD TO JUST SIT AROUND AND PASS THE TIME WHEN YOU DON'T KNOW WHAT'S GOING ON...
OUR ENEMY CAN SEE US AND WE CAN'T SEE SQUAT.
IF WE STUMBLE AROUND IN THE DARK NOW WE'LL JUST GET SHOT AND THAT WILL BE THE END OF IT.
WE HAVE TO WAIT UNTIL IT'S LIGHT OUT.
I'M GOING TO STAND WATCH. YOU GET SOME REST.
YOU THINK I CAN SLEEP NOW?
I SAID
RUSH
GET SOME
REST!
PRESS

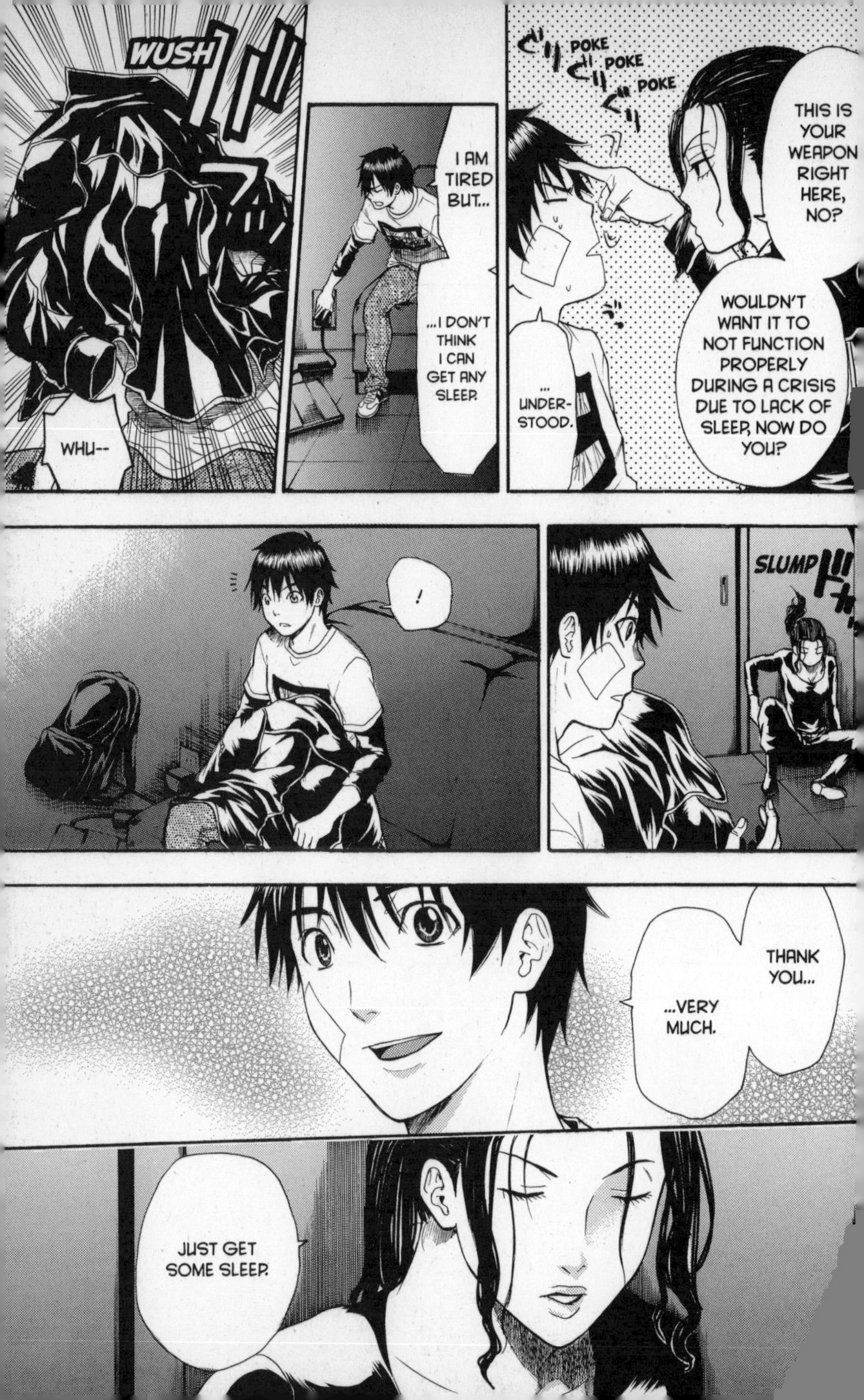
POKE POKE POKE
THIS IS YOUR WEAPON RIGHT HERE, NO?
WOULDN'T WANT IT TO NOT FUNCTION PROPERLY DURING A CRISIS DUE TO LACK OF SLEEP, NOW DO YOU?
... UNDERSTOOD.
I AM TIRED BUT...
...I DON'T THINK I CAN GET ANY SLEEP.
WUSH
WHU--
SLUMP
!
THANK YOU...
...VERY MUCH.
JUST GET SOME SLEEP.

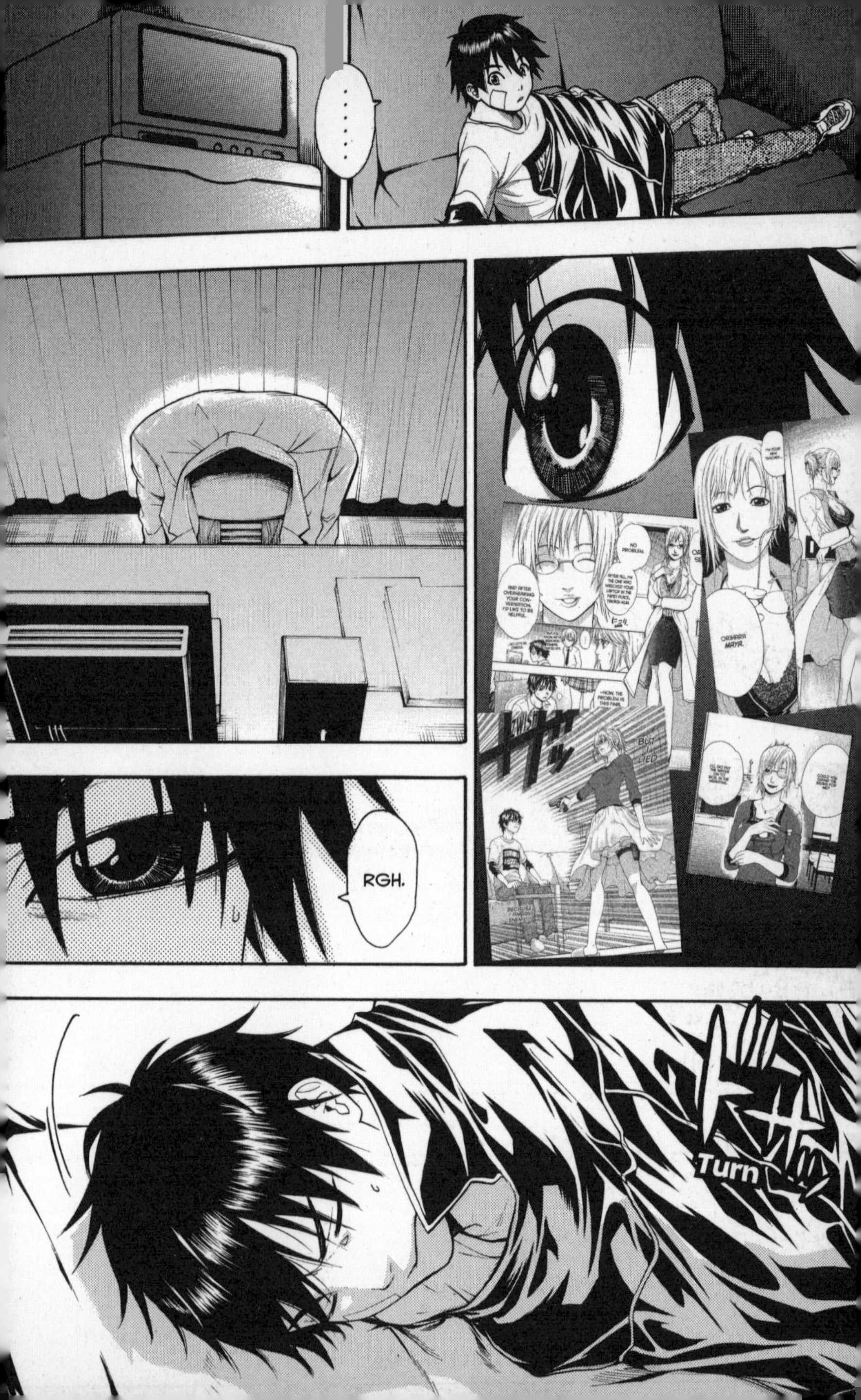
......
RGH.
I'M YOUR NEW TEACHER...
NO PROBLEM.
AND AFTER OVERHEARING YOUR CON-VERSATION, I'D LIKE TO BE HELPFUL.
BUT... I LIED
Turn

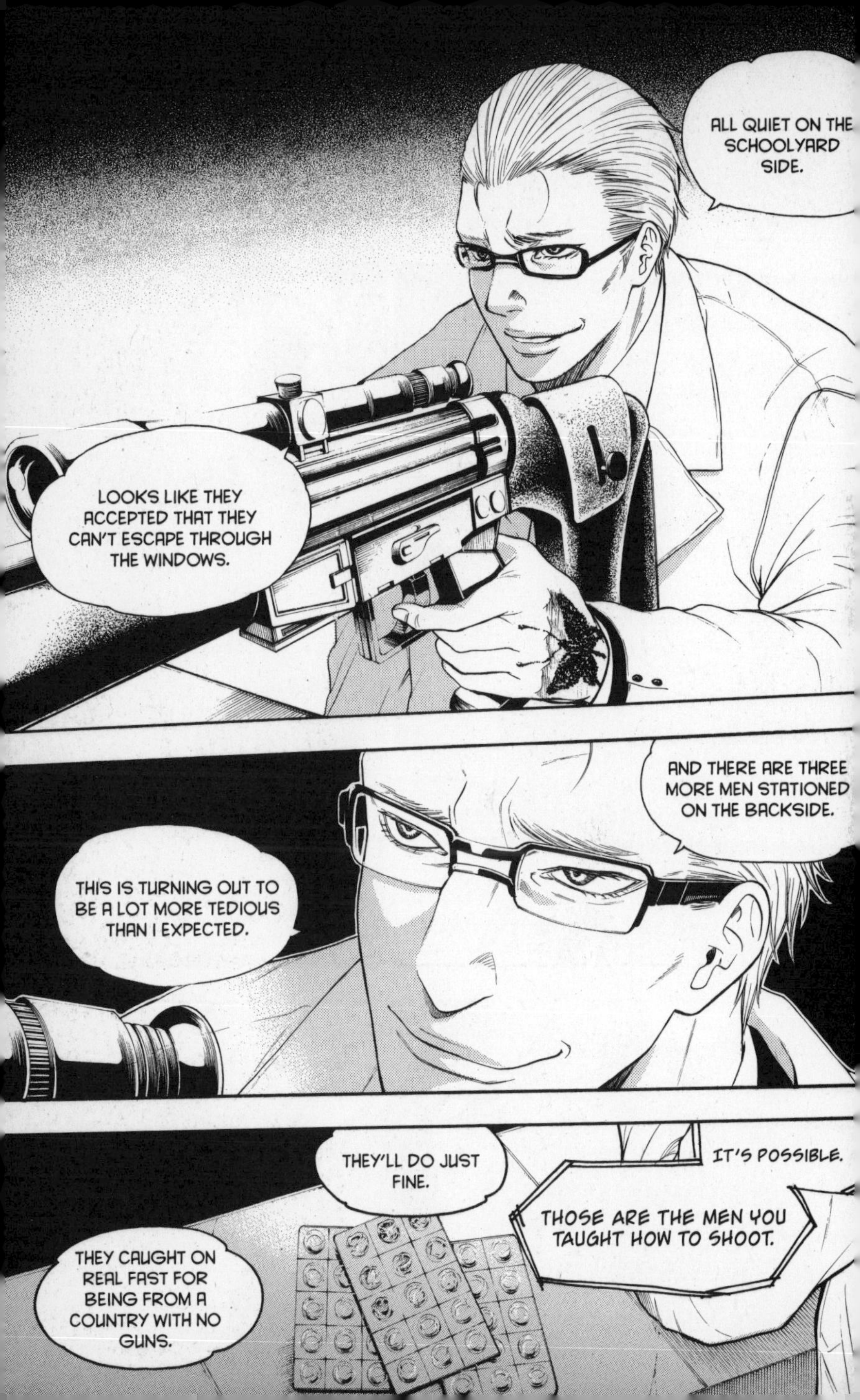
ALL QUIET ON THE SCHOOLYARD SIDE.
LOOKS LIKE THEY ACCEPTED THAT THEY CAN'T ESCAPE THROUGH THE WINDOWS.
AND THERE ARE THREE MORE MEN STATIONED ON THE BACKSIDE.
THIS IS TURNING OUT TO BE A LOT MORE TEDIOUS THAN I EXPECTED.
IT'S POSSIBLE.
THEY'LL DO JUST FINE.
THOSE ARE THE MEN YOU TAUGHT HOW TO SHOOT.
THEY CAUGHT ON REAL FAST FOR BEING FROM A COUNTRY WITH NO GUNS.

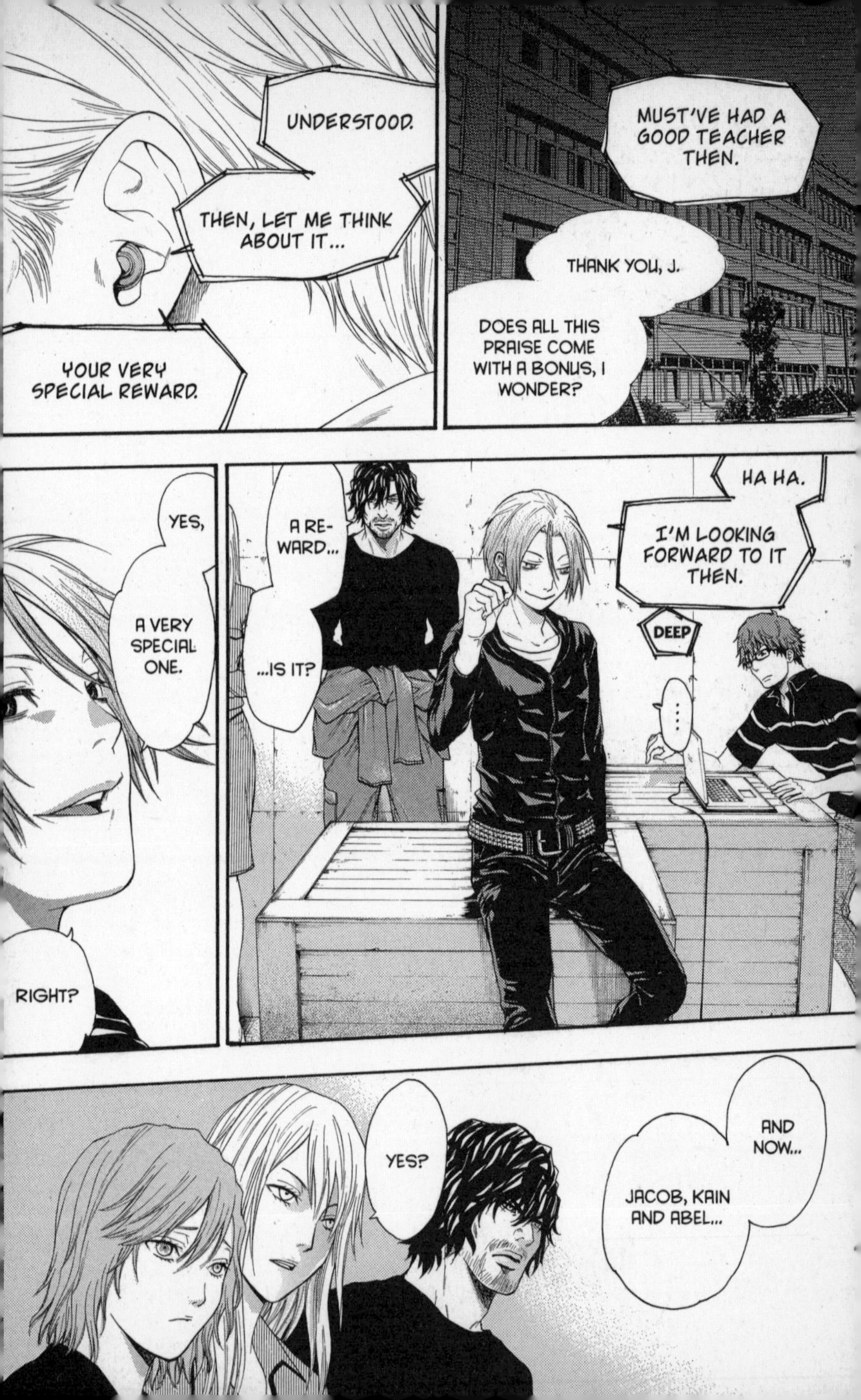
MUST'VE HAD A GOOD TEACHER THEN.
THANK YOU, J.
DOES ALL THIS PRAISE COME WITH A BONUS, I WONDER?
UNDERSTOOD.
THEN, LET ME THINK ABOUT IT...
YOUR VERY SPECIAL REWARD.
HA HA.
I'M LOOKING FORWARD TO IT THEN.
DEEP
...
A RE-WARD...
...IS IT?
YES,
A VERY SPECIAL ONE.
RIGHT?
AND NOW...
JACOB, KAIN AND ABEL...
YES?

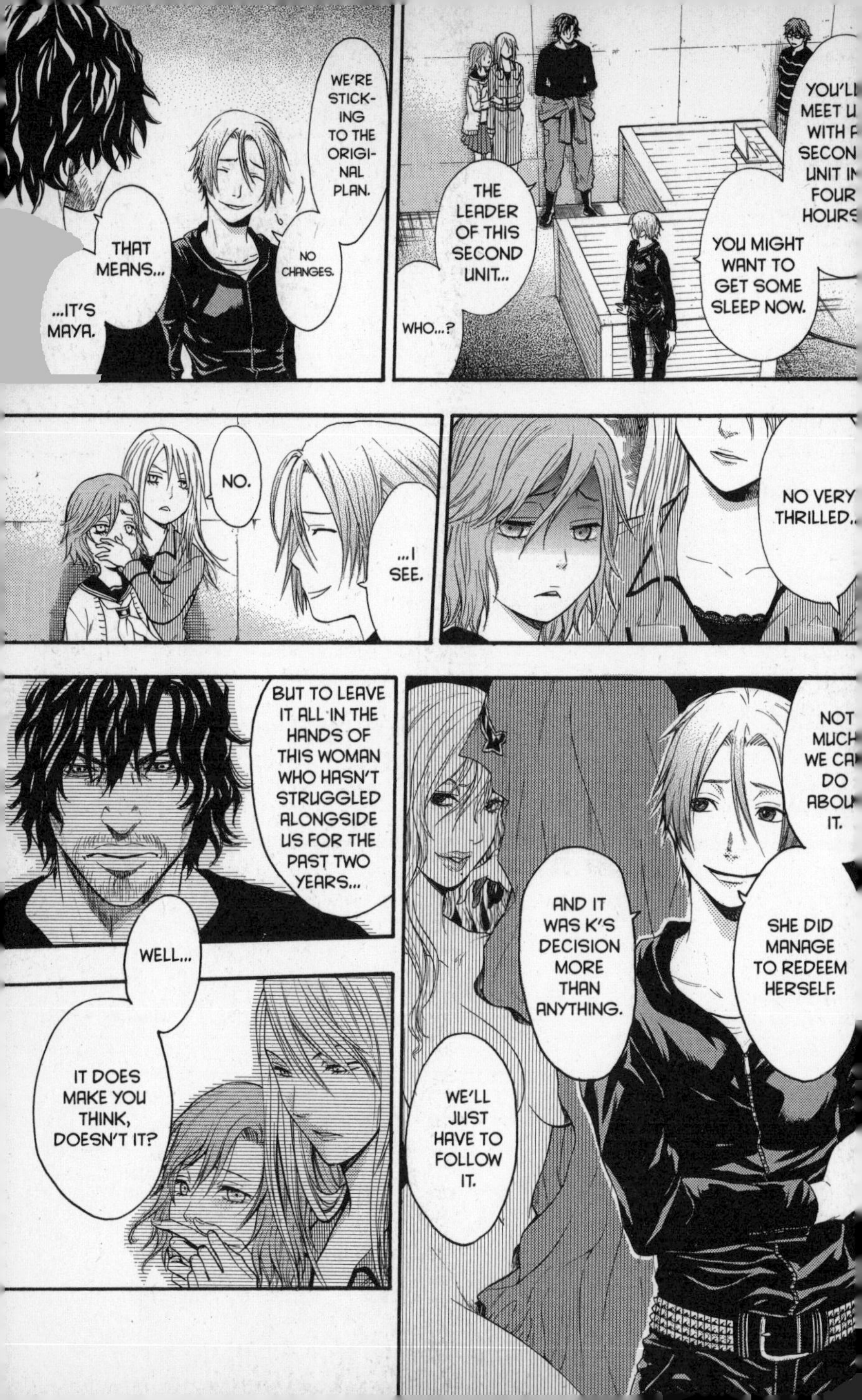
YOU'LL MEET U WITH SECON UNIT IN FOUR HOURS
YOU MIGHT WANT TO GET SOME SLEEP NOW.
THE LEADER OF THIS SECOND UNIT...
WHO...?
WE'RE STICKING TO THE ORIGINAL PLAN.
NO CHANGES.
THAT MEANS...
...IT'S MAYA.
NO VERY THRILLED...
NO.
...I SEE.
NOT MUCH WE CA DO ABOU IT.
SHE DID MANAGE TO REDEEM HERSELF.
AND IT WAS K'S DECISION MORE THAN ANYTHING.
WE'LL JUST HAVE TO FOLLOW IT.
BUT TO LEAVE IT ALL IN THE HANDS OF THIS WOMAN WHO HASN'T STRUGGLED ALONGSIDE US FOR THE PAST TWO YEARS...
WELL...
IT DOES MAKE YOU THINK, DOESN'T IT?

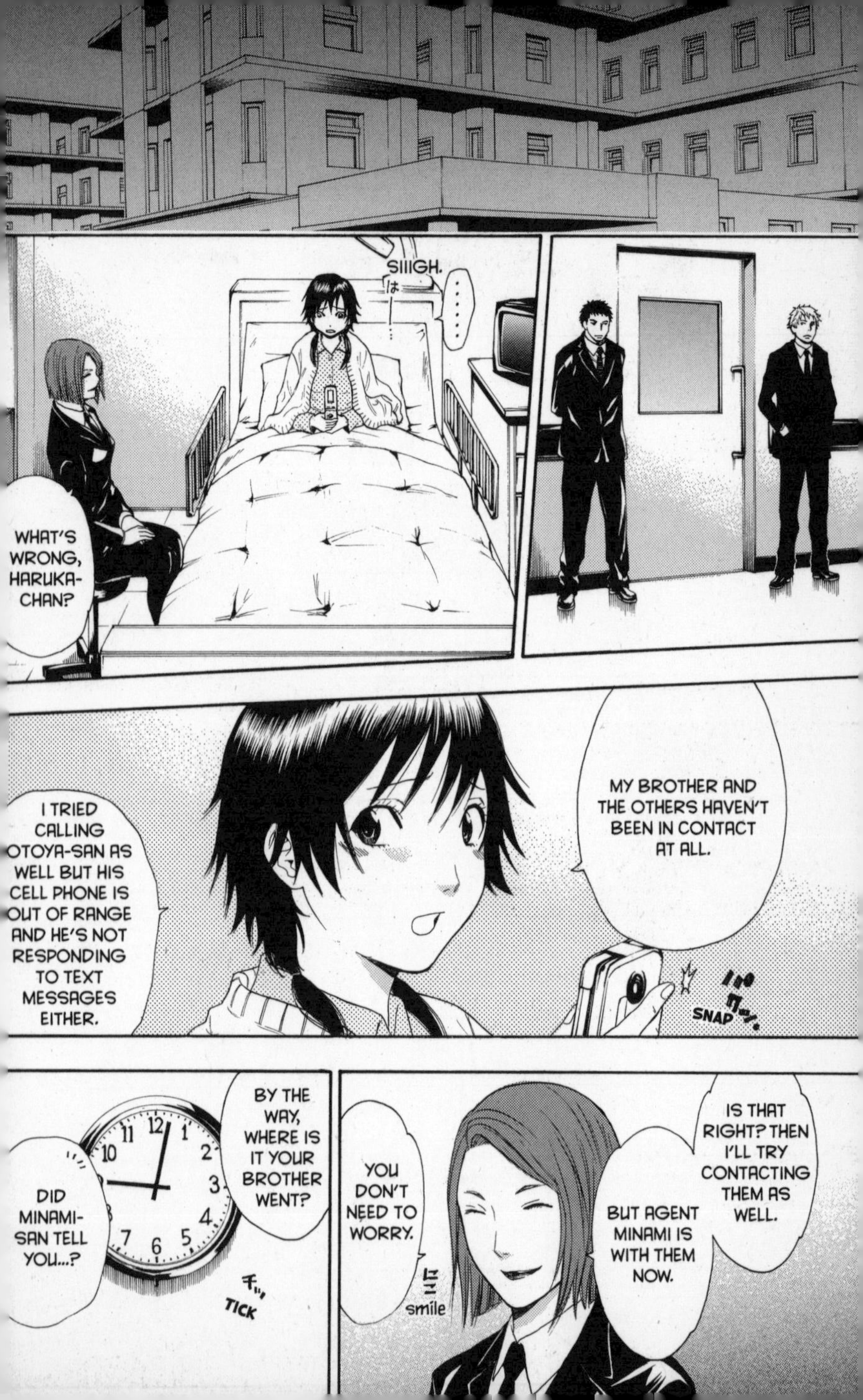
SIIGH.
は—…
……
WHAT'S WRONG, HARUKA-CHAN?
MY BROTHER AND THE OTHERS HAVEN'T BEEN IN CONTACT AT ALL.
SNAP
I TRIED CALLING OTOYA-SAN AS WELL BUT HIS CELL PHONE IS OUT OF RANGE AND HE'S NOT RESPONDING TO TEXT MESSAGES EITHER.
IS THAT RIGHT? THEN I'LL TRY CONTACTING THEM AS WELL.
BUT AGENT MINAMI IS WITH THEM NOW.
YOU DON'T NEED TO WORRY.
にこ
smile
BY THE WAY, WHERE IS IT YOUR BROTHER WENT?
DID MINAMI-SAN TELL YOU...?
TICK

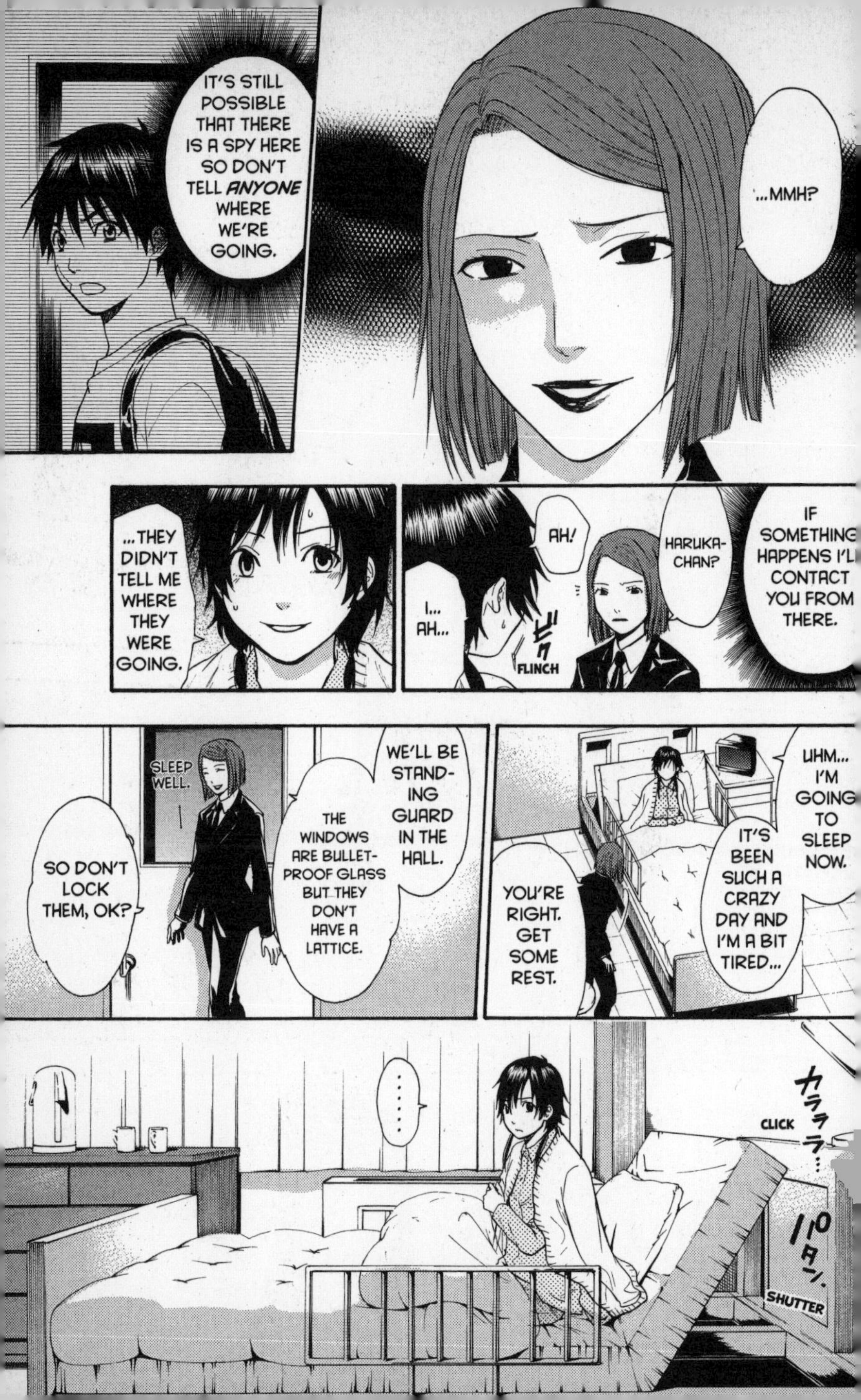
...MMH?
IT'S STILL POSSIBLE THAT THERE IS A SPY HERE SO DON'T TELL *ANYONE* WHERE WE'RE GOING.
IF SOMETHING HAPPENS I'LL CONTACT YOU FROM THERE.
HARUKA-CHAN?
AH!
I... AH...
FLINCH
...THEY DIDN'T TELL ME WHERE THEY WERE GOING.
UHM... I'M GOING TO SLEEP NOW.
IT'S BEEN SUCH A CRAZY DAY AND I'M A BIT TIRED...
YOU'RE RIGHT. GET SOME REST.
WE'LL BE STANDING GUARD IN THE HALL.
THE WINDOWS ARE BULLET-PROOF GLASS BUT THEY DON'T HAVE A LATTICE.
SO DON'T LOCK THEM, OK?
SLEEP WELL.
カラララ…
CLICK
パタン。
SHUTTER
......

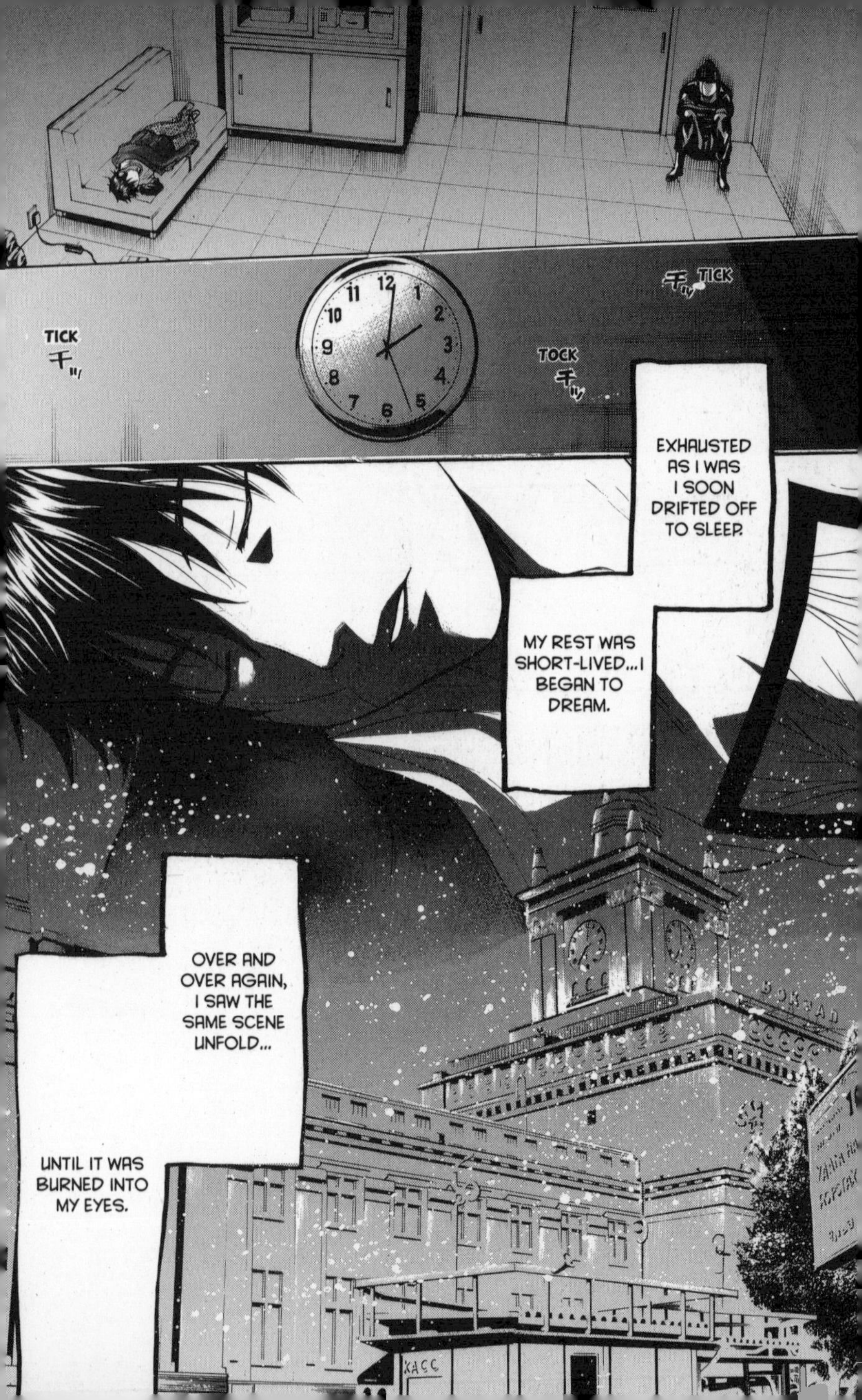

チッ TICK
TOCK チッ
TICK チッ
EXHAUSTED AS I WAS I SOON DRIFTED OFF TO SLEEP.
MY REST WAS SHORT-LIVED...I BEGAN TO DREAM.
OVER AND OVER AGAIN, I SAW THE SAME SCENE UNFOLD...
UNTIL IT WAS BURNED INTO MY EYES.

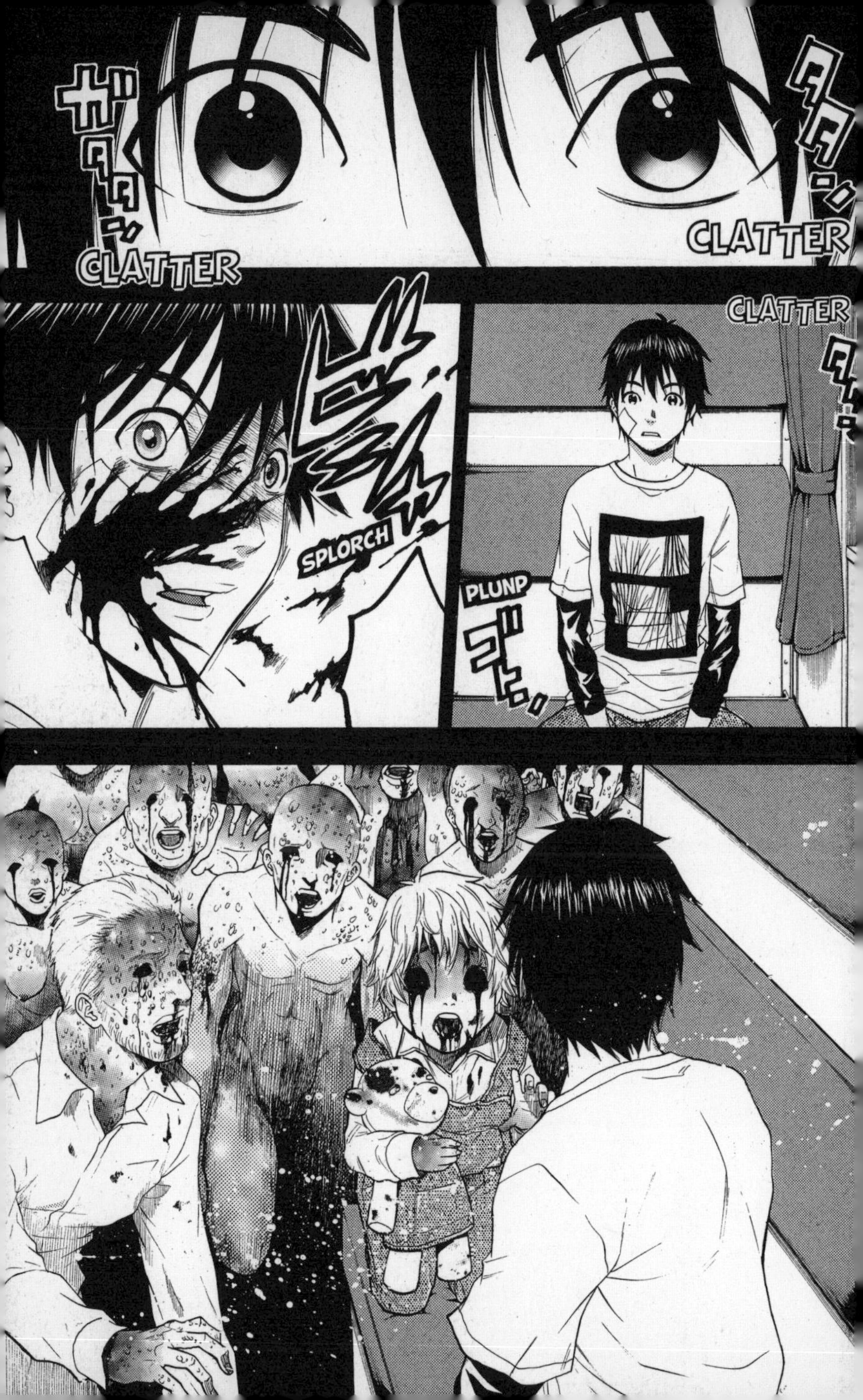
CLATTER
CLATTER
CLATTER
PLUNP
SPLORCH

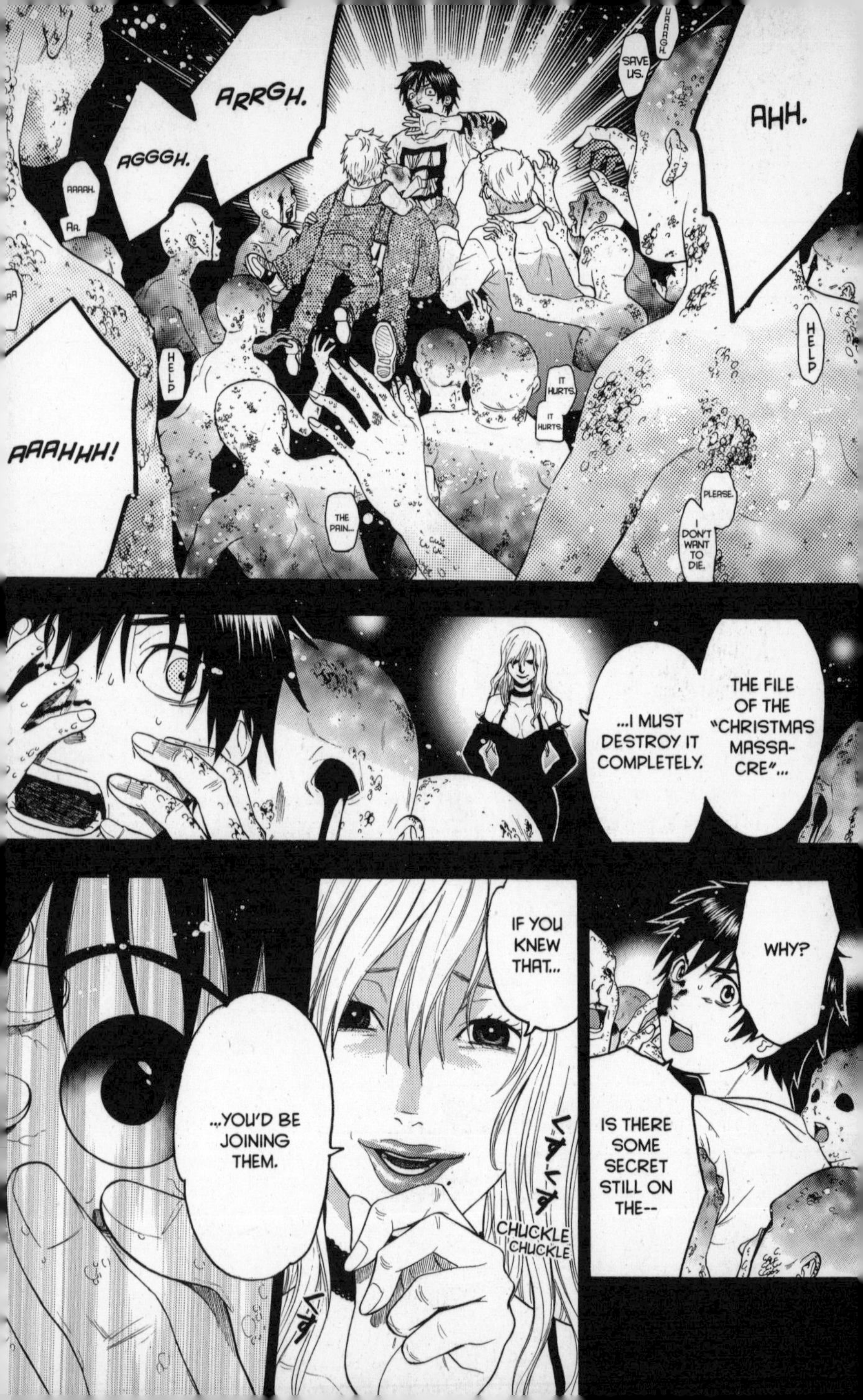
URAAGH.
SAVE US.
AHH.
ARRGH.
AGGGH.
AAAAH.
AA.
HELP
IT HURTS.
IT HURTS.
HELP
AAAHHH!
PLEASE.
I DON'T WANT TO DIE.
THE PAIN...
THE FILE OF THE "CHRISTMAS MASSA-CRE"...
...I MUST DESTROY IT COMPLETELY.
WHY?
IS THERE SOME SECRET STILL ON THE--
IF YOU KNEW THAT...
...YOU'D BE JOINING THEM.
CHUCKLE CHUCKLE

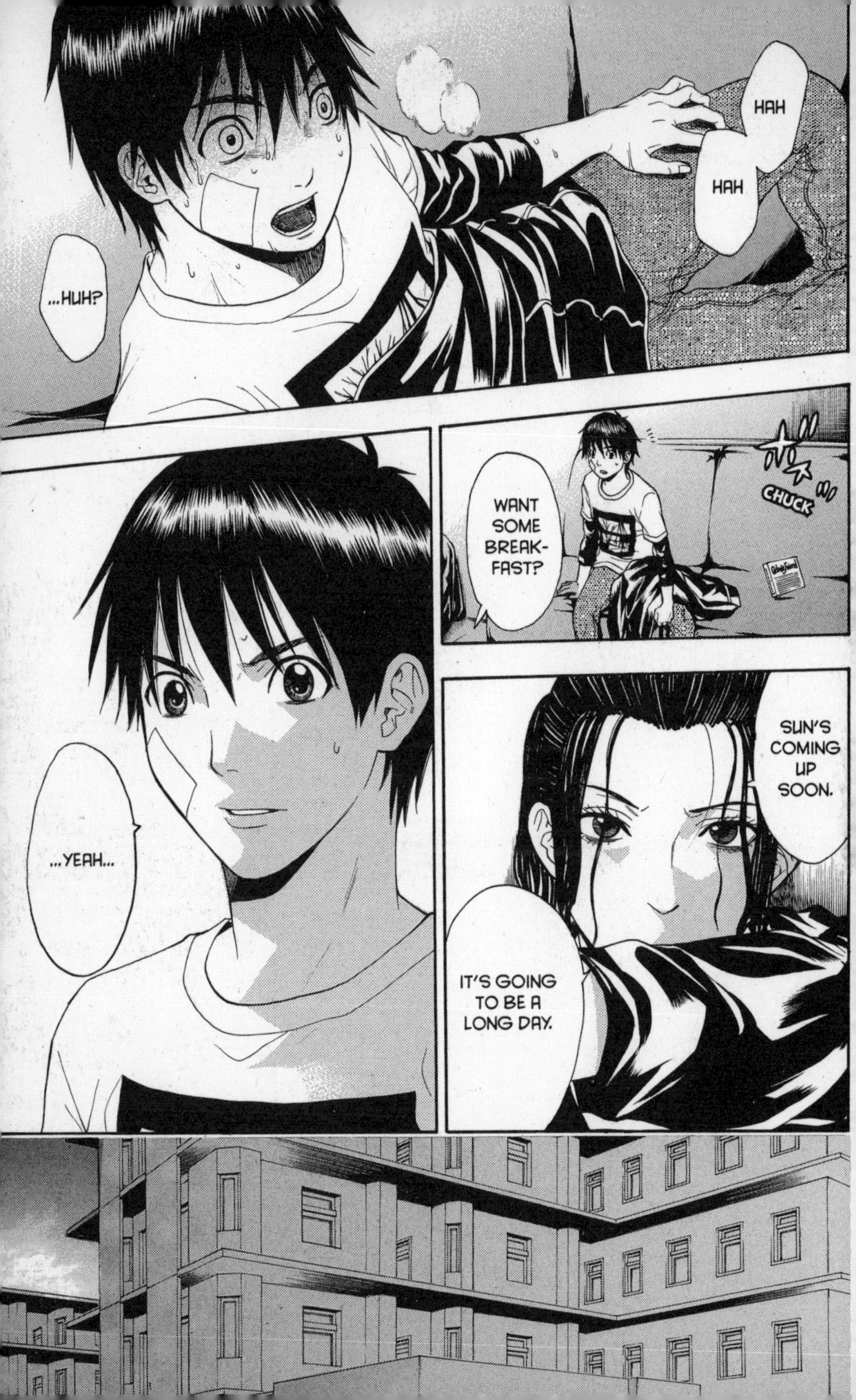
HAH
HAH
...HUH?
CHUCK
WANT SOME BREAK-FAST?
SUN'S COMING UP SOON.
IT'S GOING TO BE A LONG DAY.
...YEAH...

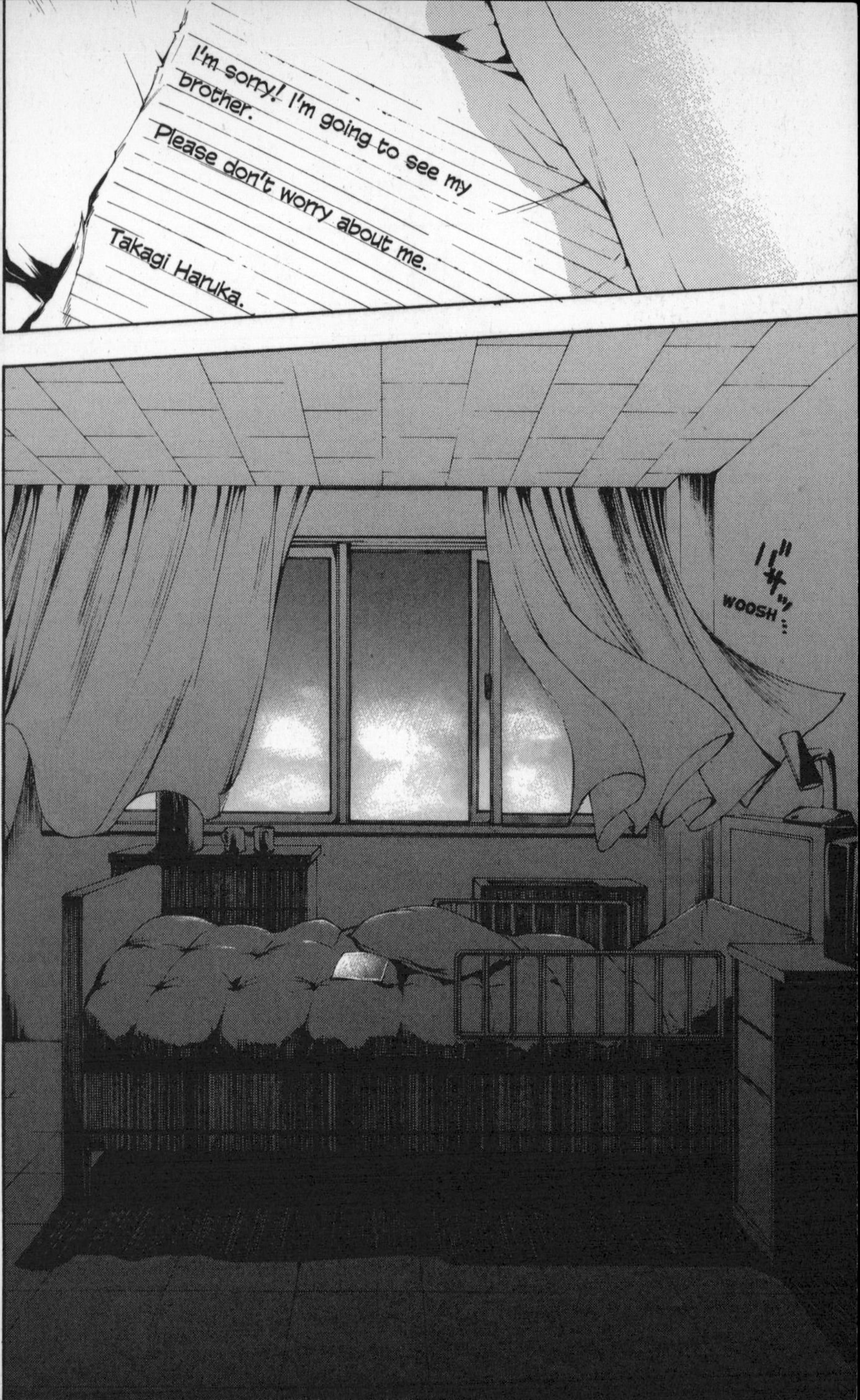
I'm sorry! I'm going to see my brother.
Please don't worry about me.
Takagi Haruka.
WOOSH

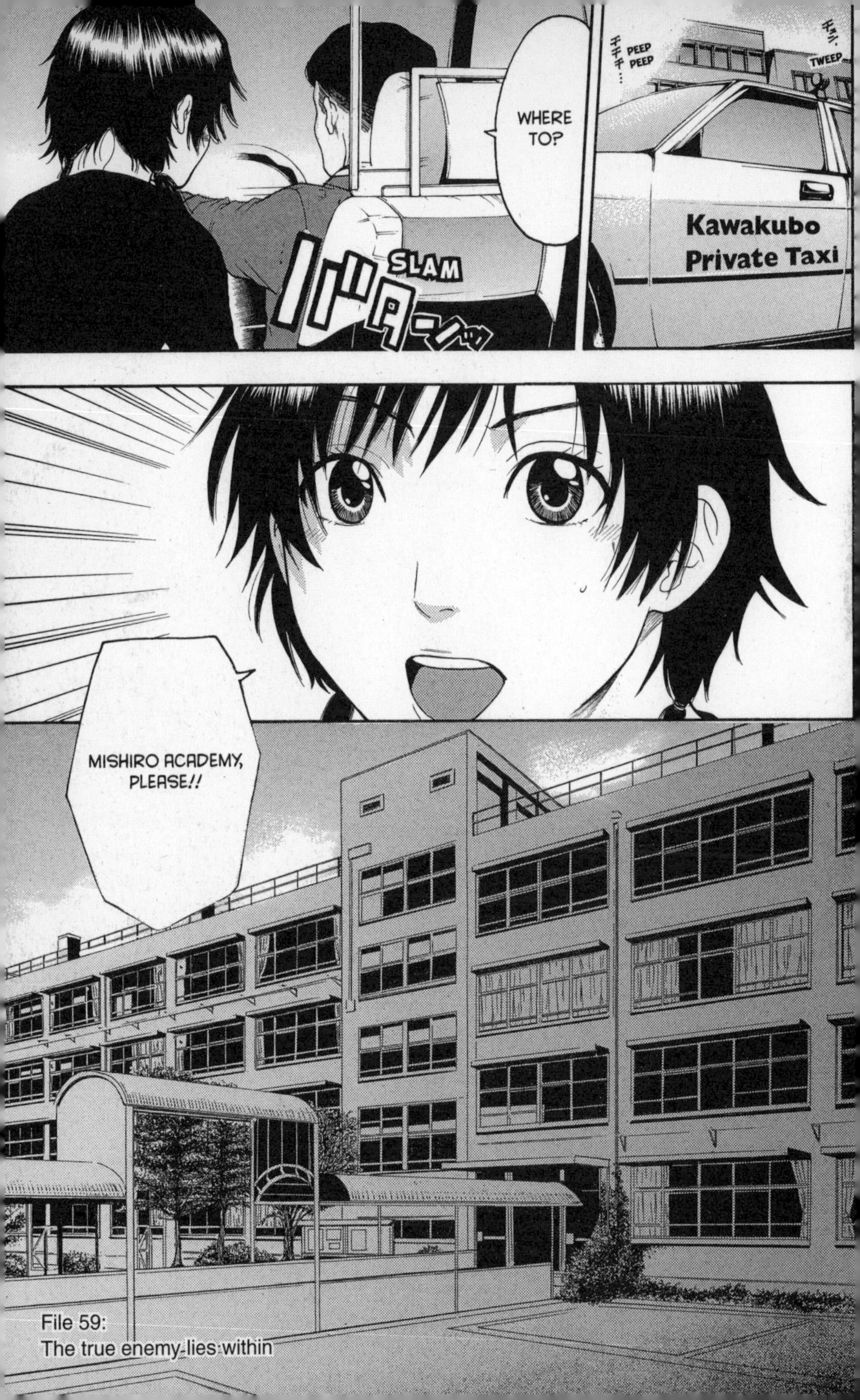
TWEEP
PEEP PEEP
WHERE TO?
Kawakubo Private Taxi
SLAM
MISHIRO ACADEMY, PLEASE!!

File 59:
The true enemy lies within

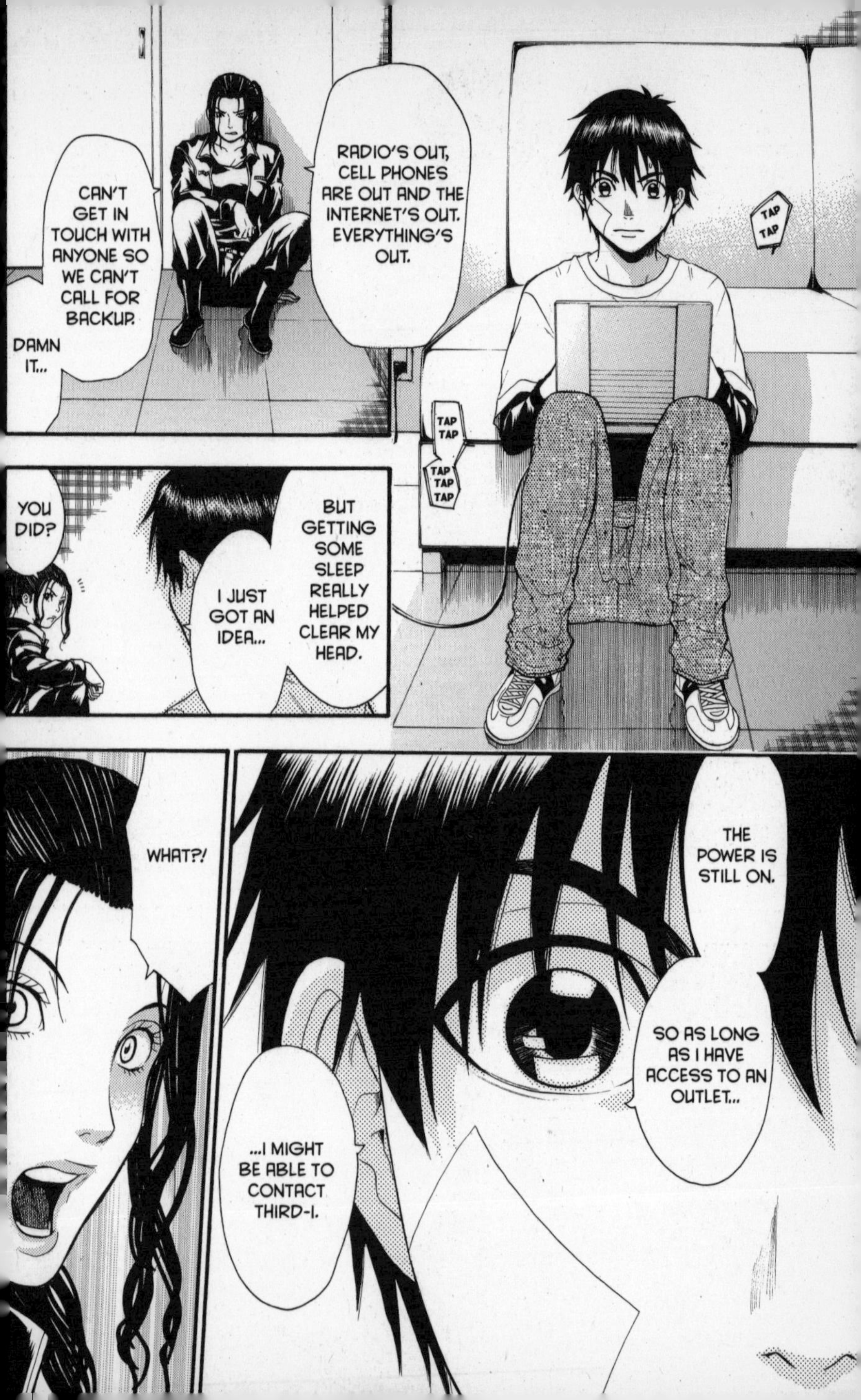
TAP TAP
TAP TAP
TAP TAP TAP
RADIO'S OUT, CELL PHONES ARE OUT AND THE INTERNET'S OUT. EVERYTHING'S OUT.
CAN'T GET IN TOUCH WITH ANYONE SO WE CAN'T CALL FOR BACKUP.
DAMN IT...
BUT GETTING SOME SLEEP REALLY HELPED CLEAR MY HEAD.
I JUST GOT AN IDEA...
YOU DID?
THE POWER IS STILL ON.
SO AS LONG AS I HAVE ACCESS TO AN OUTLET...
...I MIGHT BE ABLE TO CONTACT THIRD-I.
WHAT?!

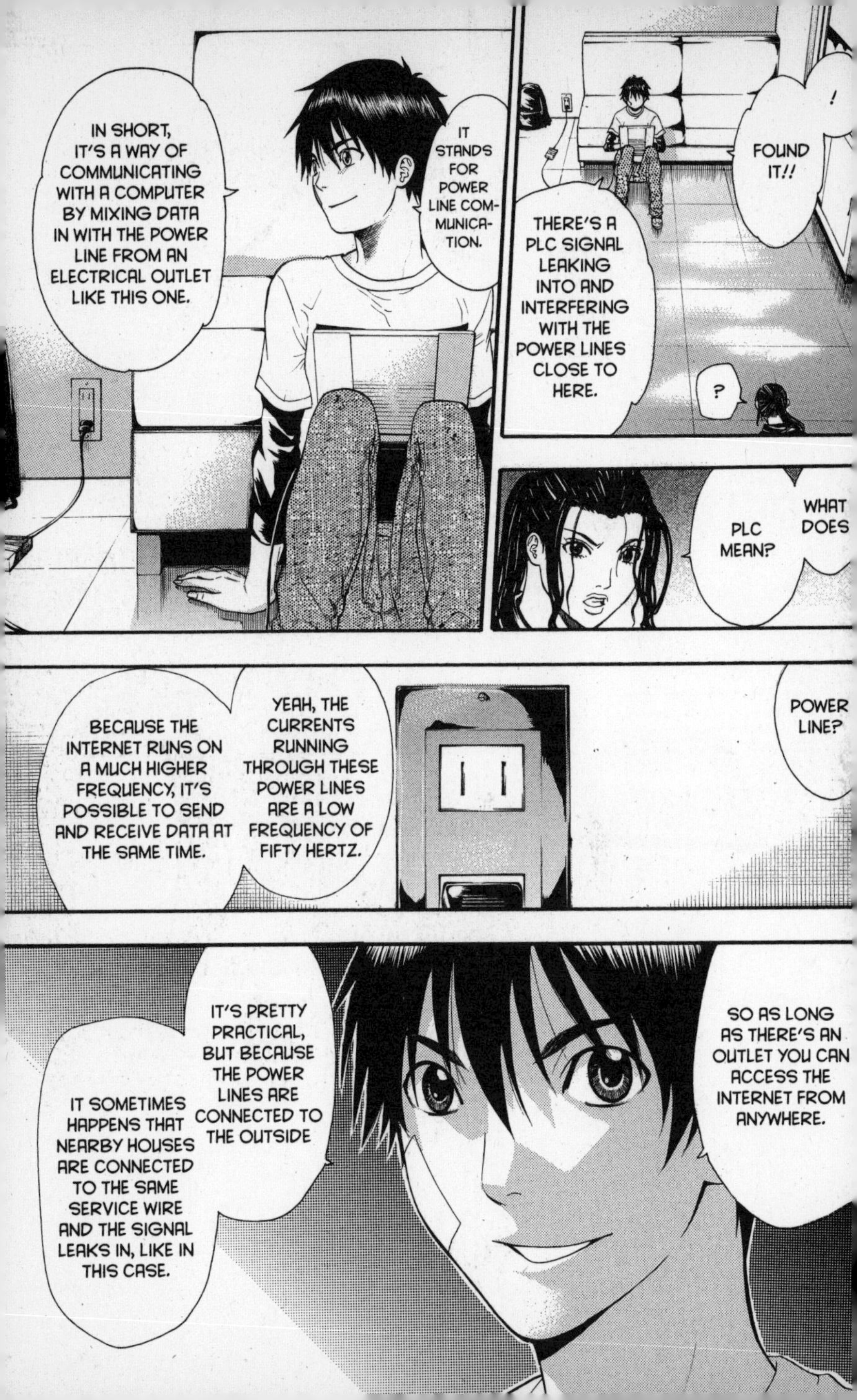
!
FOUND IT!!
THERE'S A PLC SIGNAL LEAKING INTO AND INTERFERING WITH THE POWER LINES CLOSE TO HERE.
?
WHAT DOES PLC MEAN?
IT STANDS FOR POWER LINE COMMUNICATION.
IN SHORT, IT'S A WAY OF COMMUNICATING WITH A COMPUTER BY MIXING DATA IN WITH THE POWER LINE FROM AN ELECTRICAL OUTLET LIKE THIS ONE.
POWER LINE?
YEAH, THE CURRENTS RUNNING THROUGH THESE POWER LINES ARE A LOW FREQUENCY OF FIFTY HERTZ.
BECAUSE THE INTERNET RUNS ON A MUCH HIGHER FREQUENCY, IT'S POSSIBLE TO SEND AND RECEIVE DATA AT THE SAME TIME.
SO AS LONG AS THERE'S AN OUTLET YOU CAN ACCESS THE INTERNET FROM ANYWHERE.
IT'S PRETTY PRACTICAL, BUT BECAUSE THE POWER LINES ARE CONNECTED TO THE OUTSIDE
IT SOMETIMES HAPPENS THAT NEARBY HOUSES ARE CONNECTED TO THE SAME SERVICE WIRE AND THE SIGNAL LEAKS IN, LIKE IN THIS CASE.

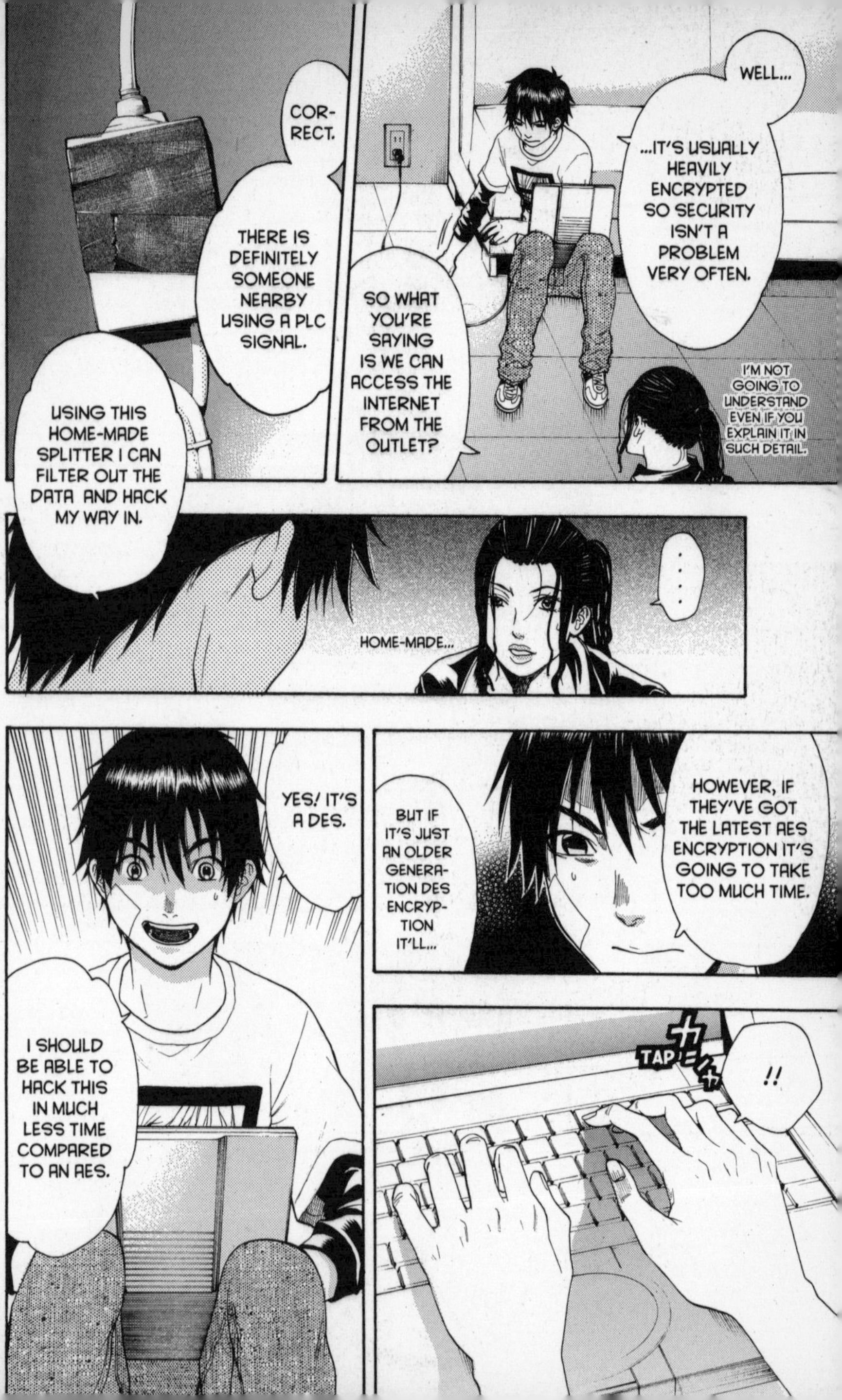
WELL...
...IT'S USUALLY HEAVILY ENCRYPTED SO SECURITY ISN'T A PROBLEM VERY OFTEN.
I'M NOT GOING TO UNDERSTAND EVEN IF YOU EXPLAIN IT IN SUCH DETAIL.
SO WHAT YOU'RE SAYING IS WE CAN ACCESS THE INTERNET FROM THE OUTLET?
COR-RECT.
THERE IS DEFINITELY SOMEONE NEARBY USING A PLC SIGNAL.
USING THIS HOME-MADE SPLITTER I CAN FILTER OUT THE DATA AND HACK MY WAY IN.
. . . .
HOME-MADE...
HOWEVER, IF THEY'VE GOT THE LATEST AES ENCRYPTION IT'S GOING TO TAKE TOO MUCH TIME.
BUT IF IT'S JUST AN OLDER GENERA-TION DES ENCRYP-TION IT'LL...
TAP
!!
YES! IT'S A DES.
I SHOULD BE ABLE TO HACK THIS IN MUCH LESS TIME COMPARED TO AN AES.

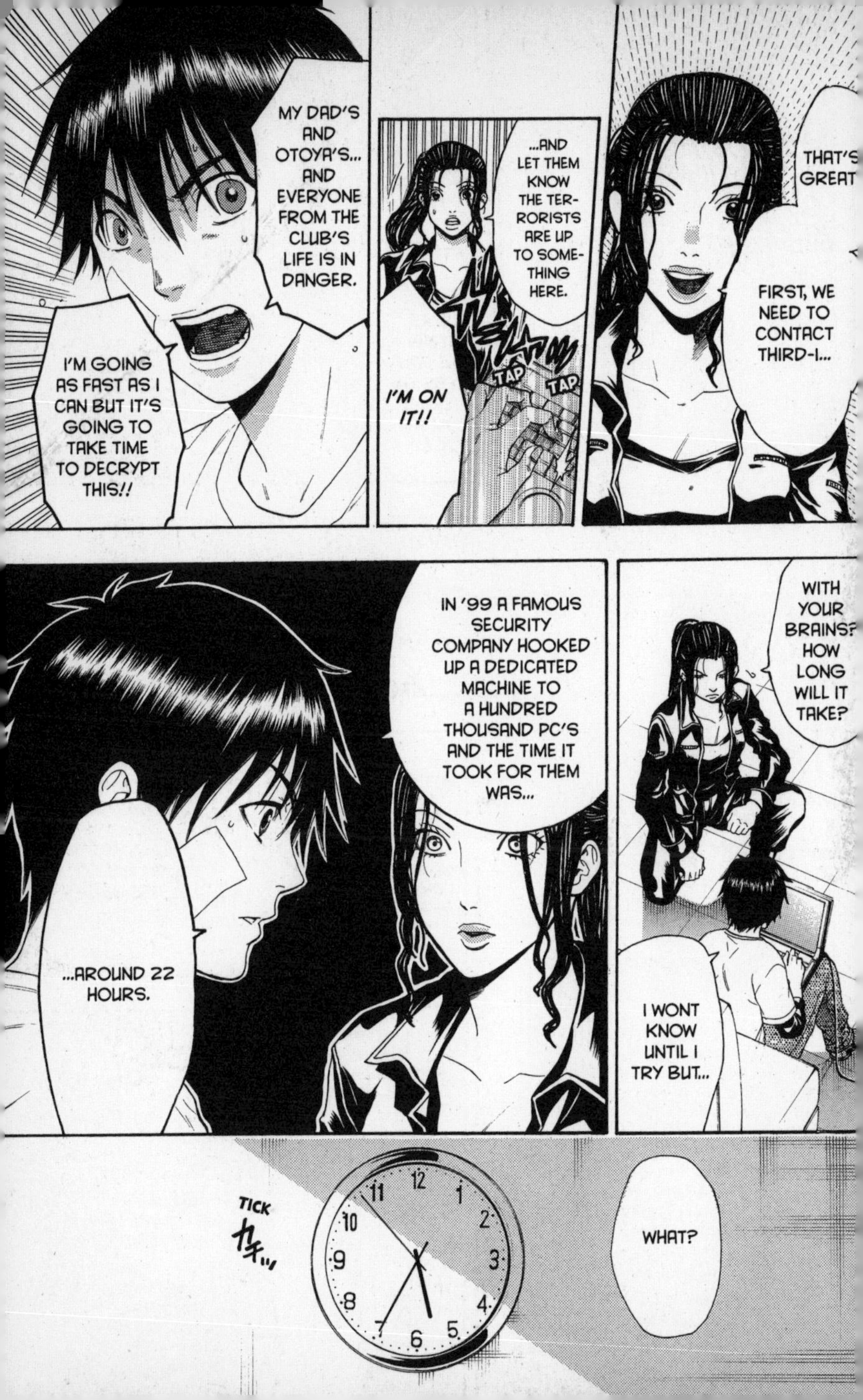
THAT'S GREAT
FIRST, WE NEED TO CONTACT THIRD-I...
...AND LET THEM KNOW THE TERRORISTS ARE UP TO SOMETHING HERE.
TAP TAP
I'M ON IT!!
MY DAD'S AND OTOYA'S... AND EVERYONE FROM THE CLUB'S LIFE IS IN DANGER.
I'M GOING AS FAST AS I CAN BUT IT'S GOING TO TAKE TIME TO DECRYPT THIS!!
WITH YOUR BRAINS? HOW LONG WILL IT TAKE?
I WONT KNOW UNTIL I TRY BUT...
IN '99 A FAMOUS SECURITY COMPANY HOOKED UP A DEDICATED MACHINE TO A HUNDRED THOUSAND PC'S AND THE TIME IT TOOK FOR THEM WAS...
...AROUND 22 HOURS.
WHAT?
TICK
カチッ

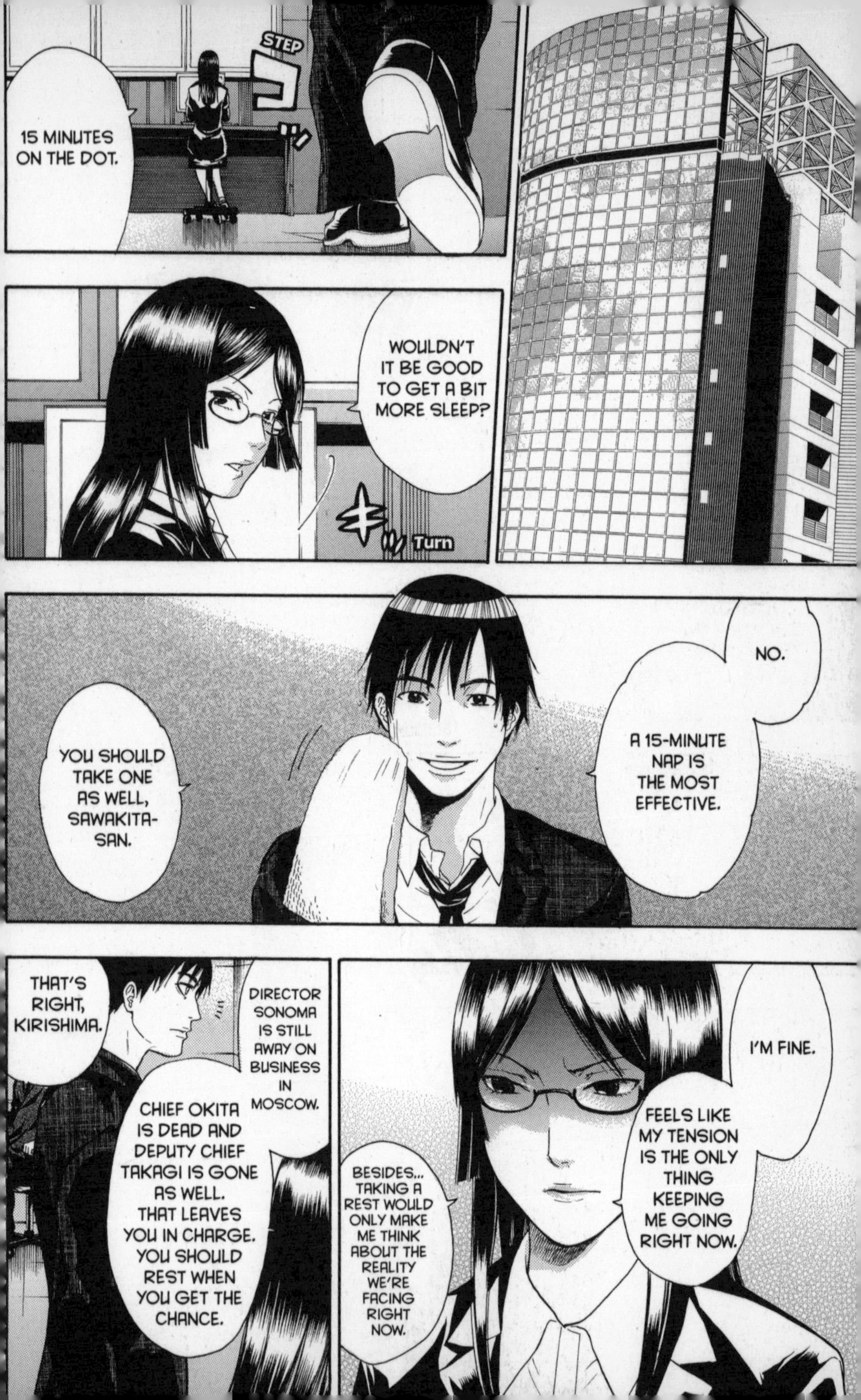
STEP
15 MINUTES ON THE DOT.
WOULDN'T IT BE GOOD TO GET A BIT MORE SLEEP?
Turn
NO.
A 15-MINUTE NAP IS THE MOST EFFECTIVE.
YOU SHOULD TAKE ONE AS WELL, SAWAKITA-SAN.
I'M FINE.
FEELS LIKE MY TENSION IS THE ONLY THING KEEPING ME GOING RIGHT NOW.
BESIDES... TAKING A REST WOULD ONLY MAKE ME THINK ABOUT THE REALITY WE'RE FACING RIGHT NOW.
THAT'S RIGHT, KIRISHIMA.
DIRECTOR SONOMA IS STILL AWAY ON BUSINESS IN MOSCOW.
CHIEF OKITA IS DEAD AND DEPUTY CHIEF TAKAGI IS GONE AS WELL. THAT LEAVES YOU IN CHARGE. YOU SHOULD REST WHEN YOU GET THE CHANCE.

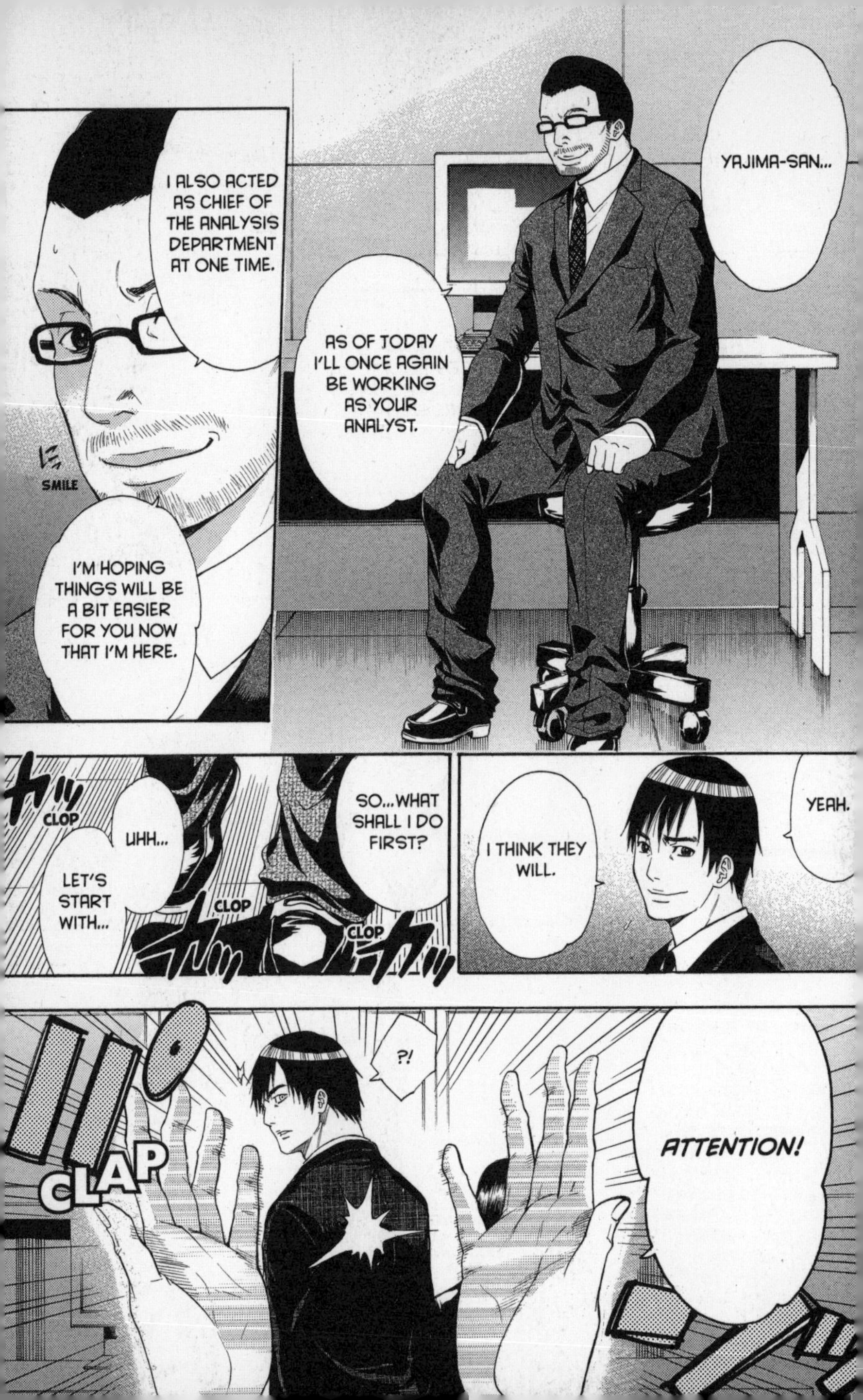
YAJIMA-SAN...
AS OF TODAY I'LL ONCE AGAIN BE WORKING AS YOUR ANALYST.
I ALSO ACTED AS CHIEF OF THE ANALYSIS DEPARTMENT AT ONE TIME.
SMILE
I'M HOPING THINGS WILL BE A BIT EASIER FOR YOU NOW THAT I'M HERE.
YEAH.
I THINK THEY WILL.
SO...WHAT SHALL I DO FIRST?
CLOP
CLOP
CLOP
UHH...
LET'S START WITH...
ATTENTION!
?!
CLAP

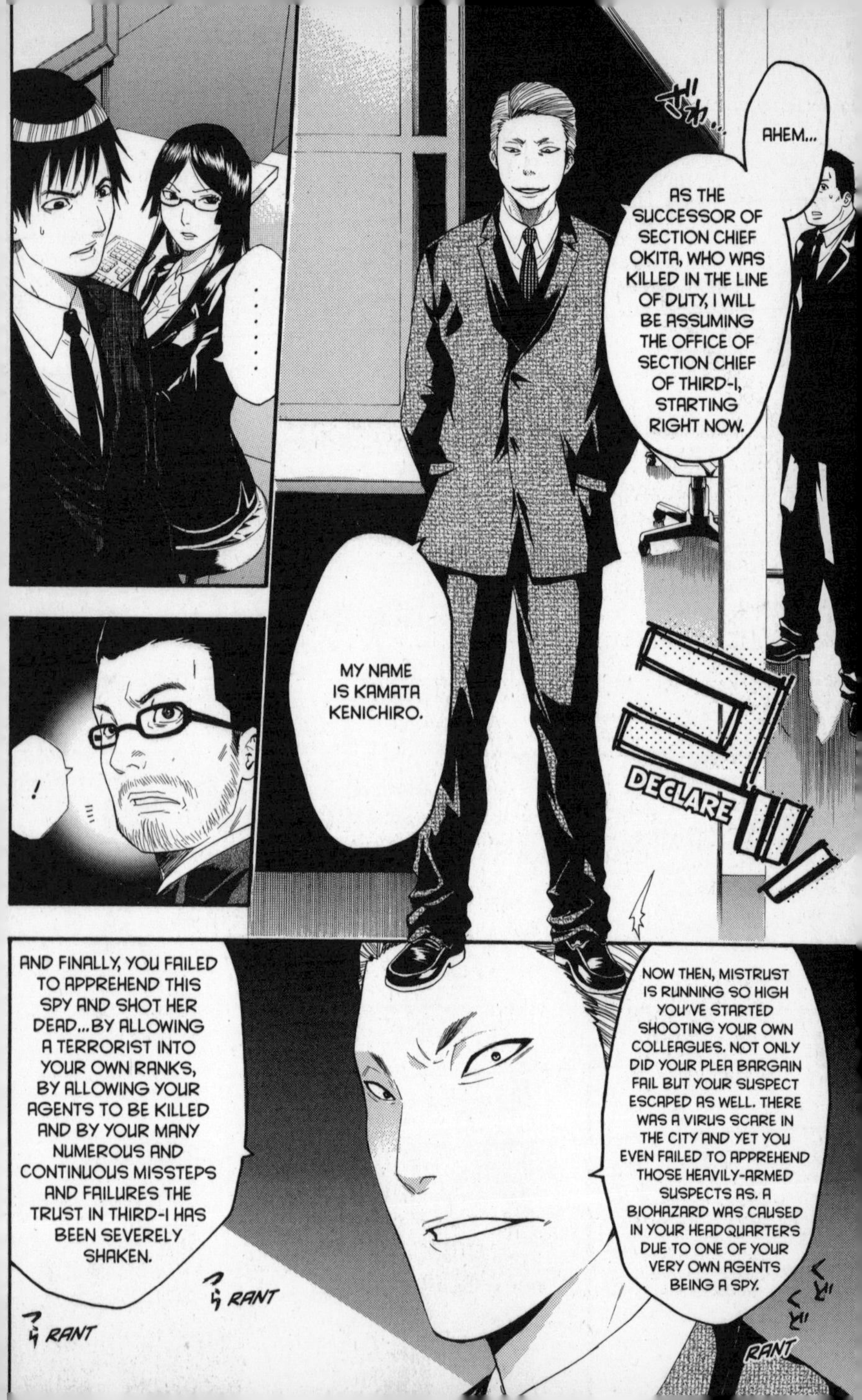
ざわ...
AHEM...
AS THE SUCCESSOR OF SECTION CHIEF OKITA, WHO WAS KILLED IN THE LINE OF DUTY, I WILL BE ASSUMING THE OFFICE OF SECTION CHIEF OF THIRD-I, STARTING RIGHT NOW.
MY NAME IS KAMATA KENICHIRO.
DECLARE
......
!
NOW THEN, MISTRUST IS RUNNING SO HIGH YOU'VE STARTED SHOOTING YOUR OWN COLLEAGUES. NOT ONLY DID YOUR PLEA BARGAIN FAIL BUT YOUR SUSPECT ESCAPED AS WELL. THERE WAS A VIRUS SCARE IN THE CITY AND YET YOU EVEN FAILED TO APPREHEND THOSE HEAVILY-ARMED SUSPECTS AS. A BIOHAZARD WAS CAUSED IN YOUR HEADQUARTERS DUE TO ONE OF YOUR VERY OWN AGENTS BEING A SPY.
くど くど
RANT
AND FINALLY, YOU FAILED TO APPREHEND THIS SPY AND SHOT HER DEAD...BY ALLOWING A TERRORIST INTO YOUR OWN RANKS, BY ALLOWING YOUR AGENTS TO BE KILLED AND BY YOUR MANY NUMEROUS AND CONTINUOUS MISSTEPS AND FAILURES THE TRUST IN THIRD-I HAS BEEN SEVERELY SHAKEN.
RANT
RANT

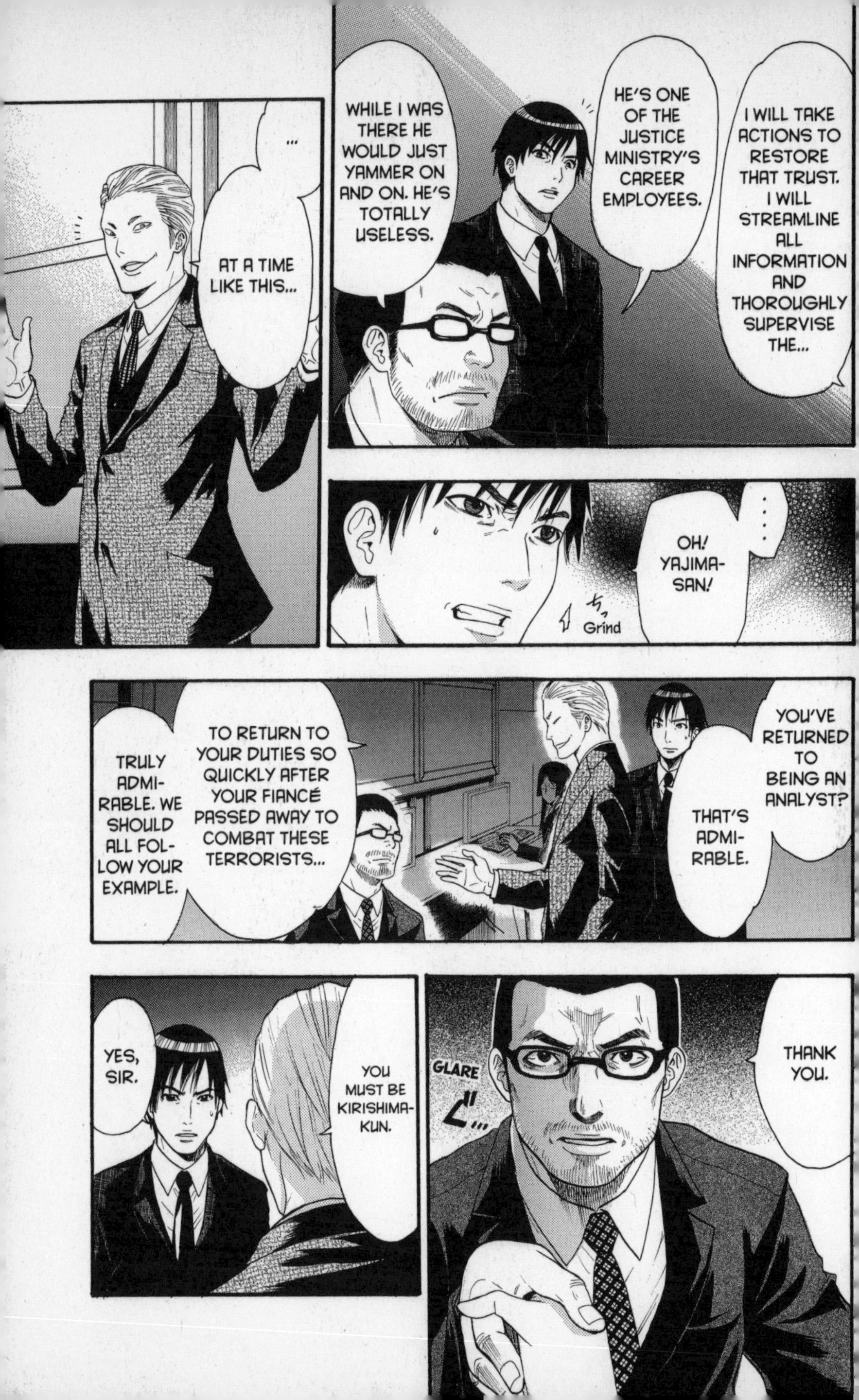
I WILL TAKE ACTIONS TO RESTORE THAT TRUST. I WILL STREAMLINE ALL INFORMATION AND THOROUGHLY SUPERVISE THE...
HE'S ONE OF THE JUSTICE MINISTRY'S CAREER EMPLOYEES.
WHILE I WAS THERE HE WOULD JUST YAMMER ON AND ON. HE'S TOTALLY USELESS.
...
OH! YAJIMA-SAN!
Grind
...
AT A TIME LIKE THIS...
YOU'VE RETURNED TO BEING AN ANALYST?
THAT'S ADMIRABLE.
TO RETURN TO YOUR DUTIES SO QUICKLY AFTER YOUR FIANCÉ PASSED AWAY TO COMBAT THESE TERRORISTS...
TRULY ADMIRABLE. WE SHOULD ALL FOLLOW YOUR EXAMPLE.
THANK YOU.
GLARE
YOU MUST BE KIRISHIMA-KUN.
YES, SIR.

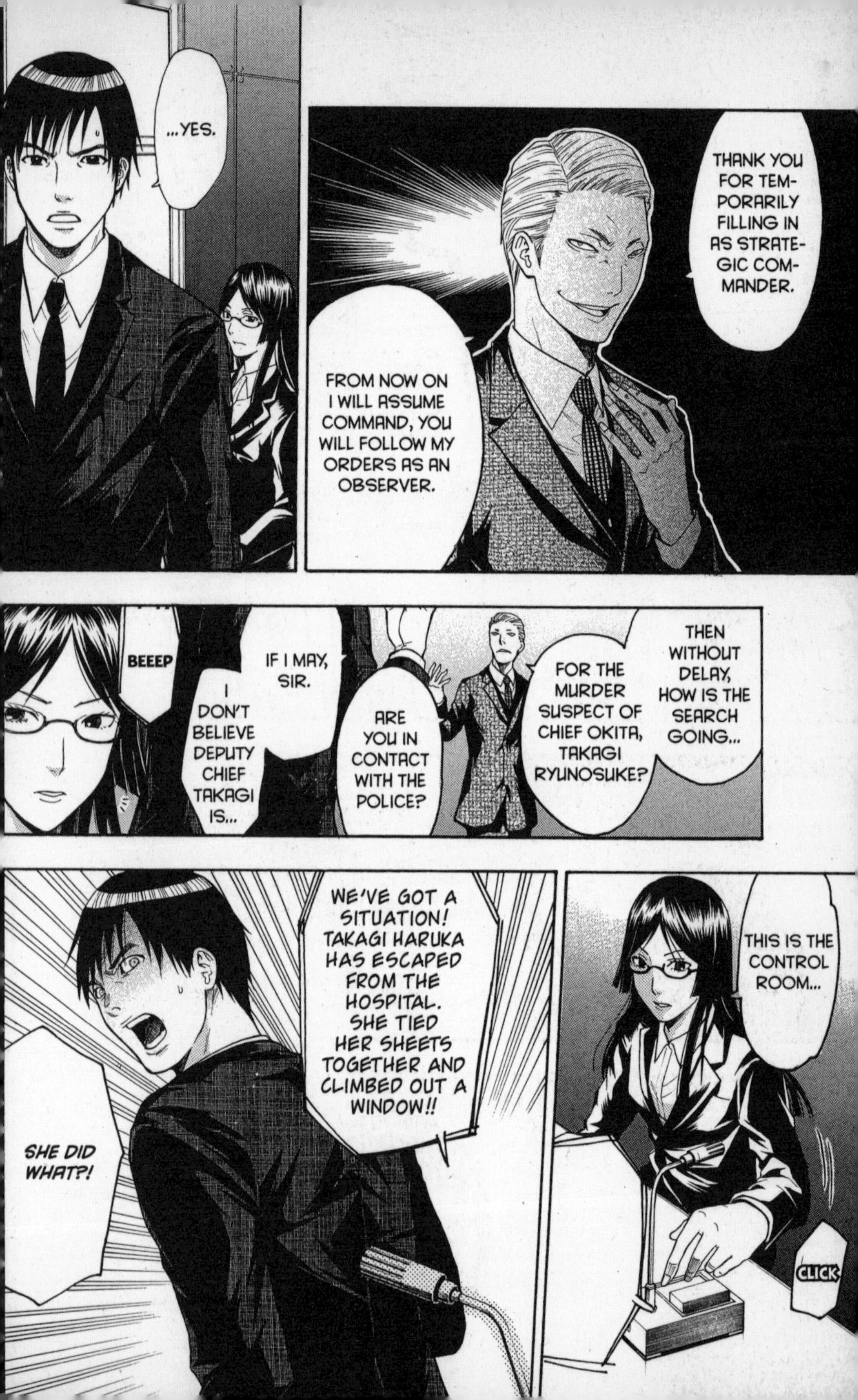
THANK YOU FOR TEMPORARILY FILLING IN AS STRATEGIC COMMANDER.
FROM NOW ON I WILL ASSUME COMMAND, YOU WILL FOLLOW MY ORDERS AS AN OBSERVER.
...YES.
THEN WITHOUT DELAY, HOW IS THE SEARCH GOING...
FOR THE MURDER SUSPECT OF CHIEF OKITA, TAKAGI RYUNOSUKE?
ARE YOU IN CONTACT WITH THE POLICE?
IF I MAY, SIR.
I DON'T BELIEVE DEPUTY CHIEF TAKAGI IS...
BEEEP
THIS IS THE CONTROL ROOM...
CLICK
WE'VE GOT A SITUATION! TAKAGI HARUKA HAS ESCAPED FROM THE HOSPITAL. SHE TIED HER SHEETS TOGETHER AND CLIMBED OUT A WINDOW!!
SHE DID WHAT?!

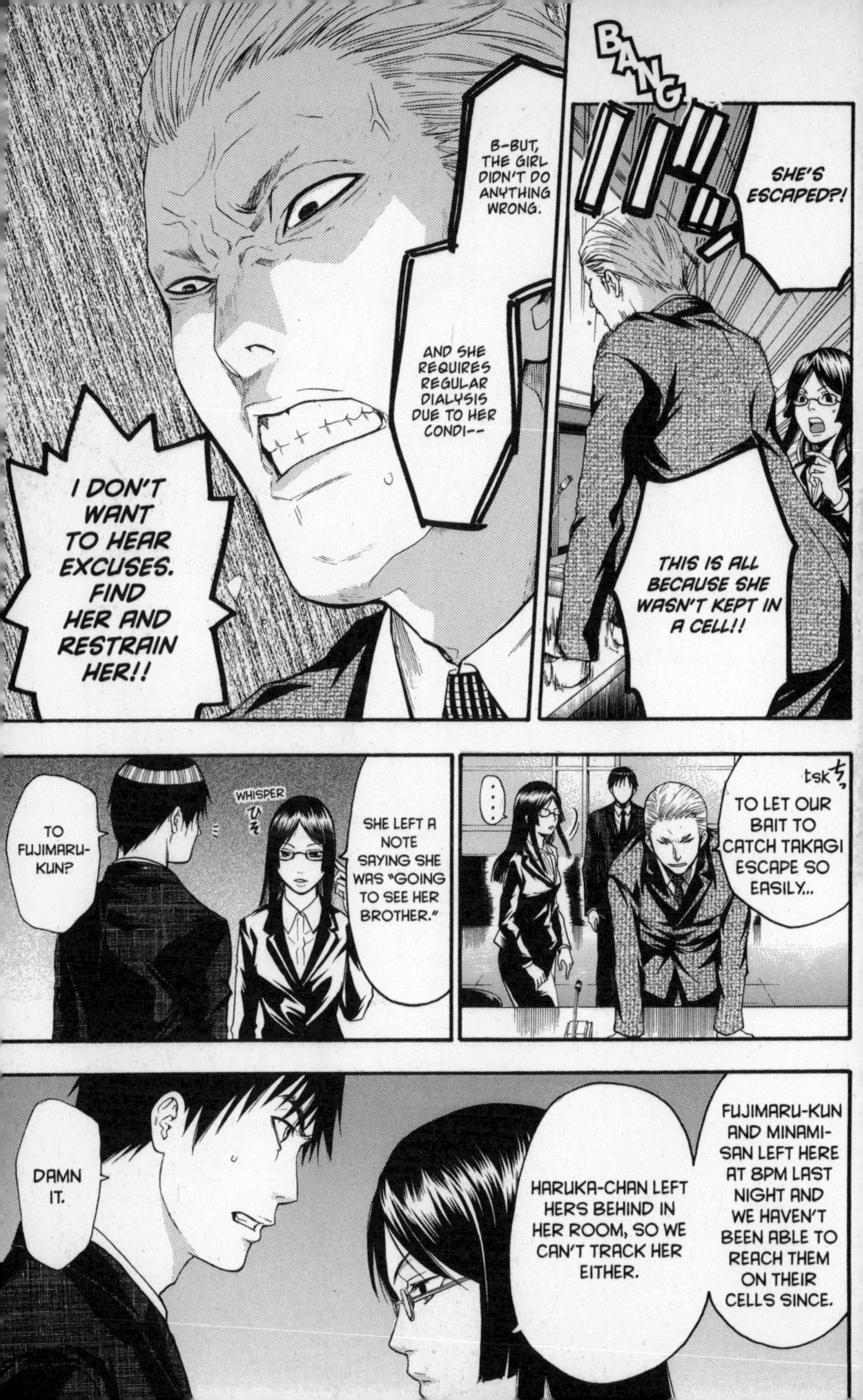
BANG!!
SHE'S ESCAPED?!
THIS IS ALL BECAUSE SHE WASN'T KEPT IN A CELL!!
B-BUT, THE GIRL DIDN'T DO ANYTHING WRONG.
AND SHE REQUIRES REGULAR DIALYSIS DUE TO HER CONDI--
I DON'T WANT TO HEAR EXCUSES. FIND HER AND RESTRAIN HER!!
tsk
TO LET OUR BAIT TO CATCH TAKAGI ESCAPE SO EASILY...
...
SHE LEFT A NOTE SAYING SHE WAS "GOING TO SEE HER BROTHER."
WHISPER
TO FUJIMARU-KUN?
FUJIMARU-KUN AND MINAMI-SAN LEFT HERE AT 8PM LAST NIGHT AND WE HAVEN'T BEEN ABLE TO REACH THEM ON THEIR CELLS SINCE.
HARUKA-CHAN LEFT HERS BEHIND IN HER ROOM, SO WE CAN'T TRACK HER EITHER.
DAMN IT.

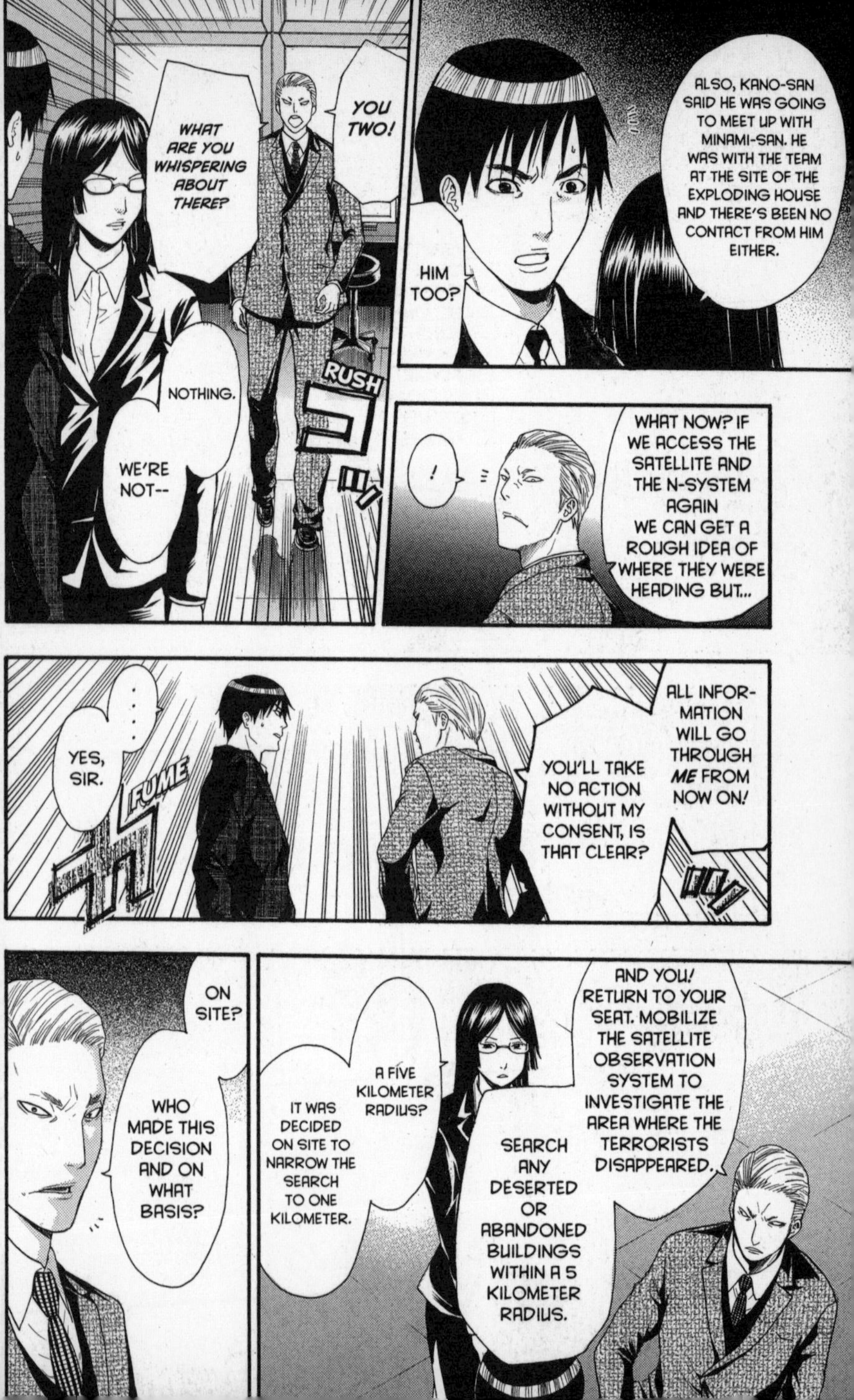
ALSO, KANO-SAN SAID HE WAS GOING TO MEET UP WITH MINAMI-SAN. HE WAS WITH THE TEAM AT THE SITE OF THE EXPLODING HOUSE AND THERE'S BEEN NO CONTACT FROM HIM EITHER.
HIM TOO?
WHAT NOW? IF WE ACCESS THE SATELLITE AND THE N-SYSTEM AGAIN WE CAN GET A ROUGH IDEA OF WHERE THEY WERE HEADING BUT...
!
YOU TWO!
WHAT ARE YOU WHISPERING ABOUT THERE?
RUSH
NOTHING.
WE'RE NOT--
ALL INFORMATION WILL GO THROUGH *ME* FROM NOW ON!
YOU'LL TAKE NO ACTION WITHOUT MY CONSENT, IS THAT CLEAR?
FUME
YES, SIR.
...
AND YOU! RETURN TO YOUR SEAT. MOBILIZE THE SATELLITE OBSERVATION SYSTEM TO INVESTIGATE THE AREA WHERE THE TERRORISTS DISAPPEARED.
SEARCH ANY DESERTED OR ABANDONED BUILDINGS WITHIN A 5 KILOMETER RADIUS.
A FIVE KILOMETER RADIUS?
IT WAS DECIDED ON SITE TO NARROW THE SEARCH TO ONE KILOMETER.
ON SITE?
WHO MADE THIS DECISION AND ON WHAT BASIS?

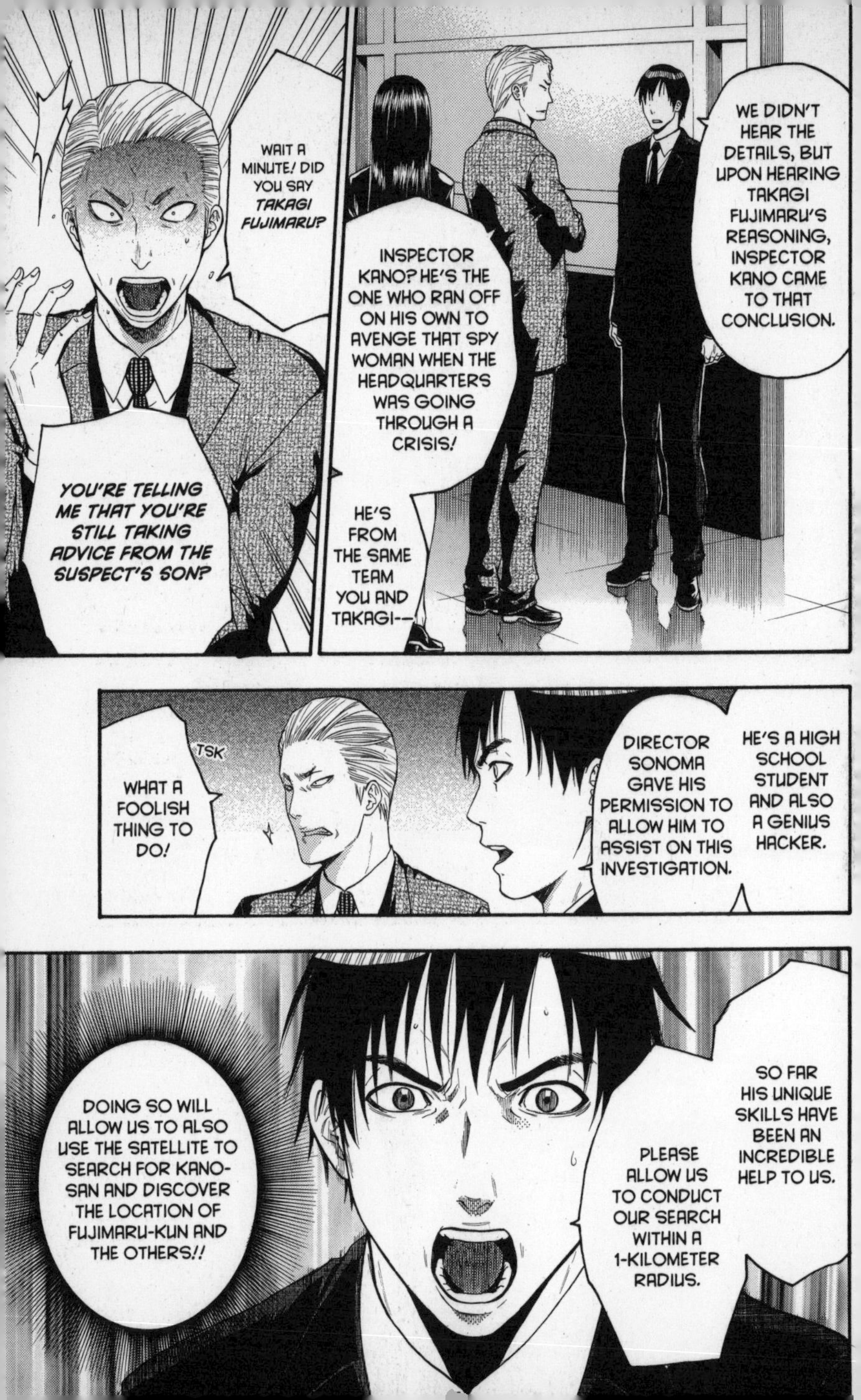
WE DIDN'T HEAR THE DETAILS, BUT UPON HEARING TAKAGI FUJIMARU'S REASONING, INSPECTOR KANO CAME TO THAT CONCLUSION.
INSPECTOR KANO? HE'S THE ONE WHO RAN OFF ON HIS OWN TO AVENGE THAT SPY WOMAN WHEN THE HEADQUARTERS WAS GOING THROUGH A CRISIS!
HE'S FROM THE SAME TEAM YOU AND TAKAGI--
WAIT A MINUTE! DID YOU SAY *TAKAGI FUJIMARU*?
YOU'RE TELLING ME THAT YOU'RE STILL TAKING ADVICE FROM THE SUSPECT'S SON?
HE'S A HIGH SCHOOL STUDENT AND ALSO A GENIUS HACKER.
DIRECTOR SONOMA GAVE HIS PERMISSION TO ALLOW HIM TO ASSIST ON THIS INVESTIGATION.
TSK
WHAT A FOOLISH THING TO DO!
SO FAR HIS UNIQUE SKILLS HAVE BEEN AN INCREDIBLE HELP TO US.
PLEASE ALLOW US TO CONDUCT OUR SEARCH WITHIN A 1-KILOMETER RADIUS.
DOING SO WILL ALLOW US TO ALSO USE THE SATELLITE TO SEARCH FOR KANO-SAN AND DISCOVER THE LOCATION OF FUJIMARU-KUN AND THE OTHERS!!

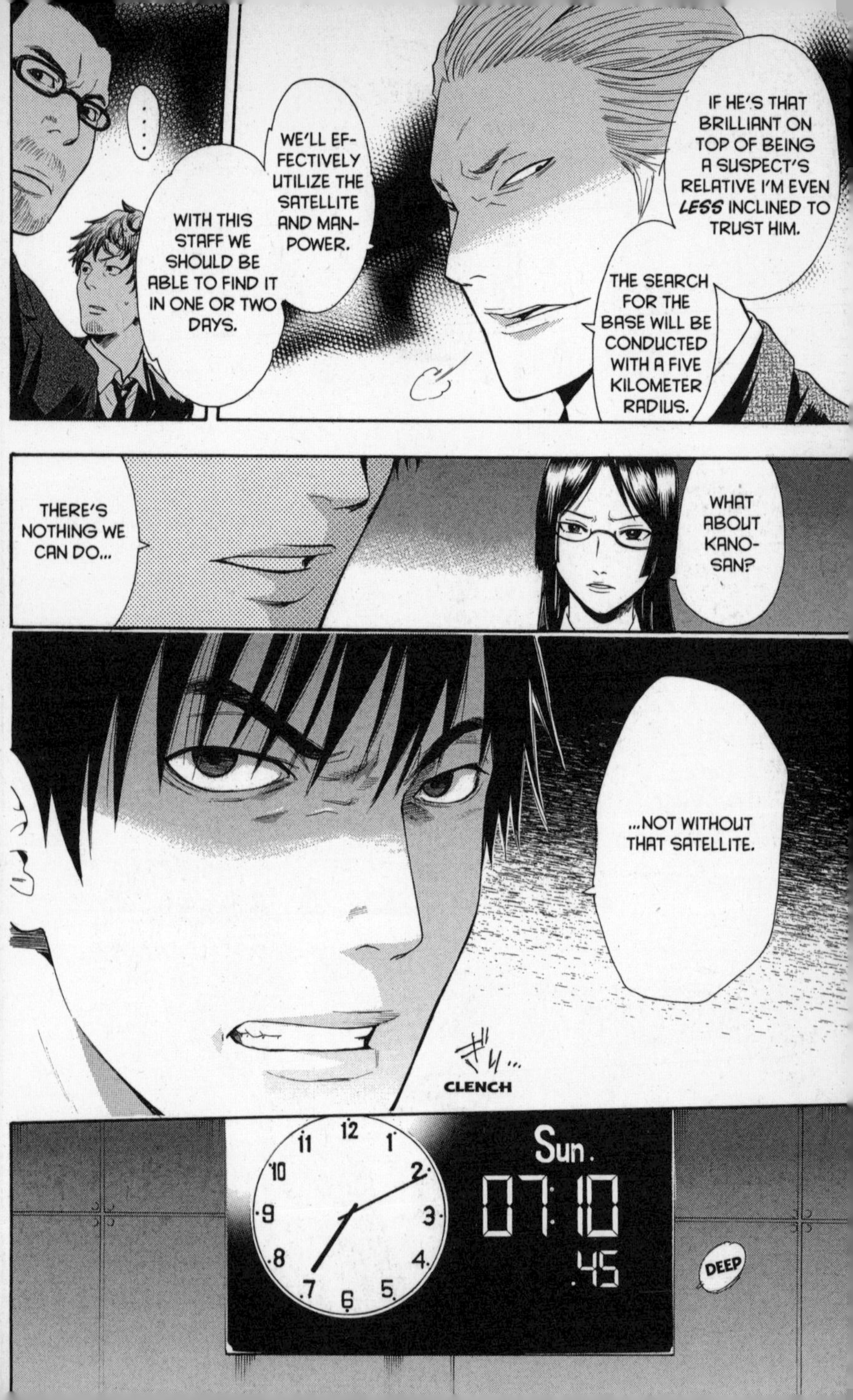

IF HE'S THAT BRILLIANT ON TOP OF BEING A SUSPECT'S RELATIVE I'M EVEN *LESS* INCLINED TO TRUST HIM.
THE SEARCH FOR THE BASE WILL BE CONDUCTED WITH A FIVE KILOMETER RADIUS.
WE'LL EF-FECTIVELY UTILIZE THE SATELLITE AND MAN-POWER.
WITH THIS STAFF WE SHOULD BE ABLE TO FIND IT IN ONE OR TWO DAYS.
....
WHAT ABOUT KANO-SAN?
THERE'S NOTHING WE CAN DO...
...NOT WITHOUT THAT SATELLITE.
CLENCH
Sun.
07:10
.45
DEEP

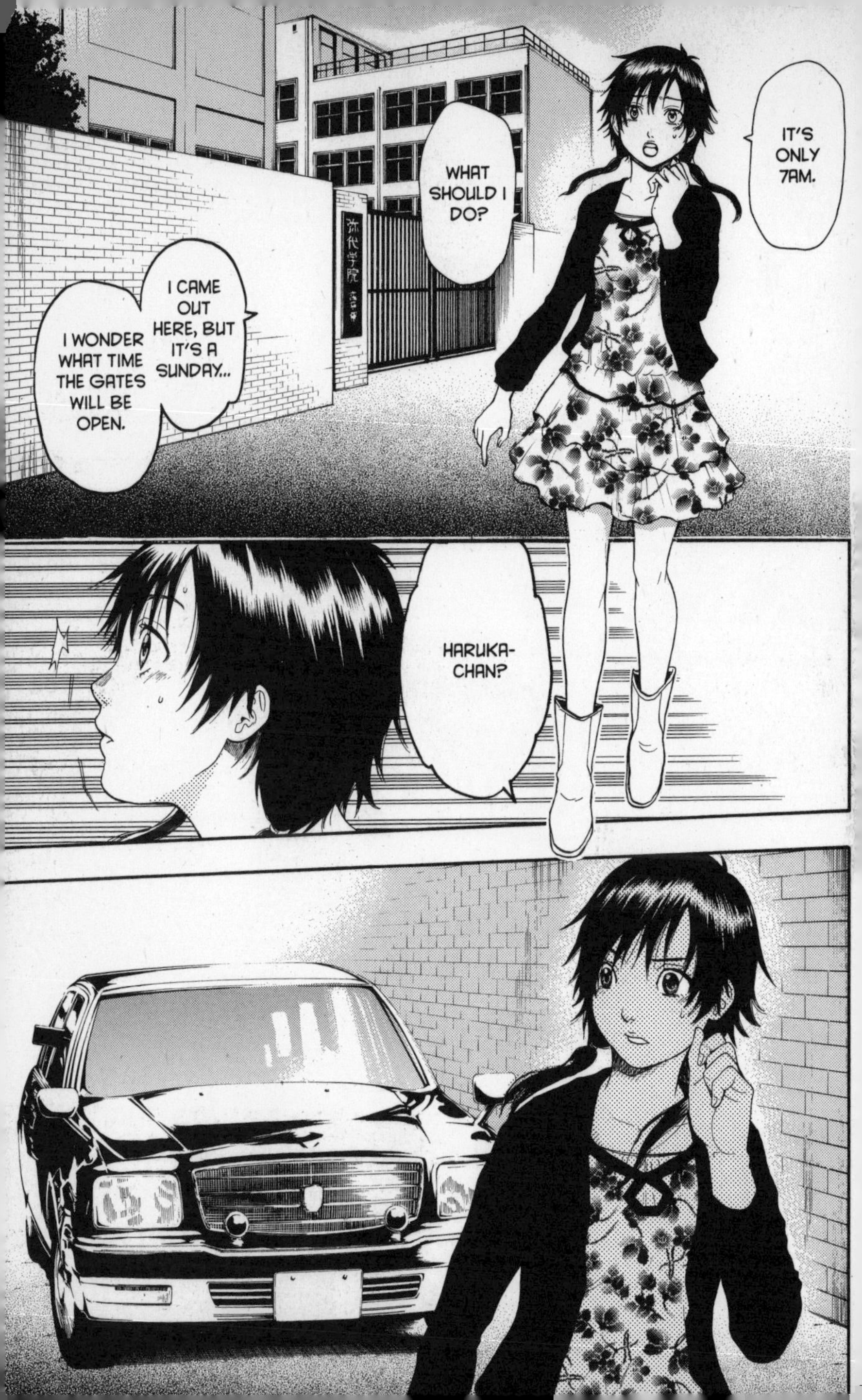
IT'S ONLY 7AM.
WHAT SHOULD I DO?
I CAME OUT HERE, BUT IT'S A SUNDAY...
I WONDER WHAT TIME THE GATES WILL BE OPEN.
HARUKA-CHAN?

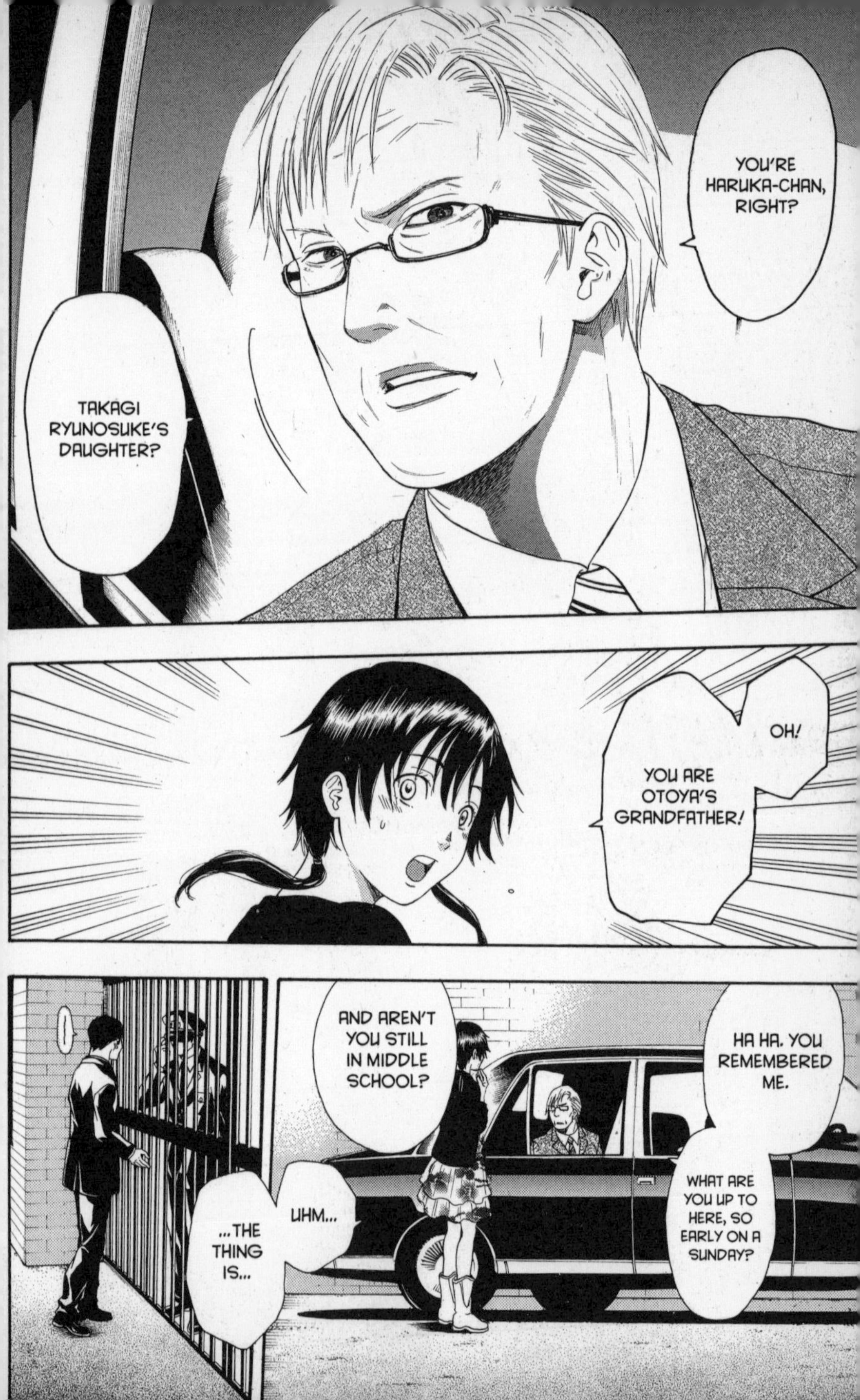
YOU'RE HARUKA-CHAN, RIGHT?
TAKAGI RYUNOSUKE'S DAUGHTER?
OH!
YOU ARE OTOYA'S GRANDFATHER!
HA HA. YOU REMEMBERED ME.
WHAT ARE YOU UP TO HERE, SO EARLY ON A SUNDAY?
AND AREN'T YOU STILL IN MIDDLE SCHOOL?
UHM...
...THE THING IS...
!

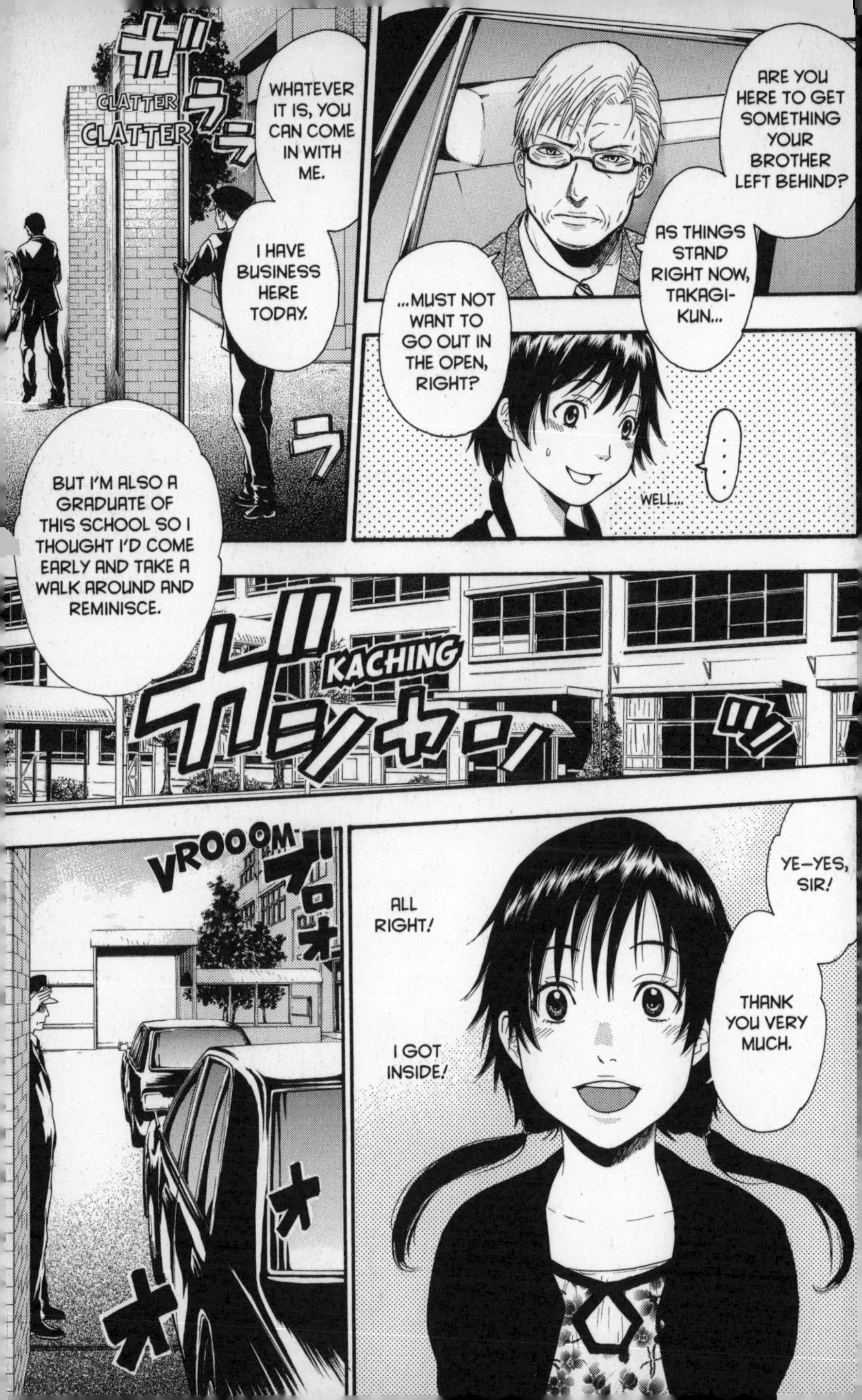

ARE YOU HERE TO GET SOMETHING YOUR BROTHER LEFT BEHIND?
AS THINGS STAND RIGHT NOW, TAKAGI-KUN...
...MUST NOT WANT TO GO OUT IN THE OPEN, RIGHT?
...
WELL...
WHATEVER IT IS, YOU CAN COME IN WITH ME.
I HAVE BUSINESS HERE TODAY.
CLATTER CLATTER
BUT I'M ALSO A GRADUATE OF THIS SCHOOL SO I THOUGHT I'D COME EARLY AND TAKE A WALK AROUND AND REMINISCE.
KACHING
YE-YES, SIR!
THANK YOU VERY MUCH.
ALL RIGHT!
I GOT INSIDE!
VROOOM

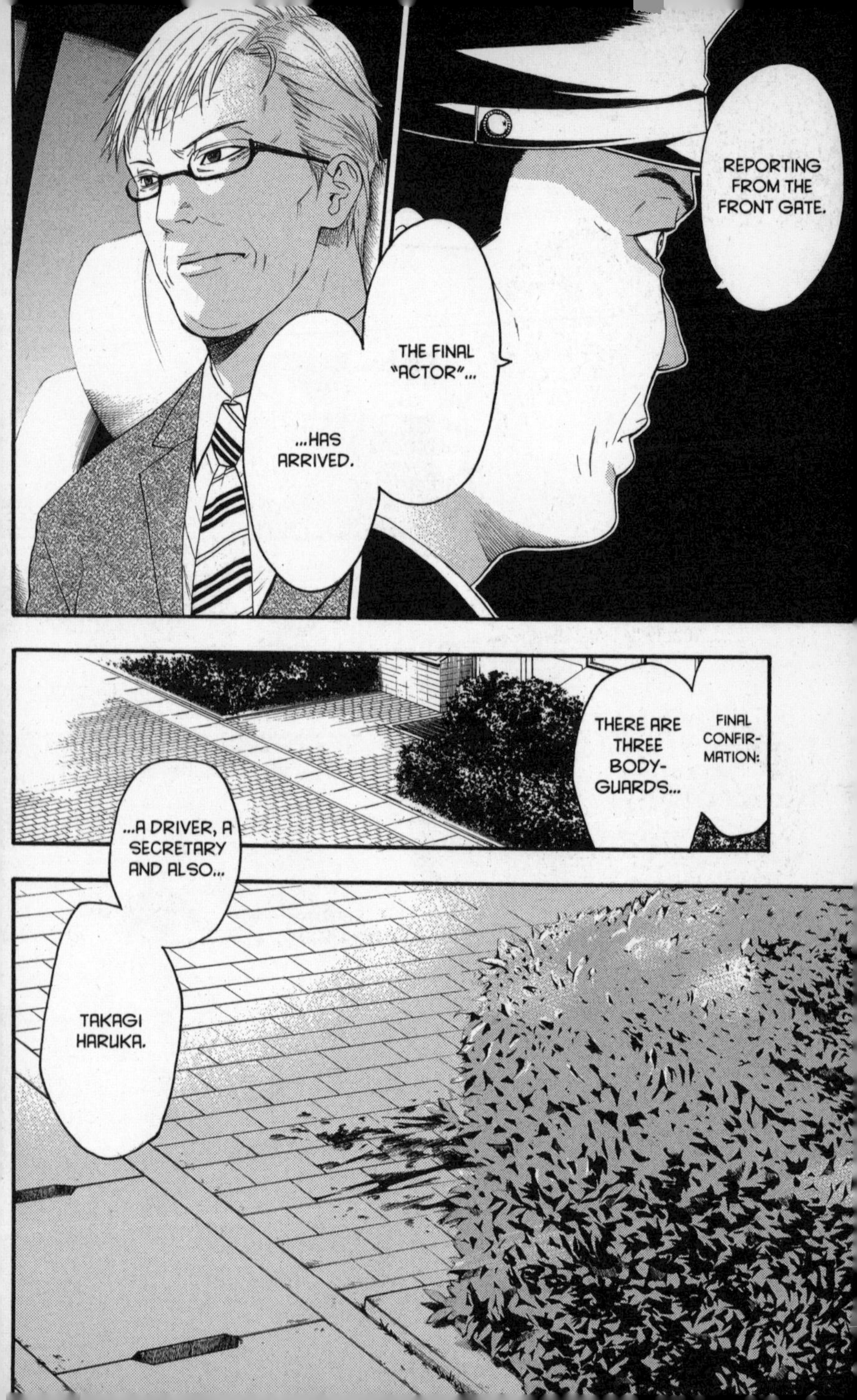
REPORTING FROM THE FRONT GATE.
THE FINAL "ACTOR"...
...HAS ARRIVED.
FINAL CONFIRMATION:
THERE ARE THREE BODYGUARDS...
...A DRIVER, A SECRETARY AND ALSO...
TAKAGI HARUKA.

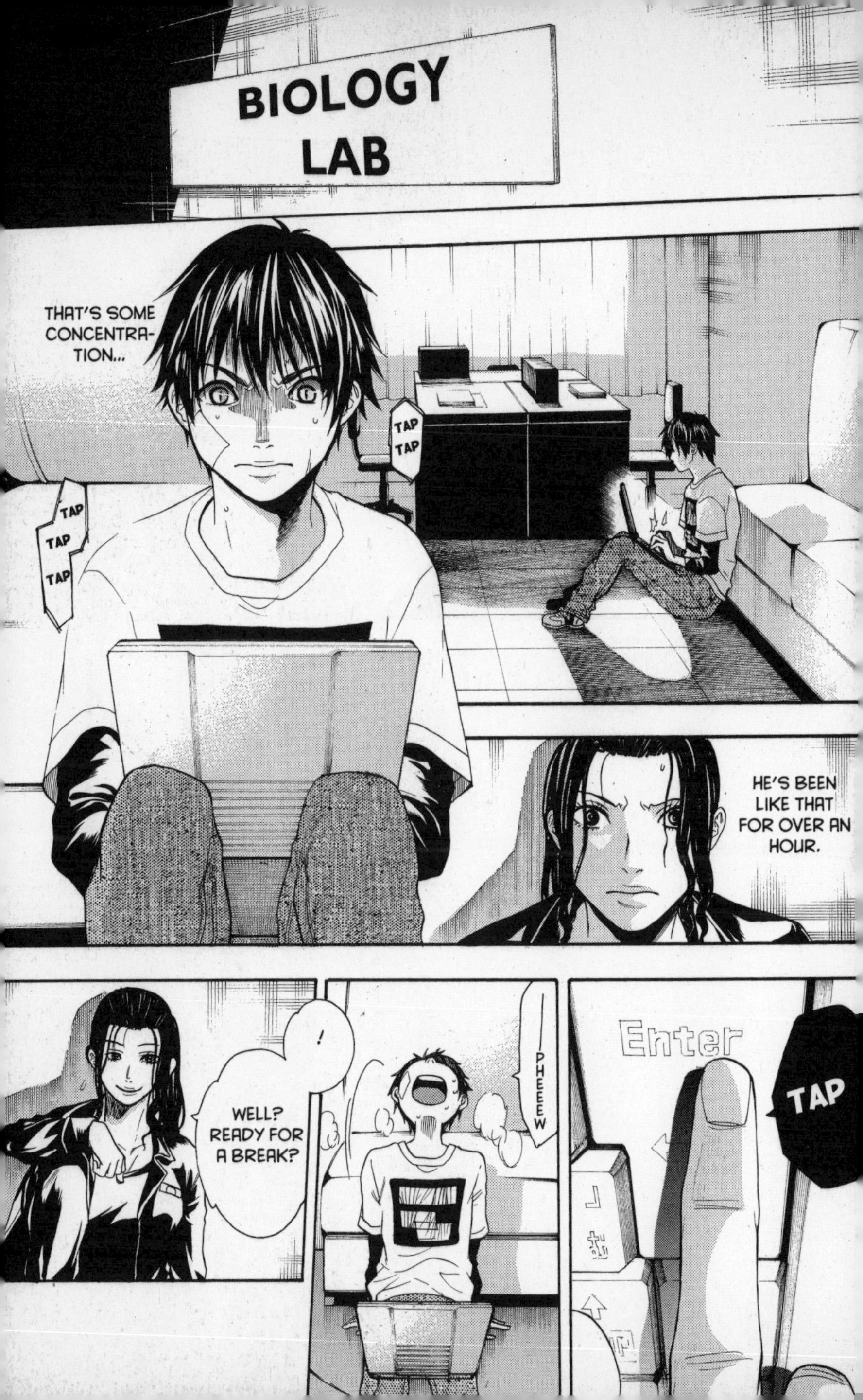
BIOLOGY LAB
TAP TAP
HE'S BEEN LIKE THAT FOR OVER AN HOUR.
THAT'S SOME CONCENTRATION...
TAP TAP TAP
Enter
TAP
PHEEEW
!
WELL? READY FOR A BREAK?

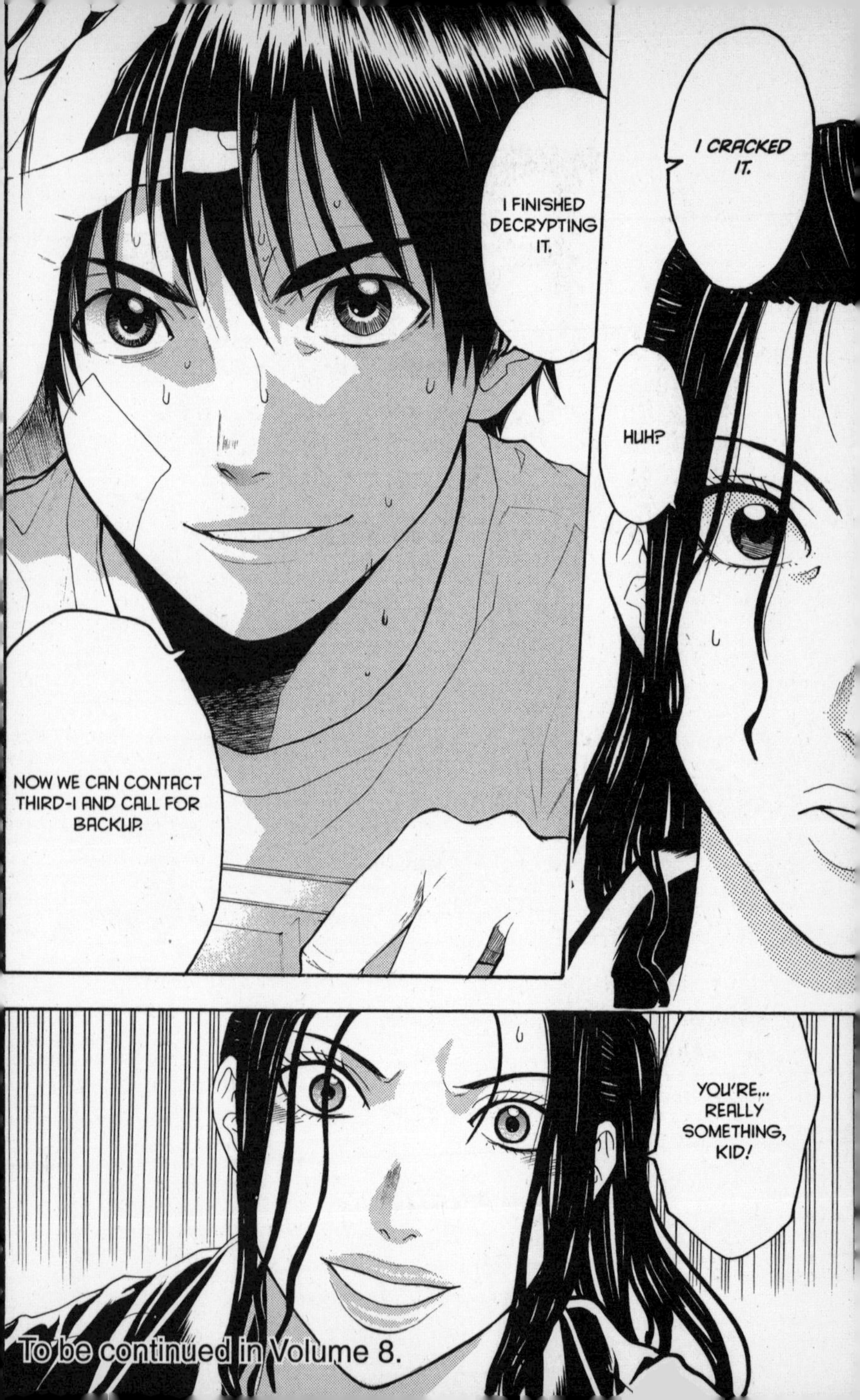
I CRACKED IT.
HUH?
I FINISHED DECRYPTING IT.
NOW WE CAN CONTACT THIRD-I AND CALL FOR BACKUP.
YOU'RE... REALLY SOMETHING, KID!
To be continued in Volume 8.

BLOODY MONDAY

Special Thanks

    Daiwa Mitsu   Kawabata Kunihiro
    Chugun   (Osaka/Daisaka) Machiko

Editorial

    Sato-san   Kawakubo-san

Comics Editorial

    Ebitani-san

Manga

    Ryumon Ryou X Megumi Kouji

THANK YOU FOR READING.

Bloody Monday volume 7 is a work of fiction. Names, characters, places, and incidents are the products of the author's imagination or are used fictitiously. Any resemblance to actual events, locales, or persons, living or dead, is entirely coincidental.

A Kodansha Comics Trade Paperback Original

Published in the United States by Kodansha Comics,
an imprint of Kodansha USA Publishing, LLC, New York.

Publication rights for this English edition arranged through Kodansha Ltd, Tokyo.

First published in Japan in 2008 by Kodansha Ltd., Tokyo.

ISBN 978-1-61262-043-5
Original cover design by Takashi Shimoyama (Red Rooster)

Printed in the United States of America.

www.kodanshacomics.com

9 8 7 6 5 4 3 2 1

Translator: Sebastian Girner
Lettering: Christy Sawyer

TOMARE!
[STOP!]

You are going the wrong way!

Manga is a completely different
type of reading experience.

To start at the *beginning,*
go to the *end*!

That's right! Authentic manga is read the traditional Japanese way—
from right to left, exactly the opposite of how American books are read.
It's easy to follow: Just go to the other end of the book, and read each
page—and each panel—from the right side to the left side, starting at
the top right. Now you're experiencing manga as it was meant to be.